D1571390

The essays in this book consider issues of tolerance and intolerance faced by Jews and Christians between approximately 200 BCE and 200 CE. The contributors ask where boundaries were drawn and where bridges were built. Several chapters are concerned with many different aspects of early Jewish–Christian relationships. Five scholars, however, take a different tack and discuss how Jews and Christians defined themselves against the pagan world. As minority groups, both Jews and Christians had to work out ways of coexisting with their Graeco-Roman neighbours. Relationships with those neighbours were often strained, but even within both Jewish and Christian circles, issues of tolerance and intolerance surfaced regularly. So it is appropriate that some other contributors should consider 'inner-Jewish' relationships, and that some should be concerned with Christian sects.

TOLERANCE AND INTOLERANCE
IN EARLY JUDAISM AND CHRISTIANITY

TOLERANCE
AND INTOLERANCE IN
EARLY JUDAISM AND
CHRISTIANITY

135009

EDITED BY

GRAHAM N. STANTON

King's College London

AND

GUY G. STROUMSA

The Hebrew University of Jerusalem

CAMBRIDGE
UNIVERSITY PRESS

Published by the Press Syndicate of the University of Cambridge
The Pitt Building, Trumpington Street, Cambridge CB2 1RP, United Kingdom

Cambridge University Press
The Edinburgh Building, Cambridge CB2 2RU, United Kingdom
40 West 20th Street, New York, NY 10011-4211, USA
10 Stamford Road, Oakleigh, Melbourne 3166, Australia

© Cambridge University Press 1998

This book is in copyright. Subject to statutory exception and to the provisions
of relevant collective licensing agreements, no reproduction of any part may
take place without the written permission of Cambridge University Press.

First published 1998

Printed in the United Kingdom at the University Press, Cambridge

Typeset in Baskerville and Greek Hellenic   [A O]

A catalogue record for this book is available from the British Library

Library of Congress cataloguing in publication data

Tolerance and intolerance in early Judaism and Christianity /
edited by Graham N. Stanton and Guy G. Stroumsa.
p.   cm.
Includes bibliographical references.
ISBN 0 521 59037 x (hardback)
1. Judaism – History – Post-exilic period, 586 B.C.–210 A.D.
2. Religious tolerance – Judaism.   3. Church history – Primitive and
early church, ca. 30–600.   4. Religious tolerance – Christianity –
History of doctrines – Early church, ca. 30–600.   5. Judaism –
Relations – Christianity.   6. Christianity and other religions –
Judaism.   I. Stanton, Graham.   II. Stroumsa, Gedaliahu A. G.
BM177.T65   1977
296.3'9 – dc21   96-51601 CIP

ISBN 0 521 59037 x hardback

Contents

Contributors

JOHN M. G. BARCLAY is Senior Lecturer in Biblical Studies, University of Glasgow. His publications include *Obeying the Truth* (1988) and *Jews in the Mediterranean Diaspora from Alexander to Trajan* (1996).

STEPHEN C. BARTON is Lecturer in New Testament in the Department of Theology, University of Durham. His most recent publications are *Discipleship and Family Ties in Mark and Matthew* (1994) and, as editor, *The Family in Theological Perspective* (1996).

RICHARD BAUCKHAM is Professor of New Testament Studies, University of St Andrews, Scotland. He has published very extensively in theology, New Testament and early Judaism. His recent books include *The Theology of the Book of Revelation* (1993), *The Climax of Prophecy* (1993) and *The Theology of Jürgen Moltmann* (1995).

ALBERT I. BAUMGARTEN is Associate Professor of Jewish History at Bar Ilan University. He has recently completed *The Emergence and Flourishing of Jewish Sects in the Maccabean Era: An Interpretation*.

FRANÇOIS BLANCHETIÈRE is Professeur d'Histoire des Religions in the Faculté des sciences historiques, Université des Sciences Humaines, Strasbourg (France). His publications include *Le Christianisme asiate aux IIe et IIIe siècles* (1981); *Aux sources de l'anti-judaïsme chrétien IIe–IIIe siècles* (1995). He is currently completing a book: *Judéo-chrétien? Nazaréen? Chrétien? Regard sur les origines juives du mouvement chrétien*.

MARCUS BOCKMUEHL is University Lecturer in Divinity and a Fellow and Tutor at Fitzwilliam College, Cambridge. His publications include *This Jesus: Martyr, Lord, Messiah* (1994) and *A Commentary on the Epistle to the Philippians* (1997).

MARTINUS C. DE BOER is Professor of New Testament, Vrije Universiteit, Amsterdam; author of *Johannine Perspectives on the Death of Jesus* (1996); and editor of *From Jesus to John: Essays on Jesus and New Testament Christology* (1993).

ANDREW CHESTER is a Fellow of Selwyn College and Lecturer in Divinity, University of Cambridge; and is co-author with R. P. Martin of *The Theology of the Letters of James, Peter and Jude*, in the New Testament Theology series (1994).

ITHAMAR GRUENWALD is Professor of Jewish Thought and Religious Studies at Tel Aviv University. His research concentrates on Jewish Apocalypticism and Mysticism. He is currently working on a book on a conceptual approach to the study of Jewish mysticism.

MOSHE HALBERTAL is Senior Lecturer in Jewish Thought and Philosophy at the Hebrew University of Jerusalem, and a Fellow at the Shalom Hartman Institute. He co-authored (with Avishai Margalit) *Idolatry* (1992) and recently published *People of the Book: Canon, Meaning, and Authority* (1997).

WILLIAM HORBURY is Reader in Jewish and Early Christian Studies, University of Cambridge, and a Fellow of the British Academy. His publications include *Jewish Inscriptions of Graeco-Roman Egypt* (with David Noy), a revised and supplemented edition of Samuel Krauss, *The Jewish–Christian Controversy* (1996) and *Jews and Christians in Contact and Controversy* (1997).

JUDITH M. LIEU is Senior Lecturer in History in the School of Philosophy and Politics, Macquarie University, Sydney. She studied at Durham, Birmingham and Oxford Universities. She is author of *The Second and Third Epistles of John* (1986), *The Theology of the Johannine Epistles* (1991), *Image and Reality: The Jews in the World of the Christians in the Second Century* (1996) and co-editor with J. North and T. Rajak of *The Jews among Pagans and Christians* (1992).

MICHAEL MACH is Senior Lecturer in Jewish Philosophy and Religious Studies at Tel Aviv University. Previous publications

include: *Entwicklungsstadien des judischen Engelglaubens in vorrabbinischer Zeit* and articles concerning ancient Jewish and early
Christian thought.

JOEL MARCUS is Lecturer in Biblical Studies, University of Glasgow. He is the author of *The Mystery of the Kingdom of God* (1986)
and *The Way of the Lord: Christological Exegesis in the Gospel of Mark*
(1992). He is currently at work on the Anchor Bible Commentary on Mark.

MAREN R. NIEHOFF is Lecturer in the Department of Jewish
Thought, the Hebrew University of Jerusalem. She has published in the fields of Jewish Hellenism and rabbinic literature,
including *The Figure of Joseph in Post-Biblical Jewish Literature*
(1992). She has also published in the field of modern Jewish
scholarship.

DANIEL R. SCHWARTZ is Professor in the Department of Jewish
History, the Hebrew University of Jerusalem. Major publications: *Agrippa I: The Last King of Judaea* (1990) and *Studies in the
Jewish Background of Christianity* (1992). He is currently completing a translation of and commentary upon 2 Maccabees.

GRAHAM N. STANTON is Professor of New Testament Studies at
King's College, University of London. His recent books include
The Gospels and Jesus (1989), *A Gospel for a New People: Studies in
Matthew* (1992) and *Gospel Truth? New Light on Jesus and the Gospels*
(1995). In 1998 he takes up the Lady Margaret's Professorship of
Divinity at the University of Cambridge.

GUY G. STROUMSA is Martin Buber Professor of Comparative
Religion at the Hebrew University of Jerusalem. Among his
publications: *Another Seed: Studies in Gnostic Mythology* (1984), *Savoir
et Salut* (1992), *Hidden Wisdom: Esoteric Traditions and the Roots of
Christian Mysticism* (1996).

JUSTIN TAYLOR SM is Professor of History at the Ecole Biblique
et Archéologique Francaise in Jerusalem. He has published two
volumes of a historical commentary on the Acts of the Apostles,
Les actes des deux Apôtres 1992 and 1996.

Abbreviations

AB	Anchor Bible
AGAJU	Arbeiten zur Geschichte des antiken Judentums und des Urchristentums
ANRW	*Aufstieg und Niedergang der römischen Welt*, eds. H. Temporini and W. Haase (Berlin 1972—)
BA	*Biblical Archaeologist*
BETL	Bibliotheca ephemeridum theologicarum lovaniensium
BhTh	Beiträge zur historischen Theologie
BJRL	*Bulletin of the John Rylands Library, Manchester*
BWANT	Beiträge zur Wissenschaft vom Alten und Neuen Testament
BZ	*Biblische Zeitschrift*
CBQ	*Catholic Biblical Quarterly*
CBQMS	Catholic Biblical Quarterly Monograph Series
CIJ	Corpus Inscriptionum Judaicarum
CPJ	Corpus Papyrorum Judaicarum
CRINT	Compendium rerum iudaicarum ad Novum Testamentum
DJD	*Discoveries in the Judean Desert*
E.tr.	English translation
FRLANT	Forschungen zur Religion und Literatur des Alten und Neuen Testament
FS	Festschrift
HSS	Harvard Semitic Studies
HTR	*Harvard Theological Review*
HUCA	*Hebrew Union College Annual*
IEJ	*Israel Exploration Journal*
IOS	*Israel Oriental Studies*
JBL	*Journal of Biblical Literature*

JJS	*Journal of Jewish Studies*
JQR	*Jewish Quarterly Review*
JRS	*Journal of Roman Studies*
JSHRZ	*Judische Schriften aus hellenistisch-römischer Zeit*, ed. W. G. Kümmel et al. (Gütersloh, 1973—)
JSJ	*Journal for the Study of Judaism in the Persian, Hellenistic, and Roman Period*
JSNT	*Journal for the Study of the New Testament*
JSNTSS	Journal for the Study of the New Testament Supplement Series
JSOTSS	Journal for the Study of the Old Testament Supplement Series
JSPSS	Journal for the Study of the Pseudepigrapha Supplement Series
JSS	*Jewish Social Studies*
JTS	*Journal of Theological Studies*
KAV	Kommentar zu den Apostolischen Vätern
LCL	Loeb Classical Library
LXX	Septuagint
MGH	Monumenta Germaniae Historica
MT	Masoretic Text
NJB	New Jerusalem Bible
NovT	*Novum Testamentum*
NovTSup	Supplements to *Novum Testamentum*
NTAbh	Neutestamentliche Abhandlungen
NTOA	Novum Testamentum et Orbis Antiquus
NTS	*New Testament Studies*
OGIS	*Orientis Graecae Inscriptiones Selectae*, ed. W. Dittenberger (Leipzig, 1903–5, repr. Hildesheim, 1970)
PG	*Patrologia Graeca*, ed. J. P. Migne (Paris, 1844–55)
PL	*Patrologia Latina*, ed. J. P. Migne (Paris, 1844–64)
RAC	Reallexicon für Antike und Christentum
RB	*Revue Biblique*
REB	Revised English Bible (1989)
REJ	*Revue des études juives*
RHPR	*Revue d'histoire et de philosophie religieuses*
RHR	*Revue de l'histoire des religions*
RQ	*Revue de Qumran*
RSR	*Recherches de science religieuse*
SBLDS	Society for Biblical Literature Dissertation Series

SC	Sources Chrétiennes
SEG	Supplementum Epigraphicum Graecum
SHR	Studies in the History of Religions
SJ	Studia Judaica
SJLA	Studies in Judaism in Late Antiquity
SJOT	*Scandinavian Journal of the Old Testament*
SNTSMS	Society for New Testament Studies Monograph Series
SNTW	Studies in the New Testament and its World
SPB	Studia postbiblica
ST	*Studia Theologica*
STDJ	Studies on the Texts of the Desert of Judah
SPap	*Studia papyrologia*
SUNT	Studien zur Umwelt des Neuen Testaments
SVTP	Studia in Veteris Testamenti Pseudepigrapha
TSAAJ	*Texts and Studies: American Academy for Jewish Research*
TSAJ	Texte und Studien zum antiken Judentum
TU	Texte und Untersuchungen zur Geschichte der altchristlichen Literatur
VC	*Vigiliae christianae*
VT	*Vetus Testamentum*
WMANT	Wissenschaftliche Monographien zum Alten und Neuen Testament
WUNT	Wissenschaftliche Untersuchungen zum Neuen Testament
ZNW	*Zeitschrift für die neutestamentliche Wissenschaft*
ZThK	*Zeitschrift für Theologie und Kirche*

Introduction

Graham N. Stanton

The essays in this book consider issues of tolerance and intolerance faced by Jews and Christians between approximately 200 BCE and 200 CE. Where were boundaries drawn and bridges built? Although this theme is explored primarily from a historical perspective, for both Jews and Christians it resonates down through the centuries right up to the present day. Communities, groups or nations with rigid boundaries of intolerance quickly become sterile: where there is no vision, people perish. So bridges must be built. On the other hand, unless clear boundary lines are drawn, bridges of tolerance which straddle political, ethnic or religious boundaries are always vulnerable both to sudden attack and to steady erosion. The location of boundaries and bridges raised particularly acute problems for both Jews and Christians in the period under discussion in this book, but the issues at stake will always be with us. The contributors hope to stimulate further research on their chosen topics, as well as reflection on the wider implications of their essays.

This book is distinctive both in its concentration on a theme of perennial concern for humanity, and also in the breadth of the essays. As might be expected in a volume on tolerance and intolerance in antiquity, several chapters are concerned with many different aspects of early Jewish–Christian relationships. Five scholars, however, take a different tack and explore wider horizons: they discuss ways Jews and Christians defined themselves over against the pagan world. As minority groups, both Jews and Christians had to work out ways of coexisting with their Graeco-Roman neighbours. Relationships with those neighbours were often strained, but even within Jewish and Christian circles, issues of tolerance and intolerance surfaced regularly. So it is appropriate

I

that several essays should consider 'inner-Jewish' relationships, and that several should be concerned with Christian 'sects'.

The opening essay, by Ithamar Gruenwald, explores the delicate interplay between intolerance and martyrdom. With a wide range of examples, he shows that 'they are not as sharply separated in human conduct as a liberal mind would wish them to be' (p. 15). The deaths of Socrates and Rabbi 'Aqiva are singled out for extended discussion, 'for each one in his own way ... marks the way from philosophical self-resignation to religious martyrdom' (p. 20). In concluding comments with which every reader will concur, Gruenwald insists that in the last resort the unwavering declaration of faith and the total rejection of evil are most potent means of destabilizing the sophisticated machinery of evil.

The 'boundaries and bridges' between Jews and Gentiles in the Maccabean period are discussed by Daniel R. Schwartz. Whereas 1 Maccabees presents non-Jews as basically evil, in 2 Maccabees Gentiles are broadly sympathetic towards Jews. Schwartz shows that there are even more crucial differences: in 2 Maccabees (but not in 1 Maccabees) being a Jew is not determined exclusively by one's birth, but by one's adherence to 'Judaism', a word perhaps coined by the writer. This conviction eventually won the day.

Why did groups such as Pharisees, Sadducees, Essenes and the Qumran covenanters emerge and flourish in Second Temple Judaism? Albert I. Baumgarten suggests that in some respects sectarianism is like messianism: both are part and parcel of Judaism's biblical heritage, and both tend to break out at irregular intervals. He then examines one aspect of messianic expectations, the pursuit of the millennium, in order to shed light on the broader question of sectarianism. While he accepts that millenarian movements are often born out of despair, he shows that, somewhat surprisingly, some emerged in response to a victory.

'Inner-Jewish' tensions are explored in Michael Mach's essay on the Qumran community. Here the intolerance of a group which sees itself as 'the true Israel' is evident, even though that term is not used. The 'declared conservatism' of the Qumran community is defended by means of radical theological innovation which uses divine revelation as an exegetical device as part of a new scriptural hermeneutic. Although Mach does not discuss striking partial parallels from later Jewish and Christian history, the reader will have no difficulty in supplying some of them.

How did it come about that some Jews were considered to have crossed beyond the acceptable boundaries of Judaism? John M. G. Barclay notes that this issue is considered far less frequently than the acceptance of Gentiles who wished to cross the boundary and enter the Jewish community. He discusses various individuals and groups considered to be apostate within Diaspora Judaism. He rightly notes that there are important implications for the parting of the ways between some early Christian groups and Jewish communities. One of Barclay's examples, Paul, is discussed in the two chapters which follow.

Justin Taylor asks a well-known question: Why did Paul persecute the church? After carefully assessing the main answers which this question has received, he advances the hypothesis that before his 'call' or 'conversion', Paul persecuted the church as a result of his hostility as a 'Zealot' towards a group which stood apart from the national struggle against Rome.

Stephen C. Barton warns against reading Paul's writings with modern notions of tolerance and intolerance in mind, and explores passages which reflect the theological principles with which Paul operated. Barton insists that we do not do the cause of a proper tolerance and a proper intolerance any favours if we harness Paul (or Jesus, or early Christianity) to the band-wagon of post-Enlightenment secular individualism amd pluralism.

The following three essays return to a topic raised by Daniel R. Schwartz: the boundaries and bridges drawn by Jews and Christians and the pagan world at large. Maren R. Niehoff considers Philo's views on paganism: he generally tends to stress the religious boundaries between Jewish monotheism and pagan idolatry. And yet there is irony in the way that Philo has appropriated pagan hermeneutics and philosophy in order to maintain and redefine the boundary between Judaism and paganism.

Moshe Halbertal considers the same topic from the very different second-century rabbinic perspective of the Mishnaic tractate *Avodah Zarah*. This tractate 'reflects a reality of two communities, Jewish and pagan, entangled with one another, within the setting of Hellenistic cities of the land of Israel' (p. 159). He outlines different conceptions of toleration and discusses their relations to the

4

rabbinic world, noting that coexistence of Jews and pagans is a
fact; the aim of the Mishnah 'is both to continue a form of the
struggle and distancing on the one hand and on the other hand to
create a space for legitimate interaction' (p. 166). This principle is
discussed with reference to several fascinating examples.

Guy G. Stroumsa also considers the Mishnaic tractate *Avodah
Zarah*, although his primary focus is on an almost contemporary
Christian writing, Tertullian's *De idololatria*. Stroumsa shows that
there are interesting similarities and differences between *Avodah
Zarah's* rabbinic and Tertullian's early Christian response to the
dominant pagan religious currents in the early Roman Empire.

The nine papers which form the second half of the book are all
concerned with aspects of early Jewish–Christian relationships.
François Blanchetière expounds three very different attitudes
towards Judaism held by early Christian writers. His discussion
ranges from the New Testament to Theodosius the Great at the
end of the fourth century.

The essay which follows complements Blanchetière's survey.
Joel Marcus discusses in detail the anti-Jewish polemic of one
key passage, Mark's Parable of the Vineyard (Mark 12:1–12). He
claims that under the impact of a chaotic social setting, Mark's
parable is a thoroughly polemical re-reading of the Vineyard Song
in Isaiah 5, which illustrates how highly charged the inheritance
dispute between Jews and Christians became in the first century.
Marcus distances himself from the fierce language of Mark 12:1–9
and suggests that one way forward may be by returning from
Mark 12 to Isaiah 5, for, after all, 'Isaiah's tenderly nurtured vineyard that has sprung Eden-like from God's hand' is also part of
the Christian canon (p. 223).

Richard Bauckham and Martinus C. de Boer consider two
Jewish–Christian groups where continuity with Judaism is more in
evidence than in most other strands of early Christianity. Bauckham discusses neglected evidence from the *Apocalypse of Peter* for
the existence of Jewish Christians in the land of Israel early in the
second century. He shows that the opening and closing sections of
this work fit the context of Bar Kochba's war against Rome and
that they illuminate Jewish–Christian responses to that war.

Martinus C. de Boer examines the complex evidence from
Jewish and Christian writings for the existence and influence of

the Nazoreans. There is continuity between the Nazorean 'sect' or 'party' mentioned in Acts 24:5 and the Nazoreans discussed by Epiphanius in the fourth century. By this time both Jewish and Christian authorities had come to regard them as 'heretics'; squeezed by intolerance from both sides, they failed to retain their toe-hold on history.

Second-century Christian writings of particular interest to the student of early Christian–Jewish relationships are discussed by two contributors. Graham N. Stanton claims that Justin Martyr's *Dialogue* with his Jewish opponent Trypho contains neglected evidence for the existence of Gentile 'God-fearers' with a close attachment to Judaism, even though Justin does not use a special term for this group. The *Dialogue* also shows that although both 'synagogue' and 'church' are concerned to maintain firm boundary lines, there is movement across both boundaries.

With special reference to Justin Martyr's *Dialogue* and *Apologies*, and also to the *Martyrdom of Polycarp*, Judith M. Lieu discusses the relationship between rhetoric and reality in second-century accusations of Jewish anti-Christian persecution. She insists that when we read these passages, the first question should not be, 'Did Jews persecute Christians?, but rather, 'Why did Christians perceive Jews as persecutors?' While not denying that there may be some historical reality behind the rhetoric, she shows that references to Jewish persecution of Christians have been shaped by a variety of theological concerns. The extent to which this has happened will surprise many readers.

William Horbury notes that our knowledge of Jewish worship in the ancient world is limited, and considers passages from a wide range of early Christian writings which historians must take seriously in discussions of the rise of the synagogue and of Jewish public prayer. Although he recognizes that Judith M. Lieu (and other scholars) have shown that Christian writings have been shaped by polemic and theology, he insists that assessment of the Christian sources should also take account of the invaluable if hostile observations which are often made concerning Jewish worship.

How were messianic expectations and convictions about Torah taken up and developed or reinterpreted in early Christian writings? Andrew Chester calls in question some widely accepted answers to this key question: he shows that within the main strands of the early Christian movement there was a very wide range of attitudes to Torah. In some Christian writings there is a call to intensify the demands of Torah, while at the other extreme there is a deliberate rejection, or least superseding, of Torah. So Torah both unites and divides early Judaism and early Christianity.

In the final chapter Markus Bockmuehl takes up a theme discussed in the earlier essays by Daniel R. Schwartz, Maren R. Niehoff, Moshe Halbertal and Guy G. Stroumsa: the stances Jews and Christians adopted towards the pagan world with which they had to come to terms. Bockmuehl concentrates on the many similarities and the smaller number of differences in the ways in which Jews and Christians communicated their ethical convictions to 'outsiders', i.e. within the early imperial environment of pluralistic paganism. Here, as in Andrew Chester's essay, it is the extent of the common ground between Jews and Christians which is perhaps unexpected. Bockmuehl lays particular stress on the way in which traditional Jewish halakah for Gentiles 'provides much of the chicken stock for the broth of internal Christian ethics' (p. 351). He notes that his point is regularly ignored by writers on Christian ethics who overemphasize the distinctively Christian theological factors which shaped the moral vision of early Christian writers.

This is the first time scholars from British and Israeli Universities have collaborated in a venture of this kind. The essays in this volume are revised versions of papers delivered at a symposium in Jerusalem in April 1994 which was sponsored by the Academic Study Group, a British organization which links British and Israeli scholars from a wide variety of academic disciplines. The essays have all benefited from questions and discussion initiated by colleagues from very different backgrounds. Readers will soon discover that some of the most perceptive insights into Christian writings are made by Jewish scholars, and vice versa. The contributors are grateful to the Academic Study Group for its generous financial support, and to its Director, John Levy, and to Guy G. Stroumsa, for making all the detailed arrangements for our fruitful seminars in Jerusalem.

CHAPTER I

Intolerance and martyrdom: from Socrates to Rabbi 'Aqiva

Ithamar Gruenwald

I

The terms used in the title of the present paper point to the moral polarization of philosophical norms and historical inevitabilities. Philosophical principles aim at setting clear moral norms and standards of behaviour. They are expected to guide people in their practical decisions even in the face of adverse historical and personal events. However, as is well known, adhering to one's philosophical convictions often leads to head-on clashes with practical needs and the will to survive. Thus, it turns out that matters are not as simple and as clearly defined in the cases which will be discussed in the present essay as one would wish them to be.

Martyrdom results when attempts at maintaining moral integrity in the face of evil and acts of despotism end in death or personal disaster. Those who are exposed to the martyrological ordeal are likely to become master-models of moral perseverance and standing. Their personal agony is turned into a display of public heroism. If they do not succeed in securing for themselves physical survival, they still survive in the memory of people as models of courage and moral integrity. Martyrs are likely to be viewed as heroes who could look into the face of death without succumbing to selfish desires of physical survival.

Socrates and Rabbi 'Aqiva are victims whose deaths received the limelight of historical attention. They were executed for different reasons and at different times. Their respective deaths are almost minutely recorded. Their names stand out in history as heroes whose moral standing and steadfastness are of exemplary importance. However, when intolerance is viewed in conjunction with martyrdom, matters become more complicated than they sometimes look. In principle, intolerance is the obvious opposite of martyrdom, and often its very cause. In practice, however, the distinctions between these two terms and their actual manifestations are not as clearly delineated as we would like them to be. The complexities involved in these matters are the subject of the present essay.

Let us start by stating the fact that history abounds in cases in which the potential martyr of today becomes the instigator of intolerance in the days to come. *Mutatis mutandis*, when today's propagators of intolerance are executed, they are likely to become in the eyes of their supporters the martyrs of the next day. In this respect, the martyrological situation is not as unambiguously outlined as it often appears to those who derive their notions about martyrology from a well-formulated theology of martyrdom.

There are an amazing number of cases in which dramatic changes occur in the roles enacted on the historical scene: the potential victim of today dramatically turns the tables and becomes the actual victimizer of the next historical phase. Or, to put it even more succinctly, categories of moral and immoral behaviour all too easily shift roles. Sometimes, it takes only a wink of the eye to bring about vicissitudinous changes in the respective forms of behaviour.

As a matter of moral preference, the praise, of course, goes to those who suffer and are the victims or martyrs in our historical and theological perception. That is, Socrates and Rabbi 'Aqiva stand high in our historical esteem. Our Western cultural values and religious attitudes make this an almost automatic choice. However, it belongs to the sad side of our historical consciousness when the memory of the martyrological acts is not always as enduring as it should be. In fact, when it comes to it, martyrological awareness seldom becomes an efficient tool in suppressing admiration for unrestrained political strength. We are somehow inclined to live in situations in which ambivalence prevails: moral codes enhance one set of values, while political practice sets different models of preferences and priorities. The great heroes of a nation are not always the martyrs of blessed memory, but the great conquerors that bring worldly power and success to their nations.

In spite of all the moral values that are at the heart of our Western culture and religious consciousness, we often fall into the trap of making wrong choices in regard to what real strength is and what its ideal forms of expression are. We frequently think that, because it enjoys the mere power of its sway, a certain political regime is correctly geared and should therefore be universally supported. However, sooner or later we realize that this was yet another trap into which we inadvertently fell. On other occasions, we discover (once again at a rather late moment) that our choice of a martyr was wrong. The person whom we had naively considered to be a martyr turned out to be an impostor.[1] With this we reach the heart of our problem, with all its inevitable complexities and mixed attitudes. Every example that can be given to illustrate our line of argumentation can be subjected to conflicting evaluations. Who stands for what in our evaluation of historical figures? Or, are moral choices a matter of playing around with ambivalent attitudes?

Cultural and religious values are easily proclaimed as normative forms of behaviour. More rigour and determination are demanded, though, from those who are called upon to enact these forms of behaviour in practical life. Moreover, when it comes to maintaining clear distinctions between opposites and contrasting values (to say nothing of reserving praise for, or else condemning, historical heroes), routinely marked borderlines are not always discerned, let alone consistently observed. Humans are given to quick shifts in moral judgement and behaviour. Thus, moral standards that are expected to help differentiate between a persecuted person and his persecutor are recklessly abandoned for the sake of a more opportunist stance.

As indicated above, the persecutor may even be viewed by his supporters as the sage forced to do things as a result of which he will have to suffer the criticism of his 'blindfolded' opponents. One group of people may consider him as fulfilling a historical mission in redressing evil and social injustice. The other group, belonging to the 'opposition', whether on the left or the right, is always viewed as foolish and evil. How long did it take people to realize that the so-called 'Great Light of the Nations', Joseph Stalin, was really a bloodthirsty tyrant? It is reasonable to argue that the Prince of History could have done a better job, if he had given people the chance of writing their once imprisoned later-to-become-dictators in the lists of political martyrs rather than allowing them to become the all-powerful leaders of nations.

In the light of the above, it should not appear strange that our discussion has begun by highlighting paradoxes and dialectical attitudes. History is not painted on one side of the canvas. When

we look at the reverse side, we are very likely to be struck by the
unexpected. In fact, experience shows that the unexpected should
always be expected. But when it comes to the teaching of moral
values, we hold fast to the ground on which we stand, trusting it
not to be as slippery as it sometimes proves to be. The fact that
this quite often turns out to be a self-deluding expectation is at the
very heart of our perception of the subject-matter.

Psychologically speaking, intolerance may be a manifestation of
something much more disturbing than just a failure of nerve or an
overdose of political tactics. Intolerance can reflect frustration,
impatience, fear, weakness and even despair. Admittedly, in speaking about martyrs we incline to emphasize the opposite qualities,
such as moral courage, political integrity and pious perfection.
However, the martyr, too, can be shown as the inevitable victim of
his own mental frailties: instead of finding solutions that require
all the resources of his practical shrewdness and courage, he responds with what may be described by some as paralysing despon-
dency. We still believe that moral dignity is a fortitude; those who
can carry that dignity even to their own gallows are justly called
martyrs. However, different people may have different views on
the same subject.

2

When we are able to sympathize with the victim rather than side
with the victimizer, we are inclined to see that as a sign of our own
moral integrity. But practice shows that people do not always stand
the test of their own code of moral values. An internal moral voice
tells us that we should favour the victim. The victimizer should
always be condemned as the cowardly rascal in the camp of the
enemy. One of the sad lessons that history teaches us is that it
amounts to moral blindness if intolerance is singularly detected in
'them' and never in 'us'. We morally compliment ourselves on the
preference we are able to show towards those suffering misery, dejection and the consequences of political oppression. We equally
praise ourselves for the fortitude shown in rejecting all forms of
tyranny. We Jews cannot forget for a single moment the horrors
inflicted upon our forefathers by the crusaders and the executioners
of the Spanish Inquisition. However, we should not be forgetful
of the fact that even Scripture testifies that when the Israelites

had their chance, mercy was suspended by divine decree.[2] Moral preaching can easily become the cover of latent prejudices. When double-talk is normalized as a standard form of behaviour and hypocrisy is accepted, even passively, as an inevitable historical necessity, alarms should be sounded.

It is not uncommon to find people who put their moral sensibility to sleep, then notice that, for example, their own educational system is faultless, while that of their opponents is clearly marked by moral disorientation. When this happens, it is indeed difficult to suppress cynicism in our assessment of the situation. Can we really find consolation in the fact that evil is found only in the 'other'[3]? Moreover, are the declared martyrs always as morally impeccable as their biographers wish them to appear? We cherish the divine grace shining through the written 'Acts of the Martyrs', Christian or Jewish alike. We are confident that martyrs deserve their eternal memorization. They are there to set a perfect and moral standard.

However, when it comes to more practical aspects of historical study, it is difficult to disguise tinges of admiration for the strong and lucky ones. Are we going then to tell those who care to listen that, when they open their history books, they are likely to be tempted by the glory of those who marched the globe and subjected others to their dominion? To make matters worse, neutrality verging on dejection towards the unluckiness of the conquered ones forces itself upon the minds of readers contemplating routine forms of historical discourse.

There is no way around the fact that most of our historical erudition comes from the exhilarating stories about despots who changed the course of history by means of a reckless display of power resulting in torture and coercion. Intolerance, to be sure, can thrive only when it is supported by a political 'philosophy' geared towards advocating the use of power. When the 'theology' of martyrdom has to contest against the 'philosophy' of intolerance, the results are not always predictable. Some people may delude themselves into thinking that martyrdom is the flag under which only the meekly minded believers go. By the same token, fascination with power is viewed as the vice of the strong and assertive type of people. Evidently, there is a moment in all this when a confusion of moral preferences takes over. Indeed, the more painful parts of our story deal with those who in our view should be siding with the positions taken by martyrs but instead show fascination with the options opened by the opposite position. It is indeed difficult to escape one's own moments of manic triumphalism, as a consequence of which martyrdom is likely to be ranked less highly than advocated in the official 'theologies'. What measures can, after all, be taken against hilarious jubilations, connected with outbursts of self-confidence and power, which fill our ears to the point of utter confusion?

Various ways are known to us in which the deaths of martyrs receive their desired glorification. Their death stories are told in special 'Acts', in homiletic compositions and in prayers. There is even a mystical version that tells of the legendary death of ten Jewish martyrs.[4] The story of Socrates' death, however, is told as part of Plato's philosophical oeuvre. Its theological function is rather limited. But, as we are going to see, there clearly were religious aspects in the accusations brought up against Socrates: he was a victim of a nervous society that could not cope with an exposure to probing questions of moral integrity and philosophical truth. In the final resort, though, he was accused of introducing new, and false, deities into the city. In the case of Rabbi 'Aqiva, his steadfastness in the face of religious persecution made him into a model of a God-loving martyr. Reportedly, he was ready to pay with his life for his refusal to break the rules of the Torah-law. Naturally, the sympathy of people is likely to be given to those who become the victim-heroes of political and religious persecutions.

However, the so-called objective observer may not be altogether off the track of reason when asking, 'Whose good has the ultimate right to prevail: that of the victim or that of the victimizer?' For the mere fact that a person considers himself to be the victim of a brutal political regime does not automatically guarantee the justice of his cause. We like to think that Socrates was correct; we give our vote of confidence to Rabbi 'Aqiva's perseverance in the face of religious coercion. But when taken from the points of view of the respective persecutors, are their arguments totally unreasonable? One should bear in mind that Rabbi 'Aqiva was in all likelihood deeply involved in a rebellion against the Romans; and the city had to defend itself against radical free-thinkers of the kind they thought they found in Socrates.

In the eyes of the people, there is no essential difference between intolerance as enacted by a political regime and that of a religious authority. Any ecclesiastical authority is as efficient in the activation of its coercive powers as is the secret-police of a secular state. And where a Roman Catholic Cardinal has the prerogative of withholding his *nihil obstat*, or even of putting books on the Index of forbidden books – to say nothing of feeding their pages to a bonfire – a politically appointed censor may still have a lesson to learn before receiving the acclaim of his or her superiors.

When viewed from the point of view of killer or executioner, no substantial difference is made between those who die for a religious cause, and are called 'martyrs', and those who die for a military or political cause, and are called 'victims'. In the eyes of the killer, no value distinctions are made: those who die unquestionably deserve their deaths. From the point of view of the killer, maintaining the justice of the victim is tantamount to betraying one's office and country. Not pulling the trigger when called upon to do so means contributing to the spread of anarchy and political disobedience. However, as historical experience shows, there is a professed reluctance on the part of the ruling authorities to enact their full juridical power in executing people. The reason given is always the same one: capital punishment, even when justified by the law, is likely to produce martyrs.

3

We have already alluded to the fact that cynicism inadvertently sneaks into our handling of the subject-matter. We can add here that more than just a tinge of relativism accompanies it, too. We cannot avoid noticing that when dealing with the relevant case histories the need to create argumentative coherence has sometimes to give way to moral confusion. Moreover, if the nomenclature of 'victim' and 'victimizer' is abandoned, even for the sake of the argument, the problem of siding with one party or another becomes an aggravating one indeed. The terms 'victim' and 'victimizer' entail a clear value judgement, and may, thus, induce the impression that ethical considerations dictate the respective choices and preferences. However, the very right to pass moral judgement is somehow called in question, or at least suspended, when justice has simultaneously to be done to both of the conflicting parties.

It must be admitted, though, that the mere fact that two parties are involved in a conflict does not make them equally right at one and the same time, as also to the same effect. There may well be one party that is absolutely right and another that is totally wrong. In the face of confusion, relativism and anarchy, a sense of moral order and certainty must be maintained. It does not require much to take the position of the outsider, the so-called neutral observer, in order to avoid getting seriously involved in the conflict and taking sides with one party or the other. People are sometimes inclined to think that abstract philosophical positions are a safeguard against political involvement. This may well be the case. However, political detachment, or neutrality, can sometimes become the road upon which the troops of injustice march undisturbed. Perfect balance in the face of brutal enactments of intolerance and almost suicidal outbursts of people who face barred doors may be tantamount to complying actively with criminal or violent modes of behaviour. To withhold one's judgement is one way of sanctioning injustice. If moral anarchy is to be avoided, this position has to be shunned.

Let me give you an example of what I have in mind. When the early Christians suffered martyrdom, they certainly thought that their moral perseverance when confronted by death deserved all the praise of those who valued moral tenacity. Ecclesiastical sanctification, or beatification, came in at a later stage, sometimes at a period when the church no longer needed the living examples of people verifying its creeds. Beatification set in, in fact, when the Catholic Church was in full political power and in control of historical events. Lessons, however, are selectively learned. Thus, when the mental offspring of those church-martyrs had the chance, in their capacity as the medieval crusaders, they did not think twice when enforcing a martyrological situation on other people. The Jews of Germany and France, who were the victims of such persecutions, figured in the eyes of those crusaders as no better than worthless infidels who deserved nothing but hell on earth. But the crusaders did not take into consideration one essential matter: their victims turned into martyrs, and thus contributed to counterpointing the alleged exclusivity of Christian-grounded martyrological claims.

Mutatis mutandis, in Jewish quarters there is an outspoken glorification of martyrdom. However, this glorification must be positioned against the background of religious intolerance to which ample expression was given in scriptural times. Obviously, oppressed and oppressor should not be placed on one and the same moral level. When this nevertheless happens, it can easily create moral confusion in the minds of people. Biases, we should remember, are not the prerogative of one 'privileged' side only. The enlightened mind of the historian and philosopher should be open to reading the legend on both sides of the coin. We are therefore forced to admit that in the light of historical facts, and philosophical considerations, the questions which we address here quite easily lead to relativistic positions. This, it must be reiterated, happens almost in spite of our wish not to reach this station.

Intolerance, like many other forms of vice in human nature and history, can always be rationalized by a good number of reasons. However, rationalizations aside, what should really give us concern is the fact, pointed out above, that the qualities of intolerance and martyrdom are not as sharply delineated in human conduct and practice as a liberal mind should wish them to be. It amounts to one of the mysteries of human nature that piety and brutality, the need to keep public order and the urge to maintain modes of personal freedom, even grace and frivolity, are likely to change roles instead of keeping to their own separated territories. When neighbours who have to stay behind barred doors break loose, moral confusion is the smallest damage that is done.

The fearful symmetry that so often manifests itself in acts of intolerance and martyrdom comes very close to what in another context is referred to as the irony of fate. One of the letters which the two Zionist leaders Hayyim Arlosorof and Chaim Weitzmann exchanged in 1932 had the following to say about the desired relationship between Arabs and Jews in the then Palestine:

... under the current circumstances, it is impossible to materialize Zionism without an interim period in which the Jewish minority will enact an organized revolutionary rule ... a national minority government ... will conquer the country's administration ... so as to prevent the danger of a take-over by the non-Jewish majority and an uprising against us ...

Arlosorof, who wrote this letter, gave good reasons for bringing into effect what he called 'an organized revolutionary rule' of the Jewish minority. Although he gave expression to what may be considered as his private credo only, he made it a case worth considering on a nation-wide level. This at least is what he wanted his addressee to believe. However, within a year of that letter, this

advocate of 'an organized revolutionary rule' became a victim, if
not a martyr, himself.

In a sense, Arlosorof may have paved his own way from professed intolerance to inevitable political martyrdom. In other parts
of our paper we point to cases that proceed in the opposite direction, namely, from potential martyrdom to outright intolerance.
In all those cases the legend on the two sides of the coin is the
same one. The relative and changing value of the 'coins' in question with regard to what they can 'buy' is one of the great riddles
circulating the market-place of moral confusion. The trading rules
of the market are very often dictated by opportunism and pre-
tence, to say nothing of blatant fraud. It is all too common to find
people who showed the fist but played the martyr; and, vice versa,
people who had been doomed to become potential martyrs but
ultimately engaged in what proved to be a violent display of fists.
Genuine martyrdom is a rarity; and when found, special stands
are erected to make its heroes show in all their glory.

As a rule, we know, intolerance is a sign of weakness. It reflects
the inability to show flexibility when a realistic policy requires
it. In one way or another, martyrdom shares the same faults. It
speaks for a certain reluctance on the part of the martyr to make
concessions when rigid rules and principles are enforced upon him
or her. Indeed, compromises, even when most desired, are viewed
by many as a sign of weakness. However, we shall soon discuss
views that insist on making compromises, particularly when what is
at stake are the lives of people. Not all problems require a martyr's
position to solve them. However, those who prefer the death of a
martyr to succumbing to the coercive oppression of a despot do so
because they believe that martyrdom is the only honourable way
of showing integrity and steadfastness when confronted by moral
vice and political evil. Some people are always ready to pay a high
price irrespective of what can realistically be achieved.

Although many people would share the belief that any faltering
in the face of the dictates of a despotic ruler epitomizes ignomin-
ious self-betrayal, the opposite position – namely that of the martyr
– is not always sanctioned in Jewish thought. Maimonides (1135–
1204) is a famous example of a high-ranking thinker who advocates restraint in the light of the suicidal zeal of certain people.[5]
However, Maimonides was severely criticized for his views on the
subject; and in the minds of many, martyrdom is still held as a

most prominent token of one's Jewish identity and commitment. In modern times, the Holocaust increased what may be referred to as the martyrological consciousness of the Jewish people. And the endless wars waged between Jews and Arabs in the Middle East has increased on the Jewish side the complementary sacrifice-consciousness.

4

The interplay between intolerance and martyrdom creates a unique dynamic in human history. Suffering as such becomes an underlying feature in shaping the ideological dynamics of historical change. We underline this fact, because suffering is not always viewed in the same light as presented here. There are famous examples that show how the same events are described from two self-excluding points of view. One such example is the Maccabean uprising against the so-called Greeks who ruled Israel in about 165 BCE. The earliest 'histories' describing the events of that time fall into two groups: (1) Documents, like 1 Maccabees, that glorify the wars waged and won by the Hasmonean rulers. (2) Documents, like 2 Maccabees and 4 Maccabees, that present other – i.e., basically martyrological – points of view in their stories. In that context the martyrdom of the old priest and that of the mother with her seven sons occupy a central position.

In many respects, 2 and 4 Maccabees shaped the predilection for the display of martyrological acts as they established themselves in the Judaism and Christianity of later times. Extreme modes of martyrdom, and self-sacrifice, are also found in Islam. It becomes yet another paradox that characterizes our subject-matter, when we realize that the same religions that are the cradle in which martyrdom grows are also the matrix in which acts of intolerance are sanctioned for certain purposes. When watching the universal God splitting attention between the supplicant prayers of the victims and the self-encouraging hymns of the victimizers, the bitter smile on one's face cannot be removed. Victim and victimizer here stand on two different sides of the religious borderlines. Since we usually recognize only one God, we do not know what the God of the other side thinks when watching the events played out on terrestrial domains.

In the ancient world, the defeat of a nation implied the defeat

of its god(s). Wars were simultaneously fought in heaven and on
earth. It was evident to all that any outcome of the war reflected a
corresponding decision in heaven. Consequently, a defeated people reflected a defeated god. The god(s) of the conquerors was/
were readily adapted, since a god that failed his people in times
of war and stress was not worth the money spent on the pur-
chase of the gifts offered to him. Moreover, the gains of cultural
adaptation were considerable: accepting the hegemony of the victorious god(s) aided the process of recovery from, and adjust-
ment after, the traumas of the war. In any event, it prevented the
prolongation of blood-shedding. In other words, succumbing to
the conditions put forward by the conquering forces was instru-
mental in circumventing situations that were potentially condu-
cive to unnecessary displays of power and consequently to acts of
martyrdom.

5

One of the basic needs of any group of people, as also that of
individuals, is to define their respective identity. Identity is more
often than not created by distancing the self or the group from the
'other', that is, by creating a sense of cultural distance and exclusiveness. In many cases, exclusiveness is the matrix in which conflicts breed. Those conflicts, even when positively geared towards
the formation of territorial, and other, forms of independence, inevitably lead to massive discharges of aggression. When the God
of the Israelites is invoked to march in front of the on-marching
troops, all the nations of old Canaan are doomed to total destruction: ' . . . you must utterly destroy them; you shall make no covenant with them, and show no mercy to them'. Or: 'You must put
them to death. You must not make a treaty with them or spare
them.' The difference between those two injunctions is only a
matter of choice between two translations of the same Hebrew
text, Deuteronomy 7:2. The consequences for the Canaanites,
though, were all the same. And since we have only the reports of
the victors, we do not know what the gods of Canaan told their
believers by way of theological and political consolation.

There was no mercy shown by the Israelites towards those whom
they defeated, or expected to defeat, in war.[6] However, in condemning the Israelites one is well advised to listen to the words of

warning reportedly spoken by Jesus in the Sermon on the Mount: 'Judge not, that you be not judged ... Why do you see the speck that is in your brother's eye, but do not notice the log that is in your own eye?' (Matt. 7:1–5). Unfortunately, as can be seen in other New Testament writings, Jesus' words had no effect on later ways of thinking. Take the following as a typical example: 'Behold, I will make those of the Assembly [in Greek: *synagōgē*, often modernized as 'Synagogue'] of Satan who say that they are Jews and are not ... come down and bow down before your feet, and learn that I have loved you' (Rev. 3:9). The words reflect the newly established mood of Christian triumphalism: those who call themselves Jews, but are not, are obviously Jews who have not been converted to Christianity. This is one of the earliest, and sharpest, expressions of the Christian doctrine of *Verus Israel*. How much horror and brutality were spread through these words! They relegated the Jews who remained faithful to the religion of their ancestors to the status of the Synagogue of Satan. The very resonance of these words paved the road which innumerable Jews had to tread, being pursued to their own Golgotha.

It is certainly more than just a matter of historical coincidence, when, in the name of the person who advocated the moral principle 'Do not resist one who is evil. But if any one strikes you on the right cheek, turn to him the other also' (Matt. 5:38), religious intolerance was practised by the letter of the law. The complementary injunction to love one's neighbour as one loves God readily suggests itself as the call for religious toleration. But history often ran a different course, one that suspended the love of one's neighbour in the name of the love of one's God.

In terms of vindicating religious intolerance, Islam does not appear to lag much behind its two historical forerunners, Judaism and Christianity. The Muslims see in inflicting the wrath of God on infidels and making it as painfully felt as possible an expression of their utter commitment to their religious ideals. The Holy War, *jihad*, which Muslims are called to enact with great zeal, is also a major factor in modern politics and power games. In such cases, as in so many other ones, the unguarded borderlines between religious fanaticism and radical politics are easily transgressed. To cut a long and painful story short, it is not uncommon in the history of religions to hear the soft voice of a Jacob which slyly camouflages the harsh hands of an Esau.

6

However mind-stimulating the study of the various forms of religious and political intolerance is, our main attention here should
be given to another issue, namely, the voluntary death of two people, Socrates and Rabbi 'Aqiva.[7] Their respective deaths stand out
in Western, or Judaic-Christian, culture as models of moral steadfastness. Each in his own way, Socrates and Rabbi 'Aqiva mark in
our eyes the path from philosophical self-resignation to religious
martyrdom. For, in the case of Socrates, we find the acceptance
of death based on moral-political and philosophical principles, and,
in the case of Rabbi 'Aqiva, we encounter the fulfilment of religious
love for God as the major factor in an act of heroic martyrdom.

The path that leads from Socrates to Rabbi 'Aqiva is a long and
winding one. However, both figures stand out in the history of
Western culture and consciousness as beacons throwing exemplary
light in the direction of those who are exposed to similar ordeals
and tests of moral courage and spiritual integrity. Moreover, their
deaths became cultural models even for those who were carried
away on imaginary trips in the course of which they saw themselves exposed to extreme risks. The very preparedness to die for a
cause or an idea is tantamount in the eyes of many to actual martyrdom in whatever phase or circumstance it may occur.

It has been argued that the model for Jewish, and hence also
Christian, martyrdom was set not by the martyrs of Maccabean
times, but by their philosophically trained forerunner, Socrates.[8]
Socrates arguably showed the right way to all posterity: when the
ideas for which life is worth living are under threat of being tram-
pled down, it befits a person to consider giving up his life. Whether
Jewish and Christian indebtedness to the noble model set by Socrates is real or merely a scholarly allegation is a question that need
not be settled here. It is indeed questionable whether Rabbi 'Aqiva,
who died a martyr's death during the notorious Hadrianic persecutions in the 130s, actually knew anything about Socrates. But
he certainly was acquainted with the stories about the martyrs of
Hasmonean times, as referred to above.

Since 2 and 4 Maccabees, in which those reports are included,
were composed in a Hellenistic environment, it is conceivable that
at least in their case a Platonic influence can be expected. Admit-

tedly, since these books do not mention Socrates, they cannot be counted as building an argument relying on his prototypical death. However, the explicitly Hellenistic tone of these texts makes it very likely that their concept of martyrdom has a pagan flavour to it. Astonishingly few references to the battles of the Maccabees are contained in 2 Maccabees, whereas 4 Maccabees makes no mention of them at all! On the contrary, 4 Maccabees has a clearly defined philosophical programme: it aims at proving that spiritual qualities, such as 'devout reason' (ὁ εὐσεβὴς λογισμός), are much stronger factors in directing one's way of life than are the needs of the body. Consequently, the former have to be viewed as more praiseworthy than anything that has to do with physical survival.

What do we know of the death of Socrates? In his *Apology*, Plato tells that Socrates was accused of 'corrupting the minds of the young, and of believing in deities of his own invention, instead of the gods recognized by the state'. It should be noticed that the words used by Plato in reference to divine beings make a clear distinction between the *theous* of the state and the *daimonia kaina* in which Socrates allegedly believed. Apparently, the prosecution wanted its case to be formulated as clearly as possible, including its terminologically expressed prejudices. But in almost no time Socrates was able to show that those speaking on behalf of the prosecution had been engaging in nonsensical tautologies. Socrates defended himself by arguing that he had been unjustly accused, and that what really was at stake was his accusers' inability to live up to the moral standards that he had set for himself and his philosophical followers. In his own words, the moral, or philosophical, integrity that he preached, 'had incurred a great deal of bitter hostility, and this is what will bring about my destruction – not Meletus or Anytus, but the slander and jealousy of a very large section of the people'. *Diabole* and *Phthonos* are the key words used here for what in modern parlance would pass for 'intolerance'. In the face of such a weird situation, Socrates could not but come to a drastic resolution:

The truth of the matter is this, gentlemen: Where a man has once taken up his stand, either because it seems best to him or in obedience to his orders, there, I believe, he is bound to remain and face the danger, taking no account of death or anything else before dishonour.

The last words as quoted from Socrates' self-defence can well serve as any martyr's ideological pledge. They strike universal tones of spiritual integrity, moral courage and intellectual commitment. In a similar manner, we find in 2 Maccabees that Eleazar, an old priest and sage, defends himself for refusing to eat pork by saying, among other things:

Therefore, if I now bravely give up my life, I shall show myself worthy of my old age, as I leave to the young a noble example of how to go eagerly and nobly to die a beautiful death in the defence of our revered and sacred laws. (6:27–8)

A more philosophical tone is struck in 4 Maccabees, where the old man is quoted as saying:

I will not violate the solemn oath of my ancestors to keep the Law, not even if you gouge out my eyes and burn my entrails. I am neither so old nor short of manliness that in a matter of religion my reason should lose its useful vigour. So set the torturer's wheel turning and fan the fire to a great blaze ... I will not play you false, O Law of my teacher; I will not forswear you, beloved self-control. I will not shame you, philosophic reason, nor will I deny you, venerable priesthood and knowledge of the Law. (5:29–35)

With all its intellectual charm, such discourse can easily lose the touch of heroic pathos to propagandist sentimentality. However, in terms of one's preparedness to give up one's life for a cause, what matters most is the deed, not the poetics of the declamation. Rhetoric can do wonders. However, as we all know, the distance between rhetorical declamation and actual performance is more easily covered when evil intentions, rather than good deeds, set the intensity of the motivation.

7

Naturally, Socrates' speeches favouring death over a change of mind with respect to moral behaviour, particularly as reported in Plato's *The Phaedo*, are of a completely different spiritual nature from the one given expression to in 2 and 4 Maccabees. One should not forget, though, that the accusations against Socrates turned around religious issues, too. Moreover, the belief in the eternal nature of the soul creates an interesting link between Socrates and the 'Maccabean' martyrs.[9] In fact, it has been shown that the Jewish, and particularly rabbinic, doctrine of the immortality of the soul – and consequently the notion of the transmigration of souls and even of the future resurrection of the body – have their roots in Hellenistic beliefs and doctrines.[10]

In this connection it is interesting to notice that according to the story incorporated in Flavius Josephus' *The Jewish War* (7.320ff.), Eleazar, the leader of the Zealots at Masada, did not succeed in persuading his followers to commit suicide rather than falling into the hands of the Roman troops, before he had preached to them the Orphic sermon on the body being the walking-grave of the soul!

It is once again Socrates that first gave that Orphic idea a fully fledged philosophical expression. In Plato's *Cratylus* (400c) we find him saying:

For some say that the body is the grave (σῆμα) of the soul which may be thought to be buried in our present life ... Probably the Orphic poets were the inventors of the name, and they were under the impression that the soul is suffering the punishment of sin, and that the body is an enclosure or prison in which the soul is incarcerated, kept safe, as the name implies, until the penalty is paid.

As the history of Western philosophy and religions shows, this view could have, and actually had, far-reaching consequences in holding the body in low esteem and in treating it as the source of moral corruption.[11]

In his first speech to the besieged people of Masada, Eleazar recommended self-destruction on the basis of Jewish exclusiveness *vis-à-vis* the Romans. He argued that God had in all likelihood abandoned his chosen people and deprived them of all hopes of deliverance. When this curious mixture of elitism and defeatism proved rather slow in having its desired effects, Eleazar reportedly changed his tactics of persuasion. He made a renewed appeal to his fellow-warriors on the basis of the assumption that 'it is death which gives liberty to the soul and permits it to depart to its pure abode, there to be free from all calamity'. The reason for that, as given by Eleazar, must by now be a familiar one: ' ... but as long as it is imprisoned in a mortal body and tainted with all its miseries, it is, in sober truth, dead' (*Jewish War* 7.344). Evidently, Josephus concocts something that strikes familiar tones in the ears of his audience in Rome.

From what may be referred to as a Jewish point of view, such a
line of argumentation smells of grass grazed in alien pastures. Its
impact on Jewish – and eventually on Christian – martyrology,
though, is an interesting chapter in itself. There is no reference
to the Masada event in any of the Jewish sources stemming from
talmudic times, that is, the first Christian centuries. The Masada
story was brought up again, in all its splendour and grandiosity, in
the medieval *Book of Josippon* (Josephus Gorionides). As modern research has shown, *Josippon* almost certainly drew upon a Christian
adaptation of Josephus written sometime during the Byzantine
period. In any event, it served as a major channel through which
Jewish history of the Second Temple period came to the knowledge of Jews in the Middle Ages. Thus, it is very likely that the
Book of Josippon shaped the martyrological consciousness of the
Jews in the Rhineland and northern France, who preferred mass
martyrdom to Christian baptism. That happened during the early
days of the First and Second Crusades (1096).

It is sometimes argued that the Jewish zeal for martyrological
death was in an essential manner influenced by the Christian *exem-
pla*, that is, stories and books that are written for moral and religious edification. However, we have already referred to the fact
that martyrdom was not always universally acclaimed in Jewish
circles. When the subject of martyrdom was first introduced into
the conceptual world of the Jewish sages at the time of the
Hadrianic persecutions (132–5 CE), quite different, if not altogether polemical, tones were struck. Over against Eleazar's fascination with the subject of death, Rabbi Ishmael, who was Rabbi
'Aqiva's most prominent Tannaitic rival, had the following to say on
a rather heated issue in his days:

['You shall therefore keep my statutes and my ordinances, by doing
which] a man shall live' (Lev. 18:5) – one should not be constrained to
die because of them. This is what Rabbi Ishmael used to say: Wherefore
does one infer that if a person is told in his own privacy to worship idols
and not die, that he should worship and not die? This is what one should
infer from the verse, 'by doing which a man shall live' – [he should live]
and not die! (*b. Sanh.* 74a)

It is clear that as a point of departure Rabbi Ishmael advocates
an anti-martyrological position. However, before long matters took
a completely different turn. This happened when circumstances

changed and different considerations from the ones maintained by Rabbi Ishmael took over. For instance, the basic halakhic position changes when idol-worship, and generally the breach with the Torah-law, is enforced upon a person in 'public', that is in the presence of at least ten other people. In that case, the death of a person unwilling to commit himself to the worship of idols receives the name of *Qiddush Ha-Shem*, that is, the sanctification of the 'Name' (a current metonym for God).[12] Those who succumb to idol-worship are, thus, called 'desecrators of the Name'.

In this connection it would be of interest to notice that the term 'martyr' comes from the Greek μάρτυς, meaning 'witness'. In Hebrew, however, the term used is *Qiddush Ha-Shem*, that is, 'the sanctification of the Name/God'. Evidently, it hits a completely different semantic field from its Greek counterpart. The theological differences, though, are non-essential.[13] In Hebrew, there are quite a number of other terms which are used instead. Most of them are known from a period preceding that in which *Qiddush Ha-Shem* established itself as the major term indicating martyrdom.[14] The term, which is not found in this sense in the Hebrew Scriptures, clearly creates a new religious category. In itself it is indicative of the fact that a new type of experience and value judgement is introduced into the framework of the 'old', scriptural, terminological tradition. In any event, if we come back to the view expressed by Rabbi Ishmael according to which martyrdom is ideally restricted to extremely rare cases, then the question must be asked: Is this view a purely academic (= halakhic) one, or is it practically implying historical criticism of the martyrdom of Rabbi 'Aqiva and a few of his colleagues?

It is told of Rabbi 'Aqiva that he was tortured to death in the presence of his students in Caesarea (*b. Ber.* 61b). The context in which the story is told makes it clear that Rabbi 'Aqiva saw in his martyrdom a unique occasion for demonstrating an unselfish love of God. The presence of his students, at least in the version of the story as told in the Talmud, makes it evident that his death could be justified even in the eyes of those maintaining the most lenient halakhic position on the matter. In other words, Rabbi 'Aqiva complied even with the minimalist view as expressed by Rabbi Ishmael. Furthermore, can we say that the story of Rabbi 'Aqiva's death was written by someone representing Rabbi Ishmael's views on the subject?

What is noteworthy here is the fact that on such a delicate issue as martyrdom two opposing views could be maintained in Tannaitic circles. Evidently, martyrdom was not generally accepted as the only and best solution in case of religious, and political, persecution. Those who wanted to set a martyrological model exposed themselves to criticism. Whether that criticism of martyrdom was guided by *realpolitik*, as for instance in the case of Rabbi Yossi bar Qisma, who showed no second thoughts in giving expression to his appreciation of the Roman rulers of the land,[15] or whether that criticism came from more ideologically minded circles, it was given little chance to establish itself as a universally accepted norm of behaviour in such cases.

8

What does this survey of sources and discussion of conflicting attitudes indicate? It seems that where a certain group of people strives at maintaining its moral assertiveness in the face of a threatening opposition, the borderlines between well-calculated and spontaneous, even somewhat haphazard, forms of behaviour are easily crossed. Although martyrdom should be viewed principally in a positive manner as reflecting serenity of mind and integrity of moral behaviour, we are equally justified in regarding it as giving way to almost uncontrollably suicidal drives. If viewed from a psychological angle, martyrdom has its aggressive sides, too. It is aggression turned against oneself. A talmudic passage (*b. B. Qam.* 91a–b) takes up the subject of martyrdom in the context of self-mutilation. The point of departure appears to be one that prevents people from inflicting any kind of harm upon themselves. However, Rabbi 'Aqiva is quoted as saying that one may mutilate oneself without having to atone for it!

As a matter of fact, martyrdom has sometimes been treated in terms that seek mystical glorification. Justification, even when enacted *post factum*, had to be found for those cases of martyrological death during the Hadrianic persecutions. This was accomplished in the framework of the major text attributed to the Merkavah mystics of talmudic times, *Hekhalot Rabbati*. The legend there tells of how the Roman authorities issued a decree to the effect that four of the Tannaitic sages had to be executed. Their ransom was set at no less than the lives of eight thousand Torah-students. According to the legend, one of the Merkavah mystics[16] was sent up to heaven to enquire whether this decree had been approved by the heavenly court. To the surprise of all, the emissary found out that the actual decree involved ten such sages, named individually. Their execution, so the emissary was told, should come as an excuse to take (heavenly) revenge on Rome and bring about its total destruction.

Evidently, there are a few historical references alluded to in this story. We should also notice that execution and not martyrdom is the actual subject-matter of our legend. However, in Jewish folk-lore and liturgy those sages are commonly referred to as martyrs! In other words, the text implies that a death that is really worth dying, and has crucial historical consequences, is that of the martyr. Evidently, this can be viewed as a glorification of martyr-dom in a basically mystical context. Moreover, since actual war-fare was practically unthinkable in the case of the Jews in their exilic existence, and no other efficient manner of self-defence was tolerated on their part, the only way of vindicating their cause was that of martyrdom. If it did not succeed in winning the battle, at least it was effective in making a moral point.

In this respect, we may conclude by placing martyrdom on the same moral level as other forms of noble resistance. It was, and still is, effective in exposing the hideous dimensions of evil. In the face of one's preparedness to undergo martyrdom, evil is shown as oscillating between monstrous deformation and banal insignifi-cance. In the final resort, the unwavering declaration of faith and the total rejection of evil are most potent means of destabilizing the sophisticated machinery of evil. When it comes to it, our choice of moral preferences is with the martyr turning mortal wounds into immortality. Evil is blindfolded with its own false glitter. It should not be given any chance of survival.

NOTES

1 In an article published in *BBC Worldwide*, January 1996, p. 64, Nelson Mature writes: 'Just as there is the "loud laugh that speaks the vacant mind", so tears do not always indicate a person of warm emotions and generous sensibilities. The novelist Hugh Walpole ... recalls meeting a young man recently released from prison. "Tears poured

down his cheeks ... I felt rather maternal to him." – The young man
was Adolf Hitler.' Symptomatically, in our eyes, the title of that article is 'To Laugh or Cry'.

2 See, for instance, Deut. 7:17–26. It should be remarked that in almost
all the cases in which the book of Deuteronomy demands the destruction of the peoples of Canaan the demand is linked to the anni-
hilation of idolatry.

3 See I. Gruenwald, 'The Other Self', *IOS* 14 (1994), 7–16.

4 See G. Reeg (ed.), *Die Geschichte von den Zehn Martyren*, Tübingen, 1985.

5 Maimonides' views on martyrdom are explicated in a number of his
writings. The central position, in this respect, is occupied by the
famous 'Epistle on *Qiddush Ha-Shem*', written to a North African community that had to pretend conversion to Islam, and the halakhic
exposition in *Mishneh Torah*, 'Hilkhot Yesodei Ha-Torah' [Laws concerning the basic principles of the Torah], ch. 5. Maimonides starts
his halakhic exposition of *Qiddush Ha-Shem* saying: 'All the members
of the House of Israel are commanded to sanctify the great Name of
God.' Obviously, this is an idiosyncratic innovation, since no law in
the Torah explicitly maintains what Maimonides says. However, it
seems to me that the introductory words, '*all the members* of the House
of Israel', which are to be found almost nowhere in this great corpus
of Jewish law, aim at flattening down the impact that the words following this statement have: 'How are these precepts [to sanctify the
Name and not to profane it] to be applied? Should an idolator arise
and coerce an Israelite to violate any one of the commandments
mentioned in the Torah under the threat that otherwise he would put
him to death, the Israelite is to commit the transgression rather than
suffer death ... And if he suffered death rather than commit a transgression, he himself is to blame for his death!' In other words, contrary to what one would expect in a discussion of *Qiddush Ha-Shem*,
Maimonides radically plays down the need to undergo martyrdom!
We shall come back to this point later on.

6 See, for instance, the tones struck by the concluding verse in an
'exilic' psalm composed in Babylon: 'Happy shall be he who takes
your [i.e., Babylonian] little ones and dashes them against the rock'
(Ps. 137:9).

7 M. D. Herr, 'Persecutions and Martyrdom in Hadrian's Days', *Scripta
Hierosolymitana* 23, Studies in History 1972, 85–125, has discussed the
possible connections between the Jewish martyrdom-consciousness
and the Hellenic world. The connection between the death of Socrates
and the Jewish martyrdom has been discussed in an extensive manner
in A. J. Droge and J. D. Tabor, *A Noble Death: Suicide and Martyrdom
among Christians and Jews in Antiquity*, San Francisco, 1992, 17–51: "The
Death of Socrates and Its Legacy".

8 In this respect, it is interesting to notice that the two books containing

the earliest martyrological reports on Jewish soil, 2 and 4 Maccabees, were composed in Greek.

9 For the Greek concepts of the soul, E. Rhode, *Psyche: Selenkult und Unsterblichkeitsglaube der Griechen*, reprint, Darmstadt, 1991, is still relevant.
10 See, for instance, T. F. Glasson, *Greek Influence in Jewish Eschatology, with Special Reference to the Apocalypses and Pseudepigraphs*, London, 1961.
11 See P. Brown, *The Body and Society: Men, Women, and Sexual Renunciation in Early Christianity*, New York, 1988.
12 A survey of the theological and terminological issues related to the subject of *Qiddush Ha-Shem*, mostly used in Tannaitic sources in a non-martyrological context, can be found in I. Gruenwald, ' "Qiddush Ha-Shem", A Clarification of the Usages of the Term' (in Hebrew), *Molad*, New Series, 1 (1968), 476–84.
13 In fact, there are cases in which the Hebrew term 'witness' is used in Hebrew in a martyrological context.
14 See Gruenwald, ' "Qiddush Ha-Shem" '.
15 See *Bavli 'Avodah Zarah* 18a.
16 Interestingly, and to some extent also paradoxically speaking, he is referred to as 'Rabbi Ishmael'!

CHAPTER 2

The other in 1 and 2 Maccabees

Daniel R. Schwartz

The first two books of Maccabees are of approximately the same length, but there are numerous differences between them.[1] For example, the former covers the period from Mattathias to Johanan Hyrcanus (c. 167–135 BCE) while the latter begins somewhat earlier but ends its account even before Judas Maccabee dies (160 BCE); the former is Palestinian and the latter of the Hellenistic Diaspora; the former was composed in Hebrew and follows biblical models, the latter was composed in Greek and follows the model of 'tragic' or 'pathetic' Hellenistic historiography; the former features soldiers and the latter, martyrs. One point of comparison which is often ignored is their understanding of others, a point which has everything to do with their authors' understanding of themselves.

To some extent, this difference is dictated by the specifically Hasmonean nature of 1 Maccabees: that is, 1 Maccabees is concerned, primarily, to establish the legitimacy of the Hasmonean dynasty, and this concern is reflected by its *damnatio memoriae* of other Jewish claimants to the high priesthood; none of them is mentioned. In contrast, 2 Maccabees not only gives us a detailed account of such condemned competitors as Jason, Menelaus and Alcimus, but also – at both the opening and the conclusion of the story (see ch. 3 and 15:12–14) – praises at length the last Zadokite high priest, Onias III, thereby undercutting, although probably unintentionally, the Hasmoneans' claims to being God's choice as high priests and rulers.[2] But there are other others dealt with by both 1 and 2 Maccabees, and their different ways of dealing with them can tell us a good deal about these books, their authors and their contexts.

We shall begin by noting that 1 Maccabees opens by summarizing (1:1–9) the career of Alexander the Great and his successors, emphasizing that he became proud and haughty just as the subsequent Hellenistic kings 'brought much evil upon the world'. In contrast, the story of 2 Maccabees (after the opening epistles) opens with the proud notice (3:1–3) that in the happy 'once upon a time' before things went downhill, kings used to honour the Temple, and Seleucus IV, King of 'Asia' (the Seleucid kingdom), even defrayed the costs of the sacrificial service.[3] For 1 Maccabees, the non-Jewish world is from the outset evil; for 2 Maccabees the opposite is the case.

Correspondingly, while both 1 and 2 Maccabees immediately go on to report that the Jews' troubles with the Seleucids derived from the initiative of wicked Jews, it is only 1 Maccabees which construes their purpose as joining with Gentiles (1:15);[4] since Gentiles are wicked, according to this book, it makes sense that wicked Jews want to join them. Hence, it is only in 1 Maccabees that we find a 'positive' platform being attributed to the Hellenizers: 'Come let us make a covenant with the nations around us, because ever since we have kept ourselves separated from them we have suffered many evils' (1:11); later, accordingly, the Gentile king is reported to have issued a decree requiring 'all to become one people' (1:41–2). In 2 Maccabees, in contrast, the Hellenizers are simply wicked Jews, who violate Seleucid precedent by setting aside the royal privileges (φιλάνθρωπα βασιλικά – 4:11) and, by bribery, manoeuvre Antiochus into doing what he otherwise would never have done.

Similarly, the continuation of this chapter of 2 Maccabees reports that the Seleucids remained basically well disposed towards the Jews. This is shown by the episode of the murder in Antioch of the Jewish high priest Onias III. Here, the reader learns that the only reason Onias could be murdered was because the king was campaigning abroad so the Jewish villain, Menelaus, could get away with it. People of many nationalities, including Greeks, were outraged at the murder, and the king himself, upon his return to the capital, was enraged and personally saw to the execution of the murderer. So too, the end of this chapter tells us (v. 49), the Tyrians were outraged by the execution of Jewish elders, an execution which – like the constitutional changes in Jerusalem – occurred only as a result of Menelaus' bribes, not as the result of any basic antipathy on the part of Antiochus.

Again, when the profanation of Jerusalem and the Temple

comes, and thereafter also the decrees against Judaism, 1 Maccabees 1 has no need to offer any special explanation. Rather, it simply reports that Antiochus Epiphanes, on his way back from an Egyptian campaign, stopped off in Jerusalem and robbed the Temple, just as two years later he sent troops to plunder the city and establish a garrison, publishing at the same time a decree prohibiting the Temple cult and the practice of Judaism. Why all this? No answer is given, apart from Antiochus having been introduced as a wicked shoot sprouted from the stock of his Hellenistic forebears (1:10). From the Gentiles, who are wicked, you expect wickedness.[5] In 2 Maccabees, in contrast, Antiochus attacked Jerusalem and Judaism only after he heard that the Jews were revolting against his rule (5:11). Although the author insists this was a false rumour, it nevertheless makes Antiochus' moves rational.

Or, for our final comparison of this type, if the Greek cities of Judaea joined in the persecution of Jews, 2 Maccabees claims this was not because they were basically hostile towards the Jews, but, rather, because a Seleucid governor ordered them to do so (6:8); in the parallel at 1 Maccabees 1:54 there is no need for such a special explanation. Indeed, in contrast to 1 Maccabees 5, which dwells at length on such neighbourly persecution of the Jews, there are only two examples at all of such in 2 Maccabees: 10:15 and 12:3–9, where we read of how the Idumeans and the residents of Jaffa and Jabneh harassed the Jews; in the latter case the residents of Jaffa are said to have tricked and then drowned two hundred Jews of the town. But in both cases the author of 2 Maccabees contrives to make it seem that this persecution by neighbours was a result of the machinations of hostile Seleucid officials, whose policy contradicted that of the king and his regent: (1) the report in ch. 10 about the Idumeans comes only after the report of the suicide of a Seleucid official who had striven to preserve justice *vis-à-vis* the Jews, and his replacement by one who kept up continuous warfare against them; and (2) the report in ch. 12 about Jaffa and Jabneh comes right after we read that although Lysias made a treaty with the Jews and then went back to Antioch, and the Jews returned to their farms, several Seleucid officials would not let the Jews remain in peace.

The implication is that the Idumeans, the Jaffaites and the Jabneans were incited by villains who represented no one but themselves. Just as the Antiochenes and the Tyrians were outraged, according to 2 Maccabees 4, at the murder of Onias III and the Jerusalemite elders, so too, this book argues, the typical attitude of the Jews' neighbours, when left on their own and not misled by a few highly placed villains, is rather shown by the people of Scythopolis, who remained benevolent and peaceful towards the Jews – as the author is pleased to emphasize (12:30–1).

Thus, to summarize our argument so far, 1 Maccabees presents non-Jews as basically evil. Evil Jews, therefore, join the Gentiles. They wanted to join 'the Gentiles around us' (1:11) and the result was that 'they joined themselves to the Gentiles and so became willing slaves to evil-doing' (1:15); for, as ch. 5 argues so programmatically, 'the Gentiles around us' have only the extermination of Jews on their mind.[6] In contrast, 2 Maccabees has the Gentiles basically sympathetic towards the Jews, and it is only some bad Jews or other individual villains who bring about deviations from this basic attitude. This general exculpation of Gentiles conforms to a major theme of 2 Maccabees and one totally absent from 1 Maccabees, namely the explanation of general Jewish suffering as a result of general Jewish sinfulness, God having used the Gentiles as the rod of his anger.[7]

At this point, it is clear that both 1 and 2 Maccabees view the world as divided between Jews and non-Jews, and also between good and evil people. However, it is also clear that while theoretically the use of these two pairs of criteria should yield four types of people (good Jews and bad Jews, good non-Jews and bad non-Jews), in fact this is only the case in 2 Maccabees. In 1 Maccabees, there is hardly room for good Gentiles,[8] nor are bad Jews allowed to remain Jews; they are said to have wished to join the Gentiles. While there are 'apostates' in both 1 and 2 Maccabees, it is only in 1 Maccabees that apostates are said to have joined the heathen.

Now, 1 Maccabees' notion of a Jew joining the non-Jews should imply that being a Jew or non-Jew is a matter of personal commitment. Hence, the notion of apostasy should entail the notion of conversion. But for this to be the case, being a Jew cannot be, or cannot only be, determined by one's birth. If one defines Jews, or non-Jews, ethnically, and ethnically alone, then they can never become 'one people' as Antiochus is here said to have demanded (1 Macc. 1:41), any more than cats can become dogs, even if they learn to bark. Of our two books, however, it is not 1 Maccabees, but only 2 Maccabees which clearly subscribes to the view that to be a Jew is not determined exclusively by one's birth; to be a Jew, for 2 Maccabees, is determined by one's adherence to 'Judaism', a word perhaps coined by 2 Maccabees (2 Macc. 2:21; 8:1; 14:38). Non-Jews too can become Jews by deciding to adhere to Judaism, a point made in 2 Maccabees by none other than Antiochus IV himself, who, in his penitence before he died, is said to have decided to convert to Judaism (Ἰουδαῖον ἔσεσθαι – 9:17).

In 1 Maccabees, in contrast, we find neither 'Judaism' nor the notion of conversion to it, nor 'Hellenism' nor ἀλλοφυλισμός; such -isms appear only in 2 Maccabees and literature of similar Diaspora background, such as 4 Maccabees and Paul.[9] Correspondingly, while 1 Maccabees' tradition (ch. 6) concerning Antiochus IV's death is in some ways similar to that in 2 Maccabees, it lets him only express his regret.[10] Again, 1 Maccabees quite regularly uses genealogically oriented terms to refer to Jews and non-Jews. It most commonly refers to the Jews as an ἔθνος or a λαός, and to non-Jews as τὰ ἔθνη; all these terms are much rarer in 2 Maccabees. Similarly, the term ἀλλόφυλος appears seven times in 1 Maccabees but only twice in 2 Maccabees, both occasions (10:2, 5) in a passage which seems to be a secondary addition to the book.[11] Finally, 1 Maccabees very frequently uses 'Israel' as a term for the Jews, pointing out a common descent from a particular patriarch. In contrast, this term appears in 2 Maccabees only five times, including two in the epistles, which are Judaean texts prefixed to the work. Thus, while Bickerman may have gone too far when he claimed that all of 1 Maccabees is governed by one single idea, namely the opposition between Israel and the nations,[12] this opposition – which is virtually absent from 2 Maccabees – nevertheless is quite pervasive in 1 Maccabees and formulated in terms which seem to indicate that it is insuperable. But if this is the case, then it is unclear how Jews could ever join the Gentiles and become one people with them – which is precisely what 1 Maccabees claims.

To deal with this problem – not to resolve it logically, but only to understand it historically – we must recognize that the author of 1 Maccabees found himself boxed into a corner. It was obvious to him, as to any observer, that there were both Jewish and non-Jewish villains. But for him to say as 2 Maccabees did, that the Jewish villains remained just that, *Jewish* villains, he would have to admit that descent is not very important. To do that would not only require a level of Hellenism which was apparently far from him, but would also undermine the case which was his main point, namely that great significance indeed does attach to descent. It is that point which allows him to claim that the Hasmonean *seed* had been chosen to save Israel (1 Macc. 5:62); it is that point which allows him to claim that it made sense that Simon's descendants should rule Israel forever, and that no priest or layman (another genealogical distinction!) should be allowed to contest that claim (1 Macc. 14:41, 44, 47). To say that one's descent did not matter would undermine all of that; and note that once the Hasmoneans began accepting converts, in the generation after our book ends, they also began to run into civil conflict with Jews who contested their right to rule.[13] Whether by instinct or by experience, the Hasmoneans' court historian knew well what to avoid.

Thus, 1 Maccabees shows us a pro-Hasmonean author, in Judaea, dealing less than successfully with the complexities of Jewish identity. He had to do something about Jews who behaved like non-Jews, but he could not or would not redefine being Jewish in a way which could account for this. Moreover, he did not yet have to deal with non-Jews who behaved like Jews, so the problem was not before him in all its intensity, and he could live with it with a little fudging. His Hellenistic competitor, the author of 2 Maccabees, living in a mixed Diasporan environment, and one in which it was the rule and the ideal that people should become Greeks although they were not Greek by *genos*, was able to deal much more successfully with the issue. It was his way, which allows for both apostasy and conversion, based on the viewing of Jews as adherents of Judaism and not as Jews by birth alone, which was to become widespread not only in the Hellenistic Jewish world but also – after the Romans imposed Diaspora conditions in Palestine too[14] – throughout the Jewish world as well.

NOTES

1 For general introductions to these two books see: E. Schürer, *The History of the Jewish People in the Age of Jesus Christ (175 BC–AD 135)*, new English edn by G. Vermes, F. Millar, M. Black and M. Goodman; 3 vols.; Edinburgh, 1973–87, I, 17–19; III, 180–5 and 531–7; H. W. Attridge, 'Historiography', in M. E. Stone (ed.), *Jewish Writings*

of the Second Temple Period, Assen and Philadelphia, 1984, 171–83; and
G. W. E. Nickelsburg, '1 and 2 Maccabees – Same Story, Different
Meaning', *Concordia Theological Monthly* 42 (1971), 515–26.

2 'Probably unintentionally', because the book shows no awareness of
any conflict between Onias and Judas; on the contrary, the scene in
ch. 15 might well be construed as having Onias legitimize Judas. Similarly, the book shows no consciousness of the descendants of Onias
and Judas, much less of any competition between them. For the same
reason, however, it is difficult to follow those who suggest that 2 Maccabees should be viewed as polemicizing against the Oniad temple in
Leontopolis (although the opening epistles might serve such an end).
See, for example, U. Kahrstedt, *Syrische Territorien in hellenistischer Zeit*,
Berlin, 1926, 135–45, and, *contra*, M. Stern, in M. Amit, I. Gafni
and M. D. Herr (eds.) *Studies in Jewish History*, Jerusalem, 1991, 41 (in
Hebrew) = *Zion* 25 (1959/60), 7.

3 Note that at 2 Maccabees 5:16, correspondingly, of all the items
Antiochus stole from the Temple the only ones specified by the
author are the gifts of other kings. On this Diaspora author's rela-
tive lack of interest in the Temple, see below, n. 11; see also my
'Temple or City – What did Hellenistic Jews see in Jerusalem?', in
M. Poorthuis and Ch. Safrai (eds.), *The Centrality of Jerusalem: Historical
Perspectives*, Kampen, 122–3.

4 The joining implied here (ἐζευγίσθησαν, 'yoked up with') is very
strong; cf. Mark 10:9, συνέζευξεν (+ variant without συν-). It may be
assumed that the Hebrew version of 1 Maccabees used the root *ṣmd*
(cf. 2 Sam. 20:8 and LXX), thus pointing us to Num. 25:3 (as 1 Maccabees elsewhere points to that episode; see esp. 2:24–7, 50, 54 and
3:8; M. Hengel, *The Zealots*, Edinburgh, 1989, 150–3). Note that in
Numbers too, as in Mark, the linkage is a full sexual unification (cf.
Gen. 2:24, cited in the preceding verse in Mark).

5 See E. Bickerman, *The God of the Maccabees*, Leiden, 1979, 20: 'The
action of Epiphanes against Jerusalem is explained simply from the
fact that he is a Gentile: because he is a "sinful offspring".'

6 On this theme in 1 Maccabees, see S. Schwartz, 'Israel and the Nations Roundabout: 1 Maccabees and the Hasmonean Expansion', *JJS*
42 (1991), 16–38.

7 See especially the sermons at 5:17–20, 6:12–17 and the martyrs'
speeches in ch. 7; D. Arenhoevel, *Die Theokratie nach dem 1. und 2. Makkabäerbuch*, Mainz, 1967, 134–5, 151–2.

8 There are two exceptions: the Romans (ch. 8) and the Spartans (12:1–
23; 14:16–23). However, both are distant and no individual Romans
or Spartans function in the book. Moreover, the Spartans, at least,
are said to be of Abrahamic descent (12:19–23) – i.e., Jewish.

9 See 2 Macc. 4:13, 6:24; 4 Macc. 4:26; Gal. 1:13–14, and D. R. Schwartz,
Studies in the Jewish Background of Christianity, Tübingen, 1992, 11.

10 See D. Mendels, 'A Note on the Tradition of Antiochus IV's Death', *IEJ* 31 (1981), 53–6. Mendels suggests, on the basis of a comparison with the Prayer of Nabonid from Qumran, that the story in 2 Maccabees, which has Antiochus converting, derives from a Babylonian tradition. Such a Diasporan origin for this tradition dovetails nicely with our appreciation of 2 Maccabees on the background of its Diasporan *Sitz im Leben*. Note, however, that lack of sources prevents us from knowing whether Babylonian Jewry of the Hellenistic period moved beyond the exclusionist stance evinced by such texts as Ezra 9:1–2 and Esth. 6:13 and 10:3, which consider being Jewish as a matter of 'seed' (but cf. Esth. 9:27!). Moreover, the hypothesis that, later on, the talmudic period saw widespread conversion in Babylonia is less than well founded, as noted by I. Gafni, 'Proselytes and Proselytism in Sassanid Babylonia', in M. Stern (ed.), *Nation and History*, Jerusalem, 1983, I, 197–209 (in Hebrew). In contrast, Jewish proselytism in the Hellenistic and early Roman world is well documented; for surveys, see Schürer, *History of the Jewish People*, III, 150–76; L. H. Feldman, *Jew and Gentile in the Ancient World*, Princeton, 1993, 288–382.

11 Note esp. the way in which 10:9 abruptly continues the narrative from the end of ch. 9, and that the Hebraic style and cultic interest displayed by 10:2–3 point us more towards the Palestinian editor(s) of the letters which preface the book; contrast 2 Macc. 5:16 with 1 Macc. 1:21–3! One may surmise that 10:1–8 was inserted along with the letters (or along with one of them). See, *inter alia*, A. Momigliano, *Prime linee di storia della tradizione maccabaica*, Turin, 1931, 67–8; J. G. Bunge, 'Untersuchungen zum zweiten Makkabäerbuch' (Diss., Bonn; Bonn, 1971), 239–45.

12 Bickerman, *God of the Maccabees*, 17.

13 On the conversions under John Hyrcanus I (135/134–104 BCE), Aristobulus I (104/103 BCE) and Alexander Jannaeus (103–76 BCE), and on the rebellions against the first and the third, see, respectively, Josephus, *Antiquities* 13.257–8, 319, 397 and 13.299 (cf. *War* 1.67!), 372–83; Schürer, *History of the Jewish People*, I, pp. 207–28 *passim*.

14 Cf. D. R. Schwartz, *Agrippa I*, Tübingen, 1990, 82.

CHAPTER 3

The pursuit of the millennium
in early Judaism[1]

Albert I. Baumgarten

I

This chapter originates in research done as background for a monograph-length study of sectarianism[2] in ancient Judaism now completed, titled *The Flourishing of Jewish Sects in the Maccabean Era: An Interpretation.* That study seeks to answer the question of how and why groups such as Pharisees, Sadducees, Essenes and the Qumran covenanters[3] emerged and flourished at the time they did. Fundamental to the larger study is the conclusion that sectarianism is endemic in Judaism. In other words, this ever-present potential is not always realized fully; in fact, sectarian schism among Jews tends to come in waves of fervent activity separated by many years, often centuries, of relative calm.[4] As such, sectarianism is similar to messianism, also a constant in Jewish life as a result of the biblical heritage, but also breaking out in waves of intense and imminent expectation. Since the pattern of the two phenomena – sectarianism and messianism – is similar, we must ask whether the path traced by the wave of one overlaps that traced by the other, and (particularly if so, and if the overlap is frequent) whether there might be an inherent connection between these two waves. Some encouragement that this might be the case is provided by a comment of Ankori's, writing about the period which saw the emergence of Karaism:

Indeed, messianism and sectarianism during the early Muslim era march inseparably hand in hand in an endeavor to remold the fate of the Jewish people and the heart of that people as well.[5]

A preliminary assessment of the data for Judaism in the Second Temple period indicates that a similar conclusion is likely. An initial attempt on my part to treat these questions indicated that messianic expectations were an important component in the constellation of factors which contributed to the emergence of Qumran sectarianism.[6] A deeper understanding of this possible connection therefore seemed essential. Accordingly, I sought to learn as much as possible concerning the pursuit of the millennium, as it has been experienced by Jews and others. One part of the results of my investigations is presented here.

2

Before beginning discussion of the subject, a word on the use of the term 'millennium' and its cognates is necessary. Technically, the term refers to a belief in the coming of a thousand-year period somehow connected with (usually inaugurating) the ultimate cosmic redemption. Another sense, although technically incorrect, has, however, become widespread: millennial movements are those that believe in the *imminent* change (usually, the *radical* change) of existing conditions as a result of divine intervention. This intervention will bring about a this-worldly collective salvation.[7] As such, these movements share the messianic beliefs in national and/or cosmic salvation common in the biblical tradition; what makes them special is their expectation that these events are to occur in the *immediate* future.[8] Millennial movements are thus a subcategory of messianic ones.[9]

In contrast to others who have studied these groups,[10] this definition leaves two points deliberately vague. First, it does not specify a particular notion of how the world will be organized in those great days as a necessary feature of millennialism. For example, I would not require that a movement assert that all will be equal at that time in order for it to be considered millennial. Furthermore, this definition does not limit millennial movements to those which behave in some specific way in the here and now, in anticipation of imminent salvation. I believe that we can understand the phenomenon fully only when we include in our focus a wide variety of visions of the glorious end and a broad range of prescriptions for behaviour in the last days of the unredeemed world. This flexibility in definition will permit us to recognize the full extent to which people of differing social and economic backgrounds, or varying religious outlooks, have been swept up in enthusiastic anticipation of an imminent grand finale.[11] It will also allow us to see that more than one type of answer has been offered over the ages to the question of how people ought to behave on the eve of salvation.[12]

When millennial movements are defined as proposed above, they share much with apocalyptic texts and the circles which produced the latter, to the extent that the differences may be close to insignificant. Apocalypses are revelations concerned with two principal issues: (1) the removal of evil from humankind and the world, and (2) the achievement of the ideal humanity.[13] All this is usually expected to occur in the immediate future.[14] As such, apocalyptic movements have much in common with millennial groups:[15] the content of apocalyptic revelation is regularly millenarian.

Millennial studies have enjoyed a certain popularity in the past decades, as a result of which these beliefs have lost their association with the 'lunatic fringe' and are now understood as a serious response (in part, at the very least) to specific political, religious or social situations.[16] Research on millennial hopes has, however, regularly stressed one conclusion. These aspirations, scholars assert, are normally found among those who are oppressed or disadvantaged in some sense of those terms. Thus Burridge begins his study with a quote from Chinnery and Haddon explaining that:

the weakening or disruption of the old social order may stimulate new and often bizarre ideals ... Communities *that feel themselves oppressed* anticipate the emergence of a hero who will restore their prosperity and prestige.[17]

Burridge elaborates, specifies and qualifies the senses in which he understands these ideas throughout his work,[18] but his fundamental commitment to understanding millenarian hopes as a result of oppression is unaffected.

Much the same is true of the view of Tuveson,[19] who sees millennial aspirations among Christians as part of their Jewish heritage, especially meaningful in the years of their persecution, and then tapering off when their movement becomes the dominant religion of the Roman world.[20] Millennial thought, according to Tuveson, will be revived at the time of the Protestant Reformation, but that will be as part of an attempt to understand why things had gone so wrong and now needed to be (and were being) set right.[21] Tuveson recognizes that there was what he calls an optimistic millennialism in the seventeenth century,[22] but he is little interested in exploring the situations which helped produce those views, and focuses instead on the main theme of his book – the connection between millennial thought and the idea of progress.[23] In short, nowhere in the book do we get more than a hint that anything but despair can promote millennial hopes.

A similar conclusion can be found in the analysis of Worsley. Confronted by the fact that the leaders of some millenarian groups were of upper-class origin, he nevertheless remains 'unrepentant' in his conviction that millenarian movements which have been historically important were movements of the disinherited.[24] The same view can be found in the work of John Gager, who, apparently appealing to the research of Aberle on the connection between millenarianism and relative deprivation,[25] concedes that relative deprivation is sufficient to call forth millenarianism.[26]

Talmon's conclusions are no different. She too insists on viewing millennial groups as the result of despair. As she summarizes matters: 'millenarianism is born out of great distress coupled with political helplessness'.[27] Talmon is reluctant to reduce millenarianism to class interest, and she acknowledges the presence of a frustrated secondary elite among the leaders of these movements.[28] She realizes that the Sabbatean example is one in which Jews who lived in comparative peace participated; some who were well off even joined enthusiastically.[29] Nevertheless, when summarizing her position, she continues to write in terms of 'precipitating crises'.[30]

A final indication of this mind-set among scholars is provided by the introduction by S. Thrupp to her collection *Millennial Dreams in Action*. At least one essay in that volume – the study of the Savonarola movement by Weinstein, to be discussed more fully below – does not fit the pattern of millennial hopes flourishing among the oppressed. Nevertheless, the implications of that essay are entirely overlooked by Thrupp when summarizing the results of the papers.[31] Thus, Thrupp notes the connection between the Savonarola movement and Joachite prophecies, as well as Savonarola's appeal to civic patriotism and naive self-glorification, but does not mention that all this was called forth, according to Weinstein, by very different circumstances from those found in most other millennial movements analysed in the volume.[32] Her theory is unaffected by the facts.[33]

From a Jewish perspective, scholarly insistence on seeing messianism as a response to crisis and despair has much to recommend it. As we learn from *m. Sota* 9.15:

With the footprints of the Messiah presumption shall increase and dearth reach its height ... the empire shall fall into heresy and there shall be none to utter reproof ... The face of this generation is as the face of a dog and the son will not be put to shame by his father.

Nevertheless, I find this scholarly consensus unsatisfying for two principal reasons. First, and less important, is the emphasis on relative deprivation. I find that notion so vague as to be close to useless as an explanation of why millenarian hopes flourish in certain circumstances. Anyone, anywhere, I would maintain, can always feel relatively deprived by comparison to someone else in some other place. If that is the case, however, what use is relative deprivation in explaining why millenarian movements emerge at specific times and places among particular groups? As Harrison has remarked:

As it is, the theory of relative deprivation (like the theory of stress and strain) is in danger of accounting for everything and nothing. Almost every millenarian, one suspects, might be shown to be relatively deprived in some way. But why should he or she react to deprivation by becoming a millenarian, and not something else remains obscure.[34]

Even more pertinent are the comments of Rayner:

The net of relative deprivation is being cast so wide as to render it logically vacuous as a general explanation of millenarianism ... Relative deprivation does not stand the test of the negative case where it exists without producing millenarian activity. In this case, relative deprivation may produce a variety of non-millenarian responses ... On the other hand, relative deprivation may produce no coherent movement at all, whilst some forms of utopian activity may appeal to members of society who cannot be usefully or sympathetically described as relatively deprived in any sense.[35]

More importantly, however, the focus on millenarianism among the dispossessed overlooks an important group of historical examples which indicate the existence of a second route leading people to hopes of imminent divine redemption. Weinstein's essay on the Savonarola movement in the Thrupp volume is a convenient place to start. As Weinstein notes, 'Here is a case of millenarianism that did not arise out of the protests of the poor and cannot be explained by economic crisis.'[36] Instead, Weinstein proposes to understand the results in other terms:

As Savonarola emerged as a political leader his prophecy and his doctrine underwent fundamental transformations. Right up to the time of the Medici expulsion he had continued to foretell disaster for Florence ... After the revolt, however, ... [he] became much more optimistic about the future of Florence ... The events of those crucial days seem to have persuaded him that Florence was chosen to lead the way to reform ... The French invasion was the opening of the fifth age of the world, the age of Antichrist and of the universal conversion to Christianity. Both his own mission and the Florentine revolt, he now saw, were part of God's plan.[37]

In other words, millenarian hopes – *particularly the belief in imminent salvation* (one of the crucial defining characteristics of a millenarian movement) – were encouraged by a *victory which convinced Savonarola and his followers that God's plans for redeeming the world must now be in the final stages.*

There is significant confirmation for my approach in a study of medieval Jewish messianism written a number of years ago by Gerson D. Cohen.[38] Cohen begins by noting that medieval Sephardi Jews experienced a number of messianic movements, while their Ashkenazi counterparts did not encounter a single case of a messianic movement or pseudo-messiah until the beginning of the sixteenth century.[39] Sephardi messianism, Cohen insists, was not the quirk of a few cranks or crackpots, and must be taken seriously.[40] Ashkenazi Jews, by contrast, were free of such movements but did engage in speculation about when the Messiah will come as part of their exegesis of the Bible. Their dates for his arrival, however, were regularly far in the future, well beyond the lifetime of those proposing these interpretations. Their activities in this vein were therefore the 'very antithesis of millenarist excitation'.[41] Most important for our purposes are the social conclusions Cohen draws from his data:

Contrary to popular impression, there is no discernible connection between persecution and messianic movements. Jewish messianic movements were not 'the religion of the oppressed' ... Active messianism or quiescence must have derived from sources other than political or economic.[42]

Cohen therefore asks, 'What in Jewish culture oriented one group to intellectual or physical activism and the other to basic passivity?'[43]

His answer is appropriately nuanced, and concentrates on aspects of medieval Jewish life not particularly relevant to our topic here. One factor which he notes touches directly on the previous discussion: 'the political successes of Jews in Spain must have whetted the appetites of the elite for even further conquests'.[44] That is, as I have been arguing above, one can enter the palace of millenarian hopes through a door over whose portals the words 'success' or 'victory' are inscribed.

To consider a non-Jewish case, millenarian ideas in seventeenth-century Britain, as Lamont has shown, were quite widespread:[45]

The philosophical assumptions (though not the political conclusions drawn from them) of Fifth Monarchy men were acceptable to the orthodox mainstream of religious thought of the time ... our concern is with a quieter sort of men; men who were no less millenarian but who did not see why the forthcoming end of the world should mean the forthcoming end of traditional political allegiances. Their millenarian faith was implicit; there was no reason why it should be made explicit. For that reason it is extraordinarily difficult to track down. This study is an attempt to hunt for this subtler form of millenarianism, but the quarry is elusive.[46]

Furthermore, there were certain periods when millenarian aspirations were particularly prominent. As Keith Thomas writes:

It is hard to say for certain just why this brief but notable shift from passive to active millenarianism should have occurred during the Interregnum. Probably more important than the effects of high prices and other economic hardships ... was the apocalyptic sense generated by an awareness of living in a time of unprecedented political change ... It also accounts for the conviction held by so many of the Civil War sects that the period in which they lived was somehow the climax of human history, the era for which all previous events had been mere preparation. For the Fifth Monarchy men it was above all the execution of King Charles which left the way open for King Jesus.[47]

In a similar vein Christopher Hill notes that:

Emigration to New England ceased, John Winthrop tells us, because the excitement of the revolution made 'all men to stay in England in expectation of a new world'.[48]

These ideas formed the core of preaching before the Long Parliament, as studied by Wilson.[49] Most pertinent to my perspective are the comments of Liu, who deliberately raises and rejects the interpretation of Puritan millenarianism in terms of movements of the disinherited:

> The millenarian strain in Puritanism has usually been considered in the past as an aberration rather than an essential part of the Puritan mind ... To Haller, [it] represented the hope of the meaner sort of people in the Puritan Revolution. 'Out of the desperation of the poor and humble,' writes Haller, 'arose hope of the millennium.'[50]

Liu continues:

> The Puritan vision of a glorious millennium of Christ's kingdom here on earth is no longer regarded merely as the ideology of the reckless Fifth Monarchy men; on the contrary, it is now considered a central theme in Puritanism during the whole course of the Puritan revolution. Historians now understand that millenarianism was *not merely the fantasy of the alienated who had no command of the reality of society but also a dynamic force in the minds of men who were totally involved in the reconstruction of the world.*[51]

A further instance in which imminent hopes of national redemption are connected with victory is supplied by modern Israel since the 1967 war. As many observers have seen, beliefs that the final drama must be well under way and close to its glorious finale were raised, and continue to inspire large groups of Israelis as a result of those events.[52] These convictions have been translated into programmes of political and strategic action on a broad scale by well-educated, socially advantaged and highly motivated leaders, not connected in any way with the dispossessed. This conclusion emerges with particular clarity from the study of Habad messianism recently completed by Ravitzky.[53] In a word, this is a millenarianism of the victors, not the vanquished.

To put this point in other terms, let us return to Burridge. Towards the end of his essay he suggests the following:

> The main theme [of millenarian activities] is moral regeneration ... the creation of a new man defined in relation to more highly differentiated criteria. The process involves the creation of new unities, a new community, a new set of assumptions within terms of which men and women may exploit the resources of their environment and order their relations with one another.[54]

True to the premises of his study, Burridge continues and restricts these insights to movements of the oppressed and to cases where the old values have been challenged by various crises. I would insist, however, that, as the examples discussed above show, the activities Burridge summarizes have sometimes also been responses to victory.

Closest to my position are the comments of Wayne Meeks.[55] Meeks defines millenarianism and discusses its roots in deprived groups in terms derived from the work of Burridge and others. Nevertheless, he recognizes that this theoretical model accords poorly with what is known of the social level of Pauline Christians, and therefore proposes to understand millenarian hopes in terms derived loosely from the work of Leon Festinger, based on the concept of cognitive dissonance.[56] 'Apocalyptic movements', Meeks suggests, 'provide relief from cognitive dissonance by offering a new or transformed set of fundamental images of the world and of relationships.'[57] Meeks continues by speculating that

people *who have advanced or declined* [emphasis mine] socially, who find themselves in an ambiguous relation to hierarchical structures, might be receptive to symbols of the world as itself out of joint and on the brink of radical transformation. They might be attracted to a group that undertook to model its own life on that new picture of reality.[58]

Fundamental to these comments, from my perspective, is the clear recognition that one can enter the realm of apocalyptic/ millenarian hopes as a result of an advance or a decline in status, that the dispossessed as well as the victors may choose to understand their somewhat disconcerting experiences (different as these may be from each other) in terms of a belief that the grand finale of the old world is soon to come.

If my criticisms of those who have ignored the victorious sort of millenarianism are correct, the reason for their error should also be apparent. I believe that the source of the error lies in choosing the paradigms of millenarianism too narrowly, in focusing on too small a group of cases as providing the archetype. More specifically, those who have studied the topic have restricted themselves too exclusively to groups whose members were often ignorant and inarticulate, who did not leave behind a satisfactory written account of their movement.[59] This description simply does not fit the ancient Jewish examples (consider the Dead Sea Scrolls, for example, where literacy was a virtual requirement for membership of the group),[60] the Puritans, or modern Habad. Another sort of millenarianism – the victorious kind – was possible in the different circumstances in which these groups arose, and that sort of millenarianism attracted members to groups with a different social composition.

To summarize, I have no quarrel with the conclusion that millenarianism is often a phenomenon of the deprived or the 'down and outs' of various sorts. I maintain, however, that we should not overlook another type – less prevalent, perhaps, but nevertheless existent in certain circumstances – the triumphant version which emerges as a result of events which produce the conviction that we humans and God are now marching together towards the most glorious of all possible new worlds. As victories rarely occur without some prior sense of crisis, the difficulties which precede the triumph may serve to prepare the ground for the millenarianism of the victors. Nevertheless, what remains crucial about this second sort is the fact that the impulse for the immediate inspiration is the sense of victory. Social scientists, I believe, will need to adjust their theory to account for the full range provided by historical example, while historians of Judaism and other religions should be prepared to encounter both varieties in the past.

3

I would like to continue with a brief discussion of one specific ancient example of the advantages to be derived from an awareness of the varied nature of millennial or apocalyptic movements.[61] The prophet Haggai wrote at a time of great upheaval, urging the Jews to complete the rebuilding of the Temple after the return from the Babylonian exile.[62] Having succeeded in convincing his contemporaries to commence work, he now turns to events for confirmation that these actions are desired by God and asserts that the blessings of the most recent past prove that famine and punishment are over (2:15–19). A second oracle given on the same day predicts the imminent shaking of the heavens and overthrowing of kingdoms, all to conclude with the choosing of Zerubbabel as God's signet ring, i.e. Messiah (2:20–3). Much the same atmosphere pervades the first eight chapters of Zechariah. In both cases we have hopes of imminent redemption being nurtured as a result of a conviction that *the right* actions are now being taken, that the successes of the present are the best indication that God will bring about the grand finale very soon.

The prophecies of Haggai and Zechariah pose a problem to

those who insist on seeing apocalyptic eschatology only as a result of oppression. Thus Hanson must contend with the uncomfortable fact that the images and content of these prophecies are completely appropriate to other expressions of apocalyptic eschatology, while he is committed to understanding the latter as a product of specific historical and social circumstances which do not fit the age and outlook of Haggai and Zechariah. It is awkward, from Hanson's perspective, to admit that the idiom of the vision is being applied as legitimation of a pragmatic political programme over which the spokesman's group has control, rather than as the dream of a group of down and outs. Rather than redefine the categories in the light of the data, however, Hanson attempts to explain the data away. He therefore argues that

the forms and symbols utilized on behalf of the ruling group bear a *prima facie* resemblance to the forms of deprived apocalyptic groups. But the 'use' made of them in one case is that of underpinning existing structures, in the other case that of undermining those same structures.[63]

I would prefer to make the categories fit the data, rather than the reverse, and to conclude in accordance with the discussion above, that Haggai and Zechariah are two further examples of those inspired by success to believe that the final redemption of the world is at hand. In particular, they should be compared with the manifestations of millenarianism among the ruling classes in sixteenth- and seventeenth-century Britain analysed by Lamont.[64]

4

Even more explicit are the conclusions to be derived from texts from Qumran, particularly those which have been appearing in recent years. They reveal a complex of beliefs focusing on imminent expectation of redemption, held both by members of the Dead Sea sect and by their opponents.[65] Full consideration of these conclusions is best left for another place. For the moment, I would like to end this chapter with a brief discussion of one of the most specific examples of these beliefs, to be found in 4Q471[a], recently published by E. Eshel and M. Kister.[66] Line 3 of that text quotes the opinion of unnamed opponents, likely Hasmoneans or Sadducees: 'You [our opponents] said, "We shall fight His battles, because He redeemed us."' In fact, however, the results will be very different from those hoped for or anticipated. The fragment continues, in line 4: 'Your ... will be brought low, and they [the opponents] did not know that He despised ... ' The full context of these events is beyond our knowledge owing to the fragmentary nature of this brief text. Nevertheless, one conclusion is certain: 4Q471[a] attacks the certainty of rivals that the redemption was at hand, and their willingness to draw practical conclusions on the basis of that belief. It thus testifies explicitly to the fact that some members of Jewish society of pre-Herodian times[67] viewed the *victorious* events of their era as proof that the messianic age was dawning and drew pragmatic conclusions as a result of this conviction. As in the end these very people were ultimately 'brought low', their place in society can be fixed: they were among the leaders of Jewish society of their day. The fragment 4Q471[a] therefore testifies to the existence of a triumphant messianism, motivating the *higher* groups in the social, political and religious orders of its day. This phenomenon, I conclude, can only be properly understood when we acknowledge the triumphalist trigger of millenarian hopes, for whose existence I have been arguing.

5

If my approach is accepted, it raises several potentially far-reaching questions for further research. Thus, for example, I have suggested above that there are at least a few cases in which a millenarian movement which emerged in response to a victory, as opposed to one born in despair, attracted people of the better sort, more members who enjoyed higher levels of education or economic advantage. Is this conclusion borne out by other instances and, if so, what is the connection between the circumstances in which triumphalist hopes arise and those who throw their lot in with these expectations? Another question which may be asked concerns possible correlations between the two types of conditions which provoke millenarianism and the analyses of messianism contributed by Scholem.[68] Scholem suggests that messianic movements can be divided into two sorts, those that stress realistic, earthly redemption, expecting relatively small changes in the natural order (of which the archetype may be Maimonides); and those that emphasize the coming radical cosmic upheaval, hence expecting dramatic changes in the world as a result of the redemption. Is there any connection between this way of characterizing movements and my distinction between messianism of the victors and of the vanquished? Are victors more likely to hold stronger visions of earthly redemption, as opposed to the more radical or cosmic dreams of the vanquished? Finally, this analysis may illuminate the connections between the way millenarians behave in what they believe to be the waning days of the bad old world[69] and the situations which call forth beliefs of immediate salvation. Questions such as these should help us deepen our understanding of the intimate connection between the hope of imminent redemption, one of the most powerful forces for change affecting human societies,[70] and the circumstances which promote it.

NOTES

1 A draft of this paper was presented at the Fourth Annual Canada–Israel Conference on Social Scientific Approaches to the Study of Judaism, Toronto, May 1992.

2 For purposes of the larger research project, my use of the terms 'sect' and 'sectarianism' follows the definition employed by Wilson, *Sects and Society*, 3–4. See further the discussion in Wilson, *Religious Sects*, 14–17. The Jewish groups which concern me are all examples of what Wilson, in a later work (*Magic and the Millennium*, 18–26), will call 'responses to the world'. Wilson would probably classify Pharisees and Sadducees as 'reformist' responses, while the Dead Sea Scrolls covenanters would fit his category of 'introversionist'. For the same conclusion concerning the Pharisees as a reformist group according to Wilson, see Saldarini, *Pharisees, Scribes and Sadducees in Palestinian Society*, 286.

3 As should be clear from the formulation, I believe we should distinguish as carefully as possible between the Essenes and Qumran. See further Baumgarten, 'The Rule of the Martian as Applied to Qumran'.

4 The last two hundred years before the destruction of the Second Temple were to witness the appearance of Pharisees, Sadducees, Dead Sea covenanters, Sicarii, Christians and Zealots, to mention but a few of the better-known examples. Thereafter follow several centuries of calm, until the new wave of sectarian activity in the early Muslim period. A fuller discussion of the phenomenon will be found in my monograph, for which this paper is part of the background. According to Stark and Bainbridge, (*The Future of Religion*, 114) sects are chronic in religion.

5 Ankori, *Karaites in Byzantium*, 10.
6 See Baumgarten, 'Qumran and Jewish Sectarianism in the Second Temple Period', 149–51. The argument there, based principally on ch. 23 of Jubilees, is reinforced by the concluding lines of 4QMMT in which the connection between imminent expectations of redemption and sectarian schism is made explicit. See in particular 4QMMT C: 15–34, as cited in Kapera, 'An Anonymously Received Pre-Publication of the 4QMMT', 1–12. For a first discussion of the implications of messianic hopes in 4QMMT see Schiffman, 'The New Halakhic Letter (4QMMT) and the Origins of the Dead Sea Sect', 66–7, and especially 72, n. 7.
7 This definition is largely inspired by Talmon, 'Millenarian Movements', 159.
8 See further Isenberg, 'Millenarianism in Greco-Roman Palestine', 35, 44, n. 25.
9 As I use the term 'messianic', it refers to collective redemption at the end of days, whether or not that transformation is to be brought about by a specific human leader, or messiah-figure. Cf. Talmon, 'Millenarian Movements', 169. Any number of messianic movements in the past and present are legitimately called such, even though they do not promote a specific person as their candidate for the role of Messiah. To mention four of the most obvious examples from the Second Temple period, the vision of ultimate national salvation in Ben Sira 36:1–17 does not involve a messiah-figure, nor does the expression of hopes in Tobit 14:5–7. In Daniel 12:1 the angel Michael has a crucial part in cosmic salvation, but there is no human saviour. Finally, Jubilees has much to say of the future redemption, but the absence of a messiah-figure is conspicuous. See further Nickelsburg, 'Salvation Without and With a Messiah', 49–68, esp. the summary, 65. See also Smith, 'What is Implied by the Variety of Messianic Figures?', 66–72. As the title of his article indicates, Smith emphasizes the enormous diversity which prevailed, *often in the same text*, between different visions of the final redemption. One such variation, as Smith recognizes, is between eschatological visions with and without a human saviour.

In the contemporary Jewish world at the time of writing this study there are two active messianic movements: one of Habad hasidism and the other of the religious-political right in Israel, roughly to be categorized as that of Gush Emunim. The former have a specific human candidate for the role of Messiah, and remain convinced of his appropriateness for the role in spite of the apparent absolute disconfirmation dealt their beliefs by his death, while the latter do not have a specific candidate for the role, but are nevertheless widely (and correctly) viewed as a messianic movement. I therefore find it difficult to agree with the suggestions of Green, 'Introduction: Messiah in Judaism,' 1–13 who proposes that the preoccupation with the Messiah was not a common reference point for ancient Jews. Rather, according to Green, it is a construct of modern scholarship created to establish backgrounds for Christianity. Green bases his conclusions on the too narrow evidence of word studies, and misinterprets the variety of scenarios for salvation (with and without a specific human redeemer) as evidence that there was no common pool of hope or belief on which the different scenarios drew. Thus Green can write that 'Ben Sira ... has no interest in a future redeemer', (3). That is unarguably true if we restrict our vision to a human figure, but Ben Sira 36:1–17, as noted above, has much to say about a future redemption.

10 See, e.g., Rayner, 'The Perception of Time and Space in Egalitarian Sects', 248. Rayner defines millenarianism by three characteristics: (1) the conviction that the present age is to be ending shortly; (2) the conviction that the new epoch will be established by the external intervention of some powerful agency; (3) the conviction that all men ought to be recognized as moral equals. In insisting on the third point as essential to millenarianism, Rayner and others, in my view, have had their field of vision overly and unnecessarily narrowed by studies such as Cohn, *The Pursuit of the Millennium*.

11 See the comments of Lamont, quoted below, 44.

12 See, e.g., Burridge, *New Heaven, New Earth*, 167: 'Knox's remarks concerning the alterations of scandal and rigorism characteristic of enthusiastic movements are not simply good history. The two go together, are integral parts of a transition process in which the new rules are still experimental and uncertain ... It could be argued that orgies of sexual promiscuity ... and the high idealism often connoted by the release from all desire are polar opposites. But the fact remains that both meet in precisely the same condition: that of no obligation.'

13 See Bloch, *On the Apocalyptic in Judaism*, 17.

14 See Koch, 'What is Apocalyptic?', 25: '[Apocalyptic] writings are dominated by an *urgent expectation* of the impending overthrow of all earthly conditions *in the immediate future*' (emphasis Koch's).' For a more recent definition, more elaborate but completely in line with Koch's, see Collins, 'Early Jewish Apocalypticism', 283: 'apocalypse is a genre of revelatory literature ... in which a revelation is mediated by an otherworldly being to a human recipient ... an apocalypse envisages eschatological salvation and involves a supernatural world ... an apocalypse is intended to interpret present earthly circumstances in the light of the supernatural world and of the future, and to influence both the understanding and behavior of the audience by means of divine authority'.

15 In this context it is worth noting that Bloch can quote and discuss a rabbinic prayer which looks forward to the establishment of the king-

dom of God on earth (but which has no specific revelatory character) as an example of apocalyptic influences on the Rabbis. See further Bloch, *On the Apocalyptic*, 62–3. I take this to be further evidence of the very thin (if indeed existent) boundary between apocalyptic and millennial hopes.

16 In general, as Christopher Hill has stressed, we should beware of dismissing movements as being part of the 'lunatic fringe'. See, e.g., Hill's comments in *The World Turned Upside Down*, 13–14. In a similar vein see Douglas, *Natural Symbols*, xv. See also Talmon, 'Millenarian Movements', 192–3.

17 Chinnery and Haddon, 'Five New Religious Cults in British New Guinea', 455, as quoted by Burridge, *New Heaven, New Earth*, 3.

18 See, e.g., his discussion of Jainism in *New Heaven, New Earth*, 86–96.

19 Tuveson, *Millennium and the Utopia*.

20 Ibid., 14–21.

21 Ibid., 29–30.

22 Ibid., 80.

23 Ibid., 70.

24 Worsley, *The Trumpet Shall Sound*, xlii.

25 Aberle, 'A Note on Relative Deprivation Theory as Applied to Millenarian and other Cult Movements', 209–14.

26 Gager, *Kingdom and Community*, 22, 95–6.

27 Talmon, 'Millenarian Movements', 185.

28 Ibid., 186–7.

29 Ibid., 190–1.

30 Ibid., 192.

31 See Thrupp, 'A Report on the Conference Discussion', 26–7.

32 Ibid., 21.

33 On theory dominating facts see Kuhn, *The Structure of Scientific Revolutions*, 62–5. As Kuhn makes clear, an anomaly which the paradigm accepted by the scientific community cannot explain is usually either resisted or overlooked.

34 Harrison, *The Second Coming*, 222. Harrison's comment is especially significant because of his general allegiance to the notion of relative deprivation and dependence on authors for whom this notion is central, stated at the outset of his work: 'Certain socio-economic factors and a situation in which unusual distress, anxiety, and feelings of relative deprivation can develop are also associated with the appearance of prophets and millenarian movements – and may indeed be necessary conditions for its emergence' (11). For another statement of doubts about the adequacy of explanations based on relative deprivation see Schwartz, *The French Prophets*: 'Whatever alternatives I propose, I am not the hunter of a wounded animal: I have not assumed that millenarian beliefs are the product of spiritual malaise, socio-economic deprivation or psychological festering' (216). I can only guess

that Schwartz came to this conclusion, at least in part, because of his analysis of the background of the people he studied, on which see his concluding remarks (219–33).

Relative deprivation remains a factor, regularly invoked, as an explanation of sect formation. See, e.g., Stark and Bainbridge, *Future of Religion*, 106. Compare, however, the trenchant criticisms of this conclusion in Wilson, 'Becoming a Sectarian', 193–8.

35 Rayner, 'Perception of Time and Space', 251. Rayner's own attempt to understand these movements is based on Douglas' notions of grid and group. As Rayner does not explore the possibility that the impulse to millenarian activity can be provided by a victory, his theoretical comments are not particularly helpful for my endeavour. See further below. Rayner's attitude towards millenarian cosmology may have been shaped by Douglas' approach. Douglas rejects deprivation as an explanation for the emergence of such groups, but she also stresses that they are responses to failures or crisis. See, e.g., Douglas, *Natural Symbols*, 82–3 (deprivation), xii and 104 (failure/crisis). In general, I find the analysis of these movements in *Natural Symbols* (e.g., 150–5) as a result of weak grid and group that is further unbalanced and weakened as a consequence of events to be too tightly focused on the phenomenon as known from the extremist groups of the late 1960s in the USA and to fit poorly with the material I have studied, especially with the Qumran evidence. Adequate elaboration of this point, however, would require a separate article.

36 Weinstein, 'The Savonarola Movement in Florence', 187.

37 Ibid., 194. Weinstein elaborates these themes in greater detail in *Savonarola and Florence*, esp. 114–16. While Weinstein denies the role of economic crisis in producing the results at Florence, he does insist on the effect of a political crisis in understanding the events (33).

38 Cohen, 'Messianic Postures of Ashkenazim and Sephardim', 117–56. I owe my knowledge of this article to a suggestion of Professor M. Lockshin of York University, to whom I am most grateful for the reference.

39 Cohen, 'Messianic Postures', 122–3.

40 Ibid., 153. Cf. above n. 16.

41 Ibid., 127.

42 Ibid., 143.

43 Ibid., 144.

44 Ibid., 146. Note that Cohen reaches this conclusion in spite of the significance of *m. Sota* 9.15, quoted above, 42. Compare the hopes for redemption sparked by the Muslim conquests of the Roman Empire. While these hopes were ultimately to be dashed, they are another example of expectations of salvation emerging as a result of a victory. See further Lewis, 'An Apocalyptic Vision of Islamic History', 323.

45 I have selected scholars who discuss the prevalence of these ideas

before the latter half of the seventeenth century when a sense of failure and bitterness began to prevail, lest these examples be taken as an opportunity for reintroducing the notion of relative deprivation as the cause of millenarian movements. Note that in choosing to compare Jewish millenarianism with that of seventeenth-century England I am *not* invoking an alien analogy, taken 'from left field'. Jewish and Puritan groups had much in common, in particular a devotion to the Bible and living by an explicit practical interpretation of its contents, great as may sometimes be the distance between Jewish and Puritan biblical interpretations.

46 Lamont, *Godly Rule*, 19. In his study, Lamont shows at length the ways in which millenarian beliefs in seventeenth-century Britain were shared, while being reinterpreted at the same time, in varying ways, by members of different strata of society. This aspect of Lamont's work provoked serious criticism. See Capp, '*Godly Rule* and English Millenarism', 106–17, and Lamont's response, 'Richard Baxter, The Apocalypse and the Mad Major', 68–90. In my opinion, Lamont's response is convincing. Lamont's thesis is also confirmed by studies of other millenarian movements which show that their supporters and members come from a wider social range than one might expect. See, for example, Harrison's summary, *The Second Coming*, 221; Shepperson, 'The Comparative Study of Millenarian Movements', 49.

47 Thomas, *Religion and the Decline of Magic*, 143–4. To be fair, the troubles of the Civil War period may have also had a share in awakening these hopes. Capp ('Extreme Millenarianism', 76) balances the factors as follows: 'such dreams were enticing, especially in the civil war period when political, social and economic security was destroyed and yet miraculous hopes of a new order were appearing'. Rare, however, are the victories not preceded by a sense of crisis, thus the two can be seen as sides of the same coin, as argued below.

48 Hill, *Antichrist in 17th Century England*, 100.

49 Wilson, *Pulpit in Parliament*, 190–5.

50 Liu, *Discord in Zion*, 3.

51 Ibid., 4 (italics mine).

52 On the whole, this conclusion has stood the test of the setbacks endured at the beginning of the 1973 war, and the withdrawal from Sinai, which were interpreted in such a way as not to contradict the consequences drawn from the 1967 victories. On these points, see further Aviad, 'The Contemporary Israeli Pursuit of the Millennium', 199–222.

53 See Ravitzky, *Messianism, Zionism and Jewish Religious Radicalism*, 264–70. Ravitzky distinguishes between the nature of Lubavitch messianism prior to the accession of the current Rebbe (although now deceased, Menahem Mendel Schneerson remains the current Rebbe, in Lubavitch parlance), which he characterizes as a messianism of

despair, and the current forms of Lubavitch messianism which are of the triumphalist variety. In the Lubavitch case, the victories are less those of 1967 (their movement remains ambivalent at best in its attitude towards the State of Israel and Zionism) and more the success of their leader in spreading the word of God and in achieving prophet-like qualities, so much so that a campaign to claim messianic status for him was begun, achieving particular notoriety. I would like to thank Professor Ravitzky for sharing the principal results of his research on this topic with me prior to his book's appearance in print. For an assessment of the Lubavitch messianism as at the end of June 1993 see Shaffir, 'Jewish Messianism Lubavitch Style: An Interim Report', 115–28. For an update of the analysis in the light of the illness of the Rebbe, with a postscript written after his death, see Shaffir, 'Interpreting Adversity', 43–53.

54 Burridge, *New Heaven, New Earth*, 141.
55 Meeks, *The First Urban Christians: The Social World of the Apostle Paul*, 172–4.
56 As far as I can tell, Festinger himself did not propose understanding millenarian movements in this way; this is Meeks' contribution based on Festinger's insights.
57 Meeks, *First Urban Christians*, 173–4.
58 Ibid., 174. Arjomand (*The Turban for the Crown*, 110 and 198), echoing Weber, discusses the dislocations caused by crises of prosperity.
59 See Talmon, 'The Pursuit of the Millennium', 127.
60 There was supposed to be a group of members, organized in shifts, engaged in interpreting the law on a 24-hour basis. See 1QS 6.7–8. This assumes the ability of all members to participate in this activity, which would normally demand literacy as a prerequisite.
61 A fuller discussion of the consequences of this approach, with a number of additional examples, will be found in my study on ancient Jewish sectarianism, for which this chapter is part of the background.
62 See esp. Bickerman, 'En marge de l'écriture', 331–6.
63 Hanson, *The Dawn of Apocalyptic*, 253.
64 If this argument is accepted, it may not be appropriate to define apocalyptic movements with Hanson ('Jewish Apocalyptic Against its New Eastern Environment', 32) as ones which have visions which they 'have ceased to translate into terms of plain history, real politics and human instrumentality because of a pessimistic view of reality growing out of the bleak post-exilic condition in which the visionary group found itself'. Rather, we may say that most apocalyptic beliefs fit this model, but not necessarily all.
65 Compare the range of millenarian belief in seventeenth-century Britain, stretching across different social and political groupings, discussed above.
66 Eshel and Kister, 'A Polemical Qumran Fragment', 277–81.

67 The letter forms of the script of the fragment are Herodian. As the text discusses events in the past, the events to which it refers most likely took place in pre-Herodian days. For a more extensive discussion of messianic hopes in Maccabean times see Goldstein, 'How the Authors of 1 and 2 Maccabees Treated the "Messianic" Promises', 69–96; Collins, 'Messianism in the Maccabean Period', 97–110.

68 Scholem, *The Messianic Idea in Judaism*. This work has inspired a number of studies by Scholem and others seeking to elaborate and extend the initial insight. For a critique of Scholem's approach see Taubes, 'The Price of Messianism', 595–600.

69 On the differences between groups on this point see the discussion above, n. 12.

70 If the historian regards members and especially leaders of messianic/ millenarian movements seriously, and not merely as part of the 'lunatic fringe' (see above, n. 16), then he or she is also virtually obliged to recognize that these members or leaders realize the very powerful forces their movements are evoking and that they treat these forces with the utmost gravity, as the forces deserve. That is, we should not expect to see messianic or millenarian hopes usually invoked by 'any fool' in response to the slightest provocation. Rather, in full recognition of the dangerous powers with which they are dealing, there should be a reluctance to assert messianic claims and to go 'out on a limb'. This caution is borne out by the history of Habad messianism up to 1991 (when, for various reasons, caution was thrown to the wind), as discussed by Ravitzky, *Messianism*, 267–70. Habad's diffidence may have an analogue in the messianic secret of Jesus' mission as described by the Gospels (especially Mark). Even Shabbtai Zvi, according to Scholem (*Messianic Idea*, 60), was tormented with doubt about the legitimacy of his mission before his encounter with Nathan of Gaza.

As yet one more indication of this careful attitude towards the forces unleashed, note the reluctance in the contemporary Habad messianic campaign to draw practical conclusions from their expectations – to sell their homes, pull up their financial roots or other similar activities (such as existed in previous instances of imminent expectations, as at the time of Shabbtai Zvi in the seventeenth century, or the Millerites in nineteenth-century America). On this point see Ravitzky, *Messianism*, 272–3. Perhaps the only exception to this caution in the case of Habad is the policies they urge upon the State of Israel as a consequence of their belief in imminent redemption.

In the light of these considerations, the vital questions to be asked of such movements therefore become the ones I have tried to address in this chapter: What circumstances lead their members to dare to believe and proclaim that the ultimate redemption is at hand? In spite of all the practical restraints imposed by experience, how is it that otherwise reasonable (and sometimes eminently successful) people become convinced that the *eschaton* with its attendant transformations is soon to come, and that we must begin to plan for that certainty?

BIBLIOGRAPHY

Aberle, D., 'A Note on Relative Deprivation Theory as Applied to Millenarian and other Cult Movements', in S. Thrupp (ed.), *Millennial Dreams in Action*, The Hague, 1962, 209–14.

Ankori, Z., *Karaites in Byzantium*, New York, 1957.

Arjomand, S., *The Turban for the Crown*, New York, 1988.

Aviad, J., 'The Contemporary Israeli Pursuit of the Millennium', *Religion* 14 (1984), 199–222.

Baumgarten, A., 'Qumran and Jewish Sectarianism in the Second Temple Period', in M. Broshi, S. Japhet, D. Schwartz and S. Talmon (eds.), *The Scrolls of the Judean Desert – Forty Years of Research*, Jerusalem, 1992, 139–151 [in Hebrew].

'The Rule of the Martian as Applied to Qumran', *IOS* 14 (1994), 121–42.

Bickerman, E. J., 'En marge de l'écriture', *Studies in Jewish and Christian History Part Three*, Leiden, 1986, 327–49.

Bloch, J., *On the Apocalyptic in Judaism*, Philadelphia, 1952.

Burridge, K., *New Heaven, New Earth: A Study of Millenarian Activities*, New York, 1969.

Capp, B. S., 'Extreme Millenarianism', in P. Toon (ed.), *Puritans, the Millennium and the Future of Israel: Puritan Eschatology 1600 to 1660*, Cambridge and London, 1970, 66–90.

'*Godly Rule* and English Millenarianism', *Past and Present* 52 (1971), 106–17.

Chinnery, E. and Haddon, A., 'Five New Religious Cults in British New Guinea', *The Hibbert Journal* 15 (1917), 448–63.

Cohen, G. D., 'Messianic Postures of Ashkenazim and Sephardim', *Studies of the Leo Baeck Institute*, Ungar, 1967, 117–56.

Cohn, N., *The Pursuit of the Millennium*, London, 1957.

Collins, J. J., 'Messianism in the Maccabean Period', in J. Neusner, W. Green and E. Frerichs (eds.), *Judaisms and their Messiahs*, Cambridge, 1987, 97–110.

'Early Jewish Apocalypticism', *Anchor Bible Dictionary*, New York, 1992, I, 282–8.

Douglas, M., *Natural Symbols*, New York, 1982².

Eshel, E. and Kister, M., 'A Polemical Qumran Fragment', *JJS* 43 (1992), 277–81.

Gager, J., *Kingdom and Community: The Social History of Early Christianity*, Englewood Cliffs, 1975.

Goldstein, J., 'How the Authors of 1 and 2 Maccabees Treated the

"Messianic" Promises', in J. Neusner, W. Green and E. Frerichs (eds.), *Judaisms and their Messiahs*, Cambridge, 1987, 69–96.

Green, W. S., 'Introduction: Messiah in Judaism: Rethinking the Question', in J. Neusner, W. Green and E. Frerichs (eds.), *Judaisms and their Messiahs*, Cambridge, 1987, 1–13.

Hanson, P., 'Jewish Apocalyptic Against its Near Eastern Environment', *RB* 78 (1971), 31–58.

The Dawn of Apocalyptic, Philadelphia, 1983².

Harrison, J. F. C., *The Second Coming: Popular Millenarianism 1780–1850*, New Brunswick, 1979.

Hill, C., *Antichrist in 17th Century England*, London, 1971.

The World Turned Upside Down: Radical Ideas during the English Revolution, New York, 1972.

Isenberg, S. R., 'Millenarianism in Greco-Roman Palestine', *Religion* 4 (1974), 26–46.

Kapera, J. Z., 'An Anonymously Received Pre-Publication of the 4QMMT', *The Qumran Chronicle* 2 (1990), 1–12.

Koch, K., 'What is Apocalyptic? An Attempt at a Preliminary Definition', in P. Hanson (ed.), *Visionaries and their Apocalypses*, Philadelphia, 1983, 16–36.

Kuhn, T. S., *The Structure of Scientific Revolutions*, Chicago, 1970².

Lamont, W., *Godly Rule: Politics and Religion 1603–60*, London, 1969.

'Richard Baxter, The Apocalypse and the Mad Major', *Past and Present* 55 (1972), 68–90.

Lewis, B., 'An Apocalyptic Vision of Islamic History', *Bulletin of the British School of Oriental and African Studies* 13 (1950), 308–38.

Liu, T., *Discord in Zion*, The Hague, 1973.

Meeks, W., *The First Urban Christians: The Social World of the Apostle Paul*, New Haven, 1983.

Nickelsburg, G., 'Salvation Without and With a Messiah: Developing Beliefs in Writings Ascribed to Enoch', in J. Neusner, W. Green and E. Frerichs (eds.), *Judaisms and their Messiahs*, Cambridge, 1987, 49–68.

Ravitzky, A., *Messianism, Zionism and Jewish Religious Radicalism*, Tel Aviv, 1993 [in Hebrew].

Rayner, S., 'The Perception of Time and Space in Egalitarian Sects: A Millenarian Cosmology', in M. Douglas (ed.), *Essays in the Sociology of Perception*, London, 1982, 247–74.

Saldarini, A. J., *Pharisees, Scribes and Sadducees in Palestinian Society: A Sociological Approach*, Edinburgh, 1988.

Schiffman, L., 'The New Halakhic Letter (4QMMT) and the Origins of the Dead Sea Sect', *BA* 53 (1990), 64–73.

Scholem, G., *The Messianic Idea in Judaism*, London, 1971.

Schwartz, H., *The French Prophets: The History of a Millenarian Group in Eighteenth-Century England*, Berkeley, 1980.

Shaffir, W., 'Jewish Messianism Lubavitch Style: An Interim Report', *The Jewish Journal of Sociology* 35 (1993), 115–28.

'Interpreting Adversity: Dynamics of Commitment in a Messianic Redemption Campaign', *The Jewish Journal of Sociology* 36 (1994), 43–53.

Shepperson, G., 'The Comparative Study of Millenarian Movements', in S. Thrupp (ed.), *Millennial Dreams in Action*, The Hague, 1962, 44–54.

Smith, M., 'What is Implied by the Variety of Messianic Figures?', *JBL* 78 (1959), 66–72.

Stark, R. and Bainbridge, W., *The Future of Religion: Secularization, Revival and Cult Formation*, Berkeley, 1985.

Talmon, Y., 'The Pursuit of the Millennium: The Relation Between Religious and Social Change', *Archives Européennes de Sociologie* 3 (1962), 125–48.

'Millenarian Movements', *Archives Européennes de Sociologie* 7 (1966), 159–200.

Taubes, J., 'The Price of Messianism', *JJS* 33 (1982), 595–600.

Thomas, K., *Religion and the Decline of Magic*, New York, 1971.

Thrupp, S., 'A Report on the Conference Discussion', in S. Thrupp (ed.), *Millennial Dreams in Action*, The Hague, 1962, 11–30.

Tuveson, E. L., *Millennium and the Utopia*, New York, 1964.

Weinstein, D., 'The Savonarola Movement in Florence', in S. Thrupp (ed.), *Millennial Dreams in Action*, The Hague, 1962, 187–206.

Savonarola and Florence, Princeton, 1970.

Wilson, B., *Sects and Society*, Berkeley, 1961.

Religious Sects, London, 1970.

Magic and the Millennium, London, 1973.

'Becoming a Sectarian: Motivation and Commitment', *The Social Dimensions of Sectarianism*, Oxford, 1990, 176–200.

Wilson, S., *Pulpit in Parliament*, Princeton, 1969.

Worsley, P., *The Trumpet Shall Sound: A Study of 'Cargo' Cults in Melanesia*, New York, 1968[2].

CHAPTER 4

Conservative revolution? The intolerant innovations of Qumran

Michael Mach

This chapter deals with a specific phenomenon, namely the Qum-ranites in the late Second Temple period.[1] In our discussion of the inner dialectic marked by a tendency towards conservatism and also by the development of new theological concepts, it is assumed that the Qumranites do not stand alone. The tension between both poles might be a useful frame of reference for the under-standing of other religious phenomena. Here it will be discussed within the limits of one distinguishable group.

As such the Qumranites were an actual part of the religion-historical scene of their time. Though confining ourselves to some aspects of this group, we would like to call to mind some of the characteristic elements of the broader situation which might have influenced the thoughts of the Qumranites.[2]

Right from its beginning the period of the Second Temple was marked by an ongoing debate about Jewish self-definition. This debate has different strands. The Babylonian exile contributed markedly to the self-awareness of Israel confronting other nations and religions,[3] and by doing so sharpened later controversies dur-ing the Hellenistic period.[4] Hellenistic culture was a real challenge by its sheer presence as well as its possible influence upon Juda-ism. This had consequences for Israel's relation to other nations[5] as well as for the growing 'nationalism',[6] though the forms of con-tact with Hellenism and Hellenistic people did not necessarily de-fine the amount of cultural influence.[7]

On the other hand, a split went right through the Jewish soci-ety, thus raising the questions: Are the returnees from the exile the real Israelites or is this designation to be kept for those who stayed in the country? Are the changes that occurred during the period of the exile within the religious thought of the community there to be followed by all as defining elements of Judaism?

The challenges, the inner struggle of the community for its self-definition and the confrontation with the outer world, cannot always be treated separately. They are sometimes intertwined and function together. What seems to be a reaction to outer influence might in fact be an inner conflict, too.[8] They are, in any case, to be recognized as factors in the process of group formation during this period.

Today it seems to be apparent that during this critical period there emerged some definition (though still not the term itself) of a 'true Israel'; in other words, not every Jew is naturally regarded as belonging to the defined group.[9] The Qumranites are one of the groups formed in this frame of reference.[10] However, the establishment of an independent group that denies outsiders the right to be regarded as part of the true Israel is at the same time the clearest expression of the group's intolerance towards others. By definition the departing group is usually the smaller part and is therefore called by several sometimes pejorative terms such as 'sect' and the like. But it should be remembered that such designations are given from the outside and need not necessarily correspond to the group's self-definition. On the contrary, such a group is likely to define itself by the most noble terms the majority would have liked to keep for itself, hence: 'Israel', 'the elect', etc.

Another aspect of such separations is the often-felt need of the minority to prove that it is keeping the old tradition – indeed, keeping it better than the majority – or even that it alone is keeping the old tradition. In other words, in its own eyes it is not the departing small group which is really leaving a stable majority; rather, this minority is the faithful remnant, the keeper of the old traditions, etc., whereas the majority left and abandoned what both had once agreed upon.[11] One might characterize this attitude as 'declared conservatism'. We call it 'declared' since its relation to historical reality, though possible, is nevertheless a nearly irrelevant factor. The group is forced to make the point, whether justly or not. What is of importance is the *claim* to continue the traditions of old more faithfully than others.

These more general reflections can be applied to the Qumranites who show at least some central features of a separatist group, even though a number of questions regarding the group are still hotly debated.[12] The Qumran community is, besides early Christianity, the best-attested Jewish group of the period.[13] Information about others, such as the Pharisees or the Sadducees, is either later or stems from outside sources, which often means from opposing groups (as, e.g., Pharisees and other Jewish groups mentioned in the writings of the New Testament). Yet, regardless of the quantity of texts published so far, the precise history of the Qumranites,[14] and their relation to others,[15] are still a matter of dispute among scholars.

Certain aspects seem, nevertheless, to be acknowledged by a majority of scholars. The group left the centre of Jewish religious life, namely Jerusalem and its temple, and settled at the Dead Sea shore. The manuscripts found in the surrounding caves should be attributed to the group. They reflect the library of the Qumranites which included biblical texts as well as otherwise known pseudepigrapha and writings of the group itself.[16]

However, there is no external evidence concerning the development of the Qumranites' thought or their group history. It is not clear how certain texts are to be related to the group's own ideology, and whether they were written by members of the group or brought to the place by those who joined the group or by others. The archaeological findings as such do not help us in differentiating levels of development or different ideologies within the group. We should therefore allow for some doctrines which must not automatically be combined into one system of the Qumranites' eschatology, messianology etc.[17] In fact, for a more precise description of the specific teaching of the group, their writings need to be investigated separately.

Yet it seems plausible to understand the several documents and the doctrines included therein as reflecting in a broader sense some kind of acceptable teaching for most of the group's members. That should allow us to refer to some broader themes as pointing to a specific phenomenon without going into textual details here. Instead of arguing for one theory or the other, one might fairly say that the simple fact of the group's settlement at this specific place indicates the separatists' ideology. The documents reveal a distinctive regulation for the group's inner life[18] and its contacts with outsiders, more precisely the attempt to diminish such contacts as far as possible.

The recently published 4QMMT[19] makes it abundantly clear

that the main reason for the separation lies in halakhic differences[20] between the group and, apparently, the Jerusalem priesthood.[21] For our discussion, it is important to note that the halakhic conservatism preceded the formation of the Qumranites' distinctive theological notions and led to the split from the rest of Israel.[22] Actually the group left Jerusalem and its temple, while still maintaining that Jerusalem is the biblical camp (מחנה).[23] The designation of the place of worship as biblical camp should be considered as one of the Qumranites' attempts to go back to biblical notions and hence as one of the expressions of a 'declared conservatism'.

A related item that illustrates this self-definition in the light of ancient traditions is the often-repeated term 'Sons of Zadok'.[24] This links the Qumranites with the high-priestly line from Zadok, who was appointed by David and maintained by Solomon.[25] His descendants continued to serve in the Temple[26] up to the deposition of Jason.[27] Though not all members of the group were priests, the special rank of the 'Sons of Zadok' is often stressed.[28] The discussion about the Qumranites' relation to the Sadducees has again been opened by 4QMMT, but it seems that the term 'Sons of Zadok' is to be understood not primarily in this way,[29] but rather as the covenanters' tying back to a biblical and early post-biblical authority. The priestly connection cannot be missed and might have an anchorage in historical reality, yet the term serves as a theological notion for the self-understanding of the group as continuing a specific kind of biblically legitimated priesthood.

A third often-discussed peculiarity of the Qumran writings is its distinctive solar calendar.[30] Yet this part of the tradition is not limited to the Qumranites; it was part of the Enoch tradition before.[31] It seems that this tradition influenced the author of the *Book of Jubilees*. Both pseudepigrapha are to be dated before the formation of the Qumran group. It is astonishing that, given the supposed time of composition of the 'Book of the Luminaries', i.e. 1 Enoch 72–82, the 364-day calendar was already outdated.[32] M. E. Stone concluded rightly: 'The survival and even more the cultivation of the 'Book of the Luminaries' is, therefore, a deliberate act of archaism.'[33] It goes without saying that such teaching is transmitted as divine revelation.[34] However, what are we to say about such 'archaism' in the middle of the second century BCE? The problem of the calendar is even more revealing since, as is well known, the 364-day period could not work out in practice. That problem was already felt by the author of the 'Book of the Luminaries', who addressed the problem theologically (1 Enoch 82.5–6).

The few items mentioned are only examples of the group's declared conservatism. The list might be continued. However, it is not this specific character of the Qumranites which will be discussed here, but rather the theological changes which they introduced.

It is admitted at the outset that not all these changes are necessarily the result of the Qumranites' separation from the rest of Judaism. It might be assumed that in some cases the Qumran evidence is simply the only evidence which has survived. As has already been noticed, in certain cases we have parallels to the Qumran texts elsewhere. However, it seems to be obvious that a group that left the rest of the nation and settled in the Judaean desert is likely to have adapted not only daily life but even more its theological teaching so as to explain its outstanding situation. Seen in this light, some of the peculiar developments in the Qumran community might be explained historically. Yet they conceptualize the thoughts of the Qumranites. Are such changes only historical necessities or should we explain them as consequences of the ideological basis of the Qumranites?

The term 'Sons of Zadok' and the priestly interest of the group reveal more than just a historical split between one group of priests and another. The mention of this specific priestly family has at least an eschatological overtone inasmuch as the 'Sons of Zadok' are the legitimate priests after the return from exile (Ezek. 44:15ff.). They will serve in the future temple prophesied by Ezekiel. CD 1 is one of the outstanding passages which relates to the community as the only return from the exile, as if the historical events under Ezra and Nehemiah never took place,[35] although this conception is not subsequently followed even within the CD: in 3.21–4.4 the 'Sons of Zadok' are mentioned together with the priests and the Levites. One has to see the self-designation 'Sons of Zadok' along these lines. It implies at least a rejection not only of the existing Temple but also of a longer period of Jewish history. The consequence of such a view is an ongoing expectation of Ezekiel's Temple in the future.[36]

However, what is even more striking is the reinterpretation of the group itself as a kind of substitute for the Temple.[37] The

whole tradition alluded to several times in the Scrolls is to be seen
not merely as a logical sequence following the separation from the
Jerusalem cult, but, rather, as a theological innovation of utmost
importance. As has been pointed out,[38] at least one of its motives
was the attempt to establish in Qumran 'a kingdom of priests, a
holy nation' (Exod. 19:6[39]) according to biblical prescriptions. This
is precisely the point where 'declared conservatism' defines the
need for theological innovation.

If the Qumranites saw themselves not only as biblical Israel but
as a kind of ideal priestly community,[40] it follows quite naturally
that their acts of Torah are seen as a kind of, or as a substitute for,
Temple offerings. Needless to say, such a view forced them to ex-
pand the laws concerning ritual purity,[41] and even to accept only
such members into their group who would have been acceptable for priesthood, regardless of whether or not these people are
actually priests.[42] Moreover priestly members as well as others
are bound by what was revealed to the 'Sons of Zadok, the priests
... and to the multitude of the men of their Covenant' (IQS 5,
2.9).

The last point is important, since the Qumranites assumed the
presence of angels within their community[43] – angels, it seems, instead of God himself.[44] In 1QSa 2.8–9 the presence of angels is
mentioned as reason not to accept certain people to the council;
quite similar is CD 15.15–17[45] for the community in general. According to 1QM 7.4–6 these people are not allowed to take part in
the eschatological war. The laws for exclusion of priests from their
office are based upon Leviticus 21:16ff. Other biblical texts might
have had some influence, too.[46]

However, of greater importance is the liturgical communion of
the Qumranites with the angels. We know comparatively little about
Jewish liturgy before the destruction of the Second Temple.[47] Yet
there is no doubt that the Qumranites conceived of themselves as
praying together with the angels.[48] This seems to be the most natural explanation of the sheer existence of 4QShiShabb. Within a
cycle of thirteen weeks this document offers for every Sabbath a
song which describes the angelic worship. The angels are called
here several times 'priests' or simply 'servants'.[49] This fact seems
to occupy much more attention than the actual contents of the
angelic praise.[50] In other words, the member of the community
does not so much take part in the heavenly recitation of songs

as recite a description of the heavenly worship, using the terms known from the actual earthly Temple.

This thought merges precisely with the priestly ideology of the Qumranites and their having left the Jerusalem cult.[51] Once the possibility of serving in a given cult does not exist any longer, one has to look for compensation. The heavenly praise of angels is a motif known already in biblical literature, and one that developed during the period of the Second Temple. The Qumranites might have understood their ideal participation in the heavenly liturgy as compensation for the loss of the temple service. But their newly developed idea is – though close to others – nevertheless quite unique in the frame of contemporary literature.[52]

However, the specific links of the Qumranites to the angelic worship are much richer than those in contemporary works.[53] If the angels are depicted as the true priests in the only legitimate temple, namely the heavenly one, and if the worshipper takes part in their service, it is only too natural to choose new members according to priestly criteria. More than this, the communion with the angels is not only a liturgical fiction, it governs life and even the eschatological hopes up to the eschatological war[54] which will be fought on both sides in the presence of and with the actual assistance of the angels.

All that amounts to much more than a compensation for the lost temple alone. The actual description of the heavenly worship as a way to connect the reciting community with that event includes a basic change in the understanding of religious life. This does not necessarily exclude eschatological hopes concerned with a new, pure temple on earth, yet that hope is no longer related to actual liturgical practice.

The separatist community did not stop at this point. A feature that has attracted Qumran scholars from the time of the first publication of the Scrolls is their extreme dualism.[55] The War Scroll describes the eschatological war between the 'Sons of Light' and the 'Sons of Darkness', and the Manual of Discipline divides humankind between both groups under the rulership of two corresponding angels.[56] The astonishing part of this treatise is the differentiation of good and evil even within those on the side of light.[57] It seems plausible that this dualistic division served in the first place to legitimize the Qumranites' separation from the rest of Israel. One could have expected some kind of self-definition as the elected (and perhaps as the only elected). The form of dualistic distribution we find in Qumran, however, goes much further in so far as it not only differentiates the truly elected from the rest but introduces this twofold view into the heavenly world. It might be that some Iranian influences are felt here,[58] yet that would explain only the origin, not the usage as such. The sharp dualism of the Qumranites goes far beyond comparable notions in contemporary literature and should be seen as another item in Qumran's theological revolution – which might again be due, at least in part, to historical conditions, but transcends by far what was actually needed.[59]

The vast number of biblical commentaries in Qumran is another indication that the group felt the need to base itself upon Scripture.[60] However, since this source is open to all the partners in the discussion the group would have to justify its exegesis and would therefore develop its own means of interpretation. The Qumranites used, at least at one important point, the theory of a second revelation, this time revealing not necessarily a new text but rather the interpretation of shared Scripture: 'And as for that which He said, "That he who reads may read it speedily": interpreted this concerns the Teacher of Righteousness, to whom God made known all the mysteries of the words of His servants the Prophets.'[61] The idea as such makes it impossible for others to argue about a given interpretation. Within the self-definition of the newly established group it serves other aims, too.[62] But what is of greater importance is the fact that the need for a scriptural basis leads to hermeneutical changes which in turn imply an alteration in an issue of immense theological importance.

In conclusion, then: the Qumranites defined themselves as the true priests and in this sense as a substitute for the Jerusalem Temple. As true priests they shared the angelic worship in heaven by reciting precisely that. As the true remnant of Israel they are the chosen ones and the 'others' enter into a dualistic frame as 'Sons of Darkness'. These important changes are argued for by means of a new hermeneutic which includes divine revelation as an exegetical device. It is true that not all the items are exclusively Qumranic; some have parallels, others might have had. The Qumran community belongs to the larger current of apocalypticism so typical of a number of books written at this time.[63] One should be aware of the fact that these products of eschatological thought are mostly to be compared with the literature of the extremists, who always sound louder than the masses; but the latter did not leave literary products behind. What counts is the concentrated effort of the Qumranites and their rigour in applying the newly developed ideas to the historical Israel which they believe themselves to represent. If our summarizing analysis will stand, we might find in Qumran an outstanding example for what we termed 'declared conservatism' which, we might add now, ends up in theological revolution.

NOTES

1 Qumran writings are cited according to the following editions and sigla: CD – M. Broshi (ed.), *The Damascus Document Reconsidered*, Jerusalem, 1992 (containing the edition of the text by E. Qimron); 1QM – Y. Yadin, *The Scroll of the War of the Sons of Light against the Sons of Darkness*, 2nd edn, Jerusalem, 1957; 1QS – J. Licht, *The Rule Scroll*, Jerusalem, 1965 (= Manual of Discipline); J. H. Charlesworth (ed.), *The Dead Sea Scrolls*. Hebrew, Aramaic, and Greek Texts with English Translations. Vol. I: *Rule of the Community and Related Documents*. Tübingen/Louisville 1994; 1QpHab – B. Nitzan, *Pesher Habakuk*, Jerusalem and Tel Aviv, 1986; 4QShiShabb – C. Newsome, *Songs of the Sabbath Sacrifice* (HSS 27), Atlanta, GA, 1985; 4QMMT – E. Qimron and J. Strugnell, 'Qumran Cave 4.V: Miqsat Ma'ase ha-Torah' *DJD* 10, Oxford, 1994; 11QBer – A. S. van der Woude, 'Ein neuer Segensspruch aus Qumran (11QBer)', in S. Wagner (ed.), *Bibel und Qumran. Festschrift H. Bardtke*, Berlin, 1968, 253–8. The author wishes to express his gratitude of Prof. D. Schwartz and Dr. B. Nitzan who read an earlier draft of this paper and contributed from their insights.

2 It goes without saying that in recalling these topics we do not aim at completeness either in the actual list of topics or in the bibliographical notes.

3 See, e.g., H. D. Preuss, *Verspottung fremder Religionen im Alten Testament* (BWANT 92), Stuttgart, 1971, 276–8, and more recently, from another angle, H. G. M. Williamson, 'The Concept of Israel in Transition', in R. E. Clements (ed.), *The World of Ancient Israel. Sociological, Anthropological and Political Perspectives*, Cambridge, 1989, 141–61; but see also Y. Hoffmann, *The Prophecies against Foreign Nations in the Bible*, Tel Aviv, 1977 [in Hebrew].

4 See, e.g., S. Talmon, 'The Emergence of Jewish Sectarianism in the early Second Temple Period', in S. Talmon, *King, Cult and Calendar in Ancient Israel. Collected Studies*, Jerusalem, 1986, 165–201 esp. 186ff.;

'Between the Bible and the Mishna', in S. Talmon, *The World of Qumran from Within. Collected Studies*, Jerusalem and Leiden, 1989, 11–52 esp. 48ff.; A. Rofé, 'Isaiah 66:1–4: Judean Sects in the Persian Period as Viewed by Trito-Isaiah', in A. Kort and S. Morschauer (eds.), *Biblical and Related Studies Presented to S. Iwry*, Winona Lake, 1985, 205–17; 'The Beginnings of Sects in Post-exilic Judaism', *Cathedra* 49 (1988), 13–22 [in Hebrew].

5 See the recent study by L. H. Feldman, *Jew and Gentile in the Ancient World. Attitudes and Interactions from Alexander to Justinian*, Princeton, 1993.

6 D. Mendels, *The Rise and Fall of Jewish Nationalism*, New York, 1992.

7 See M. Hengel, *Judentum und Hellenismus. Studien zu ihrer Begegnung unter besonderer Berücksichtigung Palästinas bis zur Mitte des 2.Jhs. v. Chr.* (WUNT 10), 2nd edn, Tübingen, 1973.

8 Already years ago E. Bickermann assumed that this inner factor was at work not only in theoretical discussions but as a political force; see his *Der Gott der Makkabäer. Untersuchungen über Sinn und Ursprung der makkabäischen Erhebung*, Berlin, 1937 (E.tr. *The God of the Maccabees. Studies in the Meaning and Origin of the Maccabean Revolt* (SJLA 32), Leiden, 1979. The thesis has attracted scholars over the years. For a more recent study of the inner relations of the Hasmoneans see J. Sievers, *The Hasmoneans and Their Supporters, From Mattathias to the Death of John Hyrcanus I* (South Florida Studies in the History of Judaism 6), Atlanta, GA, 1990.

9 For some implications of the processes alluded to here for ancient Jewish and early Christian self-definition, as well as for further bibliography, cf. the present writer's 'Verus Israel: Towards the Clarification of a Jewish Factor in early Christian Self-definition', *IOS* 14 (1994), 143–71.

10 It has been observed that the Qumranites regarded themselves as the true Israel, see e.g. G. Vermes, *The Dead Sea Scrolls. Qumran in Perspective*, Cleveland, 1978, 88; S. Talmon, *The Emergence of Jewish Sectarianism* (above n. 4), here esp. pp. 123–126 as well as his 'Waiting for the Messiah – The Conceptual Universe of the Qumran Covenanters', *The World of Qumran*, 273–300, esp. 280–1.

11 See e.g. the remarks of F. García Martínez and A. S. van der Woude, 'A "Groningen" Hypothesis of Qumran Origins and Early History', *RQ* 14 (1990) (= F. García Martínez (ed.), *The Texts of Qumran and the History of the Community* (Proceedings of the Groningen Congress on the Dead Sea Scrolls, 20–3 August 1989, III), 521–41, here 524, and the literature quoted there; further D. Flusser, Pharisäer, Sadduzäer und Essener im Pescher Nahum. *Qumran*. Hrsg. v. E. Grötzinger e.a. Darmstadt 1981, 129–66, here 138.

12 For recent summaries of the questions discussed see L. H. Schiffman,

'The Battle of the Scrolls: Recent Developments in the Study of the Dead Sea Scrolls', *Cathedra* 61 (1991), 3–23 [in Hebrew]; E. Tov, 'Dead Sea Scrolls in Light of New Research', *Jewish Studies* 34 (1994), 37–67 [in Hebrew]; J. C. VanderKam, *The Dead Sea Scrolls Today*, London and Grand Rapids, 1994; L. H. Schiffman, *Reclaiming the Dead Sea Scrolls. The History of Judaism, the Background of Christianity, the Lost Library of Qumran*, Philadelphia and Jerusalem, 1994.

13 It should be remarked, however, that scholarly discussion traces some of the text to pre-Qumranic origins as, e.g., 11QTemp; see *inter alia* P. R. Callaway, 'The Temple Scroll and the Canonization of Jewish Law'. *RQ* 13 (1988), 237–50 and literature quoted there.

14 See recently P. R. Callaway, *The History of the Qumran Community. An Investigation* (JSPSS 3), Sheffield, 1988; H. Stegemann, 'The Qumran Essenes – Local Members of the Main Jewish Union in Late Second Temple Times', in J. Trebolle Barrera and L. Vegas Montaner (eds.), *The Madrid Qumran Congress* (Proceedings of the International Congress on the Dead Sea Scrolls, Madrid, 18–21 March, 1991), Leiden, 1992, I, 83–166. The term 'Qumranites' is in more than one respect problematic; cp. P. R. Davies, 'The Birthplace of the Essenes: Where is "Damascus"?' *RQ* 14 (1990), 503–19.

15 See now A. I. Baumgarten, 'The Rule of the Martian as Applied to Qumran', *IOS* 14 (1994), 121–42; and see below, nn. 18–19.

16 There has been some dispute concerning the relation between the manuscripts and the settlement, see e.g. García Martínez and van der Woude, 'A "Groningen" Hypothesis'.

17 Especially at these points scholars tried for years to distinguish different levels of development. See, e.g., P. R. Davies, 'Eschatology at Qumran', *JBL* 104 (1985), 39–55; J. VanderKam, 'Messianism in the Scrolls', in E. Ulrich and J. VanderKam (eds.), *The Community of the Renewed Covenant* (The Notre Dame Symposium on the Dead Sea Scrolls), (CJAn 10), Notre Dame, 1994, 211–34. On the other side a prominent Qumran scholar like F. García Martínez can do without a system of development in such a crucial matter: 'Messianische Erwartungen in den Qumranschriften', *JBTh* 8 (1993), 171–208.

18 See M. Weinfeld, *The Organizational Pattern and the Penal Code of the Qumran Sect* (NTOA 2), Fribourg and Göttingen, 1986; L. H. Schiffman, *Sectarian Law in the Dead Sea Scrolls. Courts, Testimony and the Penal Code*, Chico, 1983, esp. 155ff; L. H. Schiffman, *The Eschatological Community of the Dead Sea Scrolls. A Study of the Rule of the Congregation* (SBLMS 38), Atlanta, GA, 1989.

19 The contents of the Scroll were made known to the public officially for the first time by E. Qimron and J. Strugnell, 'An Unpublished Halakhic Letter from Qumran', in J. Amitai (ed.), *Biblical Archaeology*

Today (Proceedings of the International Conference on Biblical Archaeology, Jerusalem, April 1984), Jerusalem, 1985, 400–7.

20 See Y. Sussmann, 'The History of Halakha and the Dead Sea Scrolls: Preliminary Observations on *Miqṣat Ma'ase ha-Torah* (4QMMT)', *Tarbiz* 59 (1989/90), 11–76 [in Hebrew], and in a shorter version his 'The History of *Halakha* and the Dead Sea Scrolls', in M. Broshi (ed.), *The Scrolls of the Judaean Desert. Forty Years of Research*, Jerusalem, 1992, 99–127 [in Hebrew]. This version is mostly identical with his 'The History of the Halakha and the Dead Sea Scrolls', Appendix 1 in Qimron's and Strugnell's edition, 179–200. The comparison of Qumran Halakha with the rabbinic one has occupied few scholars, notably J. M. Baumgarten, *Studies in Qumran Law* (SJLA 24), Leiden, 1977 and L. H. Schiffman, *The Halakha at Qumran* (SJLA 16), Leiden, 1975.

21 It is not clear that 4QMMT points to a first stage in the relations between the Jerusalem establishment and the separatists, though the theory has to be taken seriously. See Schiffman, 'Battle of the Scrolls', and 'The New Halakhic Letter (4QMMT) and the Origins of the Dead Sea Scrolls', *BA* 53 (1990), 64–73. It is even not as established as might be assumed that 4QMMT is to be labelled 'halakhic letter'; see J. Strugnell, 'MMT: Second Thoughts on a Forthcoming Edition', in E. Ulrich and J. VanderKam (eds.), *The Community of the Renewed Covenant*, 57–73, esp. 70–1.

22 Recently D. R. Schwartz argued for the application of the terms 'realism' versus 'nominalism' to denote the difference between the Qumranic and the rabbinic attitudes towards the law, characterizing the Qumranites as 'realists'; this view is not easily to be combined with our thesis here, yet, it is not necessarily inappropriate: 'Law and Truth: On Qumran–Sadducean and Rabbinic views of Law', in D. Dimant and U. Rappaport (eds.), *The Dead Sea Scrolls. Forty Years of Research*, Leiden and Jerusalem, 1992, 229–40.

23 See the end of 4QMMT. E. Qimron has recently drawn significant conclusions from the symbolic use of this term in Qumran literature. His discussion has consequences for the understanding of ritual purity in the group's theology as well; see Qimron, 'Celibacy in the Dead Sea Scrolls and the Two Kinds of Sectarians', in Barrera and Montanen (eds.), *The Madrid Qumran Congress*, 1, 287–94; regarding the specific question of celibacy see also, J. M. Baumgarten, 'The Qumran–Essene Restraints on Marriage', in L. H. Schiffman (ed.), *Archaeology and History in the Dead Sea Scrolls* (The New York University Conference in Memory of Y. Yadin), (JSPSS 8), Sheffield, 1990, 13–24.

24 See J. Liver, 'The "Sons of Zadok the Priests" in the Dead Sea Sect', *RQ* 6 (21) (1967), 3–30; for a more recent discussion cf. Baumgarten, 'The Rule of the Martian, 127 and n. 32.

25 2 Sam: 8:17–25; 15:24; 1 Kings 2:35.

26 See 2 Chron. 31:10; 1 Chron. 9:11; Neh. 11:11; the two later sources ascribe the Zadokites a higher rank within the priesthood.

27 For the historical side cf. E. Schürer, *The History of the Jewish People in the Age of Jesus Christ (175 BC–AD 135)*, new English edn rev. and ed. G. Vermes, F. Millar and M. Black, Edinburgh, 1973, 1, 148–50; for the influences not only upon the Qumranites see H. P. Hanson, 'The Matrix of Apocalyptic', in W. D. Davies and L. Finkelstein (eds.), *The Cambridge History of Judaism*, 11, *The Hellenistic Age*, Cambridge, 1989, 524–33, esp. 530–2.

28 See as one example among many others 1QSb 3.22–3: 'Words of blessing. The Master shall bless the sons of Zadok, the Priests, whom God has chosen to confirm His Covenant for ever and to inquire into all His precepts in the midst of His people, and to instruct them as He commanded; who have established His Covenant on truth and watched over all His laws with righteousness and walked according to the way of His choice.' Interestingly enough these priests are here to be blessed with the priestly blessing (Num. 6:24–6), instead of blessing others!

29 Cf. G. Vermes, *The Dead Sea Scrolls*, 118–19; and the articles by Sussmann listed in n. 18, above; for the Sadducees as a priestly sect see D. R. Schwartz, 'Philo's Priestly Descent', in: F. E. Greenspahn, E. Hilgert, B. L. Mack (eds.), *Nourished with Peace. Studies in Hellenistic Judaism in Memory of S. Sandmel*, Chico, 1984, 155–71, here: 166–8; J. M. Baumgarten, 'Sadducean Elements in Qumran Law', in E. Ulrich and J. VanderKam (eds.), *The Community of the Renewed Covenant*, 27–36, and, more pointedly, L. H. Schiffman throughout his recent writings, e.g., 'The Sadducean Origins of the Dead Sea Sect', in H. Shanks (ed.), *Understanding the Dead Sea Scrolls. A Reader from the Biblical Archaeologist Review*, New York, 1992 (= 1993), 36–49.

30 See the still important study by S. Talmon, 'The Calendar of the Covenanters of the Judean Desert' and 'The Emergence of In-stitutionalized Prayer in Israel in Light of Qumran Literature', in *The World of Qumran*, 147–85, 200–43 resp. See further Schiffman, *Reclaiming the Dead Sea Scrolls*, 301–5; H. Stegemann, 'The Qumran Essenes', here 114–22. It might well be that the *Temple Scroll* still re-flects a lunar calendar. But such interpretation is based upon an early, pre-Qumranic date of the document; see H. Stegemann, 'The Institutions of Israel in the *Temple Scroll*', in D. Dimant and U. Rap-paport (eds.), *The Dead Sea Scrolls*, 156–85, esp. 169–76; J. Vander-Kam, 'Calendrical Texts and the Origins of the Dead Sea Scroll Community', in M. O. Wise et al. (eds.), *Methods of Investigations of the Dead Sea Scrolls and the Khirbet Qumran Site. Present Realities and Future Prospects* (Annals of the New York Academy of Sciences 722), New York, 1994, 371–87.

31 For a more detailed commentary on the relevant passages in 1 Enoch
    see O. Neugebauer, *The 'Astronomical' Chapters of the Ethiopic Book of
    Enoch (72 to 82)*, transl. and comm. with additional notes on the Ara-
    maic fragments by M. Black, Copenhagen, 1981 (Kongelige Danske
    Videnskabernes Selskab, Matematisk-fysiske Meddelelser 40:10) =
    Appendix A of M. Black, *The Book of Enoch or I Enoch. A New English
    Edition with Commentary and Textual Notes* (SVTP 7), Leiden, 1985, 386–
    419; H. S. Kvanvig, *Roots of Apocalyptic. The Mesopotamian Background of
    the Enoch Figure and the Son of Man* (WMANT 61), Neukirchen, 1988,
    68ff. and the material quoted there; J. C. VanderKam, *Enoch and the
    Growth of an Apocalyptic Tradition* (CBQMS 16), Washington, 1984, 76–
    104. See also E. Rau, 'Kosmologie, Eschatologie und die Lehrautor-
    ität Henochs. Traditions- und formgeschichtliche Untersuchungen
    zum äth. Henochbuch und zu verwandten Schriften', unpublished
    Ph.D. thesis, Hamburg, 1974. Different attempts to reconcile the solar
    calendar of the Qumranites with the moon have been discussed re-
    cently; see R. T. Beckwith, 'The Essene Calendar and the Moon: A
    Reconsideration', *RQ* 15 (1992), 457–66.
32 As has been pointed out by M. E. Stone, 'Enoch, Aramaic Levi and
    Sectarian Origins', *JSJ* 19 (1988), 159–70 (= *Selected Studies in Pseudepi-
    grapha and Apocrypha with Special Reference to the Armenian Tradition* (SVTP),
    Leiden, 1991, 247–58, esp. 249–55). H. S. Kvanvig sees in this tradi-
    tion eventually a Jewish group 'that struggles to reconcile the older
    Jewish traditions ... from other cultures,' (*Roots of Apocalyptic*, 84).
33 M. E. Stone, *Selected Studies*, 252.
34 Cf. Rau, 'Kosmologie', 140–84.
35 The picture changes essentially once the historical notions of the pas-
    sage are dismissed for metrical reasons. See the discussion by P. R.
    Davies, *The Damascus Covenant. An Interpretation of the 'Damascus Docu-
    ment'*, (JSOTSS 25), Sheffield, 1983, esp. 61–3. However, such a con-
    clusion is not supported by any of the extant texts; see now Qimron's
    edition, 11.
36 This consequence has not been drawn by B. Gärtner, *The Temple and
    the Community in Qumran and the New Testament. A Comparative Study in the
    Temple Symbolism of the Qumran Texts and the New Testament* (SNTSMS 1),
    Cambridge, 1965, 5. CD 3,21–4,4 is linked *expressis verbis* to Ezechiel's
    prophecies (CD 3,20–1).
37 This tradition has been dealt with already by D. Flusser, 'The Dead
    Sea Sect and Pre-Pauline Christianity', in C. Rabin and Y. Yadin
    (eds.), *Scripta Hierosolymitana* IV: *Aspects of the Dead Sea Scrolls*, 2nd edn,
    Jerusalem, 1965, 215–66, esp. 229–36; J. Licht, *The Rule Scroll*,
    Jerusalem, 1965 (Hebr.), 171f., 175, has tried to understand it in a
    more symbolic way as indicating the firmness of the community. The
    following lines differ from such an interpretation in some respects.

B. Gärtner has dedicated a full study to the subject (*The Temple and the Community*); see also G. Klinzing, *Die Umdeutung des Kultus in der Qumrangemeinde und im NT* (SUNT 7), Göttingen, 1971, esp. 50–93. The actual character of 'substitute' was denied by D. Dimant, '*4QFlorilegium* and the Idea of the Community as Temple', in A. Caquot, M. Madas-Lebel and J. Riaud (eds.), *Hellenica et Judaica. Hommage à V. Nikiprowetzky*, Leuven and Paris, 1986, 165–89, esp. 187. However, even according to her careful reading of 4Qflor there remains at least the connection of the 'temple of men' with eschatological hopes (not necessarily the eschatological temple, as she stresses rightly), the priestly organization of the community as it were serving in the temple, and the link to the 'Sons of Zadok'. For the ongoing debate about this crucial point see further D. R. Schwartz, 'The Three Temples of 4QFlorilegium', *RQ* 10 (1979), 83–91; M. Ben-Yashar, 'Noch zum Miqdas 'Adam in 4QFlorilegium', *RQ* 10 (1981), 587–8; G. J. Brooke, *Exegesis at Qumran: 4QFlorilegium in its Jewish Context* (JSOTSS 29), Sheffield 1985, 80–204; J. J. Collins, 'Teacher and Messiah? The One Who Will Teach Righteousness at the End of Days', in E. Ulrich and J. VanderKam (eds.), *The Community of the Renewed Covenant*, 193–210, esp. 196–8; H. K. Harrington, *The Impurity Systems of Qumran and the Rabbis* (SBLDS 143), Atlanta, GA, 1992, 52–4; L. H. Schiffman, 'Purity and Perfection: Exclusion from the Council of the Community in the Serekh ha'Edah', in J. Amitai (ed.), *Biblical Archaeology Today* (Proceedings of the International Conference on Biblical Archaeology Jerusalem), Jerusalem, 1985, 373–89; J. M. Baumgarten, 'Purification after Childbirth and the Sacred Garden in 4Q 265 and Jubilees', in G. J. Brooke with F. García Martínez (eds.), *New Qumran Texts and Studies* (Proceedings of the First Meeting of the International Organization for Qumran Studies, Paris 1992), (STDJ 15), Leiden, 1994, 3–10, esp. 8f.

38 D. Dimant in '*4QFlorilegium*', esp. 188–9.

39 But see D. R. Schwartz, '"Kingdom of Priests"–a Pharisaic Slogan?', *Studies in the Jewish Background of Christianity* (WUNT 60), Tübingen, 1992, 57–80, for the Qumran references esp. 61.

40 See also Davies, *The Damascus Covenant*, 202–3.

41 Cf. *inter alia* E. Qimron, 'Celibacy in the Dead Sea Scrolls'. It has been stressed sometimes that the Qumranites did not really ask for a general priesthood but only for ritual purity comparable to that demanded from priests, see, e.g., D. R. Schwartz, 'Kingdom', 62 n. 19. Yet, at least at this point it is obvious that the Qumranites tried to extend laws regarding priestly purity to Israel in general, see, e.g., L. H. Schiffman, 'The Impurity of the Dead in the *Temple Scroll*', in L. H. Schiffman (ed.), *Archaeology and History*, 135–56. The Qumran writings contain a valuable number of texts that belong to the re-

interpretation of the concepts of purity enlarging these towards an
ethical understanding. The subject cannot be dealt with here. It is
part of the larger process of what has been called the 'spiritualization'
of cultic practices. For this development cf. D. R. Schwartz, 'Priesthood, Temple, Sacrifices: Opposition and Spiritualization in the Late
Second Temple Period', unpublished Ph.D. thesis, Jerusalem, 1979,
and Klinzing, *Die Umdeutung*, and J. Milgrom, 'Deviations from Scripture in the Purity Laws of the *Temple Scroll*', in S. Talmon (ed.), *Jewish Civilization in the Hellenistic–Roman Period*, Philadelphia, 1991, 159–
67.

42 The community consisted of priests and other people, as is obvious
from passages like, e.g., CD 14,3–6 and 1QS 6,14–23. The latter text
relates the conditions of admitting new members. It starts with the
words 'and whoever of Israel volunteers...' (thus D. R. Schwartz,
'On Two Aspects of a Priestly View of Descent at Qumran', in L. H.
Schiffman (ed.), *Archaeology and History*, 157–80, here: 158). It cannot
be decided clearly whether this openness to non-priests was the attitude of the sect throughout its history; for a possible explanation of
changes in attitude, see Schwartz's article. This is one of the many
points where the inner development of the group's theology is of
utmost importance, yet as the texts have come down to us, it is
impossible to establish such inner elaborations, if such had been
there.

43 The whole complex of 'communion with the angels' in Qumran
literature has been dealt with by several scholars, partly in disagree-
ment. See the present writer's *Entwicklungsstadien des jüdischen Engelglaubens in vorrabbinischer Zeit* (TSAJ 34), Tübingen, 1992, 159–69, 209–40,
and the literature quoted there. Add now L. H. Schiffman, *The Eschatological Community*, 49–51.

44 Already noted by P. Schäfer, *Rivalität zwischen Menschen und Engeln.
Untersuchungen zur rabbinischen Engelvorstellung*, (SJ 8) Berlin and New
York, 1975, 36 relating to 1QM 7.1–7.

45 See Qimron's edition; further 11QTemp 45.17–18 and 11QBer 13–14;
for the whole complex cf. J. A. Fitzmyer, 'A Feature of Qumran
Angelology and the Angels of I Cor. XI 10', in *Essays on the Semitic
Background of the New Testament*, London, 1971, repr. Missoula, MT,
1974, 187–217.

46 Cf. Num. 5:1ff. and Deut. 23:10ff.

47 Earlier assumptions have been attacked recently by E. Fleischer in a
series of articles; see 'On the Beginnings of Obligatory Jewish Prayer',
Tarbiz 59 (1990), 397–441 (with the 'Rejoinder to Dr Reif's Remarks',
Tarbiz 60 (1990/1), 677–81); 'Annual and Triennial Reading of the
Bible in the Old Synagogue', *Tarbiz* 61 (1991), 25–43; 'The *Shemone
Esre* – Its Character, Internal Order, Content and Goals', *Tarbiz* 62
(1993), 179–223. [All in Hebrew.]

48 Cf. 1QH 2.13; 3.19–23; 11.9–10; 1QS 11.4–9. See further Mach, *Entwicklungsstadien*, esp. 209–16, 229–35.

49 See Newsome's introduction, 26, 30; and her study 'Merkabah Exegesis in the Qumran Sabbath Shirot', *JJS* 38 (1987), 11–30, for a corrected reading of 4Q 405 20 ii.21–2; cf. further 1QM 13.3 and also A. Caquot, 'Le service des anges', *RQ* 13 (1988), 421–9; É. Puech, 'Notes sur le manuscrit des cantiques du Sacrifice du Sabbath trouvé à Massada', *RQ* 12 (1987), 575–83.

50 Cf. esp. D. C. Allison, 'The Silence of the Angels: Reflections on the Sabbath Sacrifice', *RQ* 13 (1988), 189–97.

51 The formerly widely accepted identification of the Qumranites with the Essenes as described by Josephus has caused some difficulties at this point, since according to Josephus the Essenes had not abandoned the Jerusalem Temple totally. However, not only does this identification become weaker in light of the recent discussions based mainly upon 4QMMT but even within that theory it should be borne in mind that Josephus is to be regarded as an outside source contrary to the Qumran writings themselves. I would therefore prefer to interpret the latter as far as possible independently of Josephus' account.

52 The Bible mentioned already the human demand that the heavenly beings should join in the human praise of God. The literature of the Second Temple period normally knows the angelic songs and occasionally repeats the biblical request. A liturgical communion, however, is typical of the Qumranites alone.

53 It should be noted that in light of Acts 23:8 the developed angelology of the Qumran literature makes it difficult to identify the group too easily as a Sadducean faction: 'For the Sadducees say, there is no resurrection, nor angel, nor spirit.' This verse has caused some difficulties for modern interpreters; see my study, *Entwicklungsstadien*, 167 with n. 140 and 403, and B. T. Viviano and J. Taylor, 'Sadducees, Angels, and Resurrection (Acts 23:8–9)', *JBL* 111 (1992), 496–8.

54 Since I have dealt with these traditions elsewhere (see *Entwicklungsstadien*, esp. 241–55), suffice it here to recall that the communion in war is a biblical motif largely developed and reused in the literature of the period, cf. esp. 2 Maccabees. However, an author like Jason does not know the other aspects of the angelic communion and seems not to be interested, e.g., in liturgy.

55 See already H. W. Huppenbauer, *Der Mensch zwischen zwei Welten. Der Dualismus der Texte von Qumran (Höhle I) und der Damaskusfragmente. Ein Beitrag zur Vorgeschichte des Evangeliums*, Zürich, 1959; P. von der Osten-Sacken, *Gott und Belial. Traditionsgeschichtliche Untersuchungen zum Dualismus in den Texten aus Qumran* (SUNT 6), Göttingen, 1969.

56 1QS 3.15–4.26.

57 1QS 3.21–4; 4.24–6; cf. von der Osten-Sacken, *Gott und Belial*, esp.

185–9, though 4Q 186 (published by J. Allegro, 'Qumran Cave 4. I (4Q 158–4Q 186' (*DJD* 5) Oxford, 1968, 88–91) need not necessarily be connected to this part of 1QS; it might have another *Sitz im Leben.*

58 See e.g. S. Shaked, 'Qumran and Iran', *IOS* 2 (1972), 433–46; S. Shaked, 'Iranian Influence on Judaism: First Century BCE to Second Century CE', in W. D. Davies and L. Finkelstein (eds.), *The Cambridge History of Judaism*, 1, Cambridge, 1984, 308–25, here 315–16.

59 It is yet unclear how this dualistic view relates to the other parts of Israel. The opening section of CD seems to pass over the return from the exile. CD 2.7–11 states more clearly that the others are not chosen. The expressions in 1QM might well fit into this pattern inasmuch as 1QM 12.1 names the chosen ones of the holy nation in parallelism to the chosen ones from heaven. If the Qumranites defined themselves as the true Israel, a remark like 1QM 10.9 ('Israel which you have chosen') stands in no contradiction. 1 Enoch 91.12–13 might be a parallel to this attitude, provided the judgement scene predicted here has the eschatological war in mind and not the Maccabean uprising. But the interpretation of this text is doubtful, see J. Licht, 'The Plant Eternal and the People of Divine Deliverance', in C. Rabin and Y. Yadin (eds.), *Essays on the Dead Sea Scrolls in Memory of E. L. Sukenik*, Jerusalem 1961, 49–75 [in Hebrew].

60 See already F. F. Bruce, *Biblical Exegesis in the Qumran Texts*, The Hague, 1959; O. Betz, *Offenbarung und Schriftforschung in der Qumransekte* (WUNT 6), Tübingen, 1960 ; for the *pesher* literature see M. P. Horgan, *Pesharim: Qumran Interpretations of Biblical Books* (CBQMS 8), Washington, 1979; for 4Qflor esp. cf. G. J. Brooke, *Exegesis at Qumran*, and A. Steudel, *Der Midrasch zur Eschatologie aus der Qumrangemeinde (4Q MidrEschat$^{a.b}$)* (STDJ 13), Leiden, 1994 and D. Flusser, 'Pharisäer, Sadduzäer', here 150f. For other aspects of the hermeneutical activities at Qumran cf. E. Tov, 'Biblical Texts as Reworked in Some Qumran Manuscripts with Special Attention to 4QRP and 4QParaGen-Exod', in E. Ulrich and J. VanderKam (eds.), *The Community*, 111–34; M. Kister, 'Biblical Phrases and Hidden Biblical Interpretation and *Pesharim*', in D. Dimant and U. Rappaport (eds.), *The Dead Sea Scrolls*, 27–39; J. Milgrom, 'Deviations'.

61 1QpHab 7.3–5. See the discussion by I. Gruenwald, *Apocalyptic and Merkavah Mysticism* (AGAJU 14), Leiden and Cologne, 1980, 19–25; L. H. Schiffman, 'The Temple Scroll and the Nature of its Law', in: *The Community*, 37–55, esp. 51f.

62 For related texts and some bibliography cf. the present writer's 'The Social Implications of Scripture-Interpretation in Second Temple Judaism', in J. Davies and I. Wollaston (eds.), *The Sociology of Sacred Texts*, Sheffield, 1993, 166–79.

63 See recently, J. J. Collins, 'Was the Dead Sea Sect an Apocalyptic Movement?' in: L. H. Schiffman (ed.), *Archaeology and History*, 25–51; I. Fröhlich, 'Pesher, Apocalyptic Literature and Qumran', in J. Trebolle Barrera and L. Vegas Montaner (eds.), *The Madrid Qumran Congress*, 295–305; D. Dimant, 'Apocalyptic Texts at Qumran', in E. Ulrich and J. VanderKam (eds.), *The Community*, 175–91; F. García Martínez, *Qumran and Apocalyptic. Studies on the Aramaic Texts from Qumran* (STDJ 9), Leiden, 1992.

CHAPTER 5

Who was considered an apostate in the Jewish Diaspora?

John M. G. Barclay

Tolerance has its limits in any community which wishes to preserve its identity. Boundaries which create distinctions between 'insiders' and 'outsiders' have to be established and maintained if a community is to survive, especially a minority community in a pluralist environment.[1] Most Jewish communities in the Diaspora appear to have been successful in preserving their social and religious identity, in many cases over hundreds of years. Where, then, did they fix the boundaries which defined the distinction between members and non-members? This question has often been addressed in enquiring how Gentiles were considered to have crossed the boundary and come into the Jewish community; but remarkably little attention has been paid to the opposite phenomenon, that is, how Jews were considered to have crossed the boundary and passed out of Judaism.[2] Recent studies have rightly emphasized the variety within Second Temple Judaism, its multifarious strands making it difficult to define universal standards of 'acceptability' within Judaism. Yet individual Jewish communities, however diverse they may have been, must have preserved some sense of 'proper' behaviour which made it possible to castigate actual or potential 'apostasy'. To detect where the boundaries lay in this regard would not only shed light on the maintenance of Jewish identity in the Diaspora; it would also provide some hints as to how the fateful division between early Christianity and Judaism took shape in the cities of the Graeco-Roman world.[3]

I. METHODOLOGICAL ISSUES

The wording of my title is carefully chosen: the question is not 'Who *was* an apostate . . . ?' but 'Who *was considered* an apostate . . . ?' I stress this distinction to indicate that 'apostasy' (i.e. desertion of

Judaism) is in essence not a matter of fact but a matter of perspective; it cannot be measured on any objective scale. Most discussions of our topic appear to work on the assumption that we all know what constituted (or constitutes – modern definitions often creep in here) apostasy; it is only a matter of detecting the cases which crop up in our sources. Yet to charge someone with 'apostasy' is to pin on them a label, to interpret their behaviour within the categories of one's own definition of loyalty to Judaism, which precisely in this matter is likely to be partial. To discuss who were apostates in Judaism is like discussing who were heretics in early Christianity, where, of course, different parties operated with varying definitions of 'heresy' and opposing groups often considered each other 'heretical'. Scholars have recognized that there are dangers in employing terms like 'orthodoxy' and 'heresy' in relation to Second Temple Judaism.[4] We should also acknowledge that we cannot employ the term 'apostate' as if it were an objectively defined category: it always comes loaded with the prejudices of those who use it.

One may measure with a degree of objectivity the extent to which Jews were socially assimilated to their Gentile environment, and the evidence which we shall consider suggests that all charges of 'apostasy' were somehow related to assimilation. But how they were related could vary greatly from one observer to another. A Jew who was assimilated to the extent of attending a Greek school and visiting the Greek theatre might be considered by some Jews an 'apostate', but be fully affirmed as an observant Jew by others. As we shall see, the acquisition of Greek citizenship was regarded by one of our Diaspora witnesses (3 Maccabees) as tantamount to apostasy, but there is reason to believe that this viewpoint was not shared by all Jews in the Diaspora, not even by all Jews in the environment of that witness (Alexandria). Yet the judgement of 3 Maccabees has been widely accepted by scholars as a universal norm.[5]

In fact, apostasy, like beauty, is in the eye of the beholder.[6] Jews could and did differ in where they considered other Jews to have 'crossed the boundary' out of Judaism. To observe 'apostasy' in the Diaspora is to observe how Jews in the Diaspora considered other Diaspora Jews to have stepped outside (what they took to be) legitimate Judaism.[7] Thus, the material we shall survey will be discussed, as far as possible, according to the authors in the

Diaspora who made the judgements that interest us.[8] We need to note very carefully whose verdict we are hearing when we find Diaspora Jews labelled as 'apostates'. It is only when we have collected all such verdicts that we shall be able to assess to what degree their judgements were commonly held and to what degree they were idiosyncratic.

Our procedure requires, therefore, that we (a) refuse to adopt any predetermined definition of apostasy, and (b) confine ourselves to the cases where we can hear the verdicts of Diaspora Jews about each other. This means that we shall be unable to pass comment on those assimilated Jews who appear in our sources without any indication of their status among their fellow Jews. Thus, for instance, the Jewish actor Aliturus, who was a favourite in the court of Nero and assisted Josephus in his mission there in 64 CE (*Life* 16), has frequently been regarded as an apostate.[9] But we have no means of knowing how he was regarded by the Jews in Rome and Josephus makes no comment about his Jewish standing. Similarly when we hear of Jewish ephebes in various Greek cities (e.g., Cyrene, Iasos, Hypaepa) or of Eleazar the 'guardian of the law' (νομοφύλαξ) in the civic administration of Cyrene, we cannot leap to conclusions about their status within the Jewish community.[10] Even when we find Jews in lists of donors to Greek gods, we cannot be sure how their Jewish contemporaries would have regarded them.[11]

Thus the only evidence suitable for our assessment is where we find individuals or categories of Jews actually described as 'apostates' from Judaism. This will not exactly match cases of the specific term 'apostate' (ἀποστάτης) or references where the related nouns 'apostasy' (ἀποστασία and ἀπόστασις) and verbs 'to apostasize' (ἀποστατέω and ἀφίστημι) are used. This group of terms is often used in Greek literature in a political sense referring to 'desertion' or 'revolt'. In the LXX we find such words employed also as a metaphor for Israel's religious disloyalty,[12] thus appearing, for instance, in Maccabean literature to describe the Hellenizers at the time of Antiochus IV.[13] Josephus uses the nouns only in the literal political sense of 'desertion' or 'revolt',[14] but he uses the verb ἀφίστημι in a religious as well as a political sense.[15] However, he (and others) have a range of alternative phrases with which to describe disloyalty to the Jewish community and its customs, such as 'abandoning the ancestral laws' or 'neglecting the ancestral customs'. Since many people who were known to have transgressed Jewish laws were not considered apostates, we shall list here only those cases where the verdict concerns what is taken (by the relevant source) to be a *seriously offensive* and *settled* pattern of behaviour which can be *generalized* as a desertion of Judaism. Philo tells of 'Yom Kippur Jews' who attended synagogue in Alexandria only on the Day of Atonement and whose life was not otherwise pious (οἷς κατὰ τὸν ἄλλον βίον εὐαγὲς οὐδὲν δρᾶται, *Spec. Leg.* 1.186); but such Jews, though 'worse' than others, were not (for him) in the same category as those who consistently 'disregarded' their ancestral teaching. It is these latter references to grave and consistent desertion of Judaism which we shall collect in the following survey.[16]

2. A SURVEY OF THE CHARGES OF APOSTASY

Our evidence from the Diaspora includes four authors who comment on those they consider 'apostate' (the author of 3 Maccabees; the author of Wisdom of Solomon; Philo; Josephus) and one who makes interesting hypothetical remarks on this matter (the author of 4 Maccabees). It also includes one case (Paul) where we can detect a Jew in the Diaspora being thought of as 'apostate'; the Johannine Christians whose situation is reflected in the Gospel of John may be another example of the same phenomenon.

(a) 3 Maccabees

The author of 3 Maccabees (end of first century BCE) refers to one individual and a whole group of assimilating Jews whom he considers to be apostate. The individual is Dositheos, son of Drimylos, a trusted courtier of Ptolemy Philopator. He is described as a Jew by birth who later 'rejected the law and was alienated from his ancestral beliefs' (μεταβαλὼν τὰ νόμιμα καὶ τῶν πατρίων δογμάτων ἀπηλλοτριωμένος, 1:3). The author gives no explanation of this verdict but, as we shall see, he appears to regard any close proximity to the royal court as necessitating 'apostasy'. Intriguingly, we have papyri concerning this same Dositheos (CPJ 127), which indicate that he was the memorandum-writer of Ptolemy Euergetes I and 'the priest of Alexander and the Gods Adelphoi and the Gods Euergetai' (in 222 BCE).

Besides Dositheos, a group of 'apostates' features in the narrative at the point when Ptolemy Philopator gives all Jews the choice of Alexandrian citizenship or death (2:28–33; cf. 7:10–15). Many features of this story are confused (and their relationship to historical fact highly questionable), but it appears that the author considered citizen rights, enlistment in the Dionysiac cult, proximity to the king and the abandonment of Jewish food laws as a 'package' which Jews either accepted or rejected. He describes these apostates as 'deserters of piety' (διέστησαν τῆς εὐσεβείας, 2:32) and transgressors of God's laws (7:10–12) 'for the sake of the stomach' (7:11), who have 'withdrawn' from the Jewish community and are to be considered 'enemies of the nation' (ὡς πολεμίους τοῦ ἔθνους, 2:33). They are to be 'abominated' and shunned (2:33; 3:23), and the author regards it as fitting that at the end of the story these 'defiled' apostates (three hundred of them) were slaughtered by the faithful Jews (7:10–15). It seems that for this author Alexandrian citizenship involves idolatrous worship and neglect of the Jewish food laws and thus an abandonment of Judaism.[17]

(b) Wisdom of Solomon

In a lengthy passage on the oppression of the righteous (chapters 2–5), the author of Wisdom of Solomon (100 BCE–30 CE) characterizes the ungodly oppressors with many terms of invective. In this welter of polemic it is difficult to identify 'the wicked', but it is possible that this group includes those he considers Jewish 'apostates'. It is intriguing, for instance, that the ungodly are reproached for 'sins against the law' (2:12) and are described at one point as 'rebels against the Lord' (οἱ τοῦ κυρίου ἀποστάντες, 3:10). This may be simply the application of Jewish terminology to Gentiles (cf. 6:4), but it is possible that the author's target includes those he considers to have abandoned Judaism.[18] If so, their scepticism about justice and their persecution of the righteous indicate what stark effects he considers their desertion of Judaism to have had.

(c) Philo

On several occasions Philo criticizes, either directly or indirectly, those he considers to be apostate. Sometimes, in paraphrasing the biblical text, he reveals his observations on contemporary Jewish life in Egypt (early first century CE). Thus in a telling little cameo he represents Jacob's fears for his son Joseph in Egypt, lest he change his customs (ἡ τῶν πατρίων ἐκδιαίτησις):

> for he knew how natural it is for young people to lose their footing and how easy it is for strangers in a land to sin, especially in Egypt which is blind towards the true God because of its deification of created and mortal things; moreover, he knew how wealth and glory could attack minds of little sense and that, left to himself, without an accompanying monitor from his father's house, alone and bereft of good teachers, he would be liable to change to alien ways (πρὸς τὴν τῶν ὀθνείων μεταβολήν). (*Jos.* 254)[19]

Here Philo analyses the factors which, in his view, led to apostasy: youth, desire for wealth and social acceptance, dislocation from the controlling influence of the Jewish home. His comments suggest that he considered there to be more apostasy in Egypt than in the Jewish homeland, perhaps also that the Diaspora in Egypt proved especially prone to leakage from the Jewish community. A similarly generalized comment on the causes of 'apostasy' is to be found in *Virt.* 182, where Philo contrasts with proselytes those he calls 'rebels from the holy laws' (οἱ τῶν ἱερῶν νόμων ἀποστάντες), who have 'sold their freedom' for the sake of food, drink and beauty, pandering to the pleasures of gluttony and sex.

Elsewhere, Philo alludes to three categories of Jew whom he considers to have abandoned their Jewish heritage:[20]

(i) The first category comprises those who are lured by social success into repudiation of their family traditions and Jewish practices. Commenting on Moses' exemplary loyalty even in the Egyptian palace, Philo says that some, puffed up by success, look down on their friends and relations, 'transgressing the laws according to which they were born and bred and subverting the ancestral customs, to which no blame can rightly be attached, by changing their mode of life' (*Mos.* 1.31).

(ii) The second category includes those who marry Gentiles, or at least the offspring of these exogamous alliances. In a comment on the Pentateuchal prohibition of marriage to Canaanite women, he highlights the danger of 'being conquered by conflicting customs' and thus turning aside from the true path to piety. Even if the Jewish spouse remains firm, he declares, 'there is much to be feared for your sons and daughters' lest they forget the honour due to the one God, enticed by 'spurious customs' (*Spec. Leg.* 3.29). He gives a concrete example of this phenomenon elsewhere (*Mos.* 2.193). Also in several passages he discusses the story of the Jewish liaisons with Midianite women (Num. 25), where the 'conversion' (μεταβολή) of the Jewish men took the form of idolatrous worship under pressure from their Gentile wives (*Mos.* 1.295–305; *Spec. Leg.* 1.54–58; *Virt.* 34–44).

(iii) A third type of apostasy in Philo's eyes may be found in his comments on critics of the Jewish Scriptures. Philo defends the Scriptures against many forms of criticism and it is often difficult to discern from his polemic what precisely he is reacting against. At times he talks about those who find in the Scriptures nothing superior to the stories of the Graeco-Roman world: those who consider Abraham's offering of Isaac (Gen. 22) no more significant than comparable stories in the Greek tradition (*Abr.* 178–93), or the story of Babel (Gen. 9) no different from familiar Greek myths (*Conf.* 2–13). While such criticism might have come from knowledgeable Gentiles, it is more likely to represent the views of well-educated Jews whose attitude to their Scriptures was less adulatory than that of Philo. In Philo's view, these critics 'reject the sacred writings' (*Quaest. Gen.* 3.3) and are discontented with the ancestral constitution (*Conf.* 2); they clearly stand, for him, outside the Jewish community.[21]

(d) Josephus

Josephus has occasion to comment on a wide range of Jewish practices during the course of his historical works. Several times he refers to transgressors of the law without, apparently, inferring that they had apostasized.[22] What Josephus means by apostasy is made clear in his paraphrase of 1 Maccabees where he describes the Jerusalem Hellenizers: these Jews 'abandoned the ancestral laws and the constitution established by them' (τοὺς πατρίους νόμους καταλιπόντες καὶ τὴν κατ' αὐτοὺς πολιτείαν) and wished, in following Antiochus' laws, to adopt a Greek constitution (τὴν Ἑλληνικὴν πολιτείαν ἔχειν, *Ant.* 12.240).[23] This double aspect (abandoning Jewish ways and adopting those of the Greeks) is present in almost all the cases of 'apostasy' featured by Josephus.

We may mention first the four particular cases of apostasy in the Diaspora which he identifies:

(i) Certain offspring of Alexander (descendants of Herod the Great) were brought up in Rome and, says Josephus, 'right from their birth abandoned the native customs of the Jews and transferred to those of the Greeks' (ἅμα τῷ φυῆναι τὴν θεραπείαν ἐξ-έλιπε τῶν Ἰουδαίοις ἐπιχωρίων μεταταξάμενοι πρὸς τὰ Ἕλλησι πάτρια, *Ant.* 18.141). This comment reveals the importance, for Josephus, of upbringing and family in inculcating the Jewish way of life.[24]

(ii) A different case, of a Jew brought up in an observant family but turning against his tradition, is recorded by Josephus in the story of Antiochus in Antioch (*War* 7.46–62). At the outbreak of the Jewish War, this individual accused fellow Jews, including his own father (the chief magistrate of the Jewish community), of plotting to destroy Antioch by fire. He also tried (says Josephus) to prove his 'conversion' (μεταβολή) from Judaism and his hatred of its customs by offering sacrifice according to Greek custom (τὸ ἐπιθύειν ὥσπερ νόμος ἐστὶ τοῖς Ἕλλησιν, *War* 7.50) and by requiring other Jews to do the same. He proceeded to ban the observance of the sabbath, using military force to compel the Jews to work on that day (7.51–3). We have only Josephus' account of this story, but it is at least clear what Josephus considered to be signs of apostasy: turning against the Jewish community, offering idolatrous worship and disregarding, as a matter of principle, the sanctity of the sabbath.

(iii) A third and famous case of 'apostasy' recorded by Josephus is that of Philo's nephew, Tiberius Julius Alexander. Raised in an immensely wealthy family, Alexander had a glittering career in the Roman administration, acting as *epistrategos* of the Thebaid in 42 CE and procurator of Judaea in 46–8 CE, and climbing further stages up the equestrian ladder before acquiring the massive responsibility of governor of Egypt (66–9 CE). At the end of the Jewish War he acted as Titus' second-in-command at the siege of Jerusalem and thereafter may have become prefect of the praetorian guard in Rome.[25] His periods of office required him to participate in Egyptian and Roman religion,[26] and, besides his aid to Titus at Jerusalem, he had to suppress a Jewish uprising in Alexandria (Josephus, *War* 2.487–98). Yet it is intriguing to note that Josephus does not refer to him as an 'apostate' in his *Jewish War* (late 70s CE). It is only in the *Antiquities*, published in 93 CE when Alexander was probably dead (he was born around 15 CE), that Josephus refers to his 'apostasy': 'he did not abide by his ancestral customs' (τοῖς πατρίοις οὐκ ἐνέμεινεν οὗτος ἔθεσιν, *Ant.* 20.100).[27]

(iv) The fourth case of apostasy is that of a proselyte, Polemo, the king of Cilicia, who got himself circumcised in order to marry Berenice, but when deserted by her 'was released from his adherence to Jewish customs' (τοῦ τοῖς ἔθεσι τῶν Ἰουδαίων ἐμμένειν ἀπήλλακτο, *Ant.* 20.145–6). Elsewhere Josephus suggests that there were other cases of proselytes who were unwilling to sustain the Jewish lifestyle: lacking endurance they again 'seceded' (πάλιν ἀπέστησαν, *Apion* 2.123).

Apart from these individual cases, Josephus hints at the deleterious effects of an excess of wealth and pleasure (*Ant.* 5.132–5) and makes explicit warnings about the dangers of apostasy through intermarriage when commenting on the folly of Solomon's behaviour (*Ant.* 8.190–4). He also gives a fascinating analysis of the biblical story of apostasy with the Midianite women (Num. 25; *Ant.* 4.126–55). Dramatizing the story with speeches, he attributes to the women a powerful critique of the peculiar customs of the Jews in matters of food and drink, urging the Hebrew men to be less antisocial and to join in the worship of gods common to all humankind (4.137–8). As the men revel in 'alien foods' and the worship of 'many gods', their representative, Zambrias, confronts Moses with an astonishing critique of his 'tyrannical rule' and a strong statement of personal autonomy in his choice of lifestyle. As van Unnik noted, in this remarkable scene Josephus reflects important debates about the validity of the Jewish way of life, and in Zambrias' speech gives his impression of 'what was thought by his contemporaries who broke away from the ancestral religion and gave their reasons for doing so'.[28]

(e) 4 Maccabees

4 Maccabees (end of first century CE) is a story of resistance to the temptation of apostasy, of how first Eleazar, then the seven brothers and their mother, refused to 'renounce Judaism' (4:26) or to 'deny the ancestral laws of their constitution' in 'adopting the

Greek way of life and changing their mode of life' (μεταλαβόντες Ἑλληνικοῦ βίου καὶ μεταδιαιτηθέντες, 8:7–8). The test issue here (derived from 2 Macc. 6–7) is 'eating unclean food', specifically pork and 'food offered to idols' (5:2). Faced with the choice of apostasy or death, each martyr refuses to compromise even to the smallest degree. In a subtle speech, Antiochus IV is represented as arguing that God would surely forgive such a small sin, committed under compulsion (5:13), and our author provides a hypothetical speech which an apostasizing Jew might make in these circumstances (8:16–26). The tone of the work suggests that the pressure on the author's generation is not as extreme as that recorded in the narrative (14:9). But, as Klauck has noted, it seems designed to counter the temptations to assimilate among acculturated Jews by parading the example of loyal Jews who resisted offers of social advancement (8:7; 12:5) and remained faithful to the Jewish food laws.[29] It is clear from this narrative what sort of people our author considered to be apostates.

(f) Paul[30]

It is not clear whether Paul would have recognized himself to be an apostate Jew or not: in places he vehemently asserts his Jewish identity (2 Cor. 11:22; Rom. 11:1) and his faithfulness to the Scriptures (Rom. 1:1–5; 8:4; 13:8–10 etc.), but elsewhere in his letters he talks about his '*former* life in Judaism' (Gal. 1:13–14) and describes his Jewish privileges as 'loss' and 'dung' (Phil. 3:2–11). In any case, what matters in this context is not what he thought about himself but how other Jews in the Diaspora viewed him.

From the evidence of his letters it appears that he was continually 'endangered' by Jews (2 Cor. 11:26) and felt himself 'persecuted' because of his stance on circumcision (Gal. 5:11; cf. Gal. 4:29; 6:12–13). In one passage he mentions being 'banished' and 'prevented from speaking to Gentiles' (1 Thess. 2:15 – some scholars question its authenticity), and in another (particularly revealing) comment he says he has received the synagogue punishment of the thirty-nine lashes on five occasions (2 Cor. 11:24).[31] It is clear that he was strongly opposed even by fellow Christian Jews who considered his policy on eating with Gentiles sinful (Gal. 2:11–17) and his teaching an encouragement to libertinism (Rom. 3:8). The picture we glean from Acts is consistent with this, even if the

theme of Jewish opposition has here become somewhat stereotyped. In Acts Paul meets Jewish opposition in almost every town
and is expelled from one synagogue after another (e.g. Acts 14:1–6;
17:1–15; 18:4–7). When he arrives back in Jerusalem, he is met by
anxious Jewish Christians who have been told that 'you teach
apostasy from Moses (ἀποστασίαν διδάσκεις ἀπὸ Μωϋσέως) to
the Jews who live among Gentiles, telling them not to circumcise
their children or to live by the [Jewish] customs (μηδὲ τοῖς ἔθεσιν
περιπατεῖν)' (Acts 21:21). When he enters the Temple he is recognized and denounced by Jews from Asia who accuse him of bringing Greeks into the inner courts (Acts 21:28).[32]

Thus there is strong evidence to suggest that Paul was treated
with very great suspicion in the Diaspora as a Jew who undermined Jewish fidelity to the law; apart from general comments on
'the customs', we find circumcision and food as matters of particular concern. The synagogue beatings suggest that Paul tried to
maintain his contact with the Diaspora communities, but was con-
victed on several occasions for serious breaches of the law. One
may presume that, if he maintained his stance on these controversial matters as a point of principle, he may have been considered an apostate who abandoned the Jewish customs.

(g) Johannine Christians?

It is reasonably clear from the Gospel of John that the Christians
whose experiences it reflects have been expelled from Jewish
synagogues (9:22; 12:42; 16:2). Thus they seem to belong to the
category of those who were considered to be apostates, but the
question in my subheading reflects scholarly uncertainty as to
their location, i.e. whether they belong in a discussion of the
Diaspora.[33] The degree of polemic in the Gospel makes it clear
that the Johannine Christians have been engaged in bitter disputes
with synagogue authorities, but renders it difficult to discern the
issues which originally brought about their separation.[34] There are
echoes of debates over the Temple (2:18–22) and the observance
of the sabbath (5:16; 7:19–24), but what stands in the forefront as
the issue of dispute with the synagogue is the affirmation of Jesus
as the Messiah (9:22; cf. 1:41; 20:31). How precisely this led to expulsion is somewhat obscure, but it is likely that the development
of the *birkat ha-minim* had some part to play in the synagogue re-

pudiation of these Christians.[35] Later evidence (e.g. from Justin, *Dialogue with Trypho* 16, 95–6, 110) may suggest that Diaspora synagogues developed mechanisms for rooting out Christian believers, denouncing them and their faith in Christ as incompatible with synagogue membership. Unfortunately, the precise contours of this repudiation are exceptionally hard to trace.[36]

3. CONCLUSIONS

What conclusions can we draw about the boundary-maintenance of Diaspora communities and their judgements concerning who had abandoned Judaism? It is clear that the material we have been able to gather is not very extensive and represents only a few voices. These voices probably all date from between 100 BCE and 100 CE. Some come from Egypt (3 Maccabees; Wisdom of Solomon; Philo), some from Asia/Syria (4 Maccabees; Paul; John?) and one from Rome (Josephus), and we should not presume a unity of perspective in these different locations, where the Jewish communities had very different experiences. Moreover, it is hard to tell how representative any of our voices are: would other Jews in Rome, for instance, have agreed with Josephus' views on this matter? It is clear that not all Jews would have accepted the view of 3 Maccabees that the acquisition of citizenship involved idolatry and laxity in matters of food: probably in Alexandria itself and certainly in other cities, there were Jews who enjoyed both Greek citizenship and good standing in their Jewish communities. Each of the authors we have examined writes with a particular perspective.

However, it is striking that, despite this variety of perspective, certain features recur in many of our disparate sources, and these commonalities *might* be taken to indicate a wider consensus among Diaspora communities. General charges concerning abandoning Jewish customs occur in many of our sources (Philo, Josephus, Acts (re Paul), 4 Maccabees), but two matters in particular are frequently mentioned:

(i) 'idolatry', i.e. worshipping other gods, or worshipping 'in the Greek manner' (3 Maccabees; Josephus on Antiochus, on the Midianite apostasy and on Solomon; Philo on the offspring of exogamy and on the Midianite apostasy; 4 Maccabees in relation to food offered to idols);

(ii) the Jewish food laws (3 Maccabees; 4 Maccabees; Josephus on the Midianite case (food and drink); Philo on 'the pleasures of the belly' (food and drink); Paul (at the Antioch dispute)).

Of other Jewish customs, circumcision is an issue in the case of Paul, and sabbath in the case of Antiochus (and the Johannine Christians?), but these are not highlighted in other cases; they were of course customs of central importance in the Maccabean story which was well known in certain Diaspora circles.

Otherwise, we find several cases where 'apostates' are accused of criticism of the Scriptures in general and of Moses' laws in particular: this emerges, for instance, in Philo's Scripture-critics, in Josephus' speech by Zambrias and probably in the case of Paul as well (if his letters were known). In several cases there is reference to the social distance which apostates have created between themselves and their fellow Jews, manifested in disdain of Jewish associates (Philo's social climbers) or even in political opposition to the Jewish community (3 Maccabees; Wisdom of Solomon; Antiochus). It seems that the primary basis of charges of apostasy was a process of assimilation, whereby the social ties between the Jew and his/her Jewish community were loosened. This could come about through social advancement (Philo) and the desire not to be thought peculiar (Josephus on the Midianite case) or, for proselytes, through reversion to Gentile company (Josephus' lapsed proselytes). An important feature also here is intermarriage (Philo; Josephus on the Midianite case and on Solomon) and the associated issue of the upbringing of children (Josephus on Alexander's offspring). This latter may be at issue in the attack on Paul regarding circumcision, for failure to circumcise suggests a lack of commitment to bring up one's children as Jews. Presumably also the food issue features so prominently because the Jewish food laws were the major impediment to social integration in the Graeco-Roman world, and compromise here was regarded as the first step towards renunciation of the Jewish community.

Inasmuch as we may generalize about the Diaspora (which is a dangerous thing to do) we may conclude, then, that 'apostates' were those who were considered to have abandoned their commitment to the Jewish community and its way of life through an assimilation most frequently marked by laxity on Jewish food laws and involvement in non-Jewish religion. Naturally, as we have stressed, individual observers and individual communities had different perceptions as to where the boundaries had been crossed even in such matters: an individual regarded as an 'apostate' in some circles or in one place and time could well have been acceptable as a Jew in other circles or in another place and time. I have stressed here this 'perspectival' aspect of 'apostasy' since it has been generally neglected by scholars, and I have arranged my survey of the material by author precisely in order to preserve awareness of the relativism inherent in all judgements on this matter. If my generalizing conclusions have any value, they may help to shed light on how Paul ran into trouble so often in the Diaspora synagogues and thus on the split between the early Christian movement and Judaism in the Diaspora. But the Johannine evidence, if it is relevant, should caution us that special factors may have played a part here which we are unlikely to find paralleled in other material from the Diaspora.

NOTES

1   H. Mol, *Identity and the Sacred*, 57–8: 'It is precisely the boundary ... which provides the sense of identity.'

2   For Gentile entry into Judaism see especially S. J. D. Cohen, 'Crossing the Boundary and Becoming a Jew'. In his massive *Jew and Gentile in the Ancient World*, L. H. Feldman devotes several chapters to the discussion of Gentile proselytes and sympathizers, but only a few pages (79–83) to the question of 'apostasy'. Before him, the longest treatment of this subject in relation to the Diaspora was by H. A. Wolfson, *Philo*, vol. 1, 73–85 (largely restricted to passages in Philo). The phenomenon of 'excommunication' in Second Temple Judaism has been explored by W. Horbury, 'Extirpation and Excommunication'.

3   My focus will be confined largely to the Western Diaspora in the period from Alexander to the second century CE. In relation to the Eastern Diaspora and outside these time-limits our literary sources are minimal (and epigraphic evidence provides little assistance for this particular quest). Among the studies of boundary-setting in Eretz Israel note G. Forkman, *The Limits of the Religious Community*, and F. Dexinger, 'Limits of Tolerance in Judaism: The Samaritan Example'. J. T. Sanders, *Schismatics, Sectarians, Dissidents, Deviants*, devotes surprisingly little attention to the questions raised in this chapter.

4   L. L. Grabbe, 'Orthodoxy in Judaism', rightly insists that 'orthodoxy' is a relative entity and that such a term belongs 'within confessional belief rather than historical investigation' (152–3).

5   So, e.g., J. J. Collins, who reports the view of 3 Maccabees as if it

were an objective fact: 'We should also note that the price of this parity [with Alexandrians] is religious apostasy, as was also true for Jews who became full citizens in the Roman era', (*Between Athens and Jerusalem*, 105). A prominent exponent of this mistake is A. Kasher (*The Jews in Hellenistic and Roman Egypt*), who frequently asserts that only apostates could have been interested in Alexandrian citizenship (e.g. 211–32, 312–13, 335–6).

6 The study of our subject could benefit from 'labelling' theories of deviance, which I have explored in Barclay, 'Deviance and Apostasy'. See H. S. Becker, *Outsiders*, whose work has been employed by Sanders, *Schismatics*.

7 How such Diaspora Jews viewed themselves and how they were viewed by non-Jews are different matters again. We know of cases where Romans considered Jews to have ceased to practise as Jews (e.g. Josephus, *Ant*. 14.228, 234, 240; Suetonius, *Domitian* 12.2), but we do not know how such Jews were viewed in their own communities. The case of the Jews described in an inscription from Smyrna (early second century CE) as οἱ ποτὲ ᾽Ιουδαῖοι is complex. Are we hearing the vocabulary of the Jews themselves or of the Gentile authority which recorded their donation? And does the phrase mean 'former Judaeans' (i.e. immigrants from Judaea) or 'former Jews'? See P. Trebilco, *Jewish Communities in Asia Minor*, 174–5.

8 I have confined myself here to the verdicts of Jews living in the Diaspora and reacting to other Diaspora Jews. For this reason I have included Josephus (despite his upbringing in Judaea) and excluded 2 Maccabees (which is based on the work of Jason of Cyrene but concerns Palestinian events).

9 E.g. E. M. Smallwood, *The Jews under Roman Rule*, 281 n.84: 'he was without doubt an apostate, even if he retained enough national consciousness to befriend Josephus'.

10 Ephebes in Cyrene: G. Lüderitz, *Corpus* nos. 6–7 (= SEG 20, 740–1); in Iasos: L. Robert, 'Un corpus des inscriptions juives', 85–6; in Hypaepa: CIJ 755. Eleazar, the 'guardian of the law': Lüderitz, *Corpus* no. 8 (= SEG 20, 737).

11 See e.g. Niketas son of Jason from Jerusalem who contributed to a Dionysiac festival in Iasos in the second century BCE (CIJ 749); or 'Moschos, son of Moschion, a Jew' who in the third century BCE received instructions in a dream from the gods Amphiaraos and Hygieia, and put up an inscription in Oropus (Boeotia) to record the fact (CIJ vol. 1 [2nd edition] Prolegomenon, 82).

12 E.g. LXX Jos. 22:18–29; Par. II 28:19; 29:19; Ps. 118 (119):118.

13 1 Macc. 1:15; 2:15, 19; 2 Macc. 2:3; 5:8.

14 See K. H. Rengstorf, *A Complete Concordance to Flavius Josephus*. I therefore take the reference to the ἀπόστασις of the Jews in Scythopolis at the outbreak of the War (*War* 2.467) as a political comment on

their desertion of the Jewish cause, not as a judgement concerning their religious fidelity; cf. the 'revolt' of Tiberias (against Josephus) in *War* 2.632–4. By the same token, the reference to ἀποστάται τοῦ Ἰουδαίων ἔθνους who settled in Shechem in *Ant.* 11.340 appears to be a comment on their political affiliations rather than their religious observances. But see the conclusions (below) on the link between social and religious loyalty in the case of the Diaspora communities.

15 Besides the examples noted below, see *Ant.* 1.14; 8.229, 313; 13.4.

16 Feldman, *Jew and Gentile*, 79–83, takes issue with Wolfson's interpretation of the evidence in this matter, but his own distinction between 'apostasy' and 'ceasing to observe the commandments' does not correspond to the perceptions of our sources.

17 On 3 Maccabees see further Collins, *Between Athens and Jerusalem*, 104–11, and my *Jews in the Mediterranean Diaspora from Alexander to Trajan*, 192–203.

18 See the discussion of this difficult question by C. L. W. Grimm, *Das Buch des Weisheit*, 27–30; J. P. Weisengoff, 'The Impious of Wisdom 2'; C. Larcher, *Le Livre de la Sagesse*, vol. 1, 115–17.

19 Here, as elsewhere, I give my own translation of the texts cited.

20 See also, though with some differences of emphasis, Wolfson, *Philo*, 73–85.

21 He represents these critics as referring to the Scriptures as 'your so-called holy books' (*Conf.* 2–3); see further J. Daniélou, *Philon d'Alexandrie*, 107–9.

22 E.g. the Jewish 'scoundrel' who had fled from Jerusalem to Rome because he was accused of transgressing certain laws (*Ant.* 18.81); he is not referred to in terms suggesting apostasy, perhaps because Josephus knew that he had been accepted in Rome as an interpreter of the law.

23 Cf. *Ant.* 4.309–10 and 5.113.

24 On this particular family see Smallwood, *The Jews under Roman Rule*, 391 n. 8.

25 His career has been fully described by E. G. Turner, 'Tiberius Julius Alexander', and V. Burr, *Tiberius Julius Alexander*.

26 We find Alexander in inscriptions honouring Egyptian deities in *OGIS* 663 and 669; cf. comparable papyri in CPJ 418.

27 I cannot follow Feldman (*Jew and Gentile*, 81) in taking Josephus' comment to mean anything less than apostasy; the use of the same verb ἐμμένειν in relation to Polemo (*Ant.* 20.146, see below) indicates its meaning clearly enough. Josephus' varied reactions to Alexander suggest his social sensitivity in dubbing important Jews 'apostates', a factor which may also have influenced others in their judgements on assimilated Jews.

28 W. C. van Unnik, 'Josephus' Account of the Story of Israel's Sin with Alien Women', 259.

29 H.-J. Klauck, *4. Makkabäerbuch*, 664–5.
30 I have explored this topic further in 'Paul among Diaspora Jews'.
31 See A. E. Harvey, 'Forty Strokes Save One' and S. Gallas, ' "Fünfmal vierzig weniger einen ... ' ".
32 On Jewish–Christian opposition to Paul (including later charges of apostasy) see G. Lüdemann, *Paulus, der Heidenapostel*.
33 J. L. Martyn, who first worked out a detailed hypothesis concerning the social experiences of Johannine Christians, remained non-committal on this question, *History and Theology in the Fourth Gospel*, 73 n. 100. Early Christian tradition placed John in Ephesus, but some scholars have recently favoured Galilee or Batanea (e.g. K. Wengst, *Bedrängte Gemeinde und verherrlichter Christus*). It is a matter of definition whether Batanea should be considered part of the Diaspora.
34 It is generally acknowledged that the Gospel contains layers of material reflecting different stages of the Johannine community and its theological development; for two slightly different attempts to describe the processes involved see J. L. Martyn, *The Gospel of John in Christian History*, and R. E. Brown, *The Community of the Beloved Disciple*.
35 So especially Martyn, *History and Theology*, 37–62. For a summary of the evidence and a balanced discussion of this controversial 'benediction' see W. Horbury, 'The Benediction of the *Minim* and Early Jewish–Christian Controversy'.
36 See, for a recent attempt, Sanders, *Schismatics*. I am unable to pursue here the question of methods of excommunication from the synagogue (on which see Horbury, 'Extirpation'). Some who were considered 'apostate' did not need to be expelled: they simply drifted away from the Jewish community of their own volition. Others were socially ostracized (3 Macc. 2:33; 3:23) but not necessarily formally expelled. Perhaps a formal expulsion was only required when the 'apostates' contested their treatment at the hands of the community and when legal issues of authority were at stake.

BIBLIOGRAPHY

Barclay, J. M. G., 'Deviance and Apostasy: Some Applications of Deviance Theory to First Century Judaism and Christianity', in P. F. Esler (ed.), *Modelling Early Christianity*, London, 1995.
'Paul among Diaspora Jews: Anomaly or Apostate?', *JSNT* 60 (1995), 89–120.
Jews in the Mediterranean Diaspora from Alexander to Trajan (323 BCE–117 CE), Edinburgh, 1996.
Becker, H. S., *Outsiders. Studies in the Sociology of Deviance*, New York, 1963.
Brown, R. E., *The Community of the Beloved Disciple*, London, 1979.
Burr, V., *Tiberius Julius Alexander*, Bonn, 1955.

Cohen, S. J. D., 'Crossing the Boundary and Becoming a Jew', *HTR* 82 (1989), 13–33.

Collins, J. J., *Between Athens and Jerusalem: Jewish Identity in the Hellenistic Diaspora*, New York, 1986.

Daniélou, J., *Philon d'Alexandrie*, Paris, 1958.

Dexinger, F., 'Limits of Tolerance in Judaism: The Samaritan Example', in E. P. Sanders, A. I. Baumgarten and A. Mendelson (eds.), *Jewish and Christian Self-Definition*, vol. 2, London, 1981, 88–114.

Feldman, L. H., *Jew and Gentile in the Ancient World. Attitudes and Interactions from Alexander to Justinian*, Princeton, 1993.

Forkman, G., *The Limits of the Religious Community*, Lund, 1972.

Gallas, S., ' "Fünfmal vierzig weniger einen…" Die an Paulus vollzogenen Synagogalstrafen nach 2Kor 11, 24', *ZNW* 81 (1990), 178–91.

Grabbe, L. L., 'Orthodoxy in Judaism: What are the Issues?', *JSJ* 8 (1977), 149–53.

Grimm, C. L. W., *Das Buch des Weisheit*, Kurzgefasstes exegetisches Handbuch zu den Apokryphen des Alten Testaments, Leipzig, 1860.

Harvey, A. E., 'Forty Strokes Save One: Social Aspects of Judaizing and Apostasy', in A. E. Harvey (ed.), *Alternative Approaches to New Testament Study*, London, 1985, 79–96.

Horbury, W., 'The Benediction of the *Minim* and Early Jewish–Christian Controversy', *JTS* n.s. 33 (1982), 19–61.

'Extirpation and Excommunication', *VT* 35 (1985), 13–38.

Kasher, A., *The Jews in Hellenistic and Roman Egypt. The Struggle for Equal Rights*, Tübingen, 1985.

Klauck, H.-J., *4 Makkabäerbuch*, *JSHRZ* iii.6, Gütersloh, 1989.

Larcher, C., *Le Livre de la Sagesse*, Paris, 1983.

Lüdemann, G., *Paulus, der Heidenapostel. Band II: Antipaulinismus im frühen Christentum*, Göttingen, 1983.

Lüderitz, G., *Corpus jüdischer Zeugnisse aus der Cyrenaika*, Wiesbaden, 1983.

Martyn, J. L., *The Gospel of John in Christian History*, New York, 1978.

History and Theology in the Fourth Gospel, Nashville, 2nd edition, 1979.

Mol, H., *Identity and the Sacred*, Oxford, 1976.

Rengstorf, K., *A Complete Concordance to Flavius Josephus*, Leiden, 1973.

Robert, L., 'Un corpus des inscriptions juives', *REJ* 101 (1937), 73–86.

Sanders, J. T., *Schismatics, Sectarians, Dissidents, Deviants: The First One Hundred Years of Jewish–Christian Relations*, London, 1993.

Smallwood, E. M., *The Jews under Roman Rule. From Pompey to Diocletian*, Leiden, 2nd edition, 1981.

Trebilco, P., *Jewish Communities in Asia Minor*, Cambridge, 1991.

Turner, E. G., 'Tiberius Julius Alexander', *JRS* 44 (1954), 54–64.

Van Unnik, W. C., 'Josephus' Account of the Story of Israel's Sin with

Alien Women', in M. S. H. G. Heerma van Vos et al. (eds.), *Travels in the World of the Old Testament*, Assen, 1974, 241–61.

Weisengoff, J. P., 'The Impious of Wisdom 2', *CBQ* 11 (1949), 40–65.

Wengst, K., *Bedrängte Gemeinde und verherrlichter Christus*, Neukirchen-Vluyn, 2nd edition, 1983.

Wolfson, H. A., *Philo*, Cambridge, MA, 1948.

CHAPTER 6

Why did Paul persecute the church?[1]

Justin Taylor SM

This question is seldom asked, but once put, is surprisingly diffi-cult to answer.

Let us be clear from the outset that the nature and extent of Paul's persecuting activity should not be exaggerated. The lan-guage of Acts 9:1 is bloodthirsty ('Saul was still breathing threats to slaughter the Lord's disciples'), and there is an allusion in Acts 26:10 to the death penalty. Nevertheless, there is no reason to think that Paul ever shed blood. For one thing, these two passages of Acts belong, I believe, to the latest redactional level of Acts and bring an element into the narrative which was not even implicit in its earlier stages of development.[2] The language which Paul him-self employs is not specific, and its vehement tone contributes to a rhetorical effect which Paul no doubt intended. Furthermore, when Paul refers to 'persecutions' (διωγμοί) which he himself has suffered (2 Cor. 12:10), it is in a recapitulation of his account of the hardships of many kinds which he has endured for the sake of the gospel (11:23ff.), and the only one which he certainly suffered at the hands of fellow Jews was the 'forty lashes less one', which he says he received on five occasions (11:24). It is to be presumed that he went no further when he was a persecutor.[3]

It will be useful to quote all together the four passages in Paul's own writings in which he speaks of himself as a former persecutor (tr. NJB):

(a) 1 Corinthians 15:9–10: Ἐγὼ γάρ εἰμι ὁ ἐλάχιστος τῶν ἀποσ-τόλων ὃς οὐκ εἰμὶ ἱκανὸς καλεῖσθαι ἀπόστολος, διότι ἐδίωξα τὴν ἐκκλησίαν τοῦ θεοῦ. χάριτι δὲ θεοῦ εἰμι ὅ εἰμι ...
For I am the least of the apostles and am not really fit to be called an apostle, because I had been persecuting the church of God; but what I am now, I am through the grace of God ...
(b) Galatians 1:13–14: Ἠκούσατε γὰρ τὴν ἐμὴν ἀναστροφήν ποτε ἐν

99

τῷ Ἰουδαϊσμῷ, ὅτι καθ' ὑπερβολὴν ἐδίωκον τὴν ἐκκλησίαν τοῦ θεοῦ
καὶ ἐπόρθουν αὐτήν, καὶ προέκοπτον ἐν τῷ Ἰουδαϊσμῷ ὑπὲρ πολλοὺς
συνηλικιώτας ἐν τῷ γένει μου, περισσοτέρως ζηλωτὴς ὑπάρχων τῶν
πατρικῶν μου παραδόσεων.

You have surely heard how I lived in the past, within Judaism, and
how there was simply no limit to the way I persecuted the church of God
in my attempts to destroy it; and how, in Judaism, I outstripped most of
my Jewish contemporaries in my limitless enthusiasm for the traditions
of my ancestors.

(c) Philippians 3:5b–6: κατὰ νόμον Φαρισαῖος, κατὰ ζῆλος διώκων
τὴν ἐκκλησίαν, κατὰ δικαιοσύνην τὴν ἐν νόμῳ γενόμενος ἄμεμπτος.

In the matter of the law, I was a Pharisee; as for religious fervour, I
was a persecutor of the church; as for the uprightness embodied in the
law, I was faultless.

(d) 1 Timothy 1:12–13 ('Deutero-Pauline', according to the general
view): Χάριν ἔχω τῷ ἐνδυναμώσαντί με Χριστῷ Ἰησοῦ τῷ κυρίῳ ἡμῶν,
ὅτι πιστόν με ἡγήσατο θέμενος εἰς διακονίαν τὸ πρότερον ὄντα
βλάσφημον καὶ διώκτην καὶ ὑβριστήν, ἀλλὰ ἠλεήθην, ὅτι ἀγνοῶν
ἐποίησα ἐν ἀπιστίᾳ.

By calling me into his service [Christ Jesus our Lord] has judged me
worthy, even though I used to be a blasphemer and a persecutor and
contemptuous. Mercy, however, was shown me because, while I lacked
faith, I acted in ignorance.

There is a certain similarity between passages (a) and (d), which
both contrast the fact that Paul had formerly persecuted the church
with his present status as an apostle. Neither seeks to explain why
Paul persecuted the church, although 1 Timothy 1:13 goes on to
plead in mitigation that he had 'acted in ignorance'.

Passages (b) and (c) also go together. Although the wider context
of each contrasts Paul's former life with his present, the passages
themselves concentrate on his life as a Jew, which both develop a
little and in a similar manner. Both are at pains to emphasize that
Paul had been an excellent Jew. Both associate his persecution of
the church with that excellence, and indeed compare his enthusiasm as a persecutor with his enthusiasm for his religion. Paul does
not explicitly make this point, but both passages imply that it was
precisely his quest for religious perfection that made him a persecutor. Finally, in both passages, Paul tells us that he was a Pharisee, expressly in Philippians 3:5b and by implication in Galatians
1:14, where he writes of himself as ζηλωτὴς ὑπάρχων τῶν πατρικῶν μου παραδόσεων. (Compare Matt. 15:2 and Mark 7:3, also
Josephus, *Ant.* 13.10, 6 §297.)

So Paul was such an enthusiastic, even fanatical, Pharisee that he persecuted the church; his persecuting activity was, so to speak, an expression of his Pharisaic convictions passionately held and devotedly pursued, and sprang from them as its source. Many would agree that the statement 'Paul the Pharisee, persecutor of the church' means 'Pharisee, and therefore persecutor of the church'. It seems to hang together with the usual view of the Pharisees in the Gospels as bitter enemies of Jesus. Those with a little learning will add that the opposition between Jesus and the Pharisees in the Gospels reflects also the situation in which the young church faced exclusion and hostility from the synagogue reconstructed after the catastrophe of 70 CE on strictly Pharisaic lines. From Jesus' opponents, through Paul the persecutor, to the Rabbis at Yavneh/Jamnia, there seems to be a straight line.

But there are several difficulties with this view. First, the picture of Paul the Pharisee as persecutor is in conflict with the Acts of the Apostles, in which Jewish persecution of the church comes mostly from the side of the Sadducees, but never from the Pharisees. Thus it is the priests, the captain of the Temple and the Sadducees who arrest Peter and John in Acts 4:1–3, and the high priest 'with all his supporters from the party of the Sadducees' who arrest the apostles in 5:17–18 (two episodes which are probably a doublet[4]). Stephen's enemies, on the other hand, were Hellenistic Jews (6:9) who arrested him and brought him before the Sanhedrin (6:12). The persecution which resulted against the church in Jerusalem (8:1b) is not expressly attributed to the Sadducees, but when Saul, who was active in it, decides to carry the persecution to Damascus, he obtains letters of authorization from the high priest (9:1–2). Note well that point: Saul the persecutor is depicted as a quasi-*Sadducee*, even though later on in Acts Paul declares that he is a Pharisee (23:6). James the brother of John was beheaded and Peter imprisoned by King Agrippa I, who was closely allied with the Sadducees, and it was no doubt they whom he 'pleased' by his action (12:1–4).[5] Paul himself, now a Christian, was arrested in the Temple by the Roman guards during a riot started by certain Asiatic Jews (21:27ff.), but the Sadducees soon take the lead in his prosecution. It is the high priest who comes down to Caesarea with an advocate to charge him before Felix (24:1), and, when Festus succeeds Felix as procurator, 'the chief priests and leaders of the Jews' move to have Paul brought to

Jerusalem for trial, having decided to ambush him on the way (25:2–3).

Acts is consistent: it is, for the most part, the Sadducees who persecute the church, to the point where the Pharisee Paul is pressed into a Sadducean mould in order to depict him as a persecutor. By contrast the Pharisees are not implicated in persecution. (One cannot insist on vague expressions like 'leaders of the Jews' in order to involve them.) Furthermore, on two significant occasions, Pharisees speak up for Christians on trial. Thus, in 5:34–9, 'a Pharisee called Gamaliel, who was a teacher of the Law respected by the whole people', counsels the Sanhedrin to leave the apostles alone to let time reveal whether their enterprise is human or divine. Again, Paul before the Sanhedrin successfully appeals to the Pharisee party to take his side as a believer in resurrection (23:6–10).

I think that in thus presenting the Sadducees as persecutors of the church, Acts is broadly correct. This picture is consistent with that of the Gospels, where those Jews who take a leading part in Jesus' arrest and condemnation are clearly Sadducees: 'chief priests', 'the high priest's servant', 'the high priest'. It is true that 'scribes', 'Pharisees' and 'elders' are thrown in for good measure, but they do not take any significant part. It is not difficult to see why, among the parties and groups within Judaism at the time, the Sadducees would come to see Jesus as an enemy who must be got out of the way, even though on some points of teaching he stood closer to them than to the Pharisees: they were the centre, he was coming in from the periphery to take the centre; they were established power, he seemed or could be perceived to be subversive, and so dangerous, especially if the Romans were to take fright. Jesus' prediction of the destruction of the Temple and the gesture which is usually described as the 'cleansing of the Temple' could not but have alarmed the authorities in charge of the Holy Place. John's account (John 11:46–53) of the debate at the conclusion of which the high priest Caiaphas declares that 'it is to your advantage that one man should die for the people, rather than that the whole nation should perish' may not be historical in the stricter sense of the word, but in its portrayal of *Realpolitiker* weighing up the issues it is surely true to life. A desire to nip unrest in the bud would explain any moves made by the Sadducees against Jesus' followers in Jerusalem, and, when Paul is accused before Felix, it is because 'he stirs up trouble among Jews the world over and is a ringleader of the Nazarene sect' (Acts 24:5). Shortly after the period covered by the Acts of the Apostles, the high priest Ananus II, who is expressly described by Josephus as 'a member of the sect of the Sadducees', took advantage of the interregnum between the death of Festus and the arrival of his successor Albinus to summon a council at which James the brother of Jesus was condemned to death for 'breaking the law'. This act was deplored before Agrippa II and eventually Albinus by a group of Jews who, from Josephus' description, were probably Pharisees (*Ant.* 20.9, 1 §201). There is, therefore, a line of Sadducean persecution running from the Gospels through Acts to Josephus.

But to return to Paul, who was undoubtedly both a persecutor and a Pharisee: what was there in his Pharisaism that made Paul a persecutor? That is difficult to see. It is usual to look for a point of doctrine on which Paul would have disagreed with the Christians so vehemently that he was led to try to suppress the church. Already we are in doubtful territory, since it was characteristic of Judaism to be tolerant in matters of doctrine. At any rate, on the doctrine of resurrection, of which so much is made in Acts, the Pharisees and the followers of Jesus were at one. The distinctive doctrine of the Christians, that Jesus of Nazareth was the Messiah, was, *ex hypothesi*, refused by other Jews, but that did not mean that they would necessarily persecute those who held it. After all, Jesus was not the only claimant to the title, and neither the others nor their followers were persecuted by Jews who rejected their claim, although the Roman authorities might intervene, as with Theudas (Josephus, *Ant.* 20.5, 1 §97–9). What happened to Jonathan the Weaver in Cyrenaica shows, all the same, that those among a local Jewish population who identified closely with Roman power might instigate the authorities to take action against a Jew who led a popular movement that was potentially revolutionary (Josephus, *War* 7.11, 1–2 §437–46).

The assertion is often made that Paul the Pharisee saw in the movement of Jesus and his followers – or perhaps only among the 'Hellenist' Christians – a rejection of what he regarded as the indispensable basis of true religion, namely the Torah, and therefore felt obliged to do all he could to stamp it out. This at first seems plausible. After all, is not the cardinal tenet of Paul the apostle that a person is justified by faith and not by the law? What more likely, from a certain dramatic and psychological point of view, than that this was precisely the doctrine which he had once repudiated with violence and which he now preached vigorously?

But, of course, this will not do. The view of Paul as the apostle of a 'law-free gospel' owes more to the Reformation than to the New Testament.[6] It is also hard to pin this allegedly Pauline doctrine on Jesus or his first followers, even on the 'Hellenists'. Jesus asserts the supremacy of the 'commandment of God' over 'human traditions' (Matt. 15:3; Mark 7:8) – thus siding with the Sadducees rather than with the Pharisees – even if he goes on to internalize the laws of clean and unclean (Matt. 15:10–11; Mark 7:14–15). As for Stephen the Hellenist, that he had 'made speeches against the law' is merely alleged by 'false witnesses' (Acts 6:13), and in the speech which he makes before the Sanhedrin – whatever its literary origin and historical value – he quotes the Torah frequently and claims to have the law on his side (7:53). Neither Jesus nor his first followers rejected the Torah or proclaimed a 'law-free gospel', even if they did, on a number of points, have their own halakah. But disputes over interpretation of the Torah were common in Judaism, and if they caused much ink to be spilt they caused no blood to be shed, and, as I can remember chanting when I was a child, 'Sticks and stones may break my bones, but names will never hurt me.'

So, should we simply say that Paul's Pharisaism was strictly irrelevant to his persecution, having really nothing to do with it? That, after all, it was not because he was a Pharisee that he persecuted the church, but rather some other impulse drove him to it, that it was a purely personal aberration? That would be a counsel of despair, and in any case it does not do justice to what Paul appears to imply, in Galatians and Philippians: that he persecuted the church as a Pharisee, that his persecution was an expression of his religious zeal.

The word ζῆλος occurs ten times in Paul's writings – in both positive and negative senses – with seven instances of the verb ζηλόω. Very interesting is Paul's use of the noun in Philippians 3:5b–6, where he says that he was κατὰ νόμον Φαρισαῖος, κατὰ ζῆλος διώκων τὴν ἐκκλησίαν, κατὰ δικαιοσύνην τὴν ἐν νόμῳ γενόμενος ἄμεμπτος. Here, it seems, the expression κατὰ ζῆλος should be taken to mean something more than merely 'eagerly', as a way of describing Paul's activity as a persecutor. Given the intended parallel with the expressions κατὰ νόμον and κατὰ δικαιοσύνην τήν ἐν νόμῳ, κατὰ ζῆλος stands for one of three specific categories according to which Paul wishes to describe himself as he was formerly. Thus, 'in terms of law [or Torah]' he was a Pharisee, giving the unwritten Torah – 'the traditions of the fathers' – at least equal weight with the written Torah; 'in terms of righteousness which is in law' he was perfect; and 'in terms of zeal' he was a persecutor of the church: his activity as a persecutor showed what kind of ζῆλος he had. In the parallel passage Galatians 1:13–14 Paul describes himself as περισσοτέρως ζηλωτὴς ὑπάρχων τῶν πατρικῶν μου παραδόσεων. It is clear that ζῆλος and ζηλωτής are terms which Paul regarded as especially apt to describe his former self and way of life.

It is possible, of course, to take the words in a fairly general way and translate them respectively as '(religious) fervour, devotion, enthusiasm' and 'devotee, enthusiast'. There would be a parallel to such a sense, and in particular for its application to Galatians 1:14, in Romans 10:2, where Paul says of 'his own people' μαρτυρῶ γὰρ αὐτοῖς ὅτι ζῆλον θεοῦ ἔχουσιν ἀλλ' οὐ κατ' ἐπίγνωσιν. So Paul too had formerly exhibited a similar religious devotion, and specifically on behalf of his ancestral traditions, as the Jews still exhibited on behalf of God, but he would now say that, like theirs, it had been misguided, 'not according to knowledge'.

It is also possible to give to ζηλωτής a quite precise meaning, to denote a follower of what Josephus represents as the 'fourth sect of philosophy' among the Jews, alongside Pharisees, Sadducees and Essenes (*War* 2.8, 1–2 §117–19; *Ant.* 18.1, 1–6 §1–25). Josephus, it is true, seems to reserve the name 'Zealots' for the members of the radical party in the civil war which broke out among the defenders of Jerusalem under the Roman siege. His usage is not, however, entirely consistent, and it appears reasonable to take the 'Zealots', 'bandits' and *sicarii* of various parts of Josephus' narrative as all interconnected. Whereas 'bandits' and *sicarii* are more or less terms of opprobrium and likely to have originated outside the movement, the name 'Zealot' has an honourable ancestry, being associated with Phineas and Elijah, and it is likely that rival groups within the movement would have contended for the honour of bearing it.[7] I am going to use the term 'Zealot' to mean a follower of Josephus' Fourth Philosophy, and I appear to have the authority of Martin Hengel for this usage, even though the revised edition of Schürer would restrict its use to those whom Josephus labels as 'Zealots' in his account of the siege of Jerusalem.[8] In any case, the argument which I am going to put forward does not stand or fall by whether one allows a wider or a narrower extension to the term 'Zealot'.

Josephus traces the origin of the Fourth Philosophy to the census of Quirinius, which took place as part of the reorganization of Judaea as a province on the deposition of Archelaus, and precisely to the assessment of Judaea for taxation by the procurator Coponius. On that occasion, against the advice of the high priest Joazarus to submit – advice which was generally followed – Judas the Galilean (or Gaulanite) and a Pharisee called Sadducus raised a revolt, declaring that the census represented the destruction of liberty. That there was a religious dimension to their love of liberty and rejection of the Roman tax is shown by their assertion that God was their sole ruler and that to submit to the tax amounted to putting mere mortals in the place of God. They and their followers were prepared to resort to violence. 'Zeal for God and his law' was the hallmark of the movement.

Now it is of great interest that, although Josephus makes of the followers of Judas a 'fourth philosophy' alongside Pharisees, Sadducees and Essenes, he not only names a Pharisee as co-founder of the movement, but also says expressly that its members 'had in all other things the same opinions as the Pharisees' (*Ant.* 18.1, 6 §23), and therefore on life after death, providence and free will, and oral tradition.

Josephus' account of the Fourth Philosophy in the *Antiquities* should, perhaps, be subjected to some criticism. For one thing, there is the co-founder, the Pharisee Sadducus, who is not mentioned in the parallel passage in the *War*. More serious is the tendency of Josephus in the *Antiquities*, composed when the Pharisees were the only remaining force in Judaism and were negotiating with the Romans, to rewrite history in a 'pan-Pharisaic' sense, to represent the Pharisees as more powerful in the past than they had really been, and to associate as many elements as possible – notably himself – with them.[9] It is true that in the *War*, although Josephus implicitly calls the movement of Judas the Galilean a sect of 'philosophy', he does not associate it there with the Pharisees. On the other hand, it is difficult to see what interest Josephus could have had, at the time of writing the *Antiquities*, in inventing a fictitious link between the Pharisees and a movement which, in his notice on it, he is at such pains to blame for the disasters which had come upon his people.

If, therefore, the Fourth Philosophy could be regarded as a branch of the Pharisees, or very closely associated with them, then we should be aware of the possibility that, when we read the word 'Pharisee' in a text relating to the period before 70 CE, it might refer to someone who would have identified himself with the Zealots and others in the orbit of the movement begun by Judas the Galilean.

Jesus had been in touch with this movement, and one of his inner circle, Simon, bore the surname 'the Zealot' (Matt. 10:4; Mark 3:18; Luke 6:15; Acts 1:13: Matthew and Mark in fact have ὁ Καναναῖος, which is a transliteration of the Aramaic *qan'ān*, with the same meaning as ζηλωτής). It has also been urged that the surname of Simon Peter, 'Bar Yona', meant 'ruffian' or 'bandit', and that the name 'Sons of thunder', which distinguished James and John, had a similar sense, both indicating a connection with the Zealot movement.[10] Jesus, however, carefully avoided aligning himself with the Zealots,[11] or, for that matter, with any other group within Judaism. This, I believe, is the meaning of the highly significant episode in which 'the Pharisees' and 'the Herodians' together ask him whether it is lawful or not to pay taxes to Caesar, and he extricates himself from a difficult situation with the famous, but not altogether perspicuous, response: 'Render unto Caesar the things that are Caesar's, and to God the things that are God's' (Matt. 22:15–22; Mark 12:13–17; also Luke 20:20–6, where, however, the questioners are not identified). The 'Herodians' in this scene are generally taken to be partisans of the dynasty,[12] which was closely allied with Rome, and who would have been in favour of paying the Roman taxes. The 'Pharisees' in the story presumably held that it was not lawful to do so. Now the Pharisees, as usually understood, are not known to have had any view on the lawfulness of the Roman taxes, and their approach to Jesus in this matter is often regarded as yet another example of their bad faith and desire to catch him out. On the other hand, the Zealots had a very decided view on the question of the Roman taxes, and I suggest that the 'Pharisees' here are in fact Zealots. Jesus was being challenged to declare himself for them, but, of course, in doing so he exposed himself to being accused by the Herodians of rebellion against Rome. On the other hand, if he pronounced in favour of the Herodians he became, for the Zealots, a traitor to the nation and to God. It is even possible that the incident represents an 'unholy alliance' between two parties, otherwise so opposed, to trap a common enemy and impale him on one or other horn of their dilemma.[13]

In the only other episode in the Gospels where 'Herodians' are named they are likewise consorting with 'Pharisees'. (How authentic this sounds, in contrast to the clichés of 'Pharisees and Sadducees', 'scribes and Pharisees' etc.!) In Mark 3:6 (the Herodians are not mentioned in the parallels) we read that after the cure of the man with the withered hand in the synagogue on a sabbath, 'the Pharisees went out and began at once to plot with the Herodians against [Jesus], discussing how to destroy him'. This seems an exaggerated reaction to the incident in question, and it is difficult to see why, at this point in the gospel story, the Herodians – or, for that matter, the Pharisees (or anyone) – should have wanted to destroy Jesus. It may well, however, be an accurate, if misplaced, piece of information, and in that case I suggest that once again the 'Pharisees' here are really Zealots.

Zealots would have had reason to be hostile to Jesus, to the point of wanting him out of the way. His refusal to ally himself with them, and more generally his preaching of non-violence and even of non-resistance to Roman rule (cf. Matt. 5:38–42; Luke 6:27–30), would have been offensive. Here let us note that, whereas Brandon attributes these elements in the Gospel to the church's elaboration of the image of a 'pacific Christ' which has disguised the truth of Jesus' proximity to the Zealot movement, literary analysis shows, on the other hand, that the commands to turn the other cheek and to go the extra mile belong to the earliest levels of the Matthean tradition and suppose a Semitic substratum, and that the command to love your enemies is a Q saying; so they cannot be arbitrarily dismissed.[14] Whereas to Romans, Herodians and Sadducees Jesus could appear to be a dangerous subversive, to Zealots he could appear to be a no-less-dangerous quietist, hardly better than a collaborator and a traitor. Indeed, he freely consorted with collaborators and traitors ('He eats with tax-collectors' is likely to have scandalized a Zealot more than a conventional Pharisee), and had one of them, Matthew or Levi, in his inner circle. Did he not distract the people from the great cause of the

national struggle by talk of a kingdom of God which was not sufficiently like the one the Zealots looked for, and which would not
be hastened by the means they employed?

It is in this setting, I suggest, that we should place Paul. The hypothesis that Paul was a follower of the Fourth Philosophy would
explain why he expressly puts forward his persecution of the
church as proof of his ζῆλος. But I do not want to build too much
simply on his use of the word ζῆλος in this context: the word has,
as we have seen, a much wider application, even in Paul. If I recommend the hypothesis that Paul was a Zealot, it is because I
think that hypothesis accounts better for the two known facts, that
he was a Pharisee and that he was a persecutor of the church,
than does the conventional view of him as a disciple of the Tan-
naim. Furthermore, it accords well with the impression of Paul
given in certain passages of Acts as not the apostle of the Gentiles,
but an apostle to the Jews of the Diaspora.[15] It is not simply that
he always goes first to the synagogues, and only turns to the Gentiles when he is rejected by his Jewish audience, or the majority
thereof. What has not usually been noticed is that in the synagogues Paul proclaims a message of national salvation to be
brought about by Jesus the Messiah.[16]

Of particular interest here is the long speech which Paul makes
in the synagogue at Antioch-by-Pisidia (Acts 13:17ff.), in which he
first recapitulates the history of Israel leading to the divine election of David. It is from David's progeny, Paul insists in v. 23, according to the Western text, that 'God, according to his promise,
has raised up salvation' – or, in the Alexandrian text, 'has brought
to Israel Jesus as saviour'. Further on, in vv. 32–3, Paul again
reminds his hearers of 'the promise made to our fathers' and declares that 'God has accomplished it for their [or "our"] children
by raising Jesus, as it is written in the Psalms: "Thou art my son,
this day I have begotten thee. Ask of me and I will give thee the
Gentiles as heritage, and as thy possession the ends of the earth."'
The Alexandrian text gives only the opening words of the quotation from Psalm 2, but the longer quotation of the Western text,
with its allusions to the subjection of the Gentiles and to worldwide dominion, merits consideration. It makes an interesting exercise to forget two thousand years of church history and exegesis
and try to imagine what such words would have meant to a contemporary Jewish audience. Such an audience would, I think, have

taken Paul as proclaiming the coming 'restoration of the kingship
to Israel' – words which occur in the last question put to Jesus by
his disciples before his ascension in Acts 1:6 – at the hands of Jesus
now risen from the dead.

   There are traces of the same picture in Paul's own writings.
First Thessalonians, his earliest extant letter, is pertinent. Paul reminds his converts – who include both Jews and Gentiles – that
when he preached to them he bade them turn to the living God
and await from heaven that Jesus whom God had raised from the
dead (1 Thess. 1:9–10). The return of Jesus from heaven is the
theme of a longer development later in the same epistle (4:13–17).
There it is implicit that Jesus will return as king to reign on earth
– and indeed, I would say, in Jerusalem. I leave it to Pauline spe-
cialists to integrate these elements into the fuller picture of Paul,
perhaps to trace some sort of change or development in his
thought. What I would say here is that there appears to be good
reason to think of Paul the apostle – at least at an early stage of
his career – as a Jewish religious nationalist. That, I would suggest, is what he had been before his conversion. What changed
was that, at a certain point, he came to believe that the crucified
Jesus was, after all, the Messiah.

   If Paul before his conversion was a religious nationalist, a follower of the Fourth Philosophy, in other words a Zealot, it would
be reasonable to suppose that he persecuted the followers of Jesus
for the same kinds of reasons that Zealots had to be hostile to
Jesus himself, namely that not only did they not take part in the
national struggle – which was also God's – but they were a threat
to it. Therefore the movement had to be suppressed. Can we say
more?

   At this point I should like to refer to a recent book by Martin
Hengel, *The Pre-Christian Paul*. Hengel too sees the κατὰ ζῆλος of
Philippians 3:6 as indicating 'not...so much individual emotion
as the concrete fact of "zeal for the law"' (p. 70). He expressly rejects the idea that 'the Pharisaic Jew was closely associated with
the "Zealot" movement of a Judas of Galilee', but does, however,
see Paul in this period of his life as one who was prepared to use
force for God's cause (p. 71).

   Hengel classes the pre-Christian Paul with the 'Hellenists', Diaspora Jews whose first language was Greek and who consequently
had their own synagogues in Jerusalem. Hengel suggests that

Saul/Paul would have been one of those from Cilicia who came forward to debate with Stephen, himself a 'Hellenist' who accepted Jesus as Messiah (Acts 6:9). When Stephen worsted his opponents they turned violent and lynched him, and Saul is expressly mentioned as an observer and even as approving of the deed (Acts 7:59; 8:1a). There followed a persecution which affected only the Hellenist Christians (Acts 8:1b, 4; 11:19). Hengel sees this as the setting in which Saul/Paul persecuted the church: it was an affair which took place entirely within the confines of the Hellenist community of Jerusalem, in which those Hellenists who believed that Jesus was the Messiah were persecuted by those, including Saul/Paul, who did not (pp. 69–70). I have some difficulties with this synthesis. For one thing, I believe that the passages of Acts on which it is based belong to different redactional levels and have different historical values,[17] but I shall not insist on this here. The principal difficulty with the portrait of Paul the Hellenist comes from Paul, who describes himself as a 'Hebrew born of Hebrew parents' (Phil. 3:5). We shall come back to this matter.

Hengel discusses the question, which is similar to ours, of 'the theological reasons for the persecution' (pp. 79–84). His starting-point is the conversion, for which he rejects a purely psychological explanation (e.g., that Paul denied and reacted violently against what he was secretly inclined to). He sees Paul's conversion as entailing the reversal of what he had previously stood for, and so infers that 'he persecuted the Jewish Christian Hellenists in Jerusalem because he saw what was most holy in Israel threatened by their proclamation and their conduct' (p. 80). Even so, Hengel traces the first beginnings of conflict to the invasion of the fixed social group of the Hellenistic synagogues by 'enthusiastic sectarians' with consequent upset to 'old, sound order'. How did the Jewish-Christian Hellenists of Jerusalem threaten 'what was most holy in Israel'? Hengel rejects the idea that they disputed the significance of the Torah for salvation; he does, however, find in Stephen's speech in Acts 7 'the remnants of a Jewish-Christian Hellenistic sermon' which expresses a radical criticism of the Temple that could be expected to provoke a violent reaction.

The reservations which I have already mentioned prevent me from seeing here the answer to the question of why Paul persecuted the church. Hengel's next point is of a different order, because it does not depend upon seeing Paul as a Hellenist. 'Further

offence', writes Hengel (p. 83), 'was caused by the proclamation of
the crucified Messiah.' Later, Paul was to speak of Christ crucified
as 'a stumbling block to the Jews' (1 Cor. 1:23), and Hengel supposes that this had been a particular stumbling block for Paul
himself. And indeed, if the crucified Messiah was a stumbling
block for the Jews in general, would not the notion have been
especially repugnant to a Zealot? To claim that a man who had
died on a cross was the one divinely accredited to lead the nation to
salvation would seem to be an intolerable offence to someone who
combined nationalist aspirations with zeal for God and his law.

The argument looks attractive, but may turn out to be less
strong than it appears. For one thing, would a Zealot have persecuted those who revered the memory of someone who had been
put to death by the Roman authorities on a charge of sedition, as
'king of the Jews'?[18] Would not someone thus executed have been
regarded as a martyr in the national cause? Readiness to lay down
his life, and even martyrdom, were notions not entirely foreign to
contemporary expectations about the Messiah, specifically about
the Messiah son of Joseph.[19] The idea of a 'crucified Messiah' remained, no doubt, paradoxical and might have been unacceptable
to many Jews: Paul indicates that this was so. There is some reason, however, to think that it was an idea which had been familiar
to the pre-Christian Paul, since the origin of the Pauline *theologia
crucis* may be found in a typological interpretation of the Binding
of Isaac in Genesis 22 in relation to the figure of the suffering
Servant in Isaiah 53.[20]

Somewhat later, say about 50 CE, a Jewish religious nationalist
might have persecuted Jewish Christians who consorted with
Gentile converts. But by the time Jewish religious nationalism can
be supposed to have impinged, at least indirectly, upon the mixed
community at Antioch (cf. Gal. 2:11–14), Paul himself was, of
course, a Christian. In the early 30s, there were no Gentile converts, or hardly any, and certainly not in Jerusalem.

So to explain why Paul persecuted the church, it seems that we
must fall back upon the supposed hostility of a Zealot towards a
group which stood apart from the national struggle. It is unfortunate for the present thesis that there is no direct evidence of
hostility towards the followers of Jesus on this ground. About one
hundred years after Paul persecuted the church, we are told, the

Jewish leader Simeon Bar Koziba (Bar Kochba) punished the Christians because they would not take part with him in his campaign against the Romans.[21] However, it is dangerous to read back this episode into the past; in any case, it is likely that Christian opposition to Simeon had to do with his messianic claims,[22] as well as with any doctrine of non-resistance Christians may have professed. Even without supporting documentation, therefore, I still propose this solution as offering an intelligible and not improbable answer – in the absence of any other – to the question of why Paul persecuted the church.

And now to the questions of Paul's birth and background, which, as I have already indicated, are relevant to our theme. In his speech to the Jews in the forecourt of the Temple, Paul declares: 'I am a Jew, and was born at Tarsus in Cilicia. I was brought up here in this city. It was under Gamaliel that I studied and was taught the exact observance of the Law of our ancestors' (Acts 22:3a). Elements of this information are found elsewhere in Acts. In the parallel passage in the speech made before Festus and Agrippa II Paul states: 'My manner of life from my youth, a life spent among my own people and in Jerusalem, is common knowledge among the Jews. They have known me for a long time and could testify, if they would, that I followed the strictest party in our religion and lived as a Pharisee' (26:4–5). To the tribune Claudius Lysias, Paul claims, 'I am a Jew and a citizen of the well-known city of Tarsus in Cilicia' (21:39), and the procurator Felix learns that Paul is from the province of Cilicia (23:34). Before the Sanhedrin, Paul cries out: 'Brothers, I am a Pharisee and the son of Pharisees' (23:6).

Paul himself in his own writings provides some information relating to his origins and education. We have already seen that he tells the Philippians (Phil. 3:5b) that he had been a Pharisee. Just before, he writes of himself: 'Circumcised on the eighth day of my life, I was born of the race of Israel, of the tribe of Benjamin, a Hebrew born of Hebrew parents.' He writes to the Corinthians in similar vein, 'Are they [his adversaries] Hebrews? So am I. Are they Israelites? So am I. Are they descendants of Abraham? So am I' (2 Cor. 11:22), and to the Romans: 'I too am an Israelite, descended from Abraham, of the tribe of Benjamin' (Rom. 11:1). Acts does not mention that Paul belonged to the tribe of Benjamin, but that would fit well with the name of Saul by which he is introduced in that book – a name which Paul never gives himself in his own writings.

Paul does not name or even allude to his birthplace in his letters, and so the statements attributed to him in Acts, that he was a native of Cilicia and a citizen of Tarsus, are unsupported by his own writings. Commentators generally, however, accept them, urging that there is nothing in Paul which contradicts them, and that Luke has no apparent reason for inventing them.[23] Birth and citizenship in Tarsus would be consistent with his statement that, after his visit to Jerusalem following his conversion, he went to 'places in Syria and Cilicia' (Gal. 1:21) and with the knowledge of means of communication in Asia Minor revealed by the strategy which is behind the 'first missionary journey' of Acts 13–14.[24] Some writers have discoursed at length on what his presumed Greek education at Tarsus – an important centre of Hellenistic culture – would have contributed to the formation of the apostle of the Gentiles,[25] although others are more reserved about this.[26]

But even the ability to write reasonably good Greek does not necessarily mean that Paul's first language was Greek or that he was born in the Diaspora. On these precise points, the information of Acts does not accord at all well with what Paul tells the Philippians, that he was a 'Hebrew born of Hebrew parents', and the Corinthians, 'Are they Hebrews? So am I.' If we had only these statements to go on, we would, I think, take them to mean that Paul was an Aramaic-speaking Jew and would presume that he was born in the Holy Land.

A report that Paul came from the Holy Land, and specifically from Gischala (Heb. *Gush Halav*, Arab. *Jish*), is mentioned twice by Jerome.[27] In his commentary on the epistle to Philemon, composed in 387 CE, he addresses the question why Paul refers to Epaphras as 'a prisoner with me' (v. 23):

As to who is Epaphras the fellow captive of Paul, we have received the following story. They say that the parents of the apostle Paul were from the region of Gischala in Judaea, and that, when the whole province was laid waste by the Romans, and Jews were dispersed throughout the world, they were transferred to the city of Tarsus in Cilicia; and that the adolescent Paul followed the status of his parents. And that would support what he himself declares, 'Are they Hebrews?' etc., and again else-

where, 'Hebrew of Hebrews' etc., which indicates that he was from
Judaea rather than from Tarsus.[28]

Five years later, in *De viris illustribus*, he wrote: 'The apostle
Paul...was of the tribe of Benjamin and from the town of
Gischala in Judaea, from which, when it was captured by the
Romans, he migrated with his parents to Tarsus in Cilicia.'[29]
  These statements are ignored or rejected by most scholars. Indeed, several objections can be made against the value of the report in the commentary on Philemon, whose source is in any case
unknown,[30] and which Jerome calls a *fabula* (which does not necessarily carry the implication that it is false or dubious). First, of
course, it contradicts the statements attributed to Paul in Acts,
which we have just seen, that he was born in Tarsus, statements
which Jerome himself elsewhere accepts.[31] Attempts have been
made to avoid the contradiction. The first and longer statement
says rather that the parents of Paul were 'de Giscalis regione', and
even the second, which says that Paul himself was 'de...oppido
Iudaeae Giscalis', could mean that Paul's roots were there and not
necessarily that he was born there.[32] On the other hand, the 'cum
parentibus suis Tarsum Ciliciae commigravit' of *De viris illustribus*
evidently implies that Paul was not born at Tarsus, and the same
is implied, though less clearly, by the 'parentum conditionem adolescentulum Paulum secutum' of *In Philem*. It is possible to take
only part of the information – that Paul's parents were from
Gischala and were transferred to Tarsus – and to combine it with
the assertion of Acts that Paul himself was born in Tarsus.[33] (If
Paul's parents came to Tarsus as slaves and he himself was born
there after the manumission of his father, he would have been
born a Roman citizen, as he boasted to the tribune Claudius Lysias
(Acts 23:28).) Such a solution does, however, seem gratuitous, and
it is preferable, if Jerome's information is to be taken seriously, to
proceed to the conclusion that Acts is mistaken in having Tarsus
as the birthplace of Paul (we recall that Paul never mentions the
city in his own writings).
  Another objection is that Jerome twice refers to Gischala as
being in Judaea, whereas the place is in fact in Upper Galilee,
near Meron. A study of Jerome's writings reveals, however, that
he habitually uses 'Judaea' for the entire Holy Land.[34] In Jerome's

own time the province was called 'Palaestina', but the kingdom of
Herod the Great, which included Galilee, had been called 'Judaea',
and the name continued to be used of the wider territory, even
when it was not under a single rule, and it became the name of the
province established after 70 CE.[35]

In fact the information reported by Jerome seems worthy of
being taken seriously. It is specific and circumstantial. And why
Gischala? A later Christian source trying to give Paul a Galilean
origin – for example, to create a Pauline 'Holy Place' – might
have been expected to put it at Nazareth, Magdala or Capernaum, but not at Gischala, where there is, in any case, no trace of
a Pauline *cultus*.[36] As Jerome himself remarks, the 'report' that Paul
was born at Gischala gives a good sense to his self-descriptions in
Philippians 3:5 and 2 Corinthians 11:22.

Jerome's information can also be placed in a precise historical
context. In the years following the death of Herod the Great, the
Romans, under Varus legate of Syria from 6 to 4 BCE, had to pacify
wide areas of Judaea which were in a state of unrest. In particular, Josephus recounts the subjugation of Galilee and the capture
of its capital, Sepphoris, which was burnt and its inhabitants sold
into slavery (*Ant.* 17.10, 9 §286–94; *War* 2.5, 1 §66–71). Jerome's
picture of the whole province laid waste, and Jews dispersed
throughout the world, was more literally true of Pompey's conquest in 63 BCE, but can be allowed to be an exaggeration of the
lesser, yet still notable, effects of Varus' restoration of Roman
order. The removal of Paul's family from Gischala to Tarsus – as
slaves or as refugees – would fit well into this context.

It will be recalled that the Fourth Philosophy arose in Galilee
not long afterwards. The call to militant religious nationalism
could have found an echo in the heart of a young Galilean who
had been forced to leave his home and the Holy Land by the
Roman occupying forces.

NOTES

1 An earlier version of this paper was read at a seminar on the Jewish
origins of Christianity, conducted in Jerusalem by Professors François
Blanchetière, of the French CNRS, and Moshe David Herr, of the
Hebrew University, during the academic year 1992–3, and was much
improved as the result of the discussion on that occasion. The second
version, which was read at the conference on which this volume is

based, has been further revised in the light of the comments of those who heard it then and also of colleagues who have kindly read it since. To all who have thus contributed criticisms, suggestions and further references I am grateful.

2 See M.-E. Boismard and A. Lamouille, *Les Actes des deux Apôtres*, vol. III, 127–30; 289–90.

3 Compare A. J. Hultgren, 'Paul's Pre-Christian Persecutions of the Church', esp. 107–10.

4 Thus Boismard and Lamouille, *Les Actes*, vol. II, 111.

5 See D. R. Schwartz, *Agrippa I*, 119–24.

6 See generally E. P. Sanders, *Paul and Palestinian Judaism*, esp. 33–59.

7 On the Zealot movement generally, see M. Hengel, *The Zealots*, and specifically 76–145 on the Fourth Philosophy, and 62–6 on οἱ ζηλωταί in Josephus' account of the Jewish War.

8 E. Schürer, *The History of the Jewish People in the Age of Jesus Christ (175 BC–AD 135)*, vol. II, 598–606; also R. A. Horsley and J. S. Hanson, *Bandits, Prophets and Messiahs*, 190–243. S. Freyne, 'Bandits in Galilee', argues that Josephus uses the word 'bandits' to disguise Hasmonean nobility who resisted Antipater and his son, and that later instances of 'banditry' recorded in Galilee up to 66 CE suggest local power struggles rather than a truly revolutionary movement.

9 See J. Neusner, 'Josephus's Pharisees'.

10 Thus S. G. F. Brandon, *Jesus and the Zealots*, 99, and 204–5, n. 2; followed by Schwartz, *Agrippa I*, 123, nn. 66 and 67.

11 Even Brandon, *Jesus and the Zealots*, who believes that Jesus was close to the Zealot movement and emphasizes the political significance of his triumphal entry into Jerusalem and cleansing of the Temple, does not hold that Jesus was himself a member.

12 So W. Bauer, *Griechisch–deutsches Wörterbuch*, col. 706; on the other hand, E. Bikerman, 'Les hérodiens', argues that they were rather 'des gens de la maison d'Hérode', i.e. members of the *familia* of the dynasty.

13 A. Stumpff, 'Ζῆλος, etc.', 888, takes a similar view of the incident; but compare Brandon, *Jesus and the Zealots*, 347, who thinks that Jesus' reply was 'a saying of which any Zealot would have approved'.

14 Brandon, *Jesus and the Zealots*, 309–10; compare Boismard, *Synopse des quatre Evangiles en Français*, vol. II, 143–6.

15 Thus J. Jervell, 'The History of Early Christianity and the Acts of the Apostles', can even write: 'Paul ... in Acts primarily is a missionary to the Jews' (16).

16 See D. P. Moessner, 'Paul in Acts: Preacher of Eschatological Repentance to Israel'.

17 See Boismard and Lamouille, *Les Actes*, vol. III, 108f., 113–15, 127–32, 136–7.

18 That this was the αἰτία of his execution is clear from all four Gospels: compare Brandon, *Jesus and the Zealots*, 328.

19 Agus, *The Binding of Isaac and Messiah*, esp. 207–54.
20 See G. G. Stroumsa, 'Herméneutique biblique et identité: l'exemple d'Isaac', who refers (536–7) to I. Lévi, 'Le sacrifice d'Isaac et la mort de Jésus', *REJ* 64 (1912), 161–84, and to more recent literature.
21 Eusebius, *Chron.* a. Abrah. 2149 (Armenian version); ed. Schoene, vol. ii, 168f.; followed by Orosius, *Hist.* 7.13, 4.
22 This is probably the sense of the otherwise puzzling statement by Justin Martyr (who was, of course, a contemporary), that Bar Kochba Χριστιανοὺς μόνους εἰς τιμωρίας δεινάς, εἰ μὴ ἀρνοῖντο Ἰησοῦν τὸν Χριστὸν καὶ βλασφημοῖεν, ἐκέλευσεν ἀπάγεσθαι (i *Apol.* 31 (72D)); compare Schürer, *History*, vol. i, 545.
23 Thus even the usually sceptical J. Knox, *Chapters in a Life of Paul*, 34.
24 See my 'St Paul and the Roman Empire', in *ANRW* 2.26. 3 (1996) 2436–500.
25 E.g. W. M. Ramsay, *The Cities of St Paul*, 83–244.
26 F. F. Bruce, *The Acts of the Apostles*, 245, believes that 'the cultural influence of Tarsus on Paul has often been greatly exaggerated'.
27 For a recent discussion, see Adinolfi, 'Giscala e san Paolo'.
28 *In Ep. ad Philem.* 23 (*PL* 26.617): 'Quis sit Epaphras concaptivus Pauli, talem fabulam accepimus: Ajunt parentes apostoli Pauli de Gyscalis regione fuisse Judaeae, et eos, quum tota provincia Romana vastaretur manu et dispergerentur in orbem Judaei, in Tharsum urbem Ciliciae fuisse translatos; parentum conditionem adolescentulum Paulum sequutum. Et sic posse stare illud quod de se ipse testatur "Hebraei sunt" etc., et rursum alibi "Hebraeus ex Hebraeis" et cetera, quae illum Judaeum magis indicant quam Tharsensem.' In that case, Jerome remarks, Epaphras could have been a fellow prisoner of Paul at this time, but he prefers, after also considering and rejecting a Platonizing interpretation as 'fellow prisoner in the body', to see Epaphras as a fellow prisoner with Paul in Rome.
29 *De viris illustribus* v (*PL* 23.615): 'Paulus apostolus ... de tribu Benjamin et oppido Judaeae Giscalis fuit, quo a Romanis capto cum parentibus suis Tarsum Ciliciae commigravit.'
30 One of the few exegetes to take the tradition seriously is Th. Zahn, *Einleitung in das Neue Testament*, vol. i, 49–50, who suggests, though on what grounds is not clear, that Jerome's source was Origen's commentary on Philemon.
31 See Jerome, *Ep.* 37.1 (*PL* 22.461); cited by Adinolfi, 'Giscala', 157, who mentions the date of this letter: 384 CE, which is before he wrote the commentary on Philemon.
32 Thus Adinolfi, 'Giscala', 156.
33 This is the solution adopted by Adinolfi. It appears to have been that also of Photius, *Ad Amphilochium quaestio 116* (*PG* 101.688–9), cited by Adinolfi, 'Giscala', 164, n. 50.

34 Adinolfi, 'Giscala', 161.
35 See Schürer, *History*, vol. I, 514. Cf. also the usage of the NT, e.g. Luke 1:5; 23:5. The province was renamed 'Syria Palaestina' after the suppression of the Bar Kochba revolt, and became the 'Three Palestines' under Diocletian and so in the time of Jerome.
36 Similarly, Adinolfi, 'Giscala', 163–4.

BIBLIOGRAPHY

Adinolfi, Marco, 'Gischala e san Paolo', in *Questioni bibliche di storia e storiografia* (Esegesi Biblica 5), Brescia, 1969, 155–64.
Bauer, Walter, *Griechisch–deutsches Wörterbuch zu den Schriften des Neuen Testaments und der frühchristlichen Literatur*, 6th edn fully revised by Kurt and Barbara Aland, Berlin and New York, 1988.
Bikerman, E., 'Les hérodiens', *RB* 47 (1938), 184–97.
Boismard, M.-E., *Synopse des quatre Évangiles en français*, vol. II, *Commentaire*, Paris, 1972.
Boismard, M.-E. and Lamouille, A., *Les Actes des deux Apôtres*, vols. I–III (Etudes Bibliques n.s. 12–14), Paris, 1990.
Brandon, S. G. F., *Jesus and the Zealots. A Study of the Political Factor in Primitive Christianity*, Manchester, 1967.
Bruce, F. F., *The Acts of the Apostles. The Greek Text with Introduction and Commentary*, 3rd edn rev. and enlarged, Grand Rapids and Leicester, 1990.
Freyne, Seán, 'Bandits in Galilee. A Contribution to the Study of Social Conditions in First-Century Palestine', in *The Social World of Formative Christianity and Judaism. Essays in Tribute to Howard Clark Kee*, ed. by J. Neusner and others, Philadelphia, 1988, 50–68.
Hengel, Martin, *The Zealots. Investigations into the Jewish Freedom Movement in the Period from Herod I until 70 AD*, E.tr. by David Smith of *Die Zeloten*, 2nd edn 1976, Edinburgh, 1985.
Hengel, Martin (in collaboration with Roland Deines), *The Pre-Christian Paul*, E.tr. by John Bowden of *Der vorchristliche Paulus*, London and Philadelphia, 1991.
Horsley, Richard A. and Hanson, John S., *Bandits, Prophets and Messiahs. Popular Movements in the Time of Jesus*, Minneapolis, Chicago and New York, 1985.
Hultgren, Arland J., 'Paul's Pre-Christian Persecutions of the Church: Their Purpose, Locale, and Nature', *JBL* 95 (1976), 97–111.
Jervell, Jacob, 'The History of Early Christianity and the Acts of the Apostles', in *The Unknown Paul. Essays on Luke–Acts and Early Christian History*, Minneapolis, 1984, 13–25.
Knox, John, *Chapters in a Life of Paul*, New York and Nashville, 1950.
Moessner, David P., 'Paul in Acts: Preacher of Eschatological Repentance to Israel', *NTS* 34 (1988), 96–104.

Neusner, J., 'Josephus's Pharisees', in *Ex Orbe Religionum. Studia Geo Widengren Oblata. I.* (SHR 21), Leiden, 1972, 224–44.

Ramsay, W. M., *The Cities of St Paul. Their Influence on his Life and Thought. The Cities of Eastern Asia Minor*, London, 1907.

Sanders, E. P., *Paul and Palestinian Judaism. A Comparison of Patterns of Religion*, London and Philadelphia, 1977.

Schürer, Emil, *The History of the Jewish People in the Age of Jesus Christ (175 BC–AD 135)*, a new English version revised and edited by G. Vermes, F. Millar, M. Black and M. Goodman, Edinburgh, 1973–87.

Schwartz, Daniel R., *Agrippa I. The Last King of Judaea* (TSAJ 23), Tübingen, 1990.

Stroumsa, G. G., 'Herméneutique biblique et identité: l'exemple d'Isaac', *RB* 99 (1992), 529–43.

Stumpff, Albrecht, 'Ζῆλος, etc.', in Gerhard Kittel (ed.), *Theologisches Wörterbuch zum Neuen Testament*, vol. II, Stuttgart, 1935, 879–90.

Zahn, Th., *Einleitung in das Neue Testament*, 2nd edn, Leipzig, 1900.

CHAPTER 7

Paul and the limits of tolerance[1]

Stephen C. Barton

I. INTRODUCTION

In the popular mind of Western European liberalism, Paul the
Christian apostle is often regarded as an intolerant religious bigot,
in contrast to Jesus who is seen as a figure of tolerance and love.
This tendency to polarize Jesus and Paul and to play one off
against the other is widespread. Its roots lie in various directions.
Perhaps one of the most significant lies in the tendency since the
Enlightenment to disparage institutional religion because of the
limits religion is believed to set on personal freedom. Once Paul
becomes identified as the founder of the Christian religion, a
wedge is driven between Paul and Jesus in a way that preserves
Jesus as the model teacher of universal love and demonizes Paul
as the source of the corruption of the original ideal. Thus, if we
may generalize further for a moment, we might say that whereas
the Reformation drove a wedge between Scripture and church
tradition, the Enlightenment shifted the wedge back a stage and
drove it into Scripture itself: in this case, between Jesus and Paul.
What results is another myth of the Fall, from Jesus the charis-
matic Galilean teacher of the fatherhood of God and brotherhood of man to Paul the founder of institutional Christianity.[2]
And, except within the Lutheran and Reformed traditions of the
Christian church, Paul's reputation has suffered ever since.

What I am trying to signal at the outset, therefore, is the importance of attending to the hermeneutical dimension of our
theme. If we are putting the question about tolerance and its limits to the historical representatives of early Judaism or early
Christianity, it is essential to acknowledge that the idea of toleration has a history and that we in the liberal West tend to think of
tolerance and intolerance in very particular ways, often without

any awareness of the history that has shaped those ideas so decisively.[3] It is essential, in other words, to question the question.
What do we mean by 'tolerance' and 'the limits of tolerance'?
How useful is 'tolerance' as a category of virtue for understanding
the moral world of early Judaism and Christianity? Does our concept of tolerance presuppose a secular, pluralist, individualist
ideology which belongs to the modern world but not to the world
of antiquity? To what extent are we in danger of looking down
into the well of history and finding there only the reflections of
our own images while under the illusion that we have discovered
the true source of values we now hold dear for quite different reasons? Is it possibly the case that our prior commitments to egalitarian social values and *laissez-faire* individualism predispose us to
think of tolerance as a virtue and intolerance as a vice, and to polarize the two in this mutually exclusive way?[4]

An analogy here might be helpful. Within that branch of theology known as liberation theology, it has become common to interpret the Bible as a kind of manifesto on liberation. The story of
the Exodus, in particular, has become a *locus classicus*. Here, more
than anywhere else, God is shown to be a God who sets the oppressed free, with the result that the story of the Exodus is interpreted as underpinning revolutionary political and social action by
the poor on behalf of the poor. But the question needs to be
asked: is the Exodus about liberation and, if so, liberation of what
kind? In a recent essay which is strongly critical of several liberationist readings, Jon D. Levenson puts it this way:

Nothing in the Bible so readily invites the term 'liberation' as the exodus
of the Israelites from Egypt. The essential question, however, has not
been so readily asked: In exactly what sense ought the exodus be seen as
an instance of liberation, or, to pose the same question in other words,
what is the character of the liberation typified by the exodus and how is
this type of liberation to be distinguished from other phenomena to
which the same term is presently applied?[5]

Levenson himself shows how strong is the liberationist tendency
to interpret the text in quite anachronistic ways as a story of class
struggle and popular insurrection, where 'justice' is defined in
terms of the essentially modern notion of individual and social
equality and where 'liberation' is defined in terms of political self-
determination. He then shows to the contrary that the primary
focus of the text is theological, with the consequence that the kind

of freedom being talked about 'is not freedom in the sense of self-determination, but *service*, the service of the loving, redeeming and delivering God of Israel, rather than the state and its proud king'.[6]

The point of the analogy is clear, I hope. If the danger of anachronism is acute when we come to the Bible and other ancient texts with categories like 'liberation', are the dangers not equally acute with an analogous category like 'tolerance'? Are we not at risk of subverting the subject of our study by operating within the terms of an agenda whose power is all the greater for being submerged and unacknowledged? Nevertheless, awareness of the danger of anachronistic misinterpretation does not mean that to talk of 'Paul and the limits of tolerance' is a futile exercise, any more than it is futile to talk about Paul's understanding of 'liberation' or 'freedom'. It means only that our analysis be carried out with historical sensitivity, hermeneutical circumspection and resistance to the tendency to moralize about what might appear at first sight to be 'lapses' into intolerance but which come subsequently to be seen as instances of a different dynamic altogether.

2. THE CASE OF PAUL

In turning now to Paul, the important issue is where to start. On the basis of what I have said already, I think it would be a mistake to begin with tolerance and intolerance. Better by far to start with categories native to Paul himself and central to his own self-understanding. This can be expressed variously, and there is a lively debate over what constitutes the 'centre' and what is more 'peripheral' in Paul's theology and apostolic mission.[7] But what needs to be emphasized is that Paul's categories of thought are not those of modern liberal secular pluralism. Rather, they are those of biblical monotheism transformed in the light of the knowledge of Christ crucified and risen. A bare catalogue of Pauline thought-forms would include at least the following: the kingdom of God, creation, covenant, revelation, Messiah, the land, the law, righteousness, sin, judgement, atonement, justification and reconciliation, holiness, obedience, apostleship, Spirit, resurrection and new creation. This is a world away from a post-Enlightenment liberal mentality. But it may turn out to be the case that modern debates about tolerance and its limits still have something to learn from this early Christian apostle.

(i) *Not even-handed tolerance but zeal for God*

The first point I would make, then, is that, for Paul, tolerance is not the issue. Paul was not an egalitarian individualist committed to maximizing the possibilities of self-fulfilment at the individual level and self-determination at the social level. Rather than tolerance, we must speak in theological terms of zeal for God and for the people of God. The autobiographical statement in Philippians 3:4ff. makes this abundantly clear:

> circumcised on the eighth day, of the people of Israel, of the tribe of Benjamin, a Hebrew born of Hebrews; as to the law a Pharisee, as to zeal a persecutor of the church, as to righteousness under the law blameless. But whatever gain I had I counted as loss for the sake of Christ. Indeed I count everything as loss because of the surpassing worth of knowing Christ Jesus my Lord. For his sake I have suffered the loss of all things, and count them as refuse, in order that I may gain Christ and be found in him.

In his 'pre-conversion' days (if we may still speak in those terms),[8] Paul's wholehearted commitment manifested itself in zeal for the law as a Pharisee, with persecution of the church as an inevitable corollary. After his encounter with the risen Christ, it is not the case that Saul the intolerant Pharisee is transformed into Paul the tolerant apostle. On the contrary, his zeal for the law is transformed into zeal for Christ his heavenly 'Lord'. In other words, there is continuity as well as discontinuity. The continuity lies in his single-minded devotion to the cause of God and the kingdom of God. The discontinuity lies in the fact that, whereas formerly he expressed his devotion to God through zeal for the law, after his call to be God's envoy to the Gentiles it was expressed through zeal for Christ.

Now the persecutor becomes himself persecuted; and on more than one occasion in his letters Paul 'boasts' in ironic fashion of the catastrophes that have befallen him in his new calling, catastrophes that are held up as if they were the garlands of the conquering athlete for God and his Christ (see 2 Cor. 4:7–12; 11:21–33; 12:1–10). What is so striking in these catalogues of suffering is that the experiences to which they point do not turn Paul into an advocate of toleration! Such a thought does not seem to occur to Paul, because tolerance and intolerance are not categories native to him. Instead, what we find is that Paul accepts the persecution and suffering meted out to him by his opponents as the inevitable consequence and the necessary proof of his faithful testimony to Christ. Even more, he interprets his experiences as the process by which his own life is being transformed into conformity with that of his crucified and risen Lord and made a channel for divine power to work. So, in 1 Corinthians 4:7ff., he says:

But we have this treasure in earthen vessels, to show that the transcendent power belongs to God and not to us. We are afflicted in every way, but not crushed; perplexed, but not driven to despair; persecuted, but not forsaken; struck down, but not destroyed; always carrying in the body the death of Jesus, so that the life of Jesus may also be manifested in our mortal bodies.

There is no evidence that Paul sought toleration from his adversaries.[9] Indeed, Anthony Harvey has shown that Paul's claim to have received at the hands of his fellow Jews 'the forty lashes less one' on no less than five occasions (2 Cor. 11:24) means that Paul accepted these punitive disciplinary measures against him as the price of his calling to preach Christ to Jews and Gentiles alike while remaining within the orbit of his native synagogue communities.[10] What Paul sought was not their tolerance but their conversion to the truth. If their response was one of rejection and violent opposition then that only reinforced Paul's belief that the powers of darkness had blinded their hearts and that they were in danger of forfeiting their participation in the true people of God (see 2 Cor. 4:3–4).

(ii) Not rationalistic optimism but apocalyptic hope

This leads to a second main point. The modern liberal ideal of tolerance is based upon the exaltation of independent human reason as the basis for the right ordering of human affairs. This position has as one of its corollaries a generally optimistic view of human nature and a basic trust in history as a process of gradual evolution. The associated theology of history (if there is one at all) is impersonal and deistic. Contrast, once again, the categories and lineaments of Paul's thought. For Paul, it is divine revelation not human reason which constitutes the basis for the right ordering of human affairs.[11] For Paul, wisdom is a matter not of the dispassionate exercise of the rational faculties, but instead of spiritual discernment of the stunning paradox according to which the wisdom of God is made known in the 'foolishness' of the crucified Christ (see 1 Cor. 1:18–25). For Paul also, human nature is marred on a universal scale by sin, and history is to be interpreted not in optimistic evolutionary terms, but in the cataclysmic biblical categories of salvation history and apocalyptic eschatology. No wonder, therefore, that tolerance and intolerance are not central to Paul's thought and practice. For, according to Paul, what is necessary is not tolerance of one's fellow creatures, but trust in God and obedience to the will of God, since it is only God who saves from the coming judgement through the revelation of his Son.

There is a specificity here which is worth noting. It is what Christian theologians have referred to as 'the scandal of particularity'. But the general doctrinal category is the biblical one of election and covenant. It is, of course, central to Paul's thought, as Galatians and Romans make plain. What it presupposes is a world-view quite alien to the humanistic rationalism that idealizes tolerance and democratic egalitarianism. For the thought-world of Paul is dominated by a theocratic belief in the sovereignty of God and the lordship of Christ through the Spirit, a corollary of which is a doctrine of divine grace in choosing a people to share God's glory and to mediate God's blessing and salvation to the world. Here, it is not a matter of recognizing and accepting people's differences in a spirit of toleration on the assumption that all people are equal. Rather, it is a matter of being accepted by God on the basis of God's covenanting love revealed first to the people of Israel and latterly in the death and resurrection of his Son.

The epistle to the Galatians is a particularly striking illustration of what I am claiming to be the great distance between Paul's apocalyptic theology and world-view on the one hand and the modern liberal view of history, with its idealization of tolerance and self-determination, on the other.[12] For, in Galatians, Paul is hardly a model of what we might call tolerance. On the contrary, he repeatedly pronounces an anathema on anyone who perverts the gospel of Christ (see 1:8, 9), recalls for his readers the occasion at Antioch when he 'opposed Cephas to his face' for his damaging act of ὑπόκρισις in withdrawing from Gentile table-fellowship (2:11–14), and is quite vituperative towards his opponents (e.g. 5:12)![13]

Paul's gospel, which came to him 'by revelation' (1:12; cf. 1:16;

2:2) – quite independent, therefore, of reason and consensus – is predicated upon what we may call a 'crisis view' of history.[14] It concerns the revelation of the one identified as 'our Lord Jesus Christ who gave himself for our sins to deliver us from the present evil age' (Gal. 1:4; cf. 1 Thess. 1:10). Now a new dispensation in history has been inaugurated, and this new age of the eschatological Spirit of God represents a fundamental break with all that has gone before, which now appears only as prophecy and allegory and custodian for that which has replaced it (see Gal. 3–4). Hence we note the way in which Paul's argument is built around a series of what J. Louis Martyn has identified as powerful 'apocalyptic antinomies': law versus faith/Christ, flesh versus Spirit, slavery versus freedom, circumcision/uncircumcision versus new creation, and so on.[15]

A direct corollary of this crisis view of history is that it does not permit of compromise. The matter is one of the revealed 'truth of the gospel' (2:5, 14; cf. 5:7) which must be either accepted or rejected. That is why Paul puts at stake his entire personal authority as an apostle of Christ, why he pronounces divine judgement on all who turn away from the gospel, why he pleads so movingly using the maternal imagery of childbirth that his 'children' might not apostasize (4:19), and why he accepts persecution by his opponents as an inevitable corollary of his own uncompromising stand (see 5:11; 6:17; cf. 4:13–14).

(iii) Not 'live and let live' but love with a view to transformation

Deliverance by Christ from 'the present evil age' which itself makes possible the inauguration of the age of the eschatological Spirit brings into being a new community, understood as sharing already in an anticipatory way in the 'new creation' (Gal. 6:15; cf. 2 Cor. 5:17). By what values, then, are the people of God to live? This brings me to a third main point, to do with Paul's moral teaching. Here, if anywhere, people will look for signs of an ethic of toleration and teaching about the limits of tolerance. But once again, I would argue that to talk in these terms is misleading. In a nutshell, what is important for Paul is not 'tolerance' but 'love' (ἀγάπη), not egalitarian acceptance but mutual 'upbuilding' (οἰκοδομή), not freedom to do what you like as long as it does not cause harm to a third party but freedom to serve God as a member of 'the

body of Christ'. Galatians 5:13–14 epitomizes this position: 'For
you were called to freedom, brethren; only do not use your freedom as an opportunity for the flesh, but through love be servants
of one another. For the whole law is fulfilled in one word, "You
shall love your neighbour as yourself".'

The point may be demonstrated in a number of ways. First, the
ethos, or habitual thought-forms which impart to Pauline ethics its
meaning and identity, is theocentric, christocentric and eschatological.[16] The theocentricity is what gives it its uncompromising
character as a form of what today might be called 'command
ethics'. The teaching on obedience to rulers in Romans 13 is a
good example of this. It begins: 'Let every person be subject to the
governing authorities. For there is no authority except from God,
and those that exist have been instituted by God' (13:1–2). Its
christocentricity is what makes love and sacrifice for the sake of
the truth the central imperatives of Pauline morality, rather than
tolerance. This is evident in the advice Paul gives to 'the strong' in
Romans 15:1ff.: 'let each of us please his neighbour for his good, to
edify him. For Christ did not please himself; but, as it is written,
"The reproaches of those who reproached thee fell on me".' Its
eschatological dimension is what impels Paul to work for the
transformation of the differences and diversity which create strife
in society in the direction of unity and harmony, rather than im-
pelling him to advocate a policy of indifference to diversity or
passive acquiescence to the *status quo*. As he says in Romans 14:17:
'For the kingdom of God is not food and drink but righteousness
and peace and joy in the Holy Spirit.'

Turning next to the lists of vices and virtues (e.g. 1 Thess. 4:1–
12; 1 Cor. 5:9–13; 6:9–11; Gal. 5:16–26),[17] what we discover is not
an analysis of universal human rights as the basis for mutual respect along the lines of 'live and let live', but instead a summons
to believers in Christ to 'walk by the Spirit' as heirs of the coming
kingdom of God and to shun the 'desires of the flesh' (Gal. 5:16).
If it is suggested that 'love, joy, peace, patience, kindness, good-
ness, faithfulness, gentleness, self-control' are qualities that add up
in all but name to what we mean by tolerance, what needs to be
emphasized is that the peculiarly Pauline semantic context and
thought-world give to these qualities a quite different nuance. For
Paul, it is not a matter of learning to live with others in spite of
different religious allegiances or no such allegiances at all. Rather,

it is a matter of learning to live with and for others in the power of the Spirit with a view to their transformation into the likeness of Christ (cf. Gal. 3:27–8). And Paul assumes a hierarchy of priorities of commitment here. He does not treat everyone the same. Rather, as he says in Galatians 6:10: 'let us do good to all men, and especially to those who are of the household of faith'.

Then there is the evidence from Paul's own teaching and practice as an apostle. Here we may take 1 Corinthians as exemplary, for the house-churches at Corinth were very much Paul's foundation (cf. 1 Cor. 3:5–9; 9:1–2). What is more, their unity and very viability were threatened by schisms of various kinds and factionalism compounded by the exercise of the traditional means of self-display or 'boasting'. The basic point that I wish to make is that Paul does not respond with tolerance, nor does he advocate tolerance as we understand it.[18] Instead, he responds in ways rather like that expected of any political leader in antiquity.[19]

Thus, using powerful rhetorical strategies he seeks to convince and confute his audience by appealing to their founding constitution as the basis for recalling them to unity and solidarity (e.g. 1:22–4; 2:2). In rather provocative fashion, he reminds the majority of his audience of their low social status outside the brotherhood (1:26–9), and does not hesitate to point out their spiritual immaturity as 'babes in Christ' in relation to whom Paul himself is their 'father', threatening even to visit them with a rod in his hand (see 2:6–4:21, with ἐν ῥάβδῳ at 4:21)! Nor will Paul allow himself to submit to judgement by the Corinthians: for Paul's politics are theocratic and he is unreceptive to the judgement of those whom he has fathered in the faith. 'It is the Lord who judges me', he says (4:4).

Having therefore reasserted his divinely ordained authority over them, Paul then proceeds to correct abuses in the Christian association. According to 1 Corinthians 5, the man guilty of πορνεία is to be expelled from the association. Other members are neither to associate with him nor even to eat with him: otherwise, the purity of the group as a whole will be at risk. Now, is not this intolerance on Paul's part? And, if so, is it praiseworthy or not? But the question is wrongly put. Tolerance and intolerance are part of a value system of a society where individual freedom of expression is placed at a premium. Antique society was not of that kind. There, group identity and group solidarity were the chief concerns, and defining and policing the boundaries were chief responsibilities of any leader.[20] Hence Paul's duty to give the lead in the exercise of discipline: and it is 'discipline' rather than 'intolerance' of which we should speak. There is no sense that the procedure Paul institutes is unusual or arbitrary or unlikely to find acceptance. Thus, in terms which remind us of another early Christian disciplinary code (in Matt. 18), Paul says: 'When you are assembled, and my spirit is present, with the power of our Lord Jesus, you are to deliver this man to Satan for the destruction of the flesh, that his spirit may be saved in the day of the Lord Jesus' (5:4–5).

In the same epistle, Paul deals with other issues to do similarly with the right internal ordering of the Christian association and its relations with 'the world' outside: the use of the judicial system of the πόλις for settling disputes among the believers; rules governing sexual practice, marriage and divorce; rules governing dietary matters and table-fellowship; the practice of worship, including gender-related roles and the proper exercise of χαρίσματα; how to respond to the anxieties generated by the deaths of group members; and so on. What is important to note in all of this is that Paul's overriding concern is to lay down rules and to encourage attitudes and practices which are consistent with the Christian association's primary, theological understanding of itself as 'the church of God' and 'the body of Christ' in Corinth.

Anything which militates in a different direction is outlawed with not the slightest twinge of the liberal pluralist conscience. Even individual liberty, which Paul by no means despises but rather wishes to encourage (see 1 Cor. 8–10), is qualified by his even greater concern to maintain unity in the truth.[21] Hence his own willingness to forgo personal prerogatives as an apostle for the sake of the common good: 'For though I am free from all men, I have made myself a slave to all, that I might win the more ... I have become all things to all people, that I might by all means save some' (9:19–22).[22] Hence also the value he places on athletic imagery to do with rigorous training and strenuous self-control (ἐγκράτεια), the clear implication being that such practice does not come easily (9:24–7). Hence, yet again, the overwhelming emphasis on the virtue of other-directed love (ἀγάπη), for which 1 Corinthians 13 is so justly famous. Such love has none of the neutrality and impartiality of the modern ideal of tolerance. Rather, it is love with a view to eschatological transformation, on the grounds that it is love practised in the context of 'faith' in the risen Christ and 'hope' for the coming of God's kingdom. Love does not 'abide' in splendid isolation: it 'abides' hand in hand with faith and hope (1 Cor. 13:3).[23]

3. CONCLUSION

If I appear to have frozen tolerance and the limits of tolerance out of the discussion of Paul, it is not because I do not believe in certain kinds of tolerance and certain kinds of limits to tolerance as essential virtues for life together in the societies of our modern world. No one, I hope, would wish for a return to the kinds of intolerance which gave rise in the Europe of the sixteenth and seventeenth centuries to the Wars of Religion. No one, I hope, would wish for a return to the kind of intolerance which led to the Holocaust or the kind of tolerance which acquiesced in its happening.

What I am saying is that we do not do the cause of a proper tolerance and a proper intolerance any favours if we harness Jesus or Paul or early Christianity to the bandwagon of post-Enlightenment secular individualism and pluralism.[24] If we allow that to happen, then we cut off the spiritual, theological and ecclesial roots upon which Christianity's ethic of neighbourly love depends – an ethic itself deeply rooted in the Bible and early Judaism. We undermine the distinctive identity and particular truth-claims of one of the major world religions which, by its very distinctiveness and particularity, has made a significant contribution to a right understanding of tolerance and to the possibility and practice of different peoples living together in harmony, a harmony based upon faith in and faithfulness to the one true God.

NOTES

1 I would like to dedicate this chapter to Professor Edwin A. Judge, recently retired from Macquarie University, Sydney, with deep gratitude for introducing me to the social world of St Paul.
2 For a comprehensive survey of the (predominantly German) scholarly debate of the last century and a half, see Victor Paul Furnish, 'The Jesus–Paul Debate'.
3 On the history of the idea of tolerance, see, e.g., Susan Mendus (ed.), *Justifying Toleration*. On toleration and the liberal political tradition, see Mendus, *Toleration and the Limits of Liberalism*.

4 For a recent investigation of the ethics of tolerance, see D. W. Brown, 'Tolerance: Virtue or Vice?'; also, the survey essay by J. Philip Wogaman, 'Persecution and Toleration'.

5 Jon D. Levenson, 'Exodus and Liberation', in his *Hebrew Bible*, 128.

6 Ibid., 144.

7 See, for example, E. P. Sanders, *Paul and Palestinian Judaism*; J. Christiaan Beker, *Paul the Apostle*; C. J. A. Hickling, 'Centre and Periphery in the Thought of Paul'.

8 See further Alan F. Segal's major investigation, *Paul the Convert*, esp. ch. 2, 'Paul's Ecstasy'.

9 He did, of course, seek the protection of the Roman authorities when it was available. See on this A. N. Sherwin-White, *Roman Society and Roman Law in the New Testament*. But seeking civil and judicial protection is quite different from advocating tolerance and complaining about intolerance.

10 A. E. Harvey, 'Forty Strokes Save One'.

11 This is to put the point too sharply, perhaps – especially in view of Stanley K. Stowers' recent essay, 'Paul on the Use and Abuse of Reason'.

12 On Paul's indebtedness to apocalyptic, see further, J. Christiaan Beker, *Paul the Apostle*; also, Wayne A. Meeks, 'Social Functions of Apocalyptic Language in Pauline Christianity'.

13 On the latter point, it is worth observing, in passing, that Paul shares with other early Christian writers and with Jewish writers also a well-developed rhetoric for vilifying opponents, a rhetoric which belies once again the appropriateness of attributing to Paul or his contemporaries either tolerance or intolerance. See, on this, Luke T. Johnson, 'The New Testament's Anti-Jewish Slander and the Conventions of Ancient Polemic'.

14 See further Leander E. Keck, 'Paul as Thinker', where stress is placed on the resurrection of the crucified Christ as the pivotal eschatological event in Paul's thought.

15 See further J. Louis Martyn, 'Apocalyptic Antinomies in Paul's Letter to the Galatians'.

16 On the notion of 'ethos', see L. E. Keck, 'Ethos and Ethics in the New Testament'.

17 For a useful overview, see Eduard Schweizer, 'Traditional Ethical Patterns in the Pauline and Post-Pauline Letters and their Development'.

18 On Paul's use of invective in its social context, see Peter Marshall, 'Invective'.

19 For this interpretation of Paul as a politician, I am indebted to a recent paper by R. M. Grant, 'Paul and Aristotle on Politics', presented to the New Testament Postgraduate Seminar of the Department of Theology in the University of Durham on 7 February 1994. Grant's

influence is reflected also in the essay by L. L. Welborn, 'On the Discord in Corinth' (with his acknowledgement at n. 20).

20 See further, B. J. Malina, *The New Testament World*.

21 On the analogous passage in Rom. 14:1–15:6, see J. D. G. Dunn, *Christian Liberty*, 78–105.

22 See now the definitive study of Paul's use of the terminology of slavery in self-designation: Dale B. Martin, *Slavery as Salvation*.

23 See further, Carl R. Holladay, '1 Corinthians 13'.

24 See further Jon D. Levenson's brilliant essay, 'Historical Criticism and the Fate of the Enlightenment Project' in his *Hebrew Bible*, 106–26. Pertinent also is Jacob Neusner's essay, 'Shalom: Complementarity', in his *Jews and Christians. The Myth of a Common Tradition*, 105–16, especially his comment on p. 107: 'Tolerance does not suffice. A theory of the other that concedes the outsider is right for the other but not for me invokes a meretricious relativism that religious believers cannot really mean. Religions will have to learn to think about each other, not merely to tolerate the other as an unavoidable inconvenience or an evil that cannot be eliminated ... [T]hey face the task of thinking, within their own theological framework and religious system, about the place within the structure of the other outside of it. And that is something no religion has ever accomplished up to this time.'

BIBLIOGRAPHY

Beker, J. C., *Paul the Apostle. The Triumph of God in Life and Thought*, Philadelphia, 1980.

Brown, D. W., 'Tolerance: Virtue or Vice?', in David R. Bromham et al, eds., *Ethics in Reproductive Medicine*, Springer Verlag, 1992, 201–9.

Dunn, J. D. G., *Christian Liberty. A New Testament Perspective*, Carlisle, 1993.

Furnish, V. P., 'The Jesus–Paul Debate: From Baur to Bultmann', in A. J. M. Wedderburn (ed.), *Paul and Jesus. Collected Essays*, Sheffield, 1989, 17–50.

Harvey, A. E., 'Forty Strokes Save One: Social Aspects of Judaizing and Apostasy', in A. E. Harvey (ed.), *Alternative Approaches to New Testament Study*, London, 1985, 79–96.

Hickling, C. J. A., 'Centre and Periphery in the Thought of Paul', in E. A. Livingstone (ed.), *Studia Biblica* 1978, vol. III, Sheffield, 1980, 199–214.

Holladay, C. R., '1 Corinthians 13: Paul as Apostolic Paradigm', in D. L. Balch, E. Ferguson and W. A. Meeks (eds.), *Greeks, Romans, and Christians*, Philadelphia, 1990, 80–98.

Johnson, L. T., 'The New Testament's Anti-Jewish Slander and the Conventions of Ancient Polemic', *JBL* 108 (1989), 419–41.

Keck, L. E., 'Ethos and Ethics in the New Testament', in J. Gaffney (ed.), *Essays in Morality and Ethics*, New York, 1980, 29–49.

'Paul as Thinker', *Interpretation* 47 (1993), 27–38.

Levenson, J. D., *The Hebrew Bible, The Old Testament and Historical Criticism*, Louisville, 1993.

Malina, B. J., *The New Testament World: Insights from Cultural Anthropology*, London, 1983.

Marshall, P., 'Invective: Paul and his Enemies in Corinth', in E. W. Coward and E. G. Newing (eds.), *Perspectives on Language and Text*, Winona Lake, 1987, 359–73.

Martin, D. B., *Slavery as Salvation. The Metaphor of Slavery in Pauline Christianity*, New Haven, 1990.

Martyn, J. L., 'Apocalyptic Antinomies in Paul's Letter to the Galatians', *NTS* 31 (1985), 410–24.

Meeks, W. A., 'Social Functions of Apocalyptic Language in Pauline Christianity', in D. Hellholm (ed.), *Apocalypticism in the Mediterranean World and the Near East*, Tübingen, 1983, 687–705.

Mendus, S. (ed.), *Justifying Toleration. Conceptual and Historical Perspectives*, Cambridge, 1988.

Mendus, S., *Toleration and the Limits of Liberalism*, London, 1989.

Neusner, J., *Jews and Christians. The Myth of a Common Tradition*, London, 1991.

Sanders, E. P., *Paul and Palestinian Judaism. A Comparison of Patterns of Religion*, London and Philadelphia, 1977.

Schweizer, E., 'Traditional Ethical Patterns in the Pauline and Post-Pauline Letters and their Development', in E. Best and R. McL. Wilson (eds.), *Text and Interpretation*, Cambridge, 1977, 195–209.

Segal, A. F., *Paul the Convert. The Apostolate and Apostasy of Saul the Pharisee*, New Haven, 1990.

Sherwin-White, A. N., *Roman Society and Roman Law in the New Testament*, Oxford, 1963.

Stowers, S. K., 'Paul on the Use and Abuse of Reason', in D. L. Balch, E. Ferguson and W. A. Meeks (eds.), *Greeks, Romans, and Christians*, Philadelphia, 1990, 253–86.

Welborn, L. L., 'On the Discord in Corinth: 1 Corinthians 1–4 and Ancient Politics', *JBL* 106 (1987), 85–111.

Wogaman, J. P., 'Persecution and Toleration', in James F. Childress and J. Macquarrie (eds.), *A New Dictionary of Christian Ethics*, London, 1985, 464–8.

CHAPTER 8

Philo's views on paganism[1]

Maren R. Niehoff

The question of cultural boundaries in antiquity, during the period when the Hellenistic commonwealth embraced many nations and established Koine-Greek as the *lingua franca* of both political and intellectual discourse, is extremely complex. Are we to imagine a kind of cultural amalgamation, in which national, cultural and religious boundaries recede to the extent that a felicitous syncretism replaces separate self-definitions? On this view, actual contact between different cultures diminishes the boundaries between them, and the dominant culture tends to provide an integrating framework for a variety of other cultures.[2] Alternatively, we may suppose that real coexistence of nations is based on inter-culturality, and thus involves clear identities and boundaries, on the basis of which significant dialogue and cultural exchange can take place. On this view, cultural contacts are likely to stimulate renewed assertions of national and cultural boundaries – far more so than would have been necessary in a culturally homogeneous environment.[3] Tolerance would thus be based precisely on the mutually accepted rejection of what comes to be regarded by each group as 'foreign'.

The case of Jewish Hellenism is in this respect especially interesting, because the encounter between monotheism and paganism obviously demands special solutions to the question of cultural boundaries. Philo, the most illustrious member of the Jewish community in Hellenistic Alexandria, was not the first to attempt an answer to the challenge of this encounter. In the first known generation of Jewish acculturation to Hellenistic Egypt, Philo's predecessor Artapanus proposed an approach which remained unparalleled in its radicalness and thus set the parameters for subsequent discussions.[4] According to Eusebius (*Prep. Ev.* 9.27.4–6), Artapanus acknowledged Egyptian polytheism to such an extent that he attributed its institution to Moses himself. Moses is thus said to have 'appointed for each of the nomes the god to be worshipped ... and that they [the gods] should be cats and dogs and ibises'.⁵ While Artapanus stresses in the context of the Exodus that the Jewish God is the 'master of the universe' (*Prep. Ex.* 9.27.22), and thus presumably superior to other deities, the second commandment of the Decalogue has obviously receded into the background. Rather than denying the existence of other gods besides Elohim, Artapanus suggests their pantheonic coexistence. He obviously thinks that paganism is culturally valuable and even congenial to Judaism. In his eyes idolatry almost seems to have become just another form of worship.

Philo's attitude towards paganism is considerably more reserved than Artapanus'. While himself immersed in Greek culture and applying classical philosophy to the Bible, Philo generally tends to stress the religious boundaries between Jewish monotheism and pagan idolatry.⁶ In this respect his attitude corresponds to that of the author of the Wisdom of Solomon, who significantly also belongs to the second wave of Jewish responses to Hellenistic Egypt. This author, too, accepts Hellenism in a selective way, distinguishing between philosophy and religion. While thus applying Stoic notions in particular to his discussion of Wisdom,⁷ he brands Egyptian polytheism as utter foolishness, warning Jews especially against the despicable worship of animals and stars (e.g. 12:23ff.). Yet in distinction from the author of the Wisdom of Solomon, Philo develops – for the first time in Egyptian Judaism – a philosophical position on paganism, which departs from the biblical injunctions against idolatry. For this purpose Philo makes extensive use of Greek thought, especially of Plato's notions of truth and mimetic literature. This overtly Platonic orientation, however, leads to new intercultural ambiguities, which become particularly apparent in Philo's discussion of myth.

Philo explains his concept of paganism when summarizing the second commandment of the Decalogue (Exod. 20:3), 'you shall have no other gods except me' (LXX θεοὶ ἕτεροι πλὴν ἐμοῦ):⁸

The second sums up all the enactments made concerning the works of men's hands. It forbids the fabrication of images or wooden busts and idols in general (ἀφιδρύματα), produced by baneful craftsmanship of painting and sculpture, and also the approval of invented myths (μύθων πλάσματα) about the marriages and pedigrees of deities and the numberless and shameless and very grave scandals associated with both of these. (*Dec.* 156)

It emerges that Philo regards paganism primarily as a mistaken esteem for human fabrications and fancies. Paganism consists of two aspects: on a practical level it involves the production and worship of idols, and on a literary level it means writing myths and/or accepting their authority. These two features are seen as complementary, enhancing one another's credibility.[9] Philo moreover regards idolatry and mythology as the opposite of an earnest search for the truth. Sincere philosophy, he argues, will rather rely on holy oracles and inevitably lead to the service of the uncreated Creator God.[10]

In his discussion of the Decalogue Philo further distinguishes between Egyptian and classical Greek paganism. The worst kind of paganism is said to be epitomized in the 'truly horrible' Egyptian cults, which involve the worship of irrational animals such as cats and dogs (*Dec.* 72–9). In obvious contrast to Artapanus, Philo stresses contemptuously that, even for these most foolish fancies, 'myths and wondrous stories' were invented to explain and justify them (*Dec.* 7). Anyone not used to such absurdities will, Philo asserts, 'die of laughter' and recognize that through *imitatio dei* these idolaters have themselves become 'beasts in human shape' (*Dec.* 80).

Greek paganism, though gravely mistaken, is according to Philo still preferable to Egyptian forms of worship (*Dec.* 66). Greek religion involves, he explains in philosophizing fashion, the deification of natural elements such as the stars.[11] Philo demonstrates a general familiarity with the Greek pantheon, briefly mentioning the names and functions of its main protagonists (*Dec.* 53–4).[12] His central concern, however, is to stress that these traditions 'were handed down by the myth-writers, who have put together fables skilfully contrived to deceive the hearers' (ibid.). Greek mythology has thus to do with dramatic effect rather than truth. It therefore satisfies only the 'lower' human instincts.

Throughout his work Philo occasionally mentions the main Greek deities, but he does so predominantly in the context of non-Jewish Hellenistic culture and in a distinctly ironic tone. This is particularly obvious in his criticism of the emperor Gaius, whom he rhetorically reminds of the virtues of his own gods. Poking fun at emperor worship,[13] Philo continues to reprimand Gaius that, since he considers himself a god, he should at least be as beneficent as Dionysus, the 'inventor of new bounties', or Heracles, the provider of justice (*Legatio* 78–92).[14] Such references suggest that Philo took for granted rather clear boundaries between the Jewish God and pagan cults.[15] Their sporadic, somewhat superficial, and often overtly polemical nature moreover implies Philo's distinct lack of interest in pagan cults.

While Philo's attitude towards the practical and popular aspects of paganism is straightforward and clearly negative, his views on mythology, the literary aspect of paganism, are far more complex. On the one hand, Philo relies for his conceptualization of myth on Plato's seminal discussions on the topic.[16] Sharpening Plato's criticism of mythology, Philo uses it as a distinguishing mark between paganism and Judaism. On the other hand, he also appreciates Plato's idiosyncratic notion of worthy, philosophical mythology. Indeed, he deeply admires Plato's own myths of the soul and the creation of the world. Philo even incorporates some of them into his own exegesis of Scripture, thus suggesting a significant congeniality between pagan and biblical stories.

Philo's criticism of pagan myth reflects Platonic arguments, which he sharpens with a view to stressing characteristic shortcomings of Hellenistic culture and contrasting them to Judaism. Plato had thus only denounced non-mimetic myths, such as Homer and Hesiod, criticizing them for not reflecting philosophical truth.[17] Relying on this Platonic distinction between the dramatic effect of literature and its philosophical truth value, Philo formulates his own, more radical, criticism of mythology. He generally uses the term with an overtly negative connotation and does not tire to stress that it is a human fabrication, which is by nature false and untrue.[18] Myth-making is thus contrasted with truth (ἀλήθεια), facts (πράγματα)[19] and oracles (χρημός).[20] Myth-making is furthermore associated with sophistry[21] and drama, two genres which aim at effect and persuasion rather than truth. Philo is particularly eager to point out the trappings of poetic language and the bewitching aspects of attractive form, such as metre and verse.[22]

Philo places his dichotomy between myth and truth in a larger cultural context. He identifies myth-making with paganism and especially with the poets, while truthful discourse is associated with philosophy and Judaism. Philo thus stresses that Moses was a real philosopher who, avoiding both mythology and simple legislation, opened his *opus* with an account of creation (κοσμο-ποίια)[23], thus encouraging the recognition of the One Creator God (*Opif.* 1ff.). Philo subsequently develops this fundamental insight by the following remarks:

God is an author in whose poetry (ποιητικῇ) you will find no fiction or myth (μύθον μὲν πλάσμα), but truth's inexorable rules (ἀληθείας ἀσινεῖς κανόνας) all observed as though graven in stone. You will find no metres and rhythms and tuneful verses charming the ear with their music, but nature's own consummate works (φύσεως ... ἔργα), which possess a harmony all their own. And even as the mind (νοῦς), with its ear tuned to the poems of God (θεοῦ ποιημάτων), is glad, so that the word (λόγος) accords with the conceptions of understanding (τοῖς διανοίας ἐνθυμήμασι), and if we may speak, lending its ear to them, cannot but rejoice. (*Deter.* 125)

Philo here contrasts myth with divine poetry, arguing that they differ significantly in their mimetic qualities. Mythology is said to have virtually no mimetic value, because its nature is charming by appeal to all the senses rather than imitating unchanging reality. To put it in modern terms, myth according to Philo lacks depth in the sense that there is no signifier in the text pointing to a real signified. By contrast, divine poetry is said to be mimetic to the extent that reality and truth are directly accessible to the reader, who can easily grasp the 'inexorable rules of truth' and 'nature's consummate works'. This is so because each word of divine poetry – the signifier – reflects the corresponding idea, namely the signified, as accurately as an impression of a seal in wax.[24] The reader of such truthful poetry can thus come into harmony with the world of the intellect. The pleasure that he or she derives from reading is truly philosophical and permanent, thus differing from the passing satisfaction provided by mythology. These views clearly indicate that, like Plato, Philo is not opposed to poetry in principle. He mainly demands that it be censored, stressing that only such poetry as has depth and which inculcates worthy philosophical and religious notions should be accepted.[25]

Philo further uses the figure of Esau to show the nature of myth. Esau, the symbol of the non-Jewish world in post-biblical Judaism, is thus identified with the inferior genres of literature:

He is a thing made up because the life that consorts with folly is just fiction and myth (πλάσμα καὶ μῦθος), full of the bombast of tragedy on the

one hand and of the broad jesting of comedy on the other. It has nothing
healthy (ὑγιές)[26] about it, is utterly false and has thrown the truth over-
board; it makes no account of the nature which is outside qualities and
forms and fashionings, the nature which the Man of practice (Jacob)
loves ... And therefore Esau his opposite must be homeless, and the
friend (ἑταῖρος) of fiction and made-up and mythological follies, or
rather himself a stage-effect and a myth. (*Cong.* 61)

Philo distinguishes here between myth and fiction, as used by
Esau, and nature as perceived and loved by Jacob. Philo's criticism of myth is again aimed at its dramatic effect which distracts
from the truth. While Jacob is thus said to represent unchanging
nature, a rooted home and true knowledge, Esau stands for the
opposite, namely transience, convention, homelessness[27] and illusion. The description of Esau as a ἑταῖρος of the artificial kinds of
literature may allude to Philo's notion that such culture implies a
prostitution of the mind. He had earlier stressed that Hagar is
rightly presented as Abraham's concubine, this status accurately
reflecting the inferior nature of the preliminary studies (*Cong.* 25).[28]
While Esau is said to be a somewhat passive and unproductive
ἑταῖρος, Jacob instead takes to himself a lawful wife, who symbol-
izes reason (*Cong.* 24–5).[29]

Using these archetypal figures of the Bible, Philo thus identifies
mythical fiction with the discourse of Greek culture, while worthy
literature is instead associated with Judaism. A particularly clear
formulation of this intrinsic connection between monotheism, truth
and Scripture, on the one hand, and polytheism, falsehood and
mythology, on the other, can be found in the following passage:

I have described now without any reservation the curses and penalties
which they will deservedly suffer who disregard the holy laws of justice
and piety (τῶν ἱερῶν νόμων δικαιοσύνης καὶ εὐσεβείας), who have been
seduced by polytheistic creeds (πολυθέοις δόξαις) which finally lead to
atheism and have forgotten the teachings of their race and their fathers
... to acknowledge the One in substance, the supreme God, to whom
alone must belong those who follow truth unfeigned instead of mythical
figments. (*Praem.* 162)

Both the terminology and arguments of the above passages indicate that Philo uses Platonic ideas for his distinction between
worthy and unworthy literature. Already the classical Greek philosopher considered traditional myths with suspicion and criticized Homer and Hesiod for presenting false and shameful stories,

which do not reflect the truth (*Rep.* 377a–e, 596e, 600e etc.). Stressing the importance of mimesis, Plato placed the work of the poets and the tragedians at a distance of three removes from the truth, since they are said to imitate not real being, but only phantasms (*Rep.* 597b–e, 599a). They strive therefore only after dramatic effect and quick impressions on the ignorant audience (*Rep.* 602b). While worthy poetry is said to appeal to man's reason and the higher qualities of the soul, low literature addresses, and even strengthens, the irrational and base parts of man (*Rep.* 603a–607a). Unacceptable poetry is thus compared to the product of 'a painter whose portraits bear no resemblance to his models' (*Rep.* 377e). For Plato, mythological distortions about the gods imply anthropomorphic stories concerning their battles, jealousies, marriages and emotions (*Rep.* 378a–e). Moreover, he prescribes appropriate ways to talk about the gods. These mainly involve a description of the gods' benevolence, their unchangeability and their inherent truthfulness (*Rep.* 379c–382e). Poets not conforming to these norms, such as Homer, must be excluded from the city. The welcome poet, on the other hand, will be more 'austere and less delightful' and will 'tell his tale in the patterns which we prescribed in the beginning' (*Rep.* 398b).

While Philo's use of these Platonic arguments is obvious, some innovations are also noticeable. Philo generalizes Plato's criticism of unworthy mythology, applying it to all myth, which is unequivocally banished. Worthy literature is no longer identified with truthful myth or logical dialogue, but rather associated exclusively with the Hebrew Scriptures. Philo thus suggests that Jewish faith, which assumes the place of pure intellectual insight in Plato's thought, is the only true philosophy. This replacement implies a substitution of foreign cultural values by Jewish ones. It assumes an important transition from Plato's notion of truth as relatively independent of texts to the distinctly Jewish notion of truth as intrinsically mediated through Holy Scripture.[30] However, the very fact that Philo could adopt Platonic notions of literature and apply them to Judaism indicates the degree to which he considered the two as congenial. Philo in fact considered Plato's stories about the gods as exceptional and different from poetic mythologies. Indeed, Plato's own myths and the revealed Scriptures of Judaism converge in his view to a significant degree. Attributing to Plato certain Jewish notions of Scripture, Philo can

thus tacitly acknowledge the truth of Plato's own myths, thus creating new ambiguities where he has just drawn seemingly un-
equivocal boundaries.

The best indication for Philo's profound appreciation of philosophical mythology is his extensive use of Plato's *Timaeus*. As D.
Runia has stressed, Philo refers very often to the *Timaeus* even
though he neither quotes it directly nor mentions the title of the
book.[31] The extent to which the *Timaeus* and Genesis 1 converge in
Philo's mind may be gathered from the fact that Philo relies on the
Timaeus almost in the same way as on Genesis, using both to establish the nature of the Creator God and his creation. An example of this attitude can be found in *Opif.* 21, where Philo mentions
the words of 'one of the men of old'. Referring to *Timaeus* 29e–
31d, Philo thus explicitly uses Greek myth in order to prove the
benevolent intention of the Creator, who transformed primordial
chaos into meaningful order.[32] Philo has thus supplemented the
biblical account of creation by information from Plato's *Timaeus*
and therefore admits implicitly that this philosophical myth has a
mimetic value similar to that of the Bible.

We are faced with a self-contradiction in Philo: while generally
branding myth as utter foolishness, he uses and acknowledges
some of it. Philo's position may be better appreciated in the light
of Plato's complex definition of his own myth. While generally
contrasting myth unfavourably with logical argument,[33] Plato distinguishes his own philosophical myth from the regular and inferior kind. He in fact calls it ἀληθινὸν λόγον (*Tim.* 26e) – a term
usually reserved for the dialectical argument. Defending himself
against charges of presenting nothing but 'old women's tales',
Plato insists that his myth about the soul is nothing but a 'logos':[34]

Give ear then ... to a fine story (καλοῦ λόγου), which you will regard as
a myth (μῦθον), I fancy, but I as an actual account (λόγον), for what I
am about to tell you I mean to offer as the truth (ἀληθῆ). (*Gorg.* 523a)

It emerges that a 'logical myth' is for Plato a story that conveys
truth which cannot be positively proven by dialectical enquiry or
historical evidence.[35] Its truth value is suggested indirectly, namely
by the facts that contrary propositions can be disproven and that
it has a highly positive effect on man's philosophical and moral
development. Logical myth essentially rests on correct conjecture.
In this sense Plato's myth represents an approximation to the

truth, being a 'likely story',[36] which complements the dialectical argument.[37] Plato moreover encourages his readers to take the following attitude towards his myths:

Now it would not be appropriate for a man of sense (νοῦν) to affirm (διισχυρίσασθαι) that all this is just as I have described it, but that this or something like this is true concerning our souls and their abodes, since the soul is shown to be immortal, it seems to me appropriate (πρέπειν μοι δοκεῖ) that he may worthily venture to assume this belief; for the venture is worthwhile. (*Phaedo* 114d)

It emerges from the above discussion that Plato understands his own myth as a story which conveys philosophical truths of salvific value for the individual.[38] This truth is outlined in large strokes, while the details of the story may not necessarily be correct. Therefore one should relate to it neither as a historical account nor as an allegory which entirely abandons the literal meaning and explicitly points beyond itself to the underlying sense. The reader of philosophical myth should instead take the literal story seriously and gropingly establish its implied message by a process of pondering and logical conjecture. Thus defined, Plato's notion of the 'logical myth' parallels to an astonishing degree the ancient concept of fables,[39] such as Aesop's, which were also called 'logoi' and appreciated by Plato at least in a limited way (*Phaedo* 61b).

Plato's notion of 'logical myth' parallels to a significant, yet hitherto unrecognized, degree Philo's textual assumptions in his treatment of Genesis. This resemblance pertains to the concept of the literal text as an approximation to the ideational truth and the conjectural style of interpretation. Philo's congeniality to Plato in this respect may initially be gathered from his introduction to the biblical creation myth. He says there that:

no writer in verse or prose could possibly do justice to the beauty of the ideas embodied in this κοσμοποιίας. For they transcend our capacity of speech and hearing, being too great and august to be adjusted to the tongue or ear of any mortal. Nevertheless they must not because of this be passed over in silence. For the sake of the God-beloved author we must venture to speak (ἐπιτολμητέον λέγειν) even beyond our power. (*Opif.* 4)

Philo indicates here that he will actually present a 'likely story' which transmits that amount of truth and beauty which the human mind is capable of. This position approaches Plato's notion of the somewhat limited mimetic value of mythological texts. Philo moreover applies to his scriptural exegesis further characteristics of Platonic mythology. He concludes his account of the creation of the world by summarizing the main teachings, which Moses is said to have implied,[40] stressing their importance for a happy life. These teachings have not been derived by an allegorization of Scripture. They have rather been inferred from significant portions of the literal account of creation. Philo's groping and conjectural style of argumentation is worth closer attention.

Philo opens his account of creation by referring to the philosophical axiom which led Moses to the true assumptions about the Creator God. In Platonic style he initially disproves currently popular fallacies about the relationship between God and the world.[41] He subsequently argues that Moses, philosophically trained and divinely instructed, could not fail to recognize that the universe necessarily (ἀναγκαιότατον) consists of two parts, one active and ethereal, the other passive and material (*Opif.* 8). This assumption is obviously taken from *Timaeus* 27dff., where this principal distinction is presented as Timaeus' 'opinion'. Philo has thus applied an ancient conjecture about the universe to Genesis 1, thus implying that the discourse of logical myth is appropriate also for Scripture.

Further arguing for providence in the process of creation, Philo stresses that 'it stands to reason' (αἱρεῖ λόγος) that 'what has been brought into existence should be cared for by its Father and Maker' (*Opif.* 9). It is significant that a similar, if less monotheistic, notion is presented in Plato's creation myth. There the 'men of wisdom' are said to have established it as 'the supreme originating principle (ἀρχήν) of becoming and the cosmos' (*Tim.* 29e). Also in this case, Philo does not hesitate to accept the authority of ancient conjecture and hearsay. He again applies the discourse of logical myth to Scripture, treating Genesis 1 as a congenial genre of literature.

Moreover, discussing the biblical expression 'let us make man in our image and in our likeness' (Gen. 1:26), Philo entertains the following thoughts:

the full truth about this must be that God alone knows, but we must not conceal the cause which by probable conjecture (εἰκότι στοχασμῷ) seems plausible and reasonable (πιθανὴν καὶ εὔλογον). (*Opif.* 73)

Philo clearly argues here by way of conjecture – a method appropriate to philosophical myth. His explanation – namely that God cannot be held responsible for evil and must therefore have employed assistants for man's creation (*Opif.* 75) – closely follows the relevant passage in Plato's creation myth (*Tim.* 42d–e).[42]

Referring to Genesis 2:4–5, Philo offers another conjectural interpretation. He takes the double reference to *genesis* in the biblical verse as an indication of two successive types of creation: the primary ideational and the secondary material. His exegetical style is yet again remarkable:

Is he not manifestly (ἐμφανῶς) describing the incorporeal ideas present only to the mind, by which, as by seals, the finished objects that meet our sense were moulded? For before the earth put forth its young green shoots, young verdure was present, he tells us (φησίν), in the nature of things without material shape, and before grass sprang up in the field, there was in existence an invisible grass. We must conjecture (ὑπονοητέον) that in the case of all other objects also, on which the senses pronounce judgement, the original forms and measures, to which all things that come into being owe their shape and size, subsisted before them; for even if he [Moses] has not dealt with everything in detail, aiming as he does at brevity, nevertheless what he does say gives us a few sketches (δείγματα) of universal nature. (*Opif.* 129)

Philo relies here on what he calls the 'manifest' meaning of Scripture. He then proceeds to develop his interpretation by way of conjectural argument. He takes Genesis 2:4 as an expression of the Platonic notion that material objects are a secondary derivative of the respective ideas. While this interpretation may not be an allegory, it certainly does not reflect the literal meaning either. Philo rather seems to have extrapolated ideas which he took to be implied in the biblical text. These ideas pertain to the essence of creation and show how God, the wholly Other and immaterial, could nevertheless have been involved in material creation. In this sense, Philo actually presents the moral of the story, suggesting the right way to think about God.

Finally, Philo supplies an interpretation for Genesis 2:6, which he presents in the following terms: 'This is one reason [for God's action], another one must be mentioned, which aims [at the truth] just as a guardian of the truth' (*Opif.* 132). Here Philo not only admits the conjectural nature of his interpretation, but also defines its truth value as approximate.

In all the above interpretations of Genesis Philo accepts the literal meaning of Scripture – yet not in a historical, but rather in a philosophical sense. While thus earnestly applying himself to the hermeneutic horizon of the biblical narrator,[43] Philo suggests ideas which he takes to be implied by the text. Such 'underlying' ideas pertain to theology, namely the nature of God and his creation. Parallel to Plato's 'logical myth', they indicate God's greatness and benevolence. They also suggest the right notions of worship, thus preparing the reader for a blissful life. It is no coincidence that Philo treats Genesis 1, more than any other biblical treatise, as parallel to the type of worthy myth which Plato had in mind. In discussion of this chapter, he also noticeably refrains from allegory. This special treatment is connected to a sense that the literal account of creation offers the only direct insight into God's nature, which is essentially unknowable to man.[44] Genesis 1, presenting God in his primal action, is the one truly theological treatise of the Bible. It thus emerges that for Philo – as for Plato – theology actually means purified, philosophical myth.

Philo's deep appreciation of Plato's logical myth has further ramifications for his allegory of Hebrew Scripture. It might in fact be one of the reasons why he departs from Stoic exegesis, remaining enormously hesitant about abandoning the literal meaning and making efforts to take it seriously alongside the allegorical dimension.[45] Again parallel to Plato, Philo tends to highlight the theological and spiritual (and not the physiological) meaning of ancient texts. It is at the crossroads of myth, Scripture and allegory that the complexity and inner tension of Philo's position become particularly obvious.[46] This is not surprising in view of the fact that in antiquity the allegorization of mythology had been increasingly flourishing. Philo is thus faced with a revival of the poets' myths, which could be philosophically rehabilitated. While Plato had already been familiar with the allegorization of myth and rejected it,[47] the Stoics rendered it highly popular. Philo has thus to respond particularly to the challenge posed by such biblical passages which seem distinctly mythological and thus similar to classical poetry – with respect to both the negligible value of their literal sense and the high philosophical significance of their allegorization. Philo's answers to such challenges indicate that he principally maintained the Platonic position of rejecting the allegorization of poetic mythology.[48] However, his distinction between such myth and Scripture, which he emphatically recommends for allegorization, is fragile and often based on his personal intuition rather than his intellectual conviction.

An example which may illuminate Philo's ambiguous position *vis-à-vis* myth, Scripture and allegory is his interpretation of Genesis 2:21, which deals with the creation of woman from man's rib:

The literal sense by itself (τὸ ῥητὸν ἐπὶ τούτου) is mythological (μυθῶδές ἐστι). For how could anyone accept (παραδέξαιτο) that a woman, or a human being at all, came into existence out of a man's side? And what was there to hinder the First Cause from creating woman, as He created man, out of earth? For not only was the Maker the same Being, but the material (ὕλη), too, out of which every particular part was fashioned, was practically unlimited. (*Leg. all.* II.19)

Philo indicates in his commentary on Genesis 2:21 that the biblical verse contains theologically problematic material. Philo feels that it undermines positive and respectful notions about God. This is so because according to him the biblical notion of woman's origin from the rib may imply that God was coerced by circumstances to deviate from his previous method of creation. This further raises the suspicion that there was not sufficient stuff left to create woman. It is significant that Philo wishes to rehabilitate the image of God by reference to the unlimited amount of ὕλη available to him. This point of emphasis suggests that the issue at stake here is not the notion of omnipotence in the later monotheistic sense, as developed in Judaism by systematic theologians such as Saadja Gaon. Otherwise Philo would have focused his apology of the biblical text on God's free decision to use a new method of creation.

Philo's irritation at Genesis 2:21 rather seems to be connected to the well-known myth about Prometheus forming man out of clay.[49] Pausanias stresses that according to tradition Prometheus formed 'the whole race of mankind'. He also highlights that the remains of that clay from which humanity was fashioned are still visible at a certain site. Hesiod also mentions that Prometheus formed woman from 'mother earth' (*Theogony* 570). These traditions throw new light on Philo's concern about the proper image of God. His emphasis on the unlimited amount of earthly stuff seems to counter allegations that the Jewish God was compromised by a severe lack of ὕλη, having to resort to a new and somewhat bewildering method of creation, whereas Prometheus could pride himself not only on having formed the whole human race out of clay, but also on having left behind honorific clay statues. Philo may thus have devalued the biblical account as 'mythological' because he feared that it prompts the reader to compare the Jewish God unfavourably to his pagan counterpart. It would therefore no longer fulfil the function of worthy literature, which is meant to present a positive and respectable picture of God. A further indication that Philo is motivated here by the suspicion that the Jewish God may appear weaker than Prometheus can be gathered from the fact that he does not criticize the account of *man*'s creation from clay as mythological. If he had been irritated only by the similarity between the biblical and the pagan creation myths, he would naturally have been disturbed by Genesis 2:7 – much more so than by Genesis 2:26.

After raising several objections to the plausibility of the literal meaning of Genesis 2:26, Philo offers another way of looking at the passage. It is significant that – though symbolical – this interpretation is not presented as an allegory or as the 'underlying sense'. Philo rather submits conjectures, which gradually lead up to the symbolical meaning of the passage. He himself identifies this exegetical process as an enquiry: 'what is it then, that he [Moses] wants to convey?'[50] The details of Philo's interpretation are established by reference to common sense plausibility. He points out, for example, that 'sides' is a term common for 'strength' (*Leg. all.* II.20). On the basis of this generally accepted assumption, Philo develops his allegory, explaining the creation of woman from man's rib as a metaphor of the creation of the senses after the mind has come into existence (*Leg. all.* II.20–35).

It emerges from Philo's presentation that he is relatively hesitant to offer his allegory. He suggests it as an additional and complementary dimension of the literal account, which is said to reflect its true and thus unmythological intention. He significantly operates with arguments of plausibility rather than proposing straight replacements of certain biblical items by their respective 'spiritual' equivalents. Indeed, Philo presents allegory here as an extension of the *logos* inherent in the biblical text. It thus becomes obvious that Philo's treatment of Scripture still relies on Plato's notion of philosophical myth, which intrinsically points to a theological and spiritual truth. It is, however, equally evident that Philo requires allegory not as an authentic extension of the biblical *logos*, but rather as an apology in the Stoic sense for what appears to be a straightforward myth which even suggests the inferiority of the Jewish God to his pagan competitors.

In his allegorization of the Garden of Eden, Philo's distinction between 'flat' myth and mimetic Scripture becomes even more fragile. His inner ambivalence becomes particularly clear. Referring to the serpent, he initially offers the following comments:

Now these are no mythical fictions (οὐ μύθου πλάσματα), such as poets and sophists delight in, but samples of models (δείγματα τύπων), bidding us resort to allegorical interpretation guiding our renderings by what lies beneath the surface (τὰς δι' ὑπονοιῶν ἀποδόσεις). (*Opif.* 157)

Philo consequently provides such an allegorical interpretation – the serpent representing pleasure – and he justifies this strategy as following 'a probable conjecture' (ibid.). In this context, Philo has thus affirmed the distinction between myth as an unmimetic story and Scripture as a text with a deeper and truthful message.[51] Yet, in a different treatise, Philo returns to this story, this time admitting that if taken literally it would actually have to be considered as a myth. According to Philo the allegorization of the serpent as pleasure can extricate Scripture from this realm of mythology:

But when we interpret the words by the underlying meaning, the mythological is removed out of the way (ἐκποδὼν οἴχεται), and the true sense becomes manifest. (*Agr.* 97)

This passage indicates that Philo at least occasionally thought of the literal story of the Garden of Eden as a myth. Paradoxically, he proposes here to apply allegory to myth, thereby transforming it into Holy Scripture.

Notwithstanding obvious difficulties, Philo continues to attach great importance to the criterion of 'allegorizability' to distinguish between myth and Scripture. This may be gathered from his outspoken opposition to more radical thinkers, who suggested a total equation between myth and Scripture and their respective allegorizations. In *Conf.* 2ff., for example, Philo explicitly refers to the 'impious scoffers' who question the uniqueness of the Bible by raising the following issues:

> how can you still ... speak gravely of the ordinances as containing the canons of absolute truth? For see your so-called holy books contain also myths, which you regularly deride when you hear them related by others.

His response to the above-mentioned challenge indicates that his opponents compared the biblical story of the tower of Babel to certain tales in Homer's *Odyssey* (xi.315, 318) and other works of literature. They are even said to question the meaningfulness of God's actions as related in Genesis (*Conf.* 4–13). Philo responds to these trendy modernisms by asserting the truthfulness of the biblical account and its superiority over other, superficially similar stories. His argument relies also here on the allegorical meaning of Scripture.

Philo himself is acutely aware of the fragility of the supposed dichotomy betwen myth and Scripture. He might even have had a sense of its ultimate arbitrariness. In the above-mentioned dispute with the 'impious scoffers', Philo insists that their allegations of mythology could be also refuted by arguments relying only on the literal sense of Scripture. Yet his overtly apologetic tone seems to betray a deep awareness that such literary refutations might indeed be wanting:

> Those who take the letter of the law in its outward sense and provide for each question as it arises the explanation which lies on the surface, will no doubt refute on their own principles the authors of these insidious criticisms. But we shall take the line of allegorical interpretation, not in any contentious spirit, nor seeking some means of meeting sophistry with sophistry. (*Conf.* 14)

When thus polemicizing against other exegetes, Philo no doubt referred also, and perhaps mainly, to his co-religionists.[52] One of his targets might have been Aristobulus, who belonged to the first known generation of acculturated Egyptian Jews, who tended to embrace Greek civilization wholeheartedly and without many reservations. Aristobulus himself probably introduced the method of allegory to the exegesis of the Hebrew Scriptures.[53] His programme of allegorical exegesis was precisely based on the assumption of a significant resemblance between the nature of Hebrew Scripture and Greek myth. Indeed, Aristobulus proposed in Stoic fashion 'to receive the interpretations according to the laws of nature and to grasp the fitting conception of God and not to fall into the mythical and human way of thinking about God'.[54] Those who have 'understanding to perceive the elevated beyond the letter' are invited to recognize the allegorical meaning of Scripture.[55] For Aristobulus this means replacing biblical myths about the Deity by parabolical references to his elevated nature and benevolence.[56] He thus proposes allegory as a replacement of the literal meaning, and not as its complement. Confident that Greek thought entirely relies on the Bible (*Prep. Ev.* 13.12ff.), and thus denying the otherness of the Other, Aristobulus recognizes the similarities between the allegorizations of Greek literature and Hebrew Scriptures. He even presents examples of both,[57] concluding that 'it is agreed by all the philosophers that it is necessary to hold holy opinions concerning God, a point our philosophical school makes particularly well'.[58]

Distancing himself from such more radical co-religionists, Philo rather chooses to maintain – at least on a psychological level – a firm boundary between pagan myth and Scripture. This distinction is based on his own personal intuition and on his deep appreciation of Plato. He therefore implicitly treats Genesis 1 as a logical myth, also incorporating materials from the *Timaeus*. Significantly extending the notion of the moral of the 'logical myth', Philo moreover accepts the allegorization of Scripture and often even requires it in order to demythologize the biblical text. He simultaneously rejects with Plato the allegorization of poetic myth, thus demonstrating its inferior status and lack of mimetic value. Ironically, Philo has thus appropriated pagan hermeneutics and philosophy in order to maintain and redefine the boundary between Judaism and paganism.

NOTES

1 I wish to thank Professors M. Hengel, M. Idel, J. Liebes, J. Rist and D. Winston for their helpful comments on an earlier draft of this chapter.
2 Such an integrative view of late antiquity is embraced especially by M. Hengel, *Judaism and Hellenism*, and S. Lieberman, *Greek in Jewish Palestine*; *Hellenism in Jewish Palestine*. With special regard to Jewish Hellenism in Egypt, see also: J. J. Collins, *Between Athens and Jerusalem*, 2–16. See also G. W. Bowerstock, *Hellenism in Late Antiquity*, where he

argues for a later period that Hellenism was not a colonizing force
but rather provided local cultures with new ways of self-expression.

3 The Hasmonean uprising in Palestine is an example of such increased national consciousness in reaction towards the impact of
Hellenism: see esp. V. Tcherikover, *Hellenistic Civilization and the Jews*,
39–265.

4 On Artapanus' background, see esp. J. J. Collins, 'Artapanus', 889–
95; E. Schürer, *The History of the Jewish People in the Age of Jesus Christ*,
521–5; M. Hengel, *Hellenism*, 90–94; M. Hadas, *Hellenistic Culture*, 96ff.

5 καί ἑκάστῳ τῶν νομῶν ἀποτάξαι τὸν θεὸν σεφθήσεσθαι τάτε ἱερὰ
γράμματα τοῖς ἱερεῦσιν εἶναι δὲ καί αἰλούρους καί κύνας καί ἴβες
(quoted according to K. Mras' edition, *Eusebius' Werke*, Berlin, 1954,
vol. VIII, 1, 520.

6 Cf. N. Umemoto, 'Juden, "Heiden" und das Menschengeschlecht in
der Sicht Philons von Alexandria', who recently argued that Philo's
universal and spiritual interpretation of Judaism leads to a significant
de-emphasis on the boundaries between Jews and non-Jews.

7 See D. Winston, *The Wisdom of Solomon*, 4–69, 151–209; B. L. Mack,
Logos und Sophia, 63–107.

8 Philo knew little Hebrew and his exegesis is clearly based on the
LXX; see esp.: Y. Amir, 'Philo and the Bible', 1–8; 'Authority
and Interpretation of Scripture in the Writings of Philo', 440–4; V.
Nikiprowetzky, *Le commentaire de l'écriture chez Philon d'Alexandrie*, 56–
111. The text of Philo's writings used here is that of F. H. Colson, *Philo*.

9 Note that Philo clearly regards myth as a story about the gods. This is
in contrast to G. S. Kirk's wider definition, which seeks to extract
mythology from the confines of a religious context (*The Nature of Greek
Myths*). See also J. Bremmer, 'What is a Greek Myth?'; R. L. Fox,
Pagans and Christians, 27–101.

10 *Dec.* 15, 41ff.; *Dec.* 53, 58–9, 64–5, *Opif.* 7–12 etc. Note especially the
clearly monotheistic emphasis in *Leg. all.* II.1, where Philo comments
on Genesis 2:18 ('it is not good that man should be alone'), stressing
that 'it is good that the Alone should be alone: God being one, is
alone and unique, and like God there is nothing'.

11 As W. Burkert stresses (*Greek Religion*, 119–25 and 305–11), the gods of
the Greeks originally did not represent abstract or cosmic elements,
but were rather thought of in distinctly personal terms. This means
that Philo understands Greek polytheism in terms of the later philosophical tradition, which conceptualized the pantheon of deities as
personifications of abstract forces and ideas.

12 Philo's work contains references to all the major deities of the Greek
pantheon (see also the *Index Philoneus*, ed. G. Mayer, Berlin and New
York, 1974). Yet these references tend to be fairly general, displaying
only an average knowledge. Significantly, Philo does not mention interpretative traditions concerning the gods; and therefore he does not

seem to have followed the discussion regarding the forms of pagan cults.

13 See also R. Barraclough, 'Philo's Politics', 417–553; G. Delling, 'Philon's Encomium auf Augustus', 171–92; P. M. Fraser, *Alexandria*, 282–3, who argues that Egyptian Jewry distanced itself from regular polytheism, yet found sufficiently ambiguous formulations with respect to the emperor, which would not offend the worship of his person.

14 For other examples of Philo's references to Greek deities, see esp.: *Prob.* 102 (Zeus), 130 (Zeus, Dionysus); *Leg.* 93–113 (Hermes, Ares, Apollo), *Vita* 3 (Demeter).

15 Note that Philo once in his discussion on the Decalogue uses a surprisingly inclusive phrase, when he actually demands that the Jewish God be worshipped not necessarily in an exclusive fashion, but only above other deities (*Dec.* 53, see also M. Simon, 'Jupiter–Jahve. Sur un essai de théologie pagano-juive, 40–66). Apart from this ambiguity, Philo seems very firm about the boundaries between Judaism and paganism, and the exclusive superiority of the former.

16 For the background of Plato's attitude towards myth, see esp.: P. Frutiger, *Les mythes de Platon. Etude philosophique et littéraire*; L. Edelstein, 'The Function of Myth in Plato's Philosophy', 463–81; K. Dowden, *The Uses of Greek Mythology*, 47–9; F. Buffière, *Les Mythes d'Homer et la pensée grecque*, 32–44; M. L. Morgan, *Platonic Piety*, 71–9; 'Plato and Greek Religion', 227–47; E. Asmis, 'Plato on Poetic Creativity', 338–64. Regarding Philo's close familiarity not only with Plato's work, but also with the different schools of Platonic exegesis, see esp. his remarks in *Aet.* 13–19.

17 Regarding Plato's definition of truth and its philosophical problems, see esp. G. Vlastos, 'Degrees of Reality in Plato', 1–19.

18 E.g. *Opif.* 2–3, *Cong.* 61, *Mut.* 152, 1 *Som.* 172, *Abr.* 243, *Aet.* 131 etc. Cf. A. Measson, 'Un aspect de la critique du polythéisme chez Philon d'Alexandrie, 75–107, where she argues that although Philo generally defines myth as untrue, he sometimes refers to it in a somewhat positive sense.

19 E.g. *Abr.* 243. See esp. *Fuga* 121, where Philo stresses that the biblical account is 'not inventing a myth, but indicating precisely a real fact'.

20 E.g. 1 *Som.* 172.

21 E.g. *Praem.* 8.

22 E.g. *Aet.* 58.

23 Philo uses only this general label for the account of creation, thus avoiding a clear definition of the literary genre of his account. The implications of this ambiguity will be discussed below.

24 For further details on Philo's concept of language, see: M. R. Niehoff, 'Philo's Mystical Philosophy of Language'; D. Winston, 'Aspects of Philo's Linguistic Theory'.

25 For Philo's positive evaluation of pedagogically effective poetry, see esp. *Cong.* 15: 'For grammar teaches us to study literature in the poets and historians, and will thus produce intelligence and wealth of knowledge. It will teach us also to despise the vain delusions of our empty imagination by showing us the calamities which heroes and demi-gods who are celebrated in such literature are said to have undergone.' See also *Abr.* 23 and *Sacr.* 78. Philo's more cautious, yet not principally adverse, attitude towards poetry becomes also transparent on those occasions, when he argues that poetry in its original form does not charm and delude but rather educates (*Plant.* 159, *Her.* 15, *Prob.* 98, 141–3).

26 Philo uses this term here in the Platonic sense of mental health, which corresponds to the soul's liberation from the body and implies its proximity to the ethereal realm of the ideas; see esp. Plato's remarks in his middle and later dialogues, where he has replaced his earlier Socratic notions of the unity of the soul and the teachability of virtue by a strongly dualistic, probably mystically inspired concept of ethics, e.g. *Gorg.* 464b–d, 521e–522a: evil is a disease of the soul, which can be cured by philosophy; *Phaedo* 113dff.; *Tim.* 44c: man becomes healthy through philosophical education. See also: F. Wehrli, 'Der Arztvergleich bei Platon', 206–14.

27 Note that Philo also characterizes Hagar, the symbol of the preliminary studies, as a sojourner (*Cong.* 20, 22; *Leg. all.* III.244). Philo moreover stresses that God 'drove away all the earthly ways of thinking which have no real desire to look on any heaven-sent good, and made them homeless and cityless, scattered in very truth' (*Cong.* 58).

28 Note also Philo's remark in *Cong.* 36: 'When God rains down from heaven the good of which the self is both a teacher and a learner, it is impossible that self should still live with the slavish and concubine arts, as though desiring to be the father of bastard thoughts and conclusions.'

29 Note also Philo's comments in *Cong.* 77: 'For some have been ensnared by the love lures of the handmaids and spurned the mistress, and have grown old, some doting on poetry, some on geometrical figures ... and have never been able to soar to the winning of a lawful wife.'

30 For further details, see M. R. Niehoff, 'Philo's Mystical Philosophy of Language'. On the increasing importance of Scripture in early Judaism, see especially J. Assmann, *Das kulturelle Gedächtnis*, 87–129.

31 D. Runia, *Philo of Alexandria and the Timaeus of Plato*, 365–406; M. Hengel, *Hellenism*, 171; H. F. Weiss, *Untersuchungen zur Kosmologie des hellenistischen und palästinischen Judentums*, 35–8; D. Winston, *Logos and Mystical Theology in Philo of Alexandria*, 9–25; A. Measson, *Du chair aile du Zeus à l'Arcle d'Alliance. Images et mythes Platoniciens chez Philon.*

32 See F. Cornford, *Plato's Cosmology*, 33–9; D. Runia, *Philo and Timaeus*, 131–77.

33 See P. Frutiger, *Mythes*, 17–18.

34 See also E. R. Dodds, *Plato's Gorgias*, 376–7.

35 See also. *Crit.* 110a; *Rep.* 382d.

36 *Tim.* 29d: τὸν εἰκότα μῦθον.

37 See also *Rep.* 614a, where Plato reaches the end of the dialectical argument, stressing that he will now relate a tale which will complement the aforementioned. See also L. Edelstein, 'Myth', 466–74. The complementary nature of the myth often implies that the myth reveals a truth beyond dialectical logic.

38 See also *Rep.* 621b–c: 'it will save us if we believe'.

39 See esp. B. E. Perry, 'Fable', 17–37.

40 *Opif.* 170 (ἀναδιδάσκει). The main lessons of Genesis are said to be the notions of God's eternity, unity and providence, and the world's createdness and uniqueness (ibid., 170–2). Cf. Plato's lists of the 'correct theology' which truthful poetry conveys (see above).

41 *Opif.* 7, where he counters the view that the world ought to be worshipped as a deity by reference to the obvious majesty of the Maker, which must be superior to the product he has made.

42 For additional Philonic explanations, see *Opif.* 79ff.

43 Note, however, that Philo does change the sequence of the biblical text in order to adapt it to his own interpretation. For an example, see esp. *Opif.* 134, where he transfers the creation of the first Adam as man and woman to the second account of creation which is said to refer to the earthly man, dealing with specifics rather than ideational *genera*; see also T. H. Tobin, *The Creation of Man*, 108–25.

44 Concerning God's lack of attributes, see esp. *Mos.* 1.75; *Deus* 62; *Mut.* 11; *Som.* 1. 40; *Leg. all.* 1.36. See also: D. Runia, *Philo and Timaeus*, 438–43.

45 See also: D. Dawson, *Allegorical Readers and Cultural Revision in Ancient Alexandria*, 113–26; J. Whitman, *Allegory*, 61–2. Cf. J. Amir, *Die hellenistische Gestalt des Judentums bei Philon von Alexandrien*, 107–18. Another and perhaps main reason for Philo's continued appreciation of the literal meaning is of course his commitment to Judaism as a way of life.

46 See also J. Pépin, *La tradition de l'allégorie*, 18–20; *Mythe et allégorie*, 231–41.

47 See also J. Tate, who emphasizes the philosophical and not apologetic roots of allegory, arguing that Plato also made use of it; see J. Tate, 'Plato and Allegorical Interpretation'; 'On the History of Allegorism', 105–14.

48 For possible exceptions to this principle, see: J. Amir, 'Die Übertragung griechischer Allegorien auf biblische Motive bei Philon',

119–28; R. Lamberton, *Homer the Theologian*, 44–54; J. Dillon, 'Ganymede as the Logos', 37–40.

49 Pausanias, *Description of Greece*, bk x, 4, 4.

50 *Leg. all.* II,36: βούλεται παραστῆσαι.

51 For a similar exegesis, see esp. *Gig.* 58ff., where Philo insists that 'it is no myth at all of giants that he sets before us; rather he wishes to show you that some men are earth-born, some heaven-born and some god-born'. These terms are further explained as allegories of different kinds of human characters. The more 'divine' a person is said to be, the greater is the rational, non-sensuous part in him.

52 Regarding Philo's use of the works of earlier, Jewish allegorists, who are not mentioned by name, see esp. D. M. Hay, 'Philo's References to other Allegorists', 41–75.

53 For the background on Aristobulus, see esp. N. Walter, *Der Thoraausleger Aristobulos*; 'Anfänge der alexandrinisch-jüdischen Bibelauslegung bei Aristobulos', 353–72; 'Fragmente jüdisch-hellenistischer Exegeten', 261–79; 'Jüdisch-hellenistische Literatur vor Philon von Alexandrien, 79–83 (and references there).

54 *Prep. Ev.* 8.10.2: τὸ μυθῶδες καὶ ἀνθρώπινον κατάστημα, quoted according to the edition of D. A. Denis, *Fragmenta Pseudepigraphorum quae supersunt graeca*, Leiden 1970, 217.

55 Ibid. 5. The term used in this context for allegorizing is μεταφέροντας. On the question of Aristobulus' teminology and its indebtedness to Stoic usage, see esp. N. Walter, *Thoraausleger*, 136–7.

56 Ibid. 7ff.

57 See esp. *Prep. Ev.* 13.13.3–8.

58 Ibid. 8.

BIBLIOGRAPHY

Amir, J. 'Philo and the Bible', *Studia Philonica* 2/1973.
     Die hellenistische Gestalt des Judentums bei Philon von Alexandrien, Forschungen zum jüdisch–christlichen Dialog 5, Neukirchen, 1983.
     'Die Übertragung griechischer Allegorien auf biblische Motive bei Philon', in *Die hellenistische Gestalt des Judentums bei Philon von Alexandrien*, Neukirchen, 1983. 119–128.
     'Authority and Interpretation of Scripture in the Writings of Philo', in M. J. Mulder (ed.), *Mikra*, Assen and Philadelphia, 1988, 440–4.
Asmis, E., 'Plato on Poetic Creativity', in R. Kraut (ed.), *The Cambridge Companion to Plato*, Cambridge, 1992, 338–64.
Assmann, J., *Das Kulturelle Gedächtnis. Schrift, Erinnerung und politische Identität in frühen Hochkulturen*, Munich, 1992.
Barraclough, R. 'Philo's Politics: Roman Rule and Hellenistic Judaism', *ANRW* 2.21.1, 417–553.

Bowerstock, G. W., *Hellenism in Late Antiquity*, Ann Arbor, 1990.

Bremmer, J., 'What is a Greek Myth?', in J Bremmer (ed.), *Interpretations of Greek Mythology*, London, 1990 (1st edn 1988).

Burkert, W., *Greek Religion*, Oxford, 1985.

Buffière, F., *Les mythes d'Homer et la pensée grecque*, Paris, 1956.

Charlesworth, J. H. (ed.), *The Old Testament Pseudepigrapha*, New York, 1985, vol. II, 889–95.

Collins, J. J., *Between Athens and Jerusalem: Jewish Identity in the Hellenistic Diaspora*, New York, 1983.

'Artapanus', in J. Charlesworth (ed.), *Old Testament Pseudepigrapha*, London, 1985, II, 831–42.

Colson, F. H. et al. (eds)., *Philo* (Loeb Classical Library), Cambridge, Mass., 1929.

Cornford, F., *Plato's Cosmology*, New York, 1952.

Dawson, D., *Allegorical Readers and Cultural Revision in Ancient Alexandria*, Berkeley, 1992.

Delling, G., 'Philon's Encomium auf Augustus: F. Paschke zum 60. Geburtstag zugeeignet', *Klio* 54 (1972).

Dillon, J., 'Ganymede as the Logos', *Studia Philonica* 6 (1979–80), 37–40.

Dodds, E. R., *Plato's Gorgias*, Oxford, 1959

Dowden, K., *The Uses of Greek Mythology*, London, 1992.

Edelstein, L., 'The Function of Myth in Plato's Philosophy', *Journal of the History of Ideas*, 10 (1949), 463–81.

Fox, R. L., *Pagans and Christians*, New York, 1987.

Fraser, P. M., *Alexandria*, Oxford, 1972.

Frutiger, P., *Les mythes de Platon. Etude philosophique et littéraire*, Paris, 1930.

Hadas, M., *Hellenistic Culture*, New York and London, 1959.

Hay, D. M., 'Philo's References to other Allegorists', *Studia Philonica* 6 (1979–80), 41–75.

Hengel, M., *Judaism and Hellenism*, London, 1974 (2nd rev. Germ. edn 1973).

Kirk, G. S., *The Nature of Greek Myths*, New York, 1974.

Lamberton, R., *Homer the Theologian*, Berkeley and Los Angeles, 1986.

Lieberman, S., *Greek in Jewish Palestine*, New York, 1942.

Hellenism in Jewish Palestine, New York, 1950.

Mack, B. L., *Logos und Sophia. Untersuchungen zur Weisheitstheologie im hellenistischen Judentum*, Göttingen, 1973.

Measson, A., 'Un aspect de la critique du polythéisme chez Philon d'Alexandrie: les acceptations du mot dans son oeuvre', *Centre Palèrne Mémoires* 2 (1980), 75–107.

Du chair aile du Zeus à l'Arche d'Alliance. Images et mythes platoniciens chez Philon d'Alexandrie, Paris, 1986.

Morgan, M. L., *Platonic Piety*, New Haven and London, 1990.

'Plato and Greek Religion', in R Kraut (ed.), *The Cambridge Companion to Plato*, Cambridge, 1992, 227–47.

Niehoff, M. R., 'Philo's Mystical Philosophy of Language', *Jewish Studies Quarterly* 2 (1995), 2–33.

Nikiprowetzky, V., *Le commentaire de l'écriture chez Philon d'Alexandrie*, Lille, 1974.

Pépin, J., *Mythe et allégorie*, Aubier, 1958.

La tradition de l'allégorie. De Philon d'Alexandrie à Dante, Paris, 1987.

Perry, B. E., 'Fable', *Studium Generale*, 12 (1959), 17–37.

Runia, D., *Philo of Alexandria and the Timaeus of Plato*, Leiden, 1986.

Schürer, E., *The History of the Jewish People in the Age of Jesus Christ (175 B.C.–A.D. 135)*, vol. III, 1, revised and edited by G. Vermes, F. Millar, M. Goodman, Edinburgh, 1986.

Simon, M., 'Jupiter-Jahvé. Sur un essai de théologie pagano-juive', *Numen* 23 (1976), 40–66.

Tate, J., 'Plato and Allegorical Interpretation', *Classical Quarterly* 23 (1929), 142–54 and 24 (1930), 1–10.

'On the History of Allegorism', *Classical Quarterly* 28 (1934), 105–14.

Tcherikover, V., *Hellenistic Civilization and the Jews*, New York, 1985.

Tobin, T. H., *The Creation of Man: Philo and the History of Interpretation*, Washington, 1983.

Umemoto, N., 'Juden, "Heiden" und das Menschengeschlecht in der Sicht Philons von Alexandria', in R. Feldmeier and U. Heckel (eds.), *Die Heiden, Juden, Christen und das Problem des Fremden*, WUNT 70, Tübingen 1994, 22–51.

Vlastos, G., 'Degrees of Reality in Plato', in J. Banbrough (ed.), *New Essays on Plato and Aristotle*, London and New York, 1965, 1–19.

Walter, N., 'Anfänge der alexandrinisch-jüdischen Bibelauslegung bei Aristobulos', *Helikon* 3 (1963), 353–72.

Der Thoraausleger Aristobulos, Untersuchungen zu seinen Fragmenten und zu pseudepigraphischen Resten der jüdisch-hellenistischen Literatur, Berlin, 1964.

'Fragmente jüdisch-hellenistischer Exegeten: Aristobulos, Demetrios, Aristeas', in: *JSHRZ* III, 2 1975, 261–79.

'Jüdisch-hellenistische Literatur vor Philon von Alexandrien', *ANRW* 2.20.1, 79–83.

Wehrli, F., 'Der Arztvergleich bei Platon', in *Theoria und Humanismus*, Artemis Verlag 1972 (1st edn 1952), 206–14.

Weiss, H. F., *Untersuchungen zur Kosmologie des hellenistischen und palästinischen Judentums*, TU 97, Berlin, 1966.

Whitman, J., *Allegory. The Dynamics of an Ancient and Medieval Technique*, Oxford, 1987.

Winston, D., *The Wisdom of Solomon*, AB 43, New York, 1979.

Logos and Mystical Theology in Philo of Alexandria, Cincinnati, 1985.

'Aspects of Philo's Linguistic Theory', *Studia Philonica* 1991, 109–25.

CHAPTER 9

Coexisting with the enemy: Jews and pagans in the Mishnah

Moshe Halbertal

This essay aims to analyse some aspects of the rabbinic outlook in the second century, concerning the norms that govern relationships between Jews and pagans. The Mishnah tractate *Avodah Zarah* – which is the main source for the following analysis – reflects a reality of two communities, Jewish and pagan, entangled with one another, within the setting of the Hellenistic cities of the land of Israel. The Mishnah's main concern is to create a complex set of norms which will constitute the proper response of Jews towards an environment saturated with pagan worshippers and symbols. The most extreme and telling case of such close proximity between Jews and pagans, which the Mishnah aims to address and regulate, is represented in the Mishnah's ruling concerning a Jewish house which shares a wall with a pagan temple:

If [an Israelite] has a house adjoining an idolatrous shrine and it collapsed, he is forbidden to rebuild it. How should he act? He withdraws a distance of four cubits into his own ground and there builds. [If the wall] belonged both to him and the shrine, it is judged as being half and half ... (*Avodah Zarah* 3.6)

The normative question that arises in the Mishnah is: what happens in a case where the wall which is shared by the temple and a neighbouring Jew's house has fallen, and the Jew wants to rebuild the wall? If the Jew re-erects the wall, it will involve not only rebuilding his own house, but also rebuilding a pagan temple. He therefore has to withdraw a distance of four cubits into his own ground. It is hard to imagine a case which would reflect closer contact between a Jew and a pagan temple. Entanglement of radically diverse communities is thus a given fact in the Hellenistic city, and the Mishnah aims to regulate the norms of such a shared social space.[1]

159

I do not aim to reconstruct the historical relations between Jews
and pagans in mixed cities as reflected in other documents in the
Mishnah. Nor do I intend to analyse the particular historical circumstances that led to the Mishnah's specific rulings. Rather, my
aim is internal to the text of the Mishnah, and my question is:
what sort of normative outlook guides the rulings of the Mishnah,
and what type of interaction is countenanced by the norms of the
Mishnah in the shared geographical and sometimes social space of
the mixed cities in the land of Israel?[2] This question can be answered independently of the as yet unanswered problem of to
what extent those rulings were actually obeyed by the community.
My enquiry is thus directed towards the normative conceptions of
the dominant and most articulate Jewish elite of the time, and not
to the actual behaviour of the Jewish populace.[3] The main concerns of this chapter are how such a coexistence was tolerated and
the conceptual framework which allowed sharing even to a limited
degree a social space with pagans.

In order to examine toleration and its limits in the Mishnaic
text, it is important to outline different conceptions of toleration
and their relations to the rabbinic world. The following conceptual outline will help us on the one hand to distinguish modern
ideas of toleration from ancient ones, and on the other hand to
attempt to define which of the conceptual possibilities is open to
the rabbis. The first and most radical concept of toleration is
based upon relativism concerning truth questions. Since truth is
not yet available and thus we do not have any clear way to de-
marcate truth from falsehood, no one has the legitimate right to
force someone out of his or her path. This view is expressed by
Mill, who argues that pluralism is the condition of examining and
experimenting with different ways of life in order to advance towards the truth which we do not yet have.[4] The only coercive limitation which is permitted is to stop anyone from coercing another
into his or her way of life. The relativistic argument has even
stronger formulations than Mill's, which deny not only the present access to truth but its future possibility. According to such
formulations of the relativistic approach, competing ways of life
are incommensurable, hence a future arbitration between them is
conceptually impossible. Besides the argument based on incommensurability, the relativistic argument has a postmodernist formulation grounded on Nietzsche's view that the very distinction

between true and false is power based and thus another form of enslavement.[5]

The conception of toleration supported by relativism in all its nuances cannot be attributed to a monotheist religion based on revealed truth. Indeed, the very centre of revealed monotheism is a denial of such a conception of toleration. The war between monotheists and pagans is perceived by monotheists as being between truth and falsehood. A strong case can be made that, from the biblical perspective, Gentiles are not prohibited from worshipping their gods. According to a plausible interpretation of the biblical view, the ban against idolatry is not universal, but is directed only towards Jews, since the prohibition against worshipping other gods is based upon the particular historical relationship between Israel and God, a relationship powerfully portrayed through the metaphor of marriage. Israel was taken out of Egypt to become God's kingdom of priests, and God, who is a jealous God, would not allow any worship of other gods by his people. The rest of the nations can worship their own gods, since God did not establish particular and exclusive relations with them. The only place where nations are prohibited from worship is the land of Israel, which is God's own land.[6]

In contrast to the Bible, the rabbis universalized the ban against idolatry and included it in the seven Noachite commandments.[7] Gentiles are thus prohibited from worshipping their gods, and the punishment for idolatry, whether practised by Jews or non-Jews, is death. This shift is manifested in the midrashic rereading of the verses that imply that Gentiles are entitled to worship their gods.[8] Toleration of paganism based on the limited particular obligation of Israel to worship only one God is not available to the rabbis who extended the prohibition to Gentiles. The deep hostility and intolerance towards paganism is manifested in rabbinic law which discriminates between pagans and non-pagans in legal matters. As in many other cases, universalism breeds intolerance. Neither particularism nor relativism is therefore a viable option for toleration for the second-century rabbis.

The second ground for toleration might be closer to what can be imagined as a potential argument for toleration, even within a system that rejects relativism or particularism. Yet, as I will show, this conception is still inadequate. I refer here to Locke's argument for toleration. According to Locke's argument, coercion in matters of religion is rejected since it is internally self-contradictory. The self-contradiction follows from an assumption that religious action is spiritually significant only if it is performed wilfully. Since no one can be coerced to believe or even decide to believe, coercion can achieve only external compliance. Locke thus rejects the common Christian argument for coercion which is based on saving the coerced other from his or her own sins. Such justification for coercion based on paternalism is empty according to Locke, since a coerced action would not save the other anyway. In order to have any religious meaning an action ought to be accompanied by an internal conviction of the person who performs the action, and no one can be coerced into such a state of mind. Thus, according to Locke, the paternalistic argument masks an unjustified desire for control.[9] What is interesting about this argument for toleration is that it is not based upon relativism or doubt concerning truth. Locke does not deny the truth of Christianity and the falsehood of paganism. Even if Christians are sure that the pagans are wrong, saving pagans from their own mistakes through coercion is self-contradictory.

Since Locke's argument is not based upon rejection of truth, it might yield more promise in the context of revealed monotheism. The main problem with the argument in the context of the Jewish attitude towards paganism, however, is that intolerance towards paganism in the Bible and in rabbinic literature is not based on the common Christian argument that coercing the other will do him or her good. The biblical concern is the eradication of paganism from the land of Israel, since it serves as a constant temptation to the Israelites. The war against paganism is thus based on an attempt to create a 'safe' and isolated community of worshippers, protected from the seductions of other rituals and world-views. From this perspective, the question of whether a forced conversion of the other will be effective for the other's good seems irrelevant, since the argument for eradicating or forcing the other is not based on a paternalistic approach. The second and less radical ground for toleration is therefore not an option for the biblical and rabbinical approach to the war against pagans.

The third argument for toleration involves accepting others not for who they are, but regardless, and sometimes in spite of, who they are. Such a view of toleration was central in the Enlightenment politics of emancipation. The idea was to create a common ground of humanity and citizenship shared by all regardless of their particular historical identity. Jews should be tolerated by Christians not as Jews but as humans. They should be tolerated not for who they are, but regardless of who they are. From this perspective the modern state creates a neutral ground where people from different, and sometimes opposing, religious communities meet as citizens. This approach aims to restrict particular identity and to carve out a neutral space of citizenship or humanity in order to tolerate others without validating or rejecting their particular commitments. It is doubtful that this approach to tolerance can survive serious philosophical scrutiny.[10] Nevertheless, I think it provides the conceptual key to the understanding of the Mishnaic text which we shall be analysing.

Of course, I do not want to claim that conceptions of shared humanity or citizenship allowed for rabbinic toleration of pagans in the second century: this would be completely anachronistic. But the idea of neutrality, itself essential to the Enlightenment view of toleration, was, in my opinion, present in the Mishnah, and it is the importance of creating a neutral ground which will allow for interaction with a defiled world. According to this reading of the Mishnah, its main concern is to constitute between Jews and pagans and to delineate the limits of a neutral space – a space that will enable Jews to coexist with what they perceive to be their ideological and religious enemy. In that space they will interact with pagans, but not in their capacities as pagans. Let us now turn to the Mishnah itself, and to its normative strategy in forming the neutral space and its limits.

One striking feature of the Mishnah is the lack of any normative command to destroy pagans living in the land of Israel. The avoidance of such a command is interesting since the starting-point of the biblical law is that coexistence is not allowed and that Israel ought to wage a total war against the pagans in the land of Israel:

When the Lord your God brings you into the land which you are entering to take possession of it, and clears away many nations before you, the Hittites, the Girgashites, the Amorites, the Canaanites, the Perizzites, the Hivites, and the Jebusites, seven nations greater and mightier than yourselves, and when the Lord your God gives them over to you, and you defeat them; then you must utterly destroy them; you shall make no covenant with them, and show no mercy to them. You shall not make marriages with them, giving your daughters to their sons or taking their daughters for your sons. For they would turn away your sons from following me, to serve other gods; then the anger of the Lord would be kindled against you, and he would destroy you quickly. But thus shall you deal with them: you shall break down their altars, and dash in pieces their pillars, and hew down their Asherim, and burn their graven images with fire ... (Deut. 7:1–5)[11]

The Mishnah does not reinterpret these laws to claim that this obligation is invalid, but it definitely avoids any mention of them as a viable option. In this respect the Mishnah seems to internalize the recommendation of an earlier rabbinic authority of the first century, R. Yochanan ben Zakai: 'Do not hasten to destroy the gentiles' temples so you wouldn't build with your own hands. You should not destroy brick temples since they [the Gentiles] will command you to build stone temples and you should not destroy stone temples since they will command you to build wooden temples' (Midrash Tanaim, Hofmann edition, p. 58). This advice seems to point to a completely different strategy from that of the Hasmoneans whose campaigns against Gentiles in the land of Israel included forced conversions and destruction of pagan temples and images. Instead of destroying pagan reality, a Jew has to avoid either supporting or benefiting from pagan worship directly or indirectly. In order to limit the possibility of assimilation and intermarriage without the actual destruction of the pagan community, rabbinic law made severe restrictions on intimate social interaction between Jews and pagans.[12] The norm of the Mishnah is not to destroy the pagan temple next door; the Mishnah rather deals with a different concern: if a shared wall has fallen, a Jew ought not to rebuild it in such a way that he ended up building a wall for a pagan temple.

Following a similar strategy of combat, most of the rulings in the first two chapters of the Mishnah tractate *Avodah Zarah* are oriented towards the prohibition of indirectly supporting pagan rituals or benefiting from pagan rituals. The first Mishnah prohibits Jews from engaging in any commercial interaction with a pagan three days before the pagan holiday, since the pagan would thank his god for the profit he made in such commerce. A Jew is not allowed, for example, to sell a pagan an article that will end up being sacrificed to the gods, nor is he allowed to be involved in a transaction in which part of the profits will be taxed to support pagan temples. It is a strategy of passive resistance rather than outward war. The issue is how to live within a pagan reality, and yet not be involved in benefiting from it, or indirectly supporting it. Instead of the biblical commandment to kill pagans, according to the Mishnah a Jewish midwife is not allowed to serve in a birth of a pagan since a Jew is prohibited from helping to sustain pagan worshippers around him or her: 'An Israelite woman should not act as midwife to a heathen woman' (*Avodah Zarah* 2.1).[13]

The introversion of the war against pagans is most manifest in a series of readings of the following verse in Deuteronomy: 'nor show mercy to them' (Deut. 7:2). All rabbinic readings are based on readings of the Hebrew term for mercy which is 'techonnem':

it has indeed been taught so elsewhere: 'lo techonnem' means, thou shalt not allow them to settle on the soil. Another interpretation of 'lo techonnem' is, thou shalt not pronounce them as graceful; yet another interpretation of 'lo techonnem' is, thou shalt not give them any free gift. (Babylonian Talmud *Avodah Zarah* 20a)

In its context, the commandment 'lo techonnem' means 'do not have mercy on them' (the seven pagan nations in the land of Israel), but rather destroy them completely. The rabbinic threefold reading of the verse is a word-play on 'lo techonnem'. The first reading prohibits a selling of land to pagans in the land of Israel using the term 'chanaya' which means 'settling'; the second, which prohibits pronouncing pagans as graceful, points to the connection between 'techonnem' and 'chen' which means 'grace'; the third reading extracts the term 'chinam', which means free, from 'techonnem' and prohibits giving pagans free gifts. What is common to these three readings is the introversion of aggression from waging an open war to avoiding benefit. It seems that the Mishnah attempts to continue the struggle from the position of weakness; it thus adopts the rule of avoiding rather than destroying. In its most extreme form, this attitude is manifested in the ruling that a Jew should avoid looking at an image: 'even in a regular day no one is allowed to watch images because it is said "you should not turn to the idols" (Lev. 19:4)' (*Tosefta Šabb.* 17.1).[14] For a community in conditions of weakness, in which the biblical attitude seems Utopian, avoiding eye contact with images at any price is the substitute for actually annihilating their physical presence.

Coexistence is therefore a fact, although a forced one, and the aim of the Mishnah is to continue a form of struggle, on the one hand by distancing, and on the other hand by creating a space for legitimate interaction. How can interacting be allowed in a situation where with every step a Jew makes he stumbles upon a pagan symbol? In this context the problem of neutral space is important. I want now to analyse a few cases where such a space is reconstructed. The most striking one is the following story in the Mishnah:

Proclos, son of a philosopher, put a question to Raban Gamliel in Acco when the latter was bathing in the bath of Aphrodite. He said to him, 'It is written in your Torah, and there shall cleave nought of the devoted thing to thine hand; why are you bathing in the bath of Aphrodite?' He replied to him, 'We may not answer [questions relating to Torah] in a bath' When he came out, he said to him, 'I did not come into her domain, she came into mine. Nobody says the bath was made as an adornment for Aphrodite; but he says, Aphrodite was made as an adornment for the bath. Another reason, if you were given a large sum of money you would not enter the presence of a statue reverenced by you while you were nude or had experienced seminal emission, nor would you urinate before it. But this [statue of Aphrodite] stands by a sewer and all people urinate before it. [In the Torah] it is only stated, their gods – i.e., what is treated as a deity is prohibited, what is not treated as a deity is permitted. (*Avodah Zarah* 3.4)

This story begins with Raban Gamliel who is situated in one of the social institutions of the Hellenistic city – the bath, a bath which is tainted by a pagan presence. The bath is called Aphrodite's bath, and presumably, as Proclos assumes, Raban Gamliel's presence in it involves a direct benefit from a pagan institution. At first Raban Gamliel delays his reply, since a person is not allowed to answer questions concerning Torah in the bath, thus exhibiting that he is not particularly bothered by Proclos' problem, which he anyhow perceives as merely polemical. When they come out of the bath Raban Gamliel responds to Proclos' problem. The two answers he provides to Proclos' challenge attempt to redescribe the bath as a neutral space in spite of the presence of a pagan symbol in its midst, thus allowing Raban Gamliel to use the bath. The first answer is to shift the description of the institution from Aphrodite's bath to a bath in which an image of Aphrodite is present: 'I did not come into her domain, she came into mine.'

The bath is not Aphrodite's domain which Raban Gamliel invaded, it is the other way around; it is Raban Gamliel's domain which Aphrodite invaded. Thus Raban Gamliel claims that Aphrodite is an adornment to the bath and not vice versa. The other answer redescribes the nature of the image not as a religious cultic image but rather as an aesthetic symbol, since the image is present within a completely unreverential set-up. Raban Gamliel raises a rhetorical question to make his point: 'if you were given a large sum of money you would not enter the presence of a statue reverenced by you while you were nude or had experienced seminal emission, nor would you urinate before it'.

The distinction between the religious realm and a neutral one, and, therefore, the description of images as merely aesthetic, is not simple. Those domains are intertwined with each other, since it is the aesthetic qualities of the image which are a manifestation of its divine nature, a divinity which invades all activities and aspects of life. The distinction between the cultic and the aesthetic is thus something that is important in order to create a neutral space between pagans and Jews and to allow for a broader interaction in that space. Raban Gamliel, one of the main figures of rabbinic circles, bathes in the presence of an image of Aphrodite, not because he accepts the legitimacy of paganism to a certain degree, but because he provides arguments to minimize the pervasiveness of such a religion, as if to exorcize it from the common space of the bath.[15]

The same attempt to stratify a reality which might be perceived as united and defiled is manifested in the following Mishnah: 'One should not join them in building a basilica, a scaffold, a stadium, or a platform. But one may join them in building pedestals [for altars][16] and also [private] baths. When however he reaches the cupola in which the idol is placed he must not build.' Here a distinction is made between the building and the cupola. The building itself is neutral until the builder reaches the cupola. The temple is thus redescribed as a building with an image, and not the image's building. The same tendency appears again in the Mishnah that prescribes the relations of Jews to images.

According to the halakah, Jews are not allowed to have any benefit from images that are worshipped, and the Mishnah provides actual signs that identify this kind of image. But there is no

generic prohibition on images of the kind that were worshipped,
images were prohibited only if they themselves were actually worshipped. Moreover, the Mishnah rules that a worshipper (not the
particular worshipper of the image but any worshipper) can 'annul'
the image and thus after the image is 'annulled' it is no more a
cultic object prohibited from benefit: 'An idolater can annul an
idol belonging to himself or to another idolater, but an Israelite
cannot annul the idol of an idolater' (*Avodah Zarah* 4.4). The process of annulment is described in the Mishnah: 'How does he annul
it? If he cut off the tip of its ear, the tip of its nose, or the tip of its
finger; or if he defaced it, although there was no reduction in the
mass of the material he annulled it ... If he sold or gave it as a
pledge, Rabbi says that he has annulled it, but the sages say that
he has not annulled it.' (*Avodah Zarah* 4.5). The process of annulment involves a symbolic gesture in which a pagan relates to the
image not as an object of worship and reverence; after such an act
of annulment, a Jew is allowed to use the image for all purposes.[17]

   One actual example which demonstrates the problem of existence within a space presumably saturated with pagan cultic objects, and the importance of annulment as a process of neutralization, is given in the Talmud:

The Palace of King Janaeus was destroyed. Idolaters came and set up a
Mercurius there. Subsequently other idolaters came, who did not worship Mercurius, and removed the stones with which they paved the roads
and streets. Some Rabbis abstained [from walking on them] while others
did not. (Babylonian Talmud *Avodah Zarah* 50a)

Roads were therefore paved with stones which were used as an
offering to Mercurius, and Jews had to stumble upon pagan objects where they walked. The Talmud explains that the argument
between the two opinions is whether those stones can be annulled
since, although images can become annulled, offerings cannot. The
opinion which permitted walking on these paved roads claimed
that walking on the stones is allowed since they were annulled by
pagan worshippers when they were removed from the temple. In a
seminal essay, Efraim Urbach has shown the extensive use of the
device of annulment.[18] According to Urbach, the explanation for
the growing leniency towards prohibitions of benefit from pagan
ritual and objects is connected to the economic difficulties of the

Jewish urban communities after the Bar Kochba revolt in the second century. Granting the role of economic necessity in creating the different permissions, there remains a need to understand how these permissions were justified in terms which are internal to the Mishnah itself. In the light of the foregoing analysis, it seems that the main strategy for enabling coexistence was the carving of a neutral space within the pagan reality, a space where a legitimate interaction, capable of lifting some of the economic pressures, could occur. Such a space was created by different legal moves and categories such as the distinction between the aesthetic and the cultic in the pagan object, the process of annulment as a technique of neutralization, and the redescription of social spaces not as spaces consecrated for the gods, but as neutral spaces invaded by the gods.

Another comment needs to be stressed in light of Urbach's argument. While economic necessity bears on some areas in the Mishnah, many cases in which neutral spaces are carved have no relationship to economics. Bathing in Aphrodite's bath was not motivated by the pressures of earning a livelihood, but by Raban Gamliel's desire to participate to a certain extent in the city's life. The same applies to the problem at the centre of debate between historians about how to explain the archaeological findings which show extensive use of pagan symbols in synagogues and private houses such as some drawings of *helyos* and the zodiac. I think Urbach is right that the presence of these symbols is not a sign of an underground syncretistic religion which existed independently of rabbinic authority, as Goodenough argued.[19] Yet drawing pagan symbols in synagogues or in villas was not an economic need but rather a symptom of cultural interaction independent of economic pressures. Like other interactions which involved pagan symbols and objects, the drawings in the synagogues were allowed through the distinction between ritualistic function and aesthetic meaning. The carving of the neutral space had, therefore, a far-reaching consequence resulting in the penetration of distinctly mythical and pagan symbols under the cover of their aesthetic function, not only to the market-place but to synagogues and to burial places.[20]

The chapters in the Mishnah that deal directly with our issue – from the first chapter to the middle of the fourth chapter – conclude with a haggadic, non-halakhic Mishnah, a Mishnah which

provides an account of a theological debate rather than legislation. This Mishnah raises the theological aspect of the problem
of coexistence in the boldest fashion:

The elders in Rome were asked, 'If [your God] has no desire of idolatry,
why does he not abolish it?' They replied, 'If it was something unnecessary to the world that was worshipped, he would abolish it; but people
worship the sun, moon, stars and planets; should he destroy his universe
on account of fools?' They said [to the elders], 'If so, he should destroy
what is unnecessary for the world and leave what is necessary for the
world!' They replied, '[If he did that] we should merely be strengthening
the hands of the worshippers of these, because they would say, "be sure
that these are deities, for behold they have not been abolished!"'.

The Mishnah starts with a theological problem: is not the existence of idolatry in the world a sign of God's defeat? In other
words: is not the fact that the previous legal material in the Mishnah
assumed a life in the midst of a social reality saturated with pagan
symbols a sign of the strength of idolatry in the face of God? The
Mishnah provides a highly sophisticated answer to overcome this
acute problem. The core of the elders' argument is that a total
war with idolatry is self-defeating, since the sun, the moon and the
planets are pagan symbols. Destruction of paganism will mean,
therefore, destruction of the cosmos, a cosmos which became in
the hands of the pagans a pagan symbol. 'Should God destroy his
world because of the fools?' The natural argument that follows is
that God should destroy only the unnecessary symbols of paganism. This possibility is ruled out by the elders, since pagans will
claim that although these symbols were destroyed, the others – the
sun, moon and planets – were left untouched and thus it is a sign
that they are invincible.

It is no accident that this theological reflection is the conclusion
of the unit which addresses the Mishnaic norms of interaction with
pagans. The haggadic Mishnah provides a theological representation of the two main points of the previous normative material
within the Mishnah. The idea that a total destruction of pagan
symbols would be self-defeating is parallel to the Mishnah's refusal
to recommend an active war to annihilate pagan reality, and its
acceptance of coexistence as a fact, however regrettable. The relation to the natural forces in the cosmos as forces not defined by
the 'fools', although worshipped by them, mirrors the attempt in
the Mishnah to stratify reality and to create within the social space

of the city – which is presumably saturated with paganism – a neutral space undefiled by the presence of pagan symbols. The attempt to carve the neutral space in the Mishnah represents a normative decision to avoid either of two alternative options: a declaration of open and total war until the mixed cities have been abolished; or a complete withdrawal and maximum reduction of the points of friction and contact. Both of these options were rejected as impossible, and toleration thus becomes a live option when a neutral space is constructed through the work of a complex set of norms.

NOTES

1　Concerning the mixed cities and the nature of the complicated and tense relationships between its Jews and pagans, see G. Fox, *Yavan be-Eretz Israel: Beit Shean (Skythopolis) ba-tekufah ha-helenistit veha-romit*, Jerusalem, 1983, ch. 14; U. Rapoport, 'Yahasei yehudim ve-lo-yehudim be-eretz israel ve-ha-mered ha-gadol be-romi', *Tarbitz* 47 (1978), 1–14; I. L. Levine, 'The Jewish–Greek Conflict in First-Century Caesarea', *JSS* 25 (1974), 381–97.

2　The problem of coexistence within mixed cities is not unique to the Mishnah. Tertullian in his *De idololatria* attempts to create a set of norms that will guide Christians in their interaction with pagans. On the possible connection between Tertullian's norms and the Mishnah see T. D. Barnes, *Tertullian*, Oxford, 1985, 85–115. Even if we reject the actual connection between Tertullian's text and the Mishnah, the comparison between the two is interesting and fruitful.

3　The degree of rabbinic dominance over the large population in the second century is debated among scholars. One aspect of the debate centres around the findings of second-century mosaics in synagogues, mosaics that are decorated with Hellenistic mythological symbols which presumably are prohibited by Jewish law. On this debate see E. R. Goodenough, *Jewish Symbols in the Graeco-Roman Period*, New York, 1953–1956, VI, 2–44. For a completely different understanding see E. E. Urbach, 'The Rabbinic Laws of Idolatry in the Second and Third Centuries in the Light of Archaeological and Historical Facts', *IEJ* 60 (1959), no. 3, 149ff.; no. 4, 229ff. For a balanced and extensive account of the status of the rabbinic class see I. L. Levine, *The Rabbinic Class of Roman Palestine in Late Antiquity*, New York, 1989, 98–195.

4　See J. S. Mill, *On Liberty* (1859), Cambridge, 1989, ch. 2.

5　For such postmodernist formulation see, for example, M. Foucault, *Power/Knowledge*, New York, 1980, 131. For the view of pluralism based on incommensurability of notions of the good life see I. Berlin, *The Crooked Timber of Humanity*, London, 1990, 1–19.

6 In the Bible, Gentiles are forbidden to worship idols only in the land of Israel, which is the territory of the God of Israel. The Gentiles who were exiled to Samaria were punished because they did not act according to 'the rules of the God of the land' (see 2 Kings 17:24–41). The universal vision of the prophets is a vision for the end of days and not a present prohibition of idol worship for the Gentiles. See Y. Kaufmann, *The Religion of Israel*, trans. M. Greenberg, New York, 1977, 127–32.

7 Concerning the universal prohibition of idolatry in rabbinic literature see Tosefta tractate *Avodah Zarah* 8.4; *Genesis Rabbah* 16.16; Babylonian Talmud tractate *Sanhedrin* 56a.

8 See, for example, the reading in Babylonian Talmud tractate *Avodah Zarah* 55a of Deuteronomy 4:19 – the verse that most explicitly allows Gentiles to worship other powers rather than God.

9 For a clear presentation of Locke's argument for toleration and its weakness see J. Waldron, 'Toleration and the Rationality of Persecution', in J. Horton and S. Mendus (eds.), *John Locke: A Letter Concerning Toleration in Focus*, New York, 1991.

10 For a discussion and criticism of the neutrality-based toleration see C. Taylor, *Philosophical Arguments*, Cambridge, Mass., 1995, 225–56.

11 See Deuteronomy 19:16–18 and 7:25–6; Exodus 23:24.

12 See for example Jerusalem Talmud tractate *Šabbat* 3.3.

13 In different editions of the Mishnah the following reason was added: 'because she would be delivering a child to idolatry'. This sentence does not appear in the Kaufman manuscript of the Mishnah.

14 The Talmud transmits a tradition in which saintliness is described as avoiding any visual contact with images even if the images are engraved on coins: 'And why did they call him the son of the holy? Because he would not gaze even at the image on a zuz' (Babylonian Talmud tractate *Avodah Zarah* 50a). See also an earlier and similar tradition in Jerusalem Talmud tractate *Avodah Zarah* 3.1.

15 On the relation between this Mishnah and the Mishnah in chapter 4.3 see Babylonian Talmud tractate *Avodah Zarah* 44b.

16 It seems that a more reliable version instead of 'bimosiyot', which could mean pedestals, is 'dimosiyot', which means public baths. The version of 'bimosiyot' implies a radical permission to build a pedestal for an altar. Such permission is not granted if the version of the Mishnah is 'dimosiyot'.

17 As Urbach pointed out, annulment was widely extended to allow commerce. See Urbach, 'The Rabbinic Laws'.

18 See Urbach, 'The Rabbinic Laws'.

19 See Goodenough, *Jewish Symbols*.

20 On the rabbinic material concerning the prohibition of figurative paintings see *Mekhilta de-Rabbi Ishmael* on Exodus 20.20; Babylonian Talmud tractate *Roš Haššana* 24a–b; tractate *Avodah Zarah* 43a–b.

CHAPTER 10

Tertullian on idolatry and the limits of tolerance

Guy G. Stroumsa

I

'Let one man worship God, another Jove' 'Colat alius Deum, alius Iovem'.[1] With this lapidary plea Tertullian establishes himself as one of the earliest advocates of religious tolerance in the Christian tradition. In the Roman Empire of the late second century, the Christians were in great need of some religious toleration.[2] Those Christian writers whom we call the Apologists aimed, precisely, at convincing Roman intellectuals in the corridors of power that toleration of the Christians and of their religious beliefs would in no way harm the state, and that such a toleration was, moreover, congruent with principles of reason shared, at least in theory, by all people.[3]

One of the major historical paradoxes reflected by the development of early Christianity is its transformation, during the course of the fourth century, from a *religio illicita* seeking recognition and tolerance into an established religion refusing to grant others (and its own dissenters from within, the 'heretics') what it had sought for itself until the recent past.[4] The traditional answer to our paradox is that, as long as the Christians were in need of religious toleration for themselves, they knew how to make a case for its necessity. As soon as they came to power, however, they forgot their early virtues and learned how to deprive others of what they had just acquired. Christian intolerance, in such a view of things, would be rooted in human nature, rather than in some implicit aspects of Christian theology.[5]

This explanation no doubt suffers from an oversimplification of complex phenomena. Moreover, it seems to me to be a mistake to focus only on the fourth century if we want to understand how this transformation was made possible. Indeed, an ambivalent attitude

173

to religious toleration had been inherent to Christianity from its
very beginnings. I have sought to analyse this ambivalence elsewhere, and cannot repeat my argument here.[6] In the second and
third centuries, Christian intellectuals were arguing for toleration,
and yet they were unwilling (or unable) to accept the basic premise
of religious toleration: a certain relativism in religious matters.

In these few pages, I cannot deal with the whole historical problem of early Christian tolerance and intolerance. Rather, through
the case of Tertullian (the first Christian writer to offer a lengthy
discussion of Christian attitudes to paganism, in his *De idololatria*),
I propose to reflect here on some aspects of this ambivalence towards religious tolerance in early Christian thought. I hope to shed
some light on the boundaries of Christian identity and the construction of Christian life in a pagan society, as well as the implications of such a life. Tertullian shows us how arguments in favour
of religious toleration could be developed which did not entail a
deep transformation of thought-patterns, a real internalization of
the idea of tolerance. In a sense, therefore, the following pages are
an attempt to understand how different, even contradictory, ideas
can live together in the same mind, and how they can come to
bear on wider historical issues.

Tertullian is a gifted polemicist, for whom tolerance cannot be
a major virtue. Rather, in the heat of the argument, he writes
numerous and fierce invectives against various enemies from all
sides: besides the pagans, the Jews, and Christians who happened
to establish their theology along lines different from his, such as
Praxeas or Hermogenes, as well as the traditional arch-heresiarchs
Marcion and Valentinus.

2

Interpreting the new religious pluralism under the early Empire,
John North has recently argued that we have here, throughout the
Mediterranean, a case of what he calls, in an appropriate metaphor, 'a market-place of religions'. This 'market-place' forms the
sociological background to Tertullian's thought. Perhaps for the
first time in antiquity, individuals could now choose that religious
practice and identity which best suited them.[7] No more the single
choice of following the *patrioi nomoi*, the religious tradition of the
city. To be sure, this religious pluralism remained more a matter

of fact than a recognized value. It was the Christians who gained most from that transformation of the relationships between religion and identity.

North's study develops some conclusions of A. D. Nock on conversion as a new dimension in religious history in the Hellenistic period.[8] The central fact of religion under the early Empire, according to North, can be encapsulated in his metaphor of this open competition for minds and hearts. In other words, religion was no longer a given of one's native identity, together with ethnicity. A new religious identity could be freely chosen by the individual, from different possibilities. In such a new situation of religious pluralism, the Christians had clear advantages over their competitors. More than any other group, they had the ability to formulate the need for conversion in religious discourse, and to express the higher truth value of their own religion. Such a discourse, part of their Jewish heritage, remained quite alien to their pagan adversaries, until they, too, developed a similar discourse – but this happened only under Christian influence, in the third and fourth centuries.[9] But by that time, it was too late. It is in such a broad frame that we must try to read Tertullian's plea for tolerance: a Christian intellectual in late second-century Africa sought to convince pagan readers that Christianity should be allowed in the 'religious market-place'. On the other hand, he knew that coexistence meant competition. Therefore, he tried to delegitimize (on intellectual, ethical and religious grounds – the only ones available to him) the party in power at the same time that he appealed to it. Hence the basic ambivalence in his discourse on religious tolerance. This ambivalence tells us much about the ways invented by early Christian intellectuals for living as a Christian in a pagan society.

3

The sentence quoted at the opening of this chapter stems from the famous chapter 24 of the *Apologeticus*, where Tertullian's argument for religious toleration reaches its peak:

Let one man worship God, another Jove; let this man raise suppliant hands to heaven, that man to the altar of Fides; let one (if you so suppose) count the clouds as he prays, another the panels of the ceiling; let one dedicate his own soul to his god, another a goat's. Look to it, whether

this also may form part of the accusation of irreligion – to do away with
freedom of religion, to forbid a man choice of deity (*Videte enim ne et hoc
ad inreligiositatis elogium concurrat, adimere libertatem religionis et interdicere optio-
nem divinitatis*), so that I may not worship whom I would, but am forced to
worship whom I would not. No one, not even a man, will wish to receive
reluctant worship.[10]

Tertullian eschews here the reasons for the Roman perception of
Christianity as a *religio illicita*. Now Christianity, in contrast with
native and traditional cults, considers Roman religion not as just
another, competing and legitimate tradition, but as a *false* religion. For Tertullian, Roman religion is a cult not of gods, but of
demons, which does not even deserve the name of religion. In the
same chapter Tertullian rejects the charge of treason against Roman religion hurled at the Christians: since the Roman 'gods' are
no real gods, then Roman 'religion' is not really a religion, and
the Christians cannot be accused of a crime against religion: 'Si
enim non sunt dei pro certo, nec religio pro certo est: si religio
non est, quia nec dei pro certo, nec nos pro certo rei sumus laesae
religionis.'[11] He then develops an argument according to which,
by common consent, men understand the concept of God as similar to that of the emperor, namely being ultimately one, above all
his various functions.[12] Tertullian further lists various deities in the
provinces of the Empire. Although these provinces are Roman,
their gods are not Roman. It appears, then, that religious freedom
is granted to all but the Christians. Tertullian's argument about
true and false deity ('de vera et falsa divinitate') concludes with the
statement that only the Christians, who honour the true God in
the midst of all idolaters, are forbidden to practise religion.

4

According to Tertullian, moreover, idolatry is not simply to be
defined as 'false religion'. It represents the supreme offence in the
eyes of God: 'Atquin summa offensa penes illum idololatria est.'[13]
So paganism (i.e. idolatry) is shown by Tertullian to be religiously
illegitimate. He further argues that it is also to be condemned
from an ethical point of view.[14] But what is, for him, the precise
nature of idolatry? Since Tertullian devotes an entire treatise to
this question, we should turn our attention to his *De idololatria*.

In this treatise, written before his Montanist period (probably between 203 and 206),[15] Tertullian asks the two related questions of the nature of idolatry and of the conditions of Christian life in a world filled with idols and idolaters. These two questions are related to each other since the definition and scope of idolatry will dictate Christian attitudes towards it. Moreover, one should recognize at the outset that many forms of idolatry are hidden, and should first be unveiled. The first point to be emphasized is the recognition of the incompatibility between the two realms of true religion and of idolatry. The realm of idolatry is also that of Caesar, and one cannot be at once a soldier of both Caesar and Christ. One is the camp of darkness, *castris tenebrarum*, totally opposed to the camp of light, *castris lucis*.[16] Hence, a Christian cannot swear an oath to Caesar, and is therefore forbidden from becoming a soldier in the Roman army. To use another metaphor of Tertullian, Athens and Jerusalem have nothing in common: 'Quid ergo Athenis et Hierosolymis? Quid academiae et ecclesiae?'[17]

There was a time, to be sure, when there existed no idols: 'Idolum aliquamdice retro non erat.'[18] But that was only in the *Urzeit*, before the devil 'brought into the world the makers of statues, portraits, and every kind of representation'. Through human error, everything but the Creator began to be worshipped.[19] As Tertullian argues in the *Adversus Praxean*, an *idolum* (a loan word which Tertullian introduces into Latin) is everything that functions as an intermediate entity between human beings and *daimones*. *Idololatria*, therefore, is the worship given to demons.[20] The same concept is reflected in *Apologeticus* 23.11: 'Those whom you had presumed to be gods, you learn to be demons (*daimonas esse cognoscitis*).'[21]

The most important trait of idolatry is perhaps its ubiquity. Tertullian further warns that idolatry does not even need temples and statues in order to be practised.[22] That means that idolatry is everywhere. Indeed, all sins reflect idolatry, in hidden as well as in open form, insists Tertullian in the introduction to his treatise.[23]

From this analysis follow various consequences. Idolatry is not only a product of metaphysical error; it is also morally reprehensible. And since it is ubiquitous, Christians cannot be too careful in seeking to avoid sin and idolatry. Tertullian devotes the bulk of his treatise to the ramifications of idolatry and their implications for the daily life of Christians in the Roman world. He enumerates, first of all, the professions which should be avoided by Christians, because they deal directly with idolatry. This list includes, obviously, the makers of idols, but also astrologists, teachers and traders. Secondly, he tackles the indirect forms of idolatry, contact with which is almost inevitable through participation in social life. He goes here also into great detail, seeking to delineate rules of conduct, and distinguishing between permissible and forbidden behaviour in the surrounding pagan world. How to live – and, more prosaically, how to make a living – in a world permeated with idolatry is a very serious question: the borders should be drawn in each case, and principles constantly weighed against feasibility. This discourse, it has been pointed out, is quite new in Christian literature. The fight against the *daimones*, or the pagan gods, is a very concrete one, against live adversaries rather than against a system.[24] Tertullian presents a sharp critique of Roman values: the very greatness of the Romans is linked to war (i.e. to violence and the destruction of temples). War and religion are mutually exclusive, and the very greatness of Rome comes from irreligiosity: 'de irreligiositate provenit'.[25]

5

In the course of his argument in the *De idololatria*, Tertullian comes to answer some concrete questions about daily life and religious practice, in a way not unknown in rabbinic literature of the same period. Indeed, some puzzling parallels in tone and detail exist between this treatise and Mishnah *Avodah Zara*, a more or less contemporary text, which deals with the interactions between Jews and pagans in Palestine.[26] In order to understand the nature of the similarities and differences between the two texts, we should first say a few words on the concept of λατρεία.

As we have seen, idolatry, or false religion, is the most common form of cult, of λατρεία. We have here a clue as to Tertullian's implicit line of argument. If there can be idolatry without idols, this is because for a Christian, the boundaries of 'cult' are very broad indeed. Λατρεία is, first and foremost, an affirmation, explicit or implicit, about the nature of the divinity. This affirmation is expressed in words or deeds, since Christianity itself is a religion defined through words, through the affirmation of a few truths, the *kerygma*. The Christians, more than any other religious community in antiquity, the Jews included, developed a concept of religion in which truth and its proclamation were central elements, more important even than traditional forms of cult.

For Jews, the domain of λατρεία is defined much more sharply than for Christians. Jewish λατρεία (ʿavoda in Hebrew) consists essentially of Temple sacrifices (or their equivalent, prayers, after the destruction of the Temple). Since for Jews their own cult is precisely delimited, the Jewish conception of idolatry will also be more specific than the Christian one. In rabbinic texts, it refers, mainly, to pagan *cult*, to sacrifices or prayers to idols. For the Jews, unlike the Christians, idolatry is essentially the cult of idols; it has less the quality of ubiquity. The implications of this semantic difference are significant, and reflect different approaches to new patterns of interaction between competing religious communities. Since the Christian conception of λατρεία, and hence of ἰδολο-λατρεία, is broader, there remains a smaller margin for toleration of alien patterns of thought and behaviour. For a theologian like Tertullian, almost any interaction with pagans may entail contact with idolatry, and this will involve its toleration. Such a toleration, needless to say, is to be most strictly condemned.

Early rabbinic Judaism did not really develop tolerant attitudes towards Gentiles and idolaters.[27] But various structural differences between Judaism and Christianity are reflected in some differences in the attitude of both religions to idolatry. The more stringent rabbinic definition of idolatry permitted the toleration of a broader spectrum of interaction with pagans than Tertullian was willing to admit. Such a toleration is reflected in Mishnah *Avodah Zara*.[28]

One major structural difference between the two religions is the fact that Judaism remained a *religio licita* throughout our period, while Christianity was still, of course, a *religio illicita*. It is certainly quite difficult, if not impossible, to expect a religious group which does not enjoy even a modicum of toleration to grant its persecutors any kind of recognition. Another factor emphasizing the different Jewish and Christian attitudes is the fact that in the late second century, the Jews had, for all practical purposes, abandoned serious attempts at proselytism, while proselytism was the Christians' very *raison d'être*. As has often been recognized, the violence of the clash with the pagan world was partly due to the centrality of mission in the Christian mind.[29]

A third difference between Jewish and Christian self-perception, crucial from our perspective, lies in the boundaries of collective identity. The Mishnaic tractate *Avodah Zara* was written in Palestine when Roman occupation was bitterly felt. The rabbis could not avoid acknowledging the existence of various cults and religions on the ancestral soil.[30] But it was also clear to them that the land of Israel belonged to God, and that he had given it to his people, Israel. The Romans, thus, were unambiguously considered to be invaders. They and their cult had to be avoided, but ways could be found which prevented a pollution through contact with idolatry without paralysing necessary contact (mainly in the field of commerce). In other words, Jews learned to live side by side with pagans. Such a limited interaction between the communities was not felt to endanger Jewish identity, because it had very clear ways of expressing itself, in language, territory, dress or food habits.

Such clear-cut patterns of self-definition were, of course, precluded for the Christians. It is the *Epistle to Diognetus*, perhaps, which formulated this lack of all objective criteria of Christian identity in the most meaningful way: Christians have neither a territory, nor a language, nor special dress nor food habits of their own. This strange people, without any of the usual identifying criteria of peoplehood, is like the heart in the body of nations.[31] It is precisely their complete territorial, linguistic and social osmosis with the pagan majorities (in Africa as elsewhere) which forced them into stricter rules of interaction with the pagans. One could say that Christian identity is formulated, in contrast to Jewish identity, *exclusively in religious*, and not in ethnic terms.

The combination of all these factors, it seems to me, goes a long way to explain why Tertullian's *De idololatria* seems to reflect in part a more radical rejection of interaction with pagans than does Mishnah *Avodah Zara*. The rather close similarities between the two treatises have often been emphasized. Claude Aziza, in particular, has argued for a Jewish influence on Tertullian's discourse on, and perception of, idolatry.[32] Although direct literary influences between the two texts are unlikely (Tertullian had no Hebrew), there is a distinct possibility that Tertullian was aware of the Jewish patterns of thought and behaviour towards idolatry.[33]

What is more important than the question of the sources, however, is the internal logic of the parallel discourses of the two treatises. Tertullian, who did not like the Jews, did not hesitate to say so, in strong language.[34] None the less, he has been accused by various patristic scholars of being 'too Jewish'. One may quote here, for instance, Hans von Campenhausen: '[Tertullian] ist in dem allen doch mehr ein Christ des Alten als des Neuen Testaments geblieben; er ist, theologisch geurteilt, beinahe ein Jude.'[35] One should go beyond the author's intention, which was obviously meant *in malam partem*, and enquire into the interesting parallels in Christian and Jewish attitudes towards idolatry. The narrow limits of religious tolerance, or rather the intolerance reflected in the writings of Tertullian, help us to understand better the intellectual and religious presuppositions which rendered possible, in the course of the fourth century, the progressive limitation of religious freedom and toleration.

Last, but not least, it should be pointed out that Christian intellectuals in the first centuries CE did not necessarily consider religious intolerance to be a vice. On the contrary, it could also be praised as a virtue, since it reflected a readiness to martyrdom, as Origen argues emphatically.[36] In this short chapter, I have sought to highlight a fundamental ambivalence, a double tradition within early Christian *psyche*: a demand for tolerance together with an acceptance of intolerance, its presuppositions and its consequences. This double tradition of two contradictory trends explains why a real conception of religious tolerance did not develop in late antique Christianity.

NOTES

1 *Apologeticus* 24.5 (132–3 LCL). On our problem, one can still refer with profit to T. R. Glover, *The Conflict of Religions in the Roman Empire*, London, 1909 and numerous later editions. For a recent bibliography, see, for instance, the entry on Tertullian in A. de Berardino (ed.), *Encyclopedia of the Early Church*, E.tr. New York, 1992.

2 On religious repression in the Roman Empire, see, for instance, A. Momigliano in M. Eliade (ed.), *Encyclopedia of Religion* 12, New York, 1987, 469–70, with bibliography. The classical work is of course W. H. C. Frend, *Martyrdom and Persecution in the Early Church*, Oxford, 1965.

3 Such principles the Stoics called *koinai ennoiai*. On the intellectual context of the Apologist movement, see for instance R. M. Grant, *Gods and the One God*, Philadelphia, 1986.

4 For a recent overview of the relationships of Christianity with the Roman authorities, see M. Sordi, *The Christians and the Roman Empire*, London, 1988; [the book was originally published in Italian in 1983].

5 See, for instance, R. MacMullen, *Christianizing the Roman Empire, A.D. 100–400*, New Haven and London, 1984, ch. 10: 'Conversion by Coercion'.

6 See G. Stroumsa, 'Le radicalisme religieux du christianisme ancien', in E. Patlagean and A. Le Boulluec (eds.), *Les retours aux écritures: fondamentalismes présents et passés*, Bibl. Ecole des Hautes Etudes, 99; Louvain and Paris, 1994, 357–82. E.tr. 'Early Christianity as Radical Religion: Context and Implications,' *IOS* 14 (1994), 173–93.

7 See J. North, 'The Development of Religious Pluralism', in J. Lieu, J. North and T. Rajak (eds.), *The Jews among Pagans and Christians in the Roman Empire*, London and New York, 1992, 174–93.

8 A. D. Nock, *Conversion*, Oxford, 1933.

9 This seems to be the case for the great interest devoted to the *Chaldean Oracles*, and also to some aspects of Julian's thought, and argued by G. Bowersock in his *Julian the Apostate*, Cambridge, Mass, 1978.

10 *Apol.* 24.5 (132–3 LCL).

11 *Apol.* 24.1 (130 LCL).

12 On the importance of this comparison, see E. Peterson's seminal essay, *Der Monotheismus als politisches Problem: ein Beitrag zur Geschichte der politischen Theologie im Imperium Romanum*, Leipzig, 1935, on which see A. Schindler (ed.), *Monotheismus als politisches Problem? Erik Petereson und die Kritik der politischen Theologie*, Gütersloh, 1978.

13 *De spectaculis* 2.9 (236 LCL). Cf. *De spect.* 4.4 on the cult of the dead among the pagans as equivalent to idolatry, since the dead are honoured like gods.

14 For many insights on monotheistic views of paganism, see a book written by two philosophers, M. Halbertal and A. Margalit, *Idolatry*, Cambridge, Mass., 1992, *passim*. For a more balanced historical overview, see, for instance, J.-C. Fredouille, 'Götzendienst', RAC 11 (1981), 828–95.

15 These are the dates considered most probable by the most recent editors of the *De idololatria*, J. H. Waszink and J. C. M. van Winden, p. 10.

16 *De idol.* 19.2.

17 On this, see J.-C. Fredouille, *Tertullien et la conversion de la culture antique*, Paris, 1972, ch. 6.

18 *De idol.* 3.1; cf. Rom. 1.

19 *De idol.* 4.

20 *De idol.* 18; see J. C. M. van Winden, 'Idolum and Idololatria in Tertullian', *VC* 36 (1982), 108–14; and C. A. Contreras, 'Christian Views of Paganism', *ANRW* 23.1, 974–1022, esp. 993; Cf. *De idol.* 4.2, 5.2, 15.6 for the relationships between Enoch, the fall of angels, and the origin of demons.

21 (126–7 LCL). One may note that the same assimilation of *dii* and *dae-mones* is found in Minucius Felix's *Octavius*.

22 *De idol.* 3.4

23 *De idol.* 1 and 2.

24 This point is emphasized by J.-M. Vermander, 'La polémique de Tertullien contre les dieux du paganisme', *RSR* 53 (1979), 111–23, esp. 116.

25 *Apol.* 25.14–17.

26 On these parallels, see Fredouille, 'Götzendienst', and esp. C. Aziza, *Tertullien et le Judaïsme*, Paris, 1977, 177ff. The *communis opinio* is that the Mishnah was redacted in the last decades of the second century. See brief discussion and references in G. Stroumsa, *Hidden Wisdom: Early Christian Thought and Esoteric Traditions*, SHR; Leiden, 1996, ch. 5.

27 See D. Novak, *The Image of the Non-Jew in Judaism: An Historical and Constructive Study of the Noahide Laws*, Toronto Studies in Theology, 14; New York, Toronto, 1983.

28 See further M. Halbertal's contribution to the present volume, ch. 9 above.

29 On this one can still refer to A. von Harnack, *Die Mission und Ausbreitung des Christentums in den ersten drei Jahrhunderten* (2nd ed, 1924), E.tr. *The Mission and Expansion of Christianity in the First Three Centuries*, London, 1908. On some implications of Christian proselytism, see G. G. Stroumsa, 'Philosophy of the Barbarians: On Early Christian Ethnological Representations,' in H. Cancik, H. Lichtenberger, P. Schäfer (eds.), *Geschichte–Tradition–Reflexion: Festschrift für Martin Hengel*, II Tübingen, 1996, 338–68.

30 For a survey of paganism in Roman Palestine, see D. Flusser, 'Paganism in Palestine', in S. Safrai and M. Stern (eds.), *The Jewish People in the First Century*, II, CRINT; Assen and Amsterdam, 1976, 1065–100. On rabbinic attitudes to pagan cults, see E. E. Urbach, 'The Laws of Idolatry in the Light of Historical and Archeological Facts in the Third Century', *Eretz Israel, Archeological and Geographical Studies* 5 (1958), 189–205 [Hebrew]. See further Y. Baer, 'Israel, the Christian Church, and the Roman Empire', *Scripta Hierosolymitana* 7 (1961), 79–149, esp. 88–95 (on Tertullian).

31 *Ep. Diognetus* 5–6.

32 See n. 26 above.

33 Against Aziza's opinion, see M. Turcan, ed. and transl., Tertullien, *Les spectacles*, SC 392; Paris, 1986, 51: 'Au lieu de parler d'emprunts, ne faut-il pas plutôt penser que Tertullien et les rabbins ont, chacun de leur côté, réagi aux excès dont ils étaient les témoins?' and T. D. Barnes, *Tertullian*, Oxford, 1985, 92, 'Any similarity which he displays in contemporary Judaism does not originate in direct derivation', or ibid., n. 10, 'The undeniable affinities between Tertullian and Judaism may be analogical, not genealogical.' For a clear link between

Tertullian and Jewish post-biblical literature, see W. Horbury, 'Tertullian and the Jews in the Light of *De Spectaculis* xxx. 5–6', *JTS* 23 (1972), 455–9.

34 See, for instance, beyond his *Adversus Judaeos*, a typical remark as in *De spectaculis* 30.1–7, on which see A. de Vogüé, *Histoire littéraire du mouvement monastique dans l'antiquité*, 1, Paris, 1991, 133.

35 H. von Campenhausen, *Lateinische Kirchenväter*, Stuttgart, 1983 [1960], 35–6. This is the last sentence of his chapter on Tertullian.

36 Origen, *C. Celsum* 7.64 (see H. Chadwick's translation (Cambridge, 1953, 448). On the willingness to die for the faith, see A. J. Droge and J. D. Tabor, *A Noble Death: Suicide and Martyrdom among Christians and Jews in Antiquity*, San Francisco, 1992.

BIBLIOGRAPHY

Tertullian, *Apology, De spectaculis*, transl. T. R. Glover, LCL; Cambridge, Mass., and London, 1978.

De idololatria ed. and transl., J. H. Waszink and J. C. M. van Winden, Suppl. to *VC* 1; Leiden, 1987.

CHAPTER 11

The threefold Christian anti-Judaism

François Blanchetière[1]

Whereas some writers, following the example of Gibbon, would view monotheism as a system which of itself generates intolerance, others would consider intolerance to be the very measure of faith. Monotheism cannot, in fact, be the cause of division between Jews and Christians since, as Tertullian points out, both groups share the same conception of the divine even though their manner of worship differs (*Apol.* 21.2–3). And yet, the question which is at the heart of this book is a real one: can there or should there be limits to tolerance between the two faiths? Indeed, are there already existing limits? The question can be expressed in other ways: how can the two faiths maintain their distinctiveness and coexist? And how can self-identity be preserved when, as several contributors to this volume suggest, intolerance is an indication of a feeling of uncertainty and 'a proof of weakness'? How can the transition be made from principle *de iure* to practice *de facto* when the distance from the law to the application of the law is so often a long way to travel? Is it a question of a majority–minority relationship? What justifications for intolerance can be offered, from both the Jewish and the Christian sides, if 'tolerance and acceptance of one's neighbour, especially if he is a monotheist, are fundamental religious principles of the Synagogue'[2] or if, as Y. Leibovitz has underlined, 'the Torah makes no provision for compelling by force'?[3] What is to be made of the interpretations given within the Christian tradition of the well-known *compelle intrare*, 'compel people to come in' (Luke 14:23), in order to justify religious coercion? Judaism has only once used force in all of its history, for the conversion of the Idumeans under John Hyrcanus, whereas it has been the victim of coercion on innumerable occasions. Can discrimination be founded on 'religious' grounds?

Within ancient polytheistic societies, *religio* belonged to the civil domain and fell under the jurisdiction of civil magistrates, *ius sacrum* being an integral part of *ius civile* (Sachot 1991). For the Greeks, it belonged to the habits and customs (νόμοι and νομαία) of each country (Rudhardt 1992). Judaism was a *religio* among others and inscriptions make mention of νόμος Ἐιουδαιῶν. Cicero, too, plainly speaks of 'suacuique civitati religio, nostra nobis' (*Pro Flacco* 28; Origen *C. Celsum* 5.25; *Symmaque Rel.* III.3). No one would want to contradict these facts (cf. Deut. 4:19–20). There are, however, 'theological' issues but these come within the province of philosophy. Tolerance and coexistence, in other words, are not really religious problems; strictly speaking, there is no *crimen* of atheism according to the etymological sense of the term, even if the complaint continues to be heard (Blanchetière 1985).

Furthermore, long-standing legislation allowed the Jews to 'live according to the laws of their Fathers', an expression which is found many times in Josephus.[4] According to the testimony of Tertullian, Judaism was a *religio certe licita* (*Apol.* 21.1), that is a particular religious system recognized by the authorities, these being successively the Persians, the Hellenistic sovereigns, and finally the Romans from the time of Caesar onwards. But what happened when Christianity appeared, and spread to the extent that by the end of the fourth century it had become the state religion of the Roman Empire? Was the situation the same in the *pars orientalis* and the *pars occidentalis*? And what happened when the Western Empire crumbled and the barbarian kingdoms took over power?

It is quite clearly a somewhat delicate enterprise to examine nearly two thousand years of relationships between Jews and Christians, when there has been so much conflict from the outset, such strong resentment and prejudice, all arising from the mutual misunderstanding which has been evident over the centuries. This contribution will obviously not be able to go into all the details of such a long and complicated history.

Any religious historian who examines the different notions of history applied within the Christian tradition will detect at least four of them, all reflecting different points of view concerning the history of the people of Israel and the Jews.

(i) *The providentialist theory* of *Heilsgeschichte*, that which underlies the system created by Dionysos the Small of reckoning the date from the birth of Jesus Christ, *anno Incarnationis* (Cullmann 1966), presents the Torah as a 'pedagogue' whose role is finished (Hanson 1988). It derives from one of the main ideas found in Paul's writings (Gal. 3:24; Rom. 7:7) and from the conception of the *praeparatio evangelica* which frequently appears in Christian works, especially in the more universalist outlook of Clement of Alexandria or Eusebius for example. It has continued to find expression over the centuries up to modern times, with some particularly interesting versions such as that of Heinrich Ewald who writes in his *Geschichte des Volkes Israel* (published in Göttingen, between 1843 and 1859): 'Above the grave which closed over the second great destruction of Jerusalem and Israel, there spread a deathly silence. From that time on, no real life would be possible again. The course of History had been defeated.'[5]

(ii) *The accomplishment theory* focuses on the ancient promises which are accomplished in the coming of Christ (Luke 24:25; Heb. 1:1 etc.). The veil of the Temple is torn (Luke 23:45; Matt. 27:51; Mark 15:38), 'it is finished'/*consummatum est*/τετέλεσται (John 19:30) or, as Augustine can proclaim, 'In Vetere Christus latet, in Novo Christus patet.' The role of the Jews was merely to receive and to pass on the Scriptures which belonged to them no longer since they did not know, indeed had never known, how to read and understand them. That is the position adopted by Justin (*Dialogue* 29.2), *Pseudo-Barnabas*, Melito of Sardis, and many others of the second-century Apologists, not to mention later authors.[6]

(iii) *The substitution theory* holds that since the *synagoga caeca* (2 Cor. 3:14–17), 'blind' and 'guilty of deicide' (Acts 2:23; 3:14-15), did not recognize the time of its visitation (Matt. 23:37–9; Luke 19:44), it lost its inheritance. This is the teaching of the parable of the sterile fig-tree (Luke 13:6–9) and even more so of the parable of the wicked tenants (Matt. 21:33–46; *Ps-Barnabas* 13; Hubaut 1976; Snodgrass 1983; Marcus 1997; Rokeah 1982). Jesus is the new Moses, the true prophet (Deut. 18:23ff.). The 'new covenant' has been ratified. The *Verus* Israel has replaced the *Vetus* Israel (Stroumsa 1992) and Lactantius can speak of the 'exheredatus populus', the disinherited people.

(iv) *Paul's teaching in Romans* remains to be considered (Rom. 9–11): God cannot repent of his gifts, Israel will be converted. 'All Israel will be saved' (11:5, 26). How should Christians behave towards the Jews in the meantime? It is true that they have sinned. They did not know how to read their Scriptures (Justin, *Dialogue* 29.2). They remain, nevertheless, 'Testes Veritatis nostrae', to cite

Augustine again. Under the influence of Satan, the Adversary (John 8:44), they seek to harm and to oppose Christian believers (John 15:20). They persecute them (John 15:16). In their synagogues, they curse them (Horbury 1997). Similarly, they put Christians out of the synagogues (John 9:22; 12:42).[7] However much the accounts of persecution may be exaggerations, as M. Simon has shown with respect to the martyrdom of Polycarp,[8] or as J. Parkes (1934) has shown with broader reference, it is a fact that the writers of early Christian literature, notably Justin, present the Jews as persecutors (Lieu 1997). These writers are to be regarded with a high degree of caution.

They must not, however, be exterminated nor must their rights be undermined, rights which were recognized by the official legislation of *Codex Theodosianus* XVI.8.1 in 321 CE[9] and XVI.8.9, 'Iudaeorum sectam nulla lege prohitam satis constat' in 393 CE.[10] This position was ratified by Gregory the Great in his letter to Victor of Palermo in 598 CE (MGH 11, 27) and reiterated by Pope Innocent III in his *Constitutio Pro Iudaeis* on 15 September 1199 (Grayzel 1966). The security of the juridical status of the Jews was thus ensured over a long period of time.

The teaching of Paul is, therefore, in direct opposition to the idea put forward by Leibovitz who affirms that, from its beginnings, Christianity had the goal of wiping out Judaism.[11] Paul's position is in antithesis to that of Leibovitz for two reasons: firstly, Paul says that the grafted branches cannot be cut off from the tree on to which they have been grafted, nor indirectly from its roots; secondly, Paul teaches that the eventual return or conversion of Israel, that is its submission to divine will, is a condition of the Parousia.

It nevertheless must be said that this eschatological perspective which views the safe keeping of Israel as a condition for the Last Days became less distinct with the passing of time. John Chrysostom, in his commentary on the epistle to the Romans in 392 CE, is aware of Paul's teaching, although that does not prevent him from employing insults (*Epist. ad Rom.* 19, *PG* 60.585–96; Wilken 1983). The eschatological hope in the salvation of Israel may not have disappeared completely but today it is no longer a central preoccupation in Christian teaching. It has perhaps been affected by the same decline of interest as affected the messianic hope.

Who today preaches on the article of the *credo*: 'He will come to judge the living and the dead'?

Whatever the present situation, it is good to examine afresh the earliest sources of Christian anti-Judaism, from the beginning up to the time of Theodosius the Great, and thereby seek to determine the reasons not only for anti-Judaic behaviour but, at a deeper level, the thinking which lies behind it, what some would call 'anti-Judaic theology'.

I. THE MAIN STAGES IN THE SPLIT

It is useful to begin by tracing the main stages of the split which developed in the course of the first centuries of the Common Era between the Jewish world, the cradle of Christianity, and the Christian movement itself.

The first signs of a split, indeed the first real breaks, appeared during the lifetime of Jesus, although in this respect the New Testament texts are to be treated with some caution in so far as they may well reflect to a large extent a situation and mind-set which belong to a time much later than that of the Teacher of Nazareth. This is especially true as regards the 'trial' and the death of Jesus, responsibility for which lay not with 'the Jewish people' or 'the Jews', to use terms from the Fourth Gospel, but almost certainly entirely with the Temple authorities referred to either as 'the leaders of the people' or as the Sadducees.

The Acts of the Apostles, and indirectly the Gospels, present a particularly condensed account of the early years of the Christian movement, which gives the impression that the first believers lived in fear of 'the Jews' (John 7:13; 9:22; 12:42; 20:19, 26), whereas elsewhere it is said that they continued faithfully to attend the Temple (Acts 2:46). When Acts speaks of 'persecutions' taking place in the early years of Christianity, it attributes them either to the leaders of the Temple, or else to Herod Agrippa I, who had one of Zebedee's sons, James the brother of John, put to death and Peter arrested (Acts 12:1).

Once Peter had been freed from the prison and had left Jerusalem 'to go to another place' (Acts 12:17), it was James the Just, one of the 'pillars of the Church' (Gal. 2:9), who, by virtue of his being 'the brother of the Lord', became the head of the community of the Nazarenes (Eusebius *H.E.* 2.2.2–4; Blanchetière and Pritz 1994a; de Boer 1997). This was a community which apparently was only one of many which existed both in Judaea and in Galilee. According to the controversial work the *Memoirs* of Hegesippus, partially preserved by Eusebius of Caesarea, James had acquired a reputation for asceticism and holiness among large sections of the population (Eusebius *H.E.* 2.23.4). It is also Hegesippus who says that the death of James was brought about by the intrigues of the scribes and the Pharisees. Flavius Josephus, on the other hand, states that the Temple authorities profited from the lack of a procurator (Festus had died while in power in 65 CE and Albinus had not yet taken up the post) to condemn and execute James in an expeditious manner. This act supposedly stirred up the anger of the people as well as of the Pharisees who managed to have the high priest deposed and replaced (*Ant.* 20.197–9; Nodet 1985).

There followed the dark days of the first main revolt against Rome. I have undertaken elsewhere a study based on the work of Ray Pritz (1988) which examines the question of the migration of the 'Nazarenes' to Pella. My conclusion was that the event was a historical one and took place in the following way: already in the year 66 CE, but definitely by 68 CE when the siege of Jerusalem with all its attendant atrocities began, the Nazarenes began to flee from the town in fear of their lives, as did many other people according to the testimony of Josephus. Some who gave themselves up to the Romans were made to take up residence in the town of Pella where they had to set about recreating some kind of community. At the end of the fighting following the defeat at Masada in 72 CE, and once the situation had become somewhat safer towards, as it seems, the fourth year of Vespasian's reign, some people managed to return to the Holy City where they set up places of worship, one of them possibly being on Mount Zion (Blanchetière and Pritz 1994b). In no way, then, did the refusal of the Nazarenes to participate more fully in the revolt separate them from the rest of their brethren.

It is thus apparent that at least until 72 CE the first disciples of Jesus, whether Hebrew-speaking or, as is more likely, Aramaic-speaking, those whom I call the Nazarenes rather than Jewish Christians (Blanchetière and Pritz 1994b; Mimouni 1992), remained closely involved in the cultural, political and social life of their time, both in Judaea and, to an even greater extent, in Galilee.

They were one of the elements of the ποίκιλον, the mosaic of which contemporary Jewish society was composed, one voice among a multitude of voices. They appear not to have met with serious opposition, notwithstanding Peter's and John's brush with the socio-religious authorities, namely the Temple authorities otherwise referred to as the Sadducees (Acts 4:1–22; 5:17–41). The Greek-speaking disciples, on the other hand, those who early on became known as Christians, fared not so well. Stephen met his death by stoning and Saul/Paul, described as the 'leader of the sect of the Nazarenes' (Acts 24:5), came up against frequent opposition and was only spared in the end because, as a Roman citizen, he could appeal to Caesar. It should be noticed, however, that almost no hostility was shown by the Pharisees of whom some, beginning with Saul/Paul, converted to the new teaching. What is more, Gamaliel the Elder was quick to come to their defence (Acts 5:34–40).

After the destruction of the Temple and the quashing of the revolt, Palestinian Judaism emerged without any strength, disoriented and disjointed. It had lost its centre of reference. It was in this situation that a whole restructuring process was carried out, centred around such Pharisaic teachers as Rabbi Yohanan ben Zakkai, and based at centres like Yavneh and Lydda, and extending within a short time to centres in Galilee, Usha, Beth Shearim, Sepphoris and finally Tiberias. Out of this movement grew rabbinic Judaism which was essentially in line with the Pharisaic tradition. Judaism owed its survival and continuation to this development (Oppenheimer 1996). There is every reason to suppose that it is this period which constitutes the real *Sitz im Leben* of the polemical elements of the Synoptic Gospels, and especially of Matthew, which express hostility towards the Pharisees and the scribes, or more generally towards the traditions of 'the Elders'. In contrast, the rabbinic literature of this period makes scarcely any mention of either Jesus or his disciples (Oppenheimer 1996). This factor can be explained by a host of concurrent reasons, not least the interference of church censorship in the Middle Ages. It may well also be that the rabbis, preoccupied as they were by other concerns, had little time to waste on the Nazarenes who, after all, were a fairly harmless minority sect. It is also possible, according to D. Flusser, that the general label of *min*/heretic was used to designate those who, lacking in solidarity with the Jewish people,

had separated from them, in addition to designating heretics as
such (Flusser 1992). R. Bauckham would see the term as applying
to all those who did not conform to the standards of rabbinic Judaism, among whom were the Nazarenes who were thus considered
to be enemies of Israel and excluded from eschatological rewards
(Bauckham 1998).

It would appear that it was at this same time, during the last
quarter of the century, either at Pella or at Jerusalem (it is impossible to say which), that a split occurred between the Nazarenes
proper and the Ebionites. It was likewise at this time that a strong
anti-Pauline current developed, traces of which are most clearly
seen in the Pseudo-Clementine literature. Once more, it is noticeable that the Nazarenes remained close to, and at times in support
of, what survived of the Jewish nation.

The same cannot be said of the second Jewish revolt against
Rome in 132–5 CE for, according to Justin, 'Bar Kochba, the leader
of the revolt, subjected the Christians, and the Christians alone, to
appalling tortures if they did not deny and blaspheme Jesus Christ'
(Justin, 1 *Apology* 31.6). The events of the revolt, as well as its messianic character, are well known. It is an equally acknowledged
fact that although the leader, Bar Kochba, was regarded as the
Messiah by some such as Akiba, there was by no means universal
agreement. The revolt does not seem to have involved all the population of Judaea and even less of Galilee where many rabbis took
refuge. The Nazarenes refused, along with many others, to acknowledge Bar Kochba as the Messiah. This can be seen in the
Ethiopic writing of the *Apocalypse of Peter*, which a modern editor
attributes in part to Jewish Christians (Bauckham 1985, 1998). That
they were the only ones to be persecuted for the stubbornness of
their refusal, as Justin states, is difficult to verify.

Following the destruction of the last point of resistance at Betar
and the crushing of the revolt, the Jewish city of Jerusalem became
the pagan city of Aelia Capitolina to which Jews were categorically denied access except for once a year, and even then it was
not entirely free access (Justin *Dialogue* 16.2; 1 *Apology* 47)[12]. The
rule applied to all Jews and consequently to the Nazarene community. Proof of this is found in an account written by Ariston of
Pella and transmitted by Eusebius, stating that from the year 135
'the church of the town was also composed of Gentiles and the
first leader to be appointed after the bishops of the circumcision

was Mark' (Eusebius *H.E.* 4.6.4). He was, in other words, a Greek-speaker whereas all the previous leaders had been of 'Jewish origin' and the very first ones, relatives of Jesus (Eusebius *H.E.* 3.11; 4.5.1–4; 5.12). It seems that the Nazarenes at that time withdrew into Galilee, Gaulanitis and more generally into the Transjordan regions. The *Ecclesia ex circumcisione* shared the fate of the Jews and remained in the defeated camp, becoming more and more marginalized, whereas the *Ecclesia ex Gentibus* shared in the victory of the conquerors.

A testimony of crucial importance to the evolution of Jewish–Christian relations is Justin's *Dialogue with Trypho the Jew*, a dialogue supposed to have taken place in Ephesus at the outbreak of the second revolt by the Palestinian Jews in 132–5 CE (*Dialogue* 1.3; 9.3). It owes its importance to the character of its editor, Justin the 'Philosopher and Martyr' who was born of non-Jewish parents in Neapolis/Nablus in Palestine. The importance of his witness to the growing separation and eventual split between Christianity and Judaism, abundantly appealed to in this chapter, cannot be overemphasized.

While the first literature which can be properly called Christian was beginning to appear during the early decades of the second century, there were other works being produced outside Palestine which contained a mixture of apologetic writing *adversus paganos* or 'against the Greeks' and *adversus Judaeos*, testimony in itself to communication between Christians and Jews which was not necessarily always of an antagonistic nature.[13] The gap was, however, becoming wider and deeper. Evidence of this is found in the *Epistle of Pseudo-Barnabas*, commonly dated to 135 CE, which M. Simon regards as a witness 'to the split which had already occurred (between Judaism and Christianity). If, however, it marks in this respect the end of a period, the post-apostolic age, it also opens a new era of anti-judaic controversy: if Judaism ... has ceased to be a problem *in* the Church, it now creates a problem *for* the Church, from the outside.'[14] This is because the Nazarene movement now represented a minority fringe group in the East. As for the rabbinic literature, it contains little information about any contact or controversy which may have existed between Jews and Christians, except very indirectly (Oppenheimer 1996).

We will return presently to discuss the legislation of the first Christian emperors in the fourth century, as also the decisions relating to the fixing of the date of Easter taken by the Council of Nicaea in 325 CE when the offical, irreversible break between Christianity and Judaism was made.

The truth of the matter is that the break was never really complete in the Eastern provinces of the Empire, even though there, too, polemical attacks against the Jews are to be found in the writings of such people as Aphrahat or Ephraem the Syrian. Jewish–Christian communities, which Muhammad presumably came across in the course of his wanderings, continued to exist principally in the Transjordan regions and otherwise at the frontiers of the Byzantine and Sassanian Empires right up to the tenth century, as is demonstrated by the document published by Pines in 1968.

Furthermore, the early Christians used to go to the Temple. It seems very likely that for quite some time Christians continued to join in prayer in the synagogue (Horbury 1998), as is suggested by the *birkat ha-minim* and later still by John Chrysostom in his attacks on Judaizers. Interpersonal relationships were quite clearly maintained, otherwise there would be no sense in the canons formulated at the Council of Elvira in Baetica prohibiting marriage with Jews (can. 16), the blessing of fields by Jews (can. 49) or sharing a meal with Jews (can. 50).[15]

It is also known that 'dialogues' concerning the reading and the interpretation of Scripture were held both in the East and the West, the *Dialogue with Trypho* being the most developed example. As M. Simon has pointed out, 'the common denominator of all the anti-Jewish writings is a shared method of argumentation, *viz.* the appeal to Scripture which both parties in the debate recognize as representing divine revelation and as speaking with infallible authority'.[16] In many ways, it is a quarrel over the inheritance of a Testament, since the whole controversy hinges on the authenticity and understanding of what Jews call the Torah and Christians the Old Testament. Many Christian exegetes, starting with Origen and Jerome and continuing throughout the Middle Ages, refer to rabbinic writings for the elucidation of difficult or obscure passages.

2. THE CAUSES OF THE SPLIT

It is now time to turn to a consideration of the causes which may have brought about the Jewish–Christian split.

L. Askenazi is most probably correct when he says that 'the

break which separated Christianity from the Jewish people was a socio-political event much more than a religious one', that is, it was a cultural split rather than a doctrinal one (Askenazi 1993).

The Acts of the Apostles describes tensions within the early community of the Jewish disciples of Rabbi Jeshua ben Joseph of Nazareth, between the Hebrew/Aramaic-speakers on the one hand and the Greek-speakers on the other, supposedly over problems to do with table service. The real problem was the language difference. Different customs were followed with the Nazarenes, for example, practising *mitzvot* in the manner of the Jews, unlike the Hellenistic Christians who did not. Likewise, different interpretations were made of the Scriptures, the text of reference. The same *Weltanschauung* was not shared by the two groups.

The gap grew increasingly wide. Among the various movements which made up early Christianity, the 'Hebrews' gradually went from being in the majority to become a minority group on the fringe. This shift was due to the increasing number of conversions among the 'Hellenists' (a term which originally meant the Greek-speakers and which was soon to become synonymous with 'pagan' in Christian literature). This was especially true after the uprising of 66–70 CE and the destruction of Jerusalem but even more so after 135 CE and the law forbidding Jews, Christian or not, to live in Jerusalem. The two groups refused to have anything to do with each other and the issues which provoked the Antioch 'crisis', although apparently settled at the Jerusalem council (Acts 15), were, in fact, far from resolved. They resurfaced in Galatia, and even in Corinth. They were still causing problems in the second century, as seen in Justin's *Dialogue with Trypho* 47.1–4.[17] The same issues arose in opposition to Pauline teaching, for example in the Pseudo-Clementine writings. The number of both Hellenized Jews and converted Gentiles, known as Christians first in the Hellenistic and later in the Roman world, increased in Asia Minor, Egypt, Africa and Italy until they represented by far the majority of Christian believers. As is later depicted by the mosaic in the church of St Sabine in Rome, alongside the *Ecclesia ex circumcisione* and the Semitic-speaking communities who found themselves on the fringe in the East because of the political crises of the third century and the founding of the neo-Sassanian Empire, there developed the *Ecclesia ex Gentibus* (Blanchetière and Pritz 1994a; Taylor 1994).

The paradoxical situation in which the 'Christians' *ex circum-*

cisione found themselves is admirably described by Eusebius of Caesarea:

For in the first place any one might naturally want to know who we are that have come forward to write. Are we Greeks or Barbarians? Or what can there be intermediate to these? And what do we claim to be, not in regard to the name, because this is manifest to all, but in the manner and purpose of our life? For they would see that we agree neither with the opinions of the Greeks, nor with the customs of the Barbarians.

What then may the strangeness in us be, and what the new-fangled manner of our life? ...

But sons of the Hebrews also would find fault with us, that being strangers and aliens we misuse their books, which do not belong to us at all, and because in an impudent and shameless way, as they would say, we thrust ourselves in, and try violently to thrust out the true family and kindred from their own ancestral rights. (*Praep. Ev.* 1.2.1–2, 5)

For the Christians *ex Gentibus*, Jerusalem was no longer the centre (Chadwick 1959) and there was no longer the same need to retain the original Jewish points of reference, nor did these hold the same significance any more.

It is not without interest in this context to compare, for example, the Jewish and Christian hermeneutical principles in the second and third centuries, and likewise the Mishnaic structures with the early Christian theological formulations. Such a comparison brings to light the continuity, at the same time as the ever-increasing differences, in the cultural frames of reference. Put in another way, that means that in using the same foundation of the Scriptures, the two groups, the rabbis on the one hand and the Nazarenes/Christians on the other, differed in the hermeneutical principles or *middot* which they applied to their interpretation. In the rabbinic world, the outcome was the six divisions of the Mishnah of Rabbi Yehouda ha-Nassi, centred as they were on the sanctification of the Name and on service/*avodah*. In the Christian world, recourse was had to the traditional principles of interpretation of the Greek-Hellenistic culture, to the use of allegory in particular, leading to the early formulations of Christian theology and of the *credo*. Whereas the first group retained a more existential outlook – *emounah* – the second placed more emphasis on the credo, that is on the intellectual understanding of the contents of their faith.

The Rabbinic halaka is designed for people who belong firmly to history, not for those who have one foot on earth and the other in the *eschaton*.

When the Rabbis refined the regulations of the halaka for everyday life, they drew on much older legal traditions which had been preserved in an oral form and which, with some minor modifications, derived from Judaism before 70 AD.[18]

The essence of Judaism is to serve God by holding fast to the Torah and by carrying out its commandments (*mitzvot*). The aspirations of Christianity, however, are centred on the redemption of man and not on the service/*avodah* of God by man. The concept of redemption does not, in fact, exist in Judaism. The term used in Judaism for redemption, in Hebrew *geoulah*, can be translated as 'liberation', without any metaphysical meaning. In Christianity, though, redemption means 'salvation'.[19]

Failure to grasp the complexity of a process which lasted several centuries has led several modern-day scholars, particularly from Jewish circles, to persist in declaring categorically that Christianity has nothing to do with Judaism, that it is simply a deviation of Hellenism for which Paul of Tarsus was responsible. A further sample from Y. Leibovitz's writing will serve to illustrate the point: 'Christianity did not originate in Judaism, as some would claim . . . but in Hellenism.'[20] There are many today who think otherwise, both Jewish scholars such as G. Vermes, the author of *Jesus the Jew*, and non-Jewish scholars such as E. P. Sanders or J. H. Charlesworth, whose writings include *Jesus within Judaism*. The most noteworthy and authoritative scholar to advocate a position which is contrary to that typified by Leibovitz is Professor David Flusser, the author of *Jesus* and of 'Theses on the Emergence of Christianity from Judaism'. His are works which, compared with the trend described above, are less dogmatic and more in line with the results of the scientific enquiries of the last hundred years or so concerning the origins of Christianity in Jewish tradition and history at the beginning of our era. His Thesis no. 33 may be cited by way of an example:

The typological interpretation of verses of the Bible was one of the characteristics of Judaism at the time of Jesus. It was a heuristic method, the results of which have no binding effect in Judaism either on practice or on theology. Philo based his theological philosophy on an allegorical exegesis of the Pentateuch, while the Essenes, using a typological interpretation of the Prophets and the Psalms, found confirmation for the *historia sacra* of their sect. In Christianity, right from the time of the New Testament, certain verses of the Old Testament were interpreted according to the Jewish typological method, mainly to confirm points of Christology and church practice ... Later on, the conclusions which were drawn from this typological exegesis took on a major significance for Christian belief and theology. The results of such interpretations are often understood, in Christology as well as in ecclesiology, as representing concrete historical facts. (Flusser 1993–4)

By way of comparison, could it not be maintained that the reason why Philo of Alexandria was rejected by Jewish tradition for so long was not that his writings were used by Christians, but that they were too 'Hellenistic'? Was it not for a similar type of reason, namely a cultural one first and foremost, that as the West became less and less able to speak or read Greek in the third and fourth centuries a deep split occurred between East and West within the Christian world, leading to the divisive activity of Photius in the ninth century and ultimately to that of Michel Cérulaire in 1054?

3. THREEFOLD CHRISTIAN ANTI-JUDAISM

We need to move on to examine the threefold nature of Christian anti-Judaism, but it is first of all necessary to clarify the terminology which will be used. We speak about anti-Judaism or Judaeophobia, rather than anti-Semitism which is a modern concept with racialist connotations, and therefore anachronistic and inadequate (Ruggini 1968, 1980; Gager 1983).

As F. Lovsky has suggested, it is important to discern the influence of three types of Christian anti-Judaism which were no doubt superimposed on sociological or economic forms of anti-Judaism which are more difficult to identify (Lovsky 1955; Sevenster 1975; Meleze-Modrzejeski 1981; Gager 1983). The three types may or may not have all been present together at the same time, depending on the period and the historical context.

(1) Anti-Judaism in a religious context

Just as Tertullian asserts at the end of the second century that Christians are 'related to the Jewish religion' (*Apol.* 16.3) and that Christianity 'spread under the shadow of Judaism' (21.1), so Lactantius writing as a Christian in Africa in the fourth century speaks of the Jews 'whose successors and heirs we are' (*Inst. Div.* 5.22.14). He thereby underlines the continuity of life, just as with a tree which depends on its roots as Paul of Tarsus says, but he also expresses an irreversible split: a successor implies a predecessor who has completed his role, and an heir implies one who has died!

The Christian Apologists attempted to hold the two aspects in tension: that of continuity, which they maintained by virtue of their links with the economy of the Old Testament, in opposition to Marcion or the Gnostics, for example; and that of separation, which they advocated on the basis of the new teachings introduced by Christianity. During the course of the fourth century, it was this second aspect with the insistence on what was new and different in Christianity compared with Judaism which came to predominate. Thus the biography of Hilary of Poitiers has its hero congratulated for never having sat at table with a Jew. Then there is also the polemical writing against the 'Judaizers' by John of Antioch, later to be known as John Chrysostom (Simon 1936; Wilken 1983). Should we not, in addition, regard as suspect the tendency to assimilate the Arians to the Jews, or the persistence in repeating generation after generation the notion that the Jews were guilty of 'deicide' (Melito of Sardis, *Peri Pascha*, ὁ Θεὸς πεφόνευται, 736, cf. 579; Justin, *Dialogue* 16.2–4)?[21] The accusation of deicide is historically unfounded since Jesus was condemned by Pilate and was subjected to a Roman method of killing. It is, furthermore, theologically unsound since it was precisely because the Jews refused to acknowledge Jesus as the 'Son of God' that they rejected him, and in any case it is impossible that the Giver and Author of Life should actually die. As early as 315 CE, or rather 329 CE according to A. Linder, Constantine passed an edict forbidding any act of retaliation by the Jews against any one of their people who converted to Christianity, adding that 'if, on the other hand, someone should join their wicked sect (that of the Jews) and take part in their meetings, they will receive the same punishment (of death)' (*C. Th.* XVI.8.1).[22] In other words, proselytizing by Christians was allowed, but not by Jews, should they have ever had the intention of practising it (Will and Orrieux 1992).

J.-M. Poinsotte has put forward a collection of reasons to account for the insistence on the newness of Christianity, the main ones arising from the circumstances in which the Christians found themselves: the rapid growth in the number of Christians especially in the East; the raising of the cultural level among the new converts, resulting in an output of typically Christian thought and

literature; alongside that phenomenon, the existence among some
of the less well-educated Christians of a tendency to confuse the
Old Israel with the New, and even of attempts at Judaizing. Not
all relationships between Jewish and Christian neighbours were
necessarily characterized by conflict![23]

The decision taken by the Council of Nicaea no longer to follow the Jewish system of calculating the date of the Passover, and
thereby to fix the date of Easter at a different time, was a significant one in so far as it marked the final step in separating Christianity from Judaism. The text containing the decisions taken by
the Council of Nicaea is only available today in the form published by J. B. Pitra (Cantalamessa 1978 no. 53). According to this
version, all that the Council required was for the churches to bury
their differences and to celebrate their festivals on the same date, a
decision everyone was supposedly happy to accept.

There are other documents, however, which reveal a somewhat
different story. First, there is the synodal document addressed to the
churches of Egypt, Cyrenaica and Pentapolis (present-day Libya)
and which is preserved by Socrates.[24] It makes the announcement
that the Quartodeciman community in the East, which had been
continuing to celebrate Easter on the eve of 14 Nisan in accordance with Jewish practice, had decided instead to conform to the
practice of the majority.

More revealing still is the letter attributed to Constantine and
which is preserved by Eusebius in his *Vita Constantini* (*V.C.*), Book
III. Supposedly passing on the decisions of the Council, the Emperor first of all comments on the disagreements in the observance
of the festival: 'some afflicting themselves with fastings and aus-
terities, while others devoted their time to festive relaxation' (*V.C.*
III.5). After reaffirming the need for agreement among Christians
concerning the celebration, he pursues his argument further:

First of all, it appeared an unworthy thing that in the celebration of
this most holy feast we should follow the practice of the Jews, who have
impiously defiled their hands with enormous sin, and are, therefore, deservedly afflicted with blindness of soul. For we have it in our power, if
we abandon their custom, to prolong the due observance of this ordinance to future ages, by a truer order, which we have preserved from the
very day of the passion to the present time. Let us then have nothing in
common with the detestable Jewish crowd; for we have received from
our Saviour a different way ... Beloved brethren, let us with one consent
adopt this course, and withdraw ourselves from all participation in their

baseness ... Why then should we follow those who are confessedly in grievous error? Surely we shall never consent to keep this feast a second time in the same year ... it was needful that this matter should be rectified so that we might have nothing in common with that nation of parricides who slew their Lord ... it is most fitting that all should unite ... in avoiding all participation in the perjured conduct of the Jews. In fine ... it has been determined by the common judgement of all, that the most holy feast of Easter should be kept on one and the same day ... (*V.C.* III.18–19)

Each of the arguments of this letter illustrates in turn the profound shift in attitude towards Judaism taking place at a time when the *Ecclesia ex circumcisione* had become quite plainly a minority group.

The letter first of all stresses the importance of not following the Jewish method of calculating the date of Passover, forgetting that it was a method derived from instructions given in the Old Testament and that Jesus himself, according to the Synoptic Gospels at least, celebrated the Jewish Passover. Two reasons of unequal importance are advanced on the basis that the Jews are mistaken, a highly theological thesis. They are first of all mistaken because they are blind – this is the theme of the *synagoga caeca* (cf. 2 Cor. 3:14–15) and we know with what fate that has met. They are mistaken, secondly, because they wrongly fix the time of the astronomical equinox with the result that they celebrate Passover twice one year and not at all the next. This same argument is used by Epiphanius (*Pan.* 50.3), and is also found in one of the Pseudo-Chrysostom homilies from 387 CE.[25] The question of the astronomical calculation of the date of Passover is one which was later to become a key issue, but it cannot be dealt with in more detail here.

The letter further insists with equal vehemence on the importance of having no dealings with the Jews who 'defiled their hands with enormous sin' and who are 'parricides who slew their Lord', a theme which finds particular expression in Melito's *Peri Pascha* with the first ever explicit mention of 'deicide' – ὁ θεὸς πεφόνευται (*Peri Pascha* 735 cf. 579). The variations on this theme are familiar, especially as they appear in the context of the Easter celebrations and the Good Friday lesson from John's Gospel.

The final argument employed by Constantine (as also by other writers of the time, not least Eusebius) is an attempt to show that the practice of celebrating Easter on a Sunday goes back to the earliest days of the church and to Jesus himself; it is what he calls the 'legitimate course'. He provides nothing, however, by way of proof. He offers no justification which can be compared with that put forward by Polycrates. We are therefore entitled to raise certain questions. The celebration of Easter on the fourteenth day after the first full moon of spring, in accordance with the instructions laid down in Scripture and followed by the Jews, was certainly the original practice and that which was respected by an entire group of Christian communities in the East for some time. Their practice was quite in order since originally they were simply following ancestral customs even though they invested the celebration with a fuller meaning. The celebration of Sunday as κυριάχη/*dies Domini*, as a weekly celebration of the resurrection, is as old a practice but one established in all the Christian communities of both the West and the East, replacing the sabbath at a fairly early date (Rordorf 1972). When and why, and under the influence of which factor(s), did the West feel the need to commemorate the resurrection on one particular Sunday of the year? The problem is to know what meaning should be given to the instructions 'observe'/'do not observe' τηρεῖν/μὴ τηρεῖν. Various hypotheses have been suggested by modern commentators but there is no way of deciding between them. My own preference, admittedly a wholly subjective one, is to side with those who maintain that the practice of celebrating Easter on a Sunday was unknown in Rome for several decades. Let us not forget that during the first century CE, the so-called Jewish-Christian groups were well represented in Rome by Clement. What was their Easter custom? What was the practice of the Syrian groups living in the capital of the Empire in the second century? We know too little about them to be able to answer.

With the Council of Nicaea, the process of differentiation, and thus of institutional dissociation, was complete and could not be reversed, despite the continuation of the practice labelled 'heretical' but maintained by the Quartodecimans in the East for some centuries still to come.

(2) *Anti-Judaism in a social context*

Anti-Judaism manifested itself in the social sphere when Christian leaders, chiefly bishops, took advantage of their power to structure society in accordance with gospel principles, giving expression at the same time to the theocratic ideals characteristic of the Hellenistic monarchy. In a world where it was the *pax deorum* which ensured the prosperity and influence of the city, cohesion among the different groups depended on a religious basis. The city was a tolerant institution. In the Christian Empire, however, the religious pluralism which had been acknowledged *de iure* by Galerius' edict of 311 CE and confirmed by Constantine in Milan in 313 CE (Eusebius *H.E.* 10.5.4; Lactantius *De mortibus persecutorum* XLVIII) no longer existed *de facto*. From the time of the fourth, and especially the fifth, century onwards, the ruling powers, assisted or encouraged as the case may be by the ecclesiastical hierarchy, sought to minimize anything which had the effect of breaking up the unity or cohesion of the society, using force if necessary. It is in this context that are to be understood the measures taken on the one hand against heretics or catholics according to whether the Emperor was Arian or not, and on the other against polytheists or Jews. In a world which tends, like Ambrosius of Milan, to confuse *Romanitas* with *Christianitas*, the Jew becomes 'The Other' in a whole host of ways. By way of example, we can consider the way in which John Chrysostom, writing in 386 CE, draws one after another the following parallels: Jews/Anomeans or Arians; Jews/foreigners – barbarians – Persians – enemies; Jews/pagans. The following short passage illustrates the point:

If any Roman soldier serving overseas is caught favoring the barbarians and the Persians, not only is he in danger but so also is everyone who was aware of how this man felt and failed to make the fact known to the general. Since you are the army of Christ, be overly careful in searching to see if anyone favoring an alien faith has mingled among you, and make his presence known – not so that we may put him to death as those generals did, nor that we may punish him or take our vengeance upon him, but that we may free him from his error and ungodliness and make him entirely our own. If you are unwilling to do this, if you know of such a person but conceal him, be sure that both you and he will be subject to the same penalty. (*Adv. Iud.* 1.4)[26]

(3) *Anti-Judaism in an emotional context*

This is a third area in which fear of the Jews is apparent. How irritating for Christians, and even more so for their leaders, to watch those Jews persisting in their stubborn refusal to believe in

or yield to the 'proof' which was for ever being explained to them
from the Scriptures, and more especially from the prophets; those
Jews who bore the mark of circumcision like the mark of Cain
(Justin, *Dialogue* 16.2; Blanchetière 1973); those Jews whose blindness was denounced along with their rebellious spirit, their 'stiff-
necks', their constant unfaithfulness to God's will, and whose
punishment was their dispersion in different parts of the world, far
from Jerusalem where they could no longer live nor even visit
except for once a year to weep over the ruins of the Temple, an
enduring sign of their misfortune (Blanchetière 1980a).

To borrow a very apt comparison from L. Landau, the link between Christianity and Judaism is not that which exists between a
satellite and the shuttle which puts it into orbit, the relationship
described by the thesis of the *praeparatio evangelica* and its accomplishment. It is, rather, the more existential and vital link which
exists between a tree and its roots, as in Paul's comparison. If Judaism can be understood without any reference to Christianity,
Christianity for its part cannot be understood without reference to
Judaism (as Christians said in argument against Marcion and the
Gnostics), without the Bible which stands as a living memory and
not as *geniza*, as the archives and condensed history of the Jewish
people. Y. Leibovitz, who is well known for his strenuous argumentation, may be quoted in this respect:

The existence of Christianity is of no importance to Judaism. For Christianity, however, Judaism is an integral part of Christian thought. For
the essence of Judaism, the fact that Christianity exists – this extra-
ordinary phenomenon which was responsible for the creation of the
Western world – is a fact of total indifference. Within the universe of
Jewish thought, the fact of the existence of Christianity poses not the
least difficulty [(bearing in mind, of course, the discrimination and the
coercion, the Inquisition, the forced baptisms and expulsions ...) Leibovitz continues]. For Christianity, on the other hand, the fact of the existence of Judaism creates serious and difficult problems. There is a total
asymmetry. By the very nature of things, Jews cannot perceive themselves with reference to Christianity whereas Christians are obliged to
perceive themselves with reference to Judaism.[27]

Nevertheless, the appeal to Scripture and the fresh application
of the invective of the prophets against infidelity, the sin of Israel,

were not without their dangers. The jump was made only too easily from the time of Jesus to the contemporary situation of the preacher and his listeners, and then from the present-day Jew 'in flesh and blood'/*basar va dam* back again to the Jew of John's Gospel. The implications of these shifts are the greater in view of the importance of the Fourth Gospel in the readings of Holy Week. The early homilies, both Greek and Latin, are worth re-reading in their entirety, rather than selected extracts, to see how they function from this point of view. As an example may be mentioned the care taken by Eusebius to distinguish between the Hebrews, whom he claims as the ancestors of Christians, and the Jews, whom he reviles. There are many more examples of this kind. There would be a vast amount of painstaking work to be done in this area in so far as the liturgy, preaching and catechesis, with what J. Isaac has called their 'enseignement du mépris', 'teaching of contempt', were responsible for the creation of a whole system of thought and behaviour.

In spite of all that has been said above, however, and as I have sought to demonstrate by a careful analysis of the texts collected in *Codex Theodosianus* (Blanchetière 1983), there is no foundation for following Juster in speaking of a noticeable harshening of the legislation concerning Jews and Judaism under the early Christian emperors, even less for speaking of *privilegia odiosa*.[28] Once the Empire had been divided in 395 CE, on the other hand, and especially in the reign of Theodosius (Blanchetière 1980a; Pavan 1965–6), the juridical status of the Jews quickly deteriorated. This was more true in the *pars orientalis* than in the Western part of the Empire (Linder 1983) and most especially in the areas untouched by the influence of rabbinic Judaism (Lightstone 1986). It would appear, in fact, that what started as Christian intransigence and quickly developed into intolerance, based on an underlying structure of hermeneutical and theological reflection, only found expression in concrete terms when Christianity was in a position of strength and protected by the ruling parties.

As a final word, and in order to maintain a balanced view of the situation, it needs to be remembered that intolerance was shown not only at this time towards Jews but just as much if not more so towards 'Hellenes', in other words 'pagans', and equally with regard to heretics as shown by distinction XVI in *Codex Theodosianus*.

All of this should prompt us to exercise prudence and to take care to be accurate when speaking of Christian anti-Judaism in the first centuries of our era.

NOTES

1 Translation by Dr Jenny Heimerdinger.
2 Hayoun 1993, 38.
3 Leibovitz 1994, 50–1.
4 Schmidt 1994, 97ff.; Saulnier 1981, 161–95.
5 F. Schmidt 1992, 194; T. Schmidt 1994, 37–63.
6 Blanchetière 1973, 367; Stanton 1998.
7 Blanchetière 1973, 383–4.
8 Simon 1964, 150–2.
9 Linder 1983, 87–9.
10 Ibid., 137–8.
11 Leibovitz 1994, 50.
12 Blanchetière 1973, 377ff.
13 Ibid., 336ff.
14 Simon 1964, E.tr. p. 91, n. 6.
15 Ibid., 373–83.
16 Ibid., 177; Blanchetière 1973, 364ff.
17 Blanchetière 1994, 73ff; Stanton 1998.
18 Charlesworth 1991, 74.
19 Leibovitz 1994, 52.
20 Ibid., 49.
21 Blanchetière 1973, 379ff.
22 Linder 1983, 83–4.
23 Poinsotte 1981, 78ff.
24 H.E. 1.9; Hefele and Leclerc 1907, 460.
25 Nautin 1957, 116–17.
26 Meeks and Wilken 1978, 94.
27 Leibovitz 1994, 49–50.
28 Juster 1914, 230; Rabello 1980, 691.

BIBLIOGRAPHY

Primary sources

John Chrysostom, *Discourses Against Judaizing Christians* (*Adversus Iudaeos*), in *The Fathers of the Church*, vol. 68 The Catholic University of America Press, 1979.
Eusebius, *Life of Constantine the Great* (*Vita Constantini*), in Philip Schaff and Henry Wace (eds.), *A Select Library of Nicene and Post-Nicene Fathers of the Christian Church*, Grand Rapids, 1952, Vol. 1; *The Preparation for the Gospel*, ed. E. H. Gifford, Oxford, 1903.

Secondary sources

Askenazi, L., 1993, in *L'information juive*, Oct. 1993.

Bauckham, R., 1985, 'The Two Fig Tree Parables in the Apocalypse of Peter', *JBL* 104:269–87.

1998, 'Jews and Jewish Christians in the Land of Israel at the time of the Bar Kochba War, with special reference to the *Apocalypse of Peter*', in Stanton and Stroumsa 1998.

Blanchetière, F., 1973, 'Aux sources de l'anti-judaïsme chrétien', *RHPR* 53:353–98.

1980a, 'La législation anti-juive de Théodose II: C.Th. 16.8.18. (29.5.408)', *Klêma* 5:125–9.

1980b, 'Julien Philhellène, Philo-sémite, Anti-Chrétien: l'affaire du Temple de Jérusalem', *JJS* 31:61–81.

1983, 'L'évolution du statut des Juifs sous la dynastie constantinienne', in E. Frezouis (ed.), *Crise et redressement dans les provinces européennes de l'Empire (milieu du IIIe, milieu du IVe siècles ap. J.C.)* Actes des VIIe rencontres d'Histoire romaine de Strasbourg (déc. 1981), Contributions et travaux de l'Institut d'Histoire romaine, Strasbourg, 127–41.

1985, '*Privilegia odiosa* ou non? L'évolution de l'attitude officielle à l'endroit des juifs et du judaïsme (312–395)', *RSR* 59:222–49.

1994, 'La "secte des Nazaréens" ou les débuts du Christianisme', in F. Blanchetière and M. D. Herr (eds.), *Les origines juives du Christianisme*, Jerusalem and Paris, 65–91.

Blanchetière, F., and Pritz, R., 1994a, 'La migration des "nazaréens" à Pella', in F. Blanchetière and M. D. Herr (eds.), *Les origines juives du Christianisme*, Jerusalem and Paris, 93–110.

1994b, 'Des cités des dieux à la cité sécularisée', intervention à la Deuxième semaine de la recherche française en Israël, in F. Alvarez-Pereyre (ed.), *Le politique et le religieux*, Jerusalem and Paris.

Cantalamessa, R., 1967, *L'omelia 'in s.Pasqua' dello Pseudo-Ippolito di Roma. Ricerche sulla teologia dell'Asia minore nella secunda metà dell II secolo*, Milan.

Chadwick, H., 1959, 'The Circle and the Ellipse: Rival Concepts of Authority in the Early Church', reprinted in *History and Thought of the Early Church*, London, 1982.

Charlesworth, J. H., 1989, *Jesus within Judaism*, London.

1991, 'The Foreground of Christian Origins and the Commencement of Jesus Research', in *Jesus' Jewishness. Exploring the Place of Jesus in Early Judaism*, New York, 63–83.

Cullmann, O., 1966, *Christ et le temps*, Paris.

De Boer, M. C., 1998, 'The Nazoreans: Living at the Boundary of Judaism and Christianity', in Stanton and Stroumsa 1998.

Evans, C. A., and Hagner, D. A. (eds.), 1993, *Anti-semitism and Early Christianity. Issues of Polemics and Faith*, Minneapolis.

Flusser D., 1969, *Jesus*, E.tr. New York.

    1992, '*Miqzat Maasei haTorah ve birkat-ha-minim*/Some of the Precepts of the Torah from Qumran (4QMMT) and the Benediction against the Heretics', *Tarbitz* 61:333–74 (Hebrew).

    1993, 'Thèses sur l'émergence du Christianisme', *Les Nouveaux Cahiers* no. 115, 60–5. French translation of 'Theses on the Emergence of Christianity from Judaism', *Immanuel* 5 (1975), 74–84.

Gager, J., 1983, *The Origins of Antisemitism? Attitudes toward Judaism in Pagan and Christian Antiquity*, Oxford.

Grayzel, L S., 1966, *The Church and the Jews in the XIIIth Century*, New York, 92–5.

Hanson, A. T., 1988, 'The Origin of Paul's Use of *paidadōgos* for the Law', *JSNT* 34:71–6.

Hayoun, M. R., 1993, 'Du Talmud à la Kabbale', in *Les Nouveaux Cahiers* no. 113, *Les Juifs et Jésus. Y-a-t-il une pensée juive du christianisme?*

Hefele, Ch. J., and Leclerc, H., 1907, *Histoire des conciles*, vol. 1, Paris.

Horbury, W., 1982, 'The Benediction of the Minim and the Jewish Christian Controversy' *JTS* n.s. 33:19–61.

    1998, 'The Church Fathers on Synagogue Prayers and Imprecations', in Stanton and Stroumsa 1998.

Hubaut, M., 1976, *La parabole des vignerons homicides*, Cahiers de la *Revue Biblique* no. 16, Paris.

Israel, G., 1993–4, 'La face cachée de l'accord Vatican/Israël', in *Les Nouveaux Cahiers* no. 115, 3–6.

Juster, J., 1914, *Les Juifs dans l'Empire romain. Leur condition juridique, économique et sociale*, Paris.

Leibovitz, Y., 1994, 'Entretien avec le Père M. Dubois in *Haaretz* du 17 avril 1992', in *La mauvaise conscience d'Israël. Entretiens avec Joseph*, Paris, 50–1.

Lieu, J., 1998, 'Accusations of Jewish Persecution in Early Christian Sources', in Stanton and Stroumsa 1998.

Lightstone, J., 1986, 'Christian Anti-Judaism in its Judaic Mirror: The Judaic Context of Early Christianity Revised', in S. G. Wilson (ed.), *Anti-Judaism in Early Christianity*, Vol. 11, Waterloo (Ontario), 103–32.

Linder, A., 1983, *HaYehoudim veHaYahadouth be Houqei haKeisarouth haRomith*, Jerusalem; *The Jews in Roman Imperial Legislation, Edited with introduction, translations and Commentary*, E.tr. Jerusalem, 1987.

Lovsky, F., 1955, *Antisémitisme et Mystère d'Israël*, Paris.

Marcus, J., 1998, 'The Intertextual Polemic of the Markan Vineyard Parable', in Stanton and Stroumsa 1998.

Meeks, W. A., and Wilken, R. L., 1978, *Jews and Christians in Antioch in the first Four Centuries of the Common Era*, Missoula.

Meleze-Modrzejewski, J., 1981, 'Sur l'antisémitisme païen', in M. Olender (ed.), *Pour L. Poliakov. Le racisme, mythes et sciences*, Brussels, 411–39.

Mimouni, S. C., 1992, 'Pour une définition nouvelle du Judéo-Christianisme ancien', *NTS* 38:161–86.

Nautin, P., 1957, *Homélies pascales III*, Une homélie anatolienne sur la date de Pâques en 387, SC 48, Paris.

Nodet, E., 1985, 'Jésus et Jean-Baptiste chez Josèphe', *RB* 92:321–48, 497–524.

Oppenheimer, A., 1996, 'L'élaboration de la *halacha* après la destruction du second Temple', *Annales E.S.C.*

Parkes, J., 1934, *The Conflict of the Church and the Synagogue. A Study in the Origins of Antisemitism*, New York.

Pavan, M., 1965–6, 'I Cristiani e il mondo ebraico nell'età di Teodosio il Grande', *Annali della Facolta di Lettere e Filosofia (Perughi)* 3:367–530.

Pines, Sh., 1968, *The Jewish Christians of the Early Centuries of Christianity according to a New Source*, Proceedings of the Israel Academy of Sciences and Humanities 2/13:237–310, Jerusalem.

Poinsotte, J.-M., 1981, 'Le juif dans la pensée chrétienne à l'époque constantinienne: l'obsession de la différenciation', *Annales du Centre d'études supérieures et de recherches sur les relations ethniques et le racisme européen*, 4:77–88.

Pritz, R., 1988, *Nazarene Jewish Christianity*, Jerusalem.

Rabello, A. M., 1980, 'The Legal Conditions of the Jews in the Roman Empire' in *ANRW* II 13:662–762.

Rokeah, D., 1982, *Jews, Pagans and Christians in Conflict*, Jerusalem.

Rordorf, W., 1972, *Sabbat et dimanche dans l'Eglise ancienne*, Neuchâtel.

Rudhardt, J., 1992, 'De l'attitude des Grecs à l'égard des religions étrangères', *RHR* 209:219–38.

Ruggini, L. C, 1968, 'Pregiudizi razziali, ostilita politica e culturale, intoleranza religioza nell'impero romano', *Athenaeum* 46:139–52.

—— 1980, 'Pagani, Ebrei e Cristiani: Odio sociologico e odio teologico nel Mondo Antico', in *Gli Ebrei nell'Alto Medioevo* (30 marzo–5 aprile 1978), Settimane di Studio del Centro Italiano di Studi sull'Alto Medioevo XXVI T. l 14–117, Spoleto.

Sachot, M., 1991, 'Religio/superstitio, Historique d'une subversion et d'un retournement', *RHR* 208:355–94.

Saulnier, Ch., 1981, 'Lois romaines sur les Juifs selon Flavius Josèphe', *RB* 88:161–95.

—— 1985, 'Rome et la Bible', in *Dictionnaire de la Bible Supplément* col. 886–95.

Schmidt, F., 1992, 'La coupure 70/135 ou la fin de la période du Second Temple dans les Histoires universelles du Judaïsme aux XVIIIe et XIXe siècles' in C. Grell and F. Laplanque (eds.), *La république des Lettres et l'Histoire du Judaïsme antique XVIe–XVIIIe siècles*, Paris, 185–201.

Schmidt, F., 1994, *La pensée du Temple. De Jérusalem à Qoumrân*, Paris.

Sevenster, J. N., 1975, *The Roots of Pagan Antisemitism in the Ancient World*, SNT 41.

Simon, M., 1936, 'La polémique anti-juive de Saint Jean Chrysostôme et le mouvement judaïsant d'Antioche', in *Mélanges F. Cumont*, Brussels, 403–21.

1964, *Verus Israel. Étude sur les relations entre Chrétiens et Juifs dans l'Empire romain (135–425)*, Paris. E.tr. *Verus Israel. A Study of Relations between Christians and Jews in the Roman Empire (AD 135–425)*, Oxford, 2nd edn, 1986.

Snodgrass, K., 1983, *The Parable of the Wicked Tenants*, Tübingen.

Stanton, G., 1998, 'Justin Martyr's *Dialogue with Trypho*: Group Boundaries, "Proselytes" and "God-Fearers"', in Stanton and Stroumsa 1998.

Stanton, G., and Stroumsa, G. (eds.), 1998, *Tolerance and its Limits in Early Judaism and Christianity*, Cambridge.

Stroumsa, G. G., 1992, '"Verus Israël". Les juifs dans la littérature hiérosolymitaine d'époque byzantine', in G. G. Stroumsa *Savoir et salut*, Paris, 111–23.

Taylor, J., 1994, 'Why Were the Disciples First Called "Christians" at Antioch? (Acts 11, 26)', *RB* 101:75–94.

Thornton, T. C. G., 1987, 'Christian Understanding of the Birkat-ha-Minim in the Eastern Roman Empire', *JTS* n.s. 38:419–31.

Wilken, R. L., 1983, *John Chrysostom and the Jews. Rhetoric and Reality in the Late IVth Century*, Berkeley.

Will, E., and Orrieux, Cl., 1992, '*Prosélytisme juif'? Histoire d'une erreur*, Paris, RB 100 (1993), 599–602.

CHAPTER 12

The intertextual polemic of the Markan vineyard parable

Joel Marcus

A discussion of the anti-Jewish polemic of the Gospel of Mark might profitably begin with Mark 12:9: 'What will the lord of the vineyard do? He will come and destroy the tenants, and give the vineyard to others.'[1] This verse is an important key to Mark's intention, since it may very well be his own addition to the Parable of the Vineyard.[2] There is no parallel to it in the *Gospel of Thomas* logion 65.[3] It coheres with the Markan emphasis on Jesus' concern for Gentiles or their positive reaction to him,[4] and with the theme of destruction which pervades this section of Mark (11:18; 12:12; 13:1–2).[5] The combination of the verbs δίδωμι and ἀπόλλυμι, moreover, recalls the redactional verse 3:6.[6]

The redactional verse 12:9, and the parable of which it is now a part (12:1–9), use Old Testament imagery drawn from Isaiah 5:1–7, where Israel is spoken of as the Lord's vineyard and threatened with devastation by a foreign power as a punishment for its injustice and violence. Besides the similarity in overall theme between the two passages, the language of Mark 12:1–2 closely echoes that of Isaiah 5:1–2 LXX, where eight of the same Greek words are used to describe the planting and protection of the vineyard.[7] The rhetorical question in Mark 12:9, moreover ('What will the lord of the vineyard do?'), is similar in form to the rhetorical questions in Isaiah 5:4 and in vocabulary and force to the statement in Isaiah 5:5: 'Now I will tell you what I will do to my vineyard.' Furthermore, the Markan context makes it clear that Mark is using the vineyard parable as a symbol for the fate of Israel, an equation that is explicit in Isaiah 5:7.

THE IDENTITY OF THE TENANTS AND THE 'OTHERS'

In order to understand this Markan symbolism better, it is necessary to decode the parable's allegory.[8] Who are the tenant farmers

who will be destroyed and lose the vineyard, and who are the
'others' to whom the owner will transfer it?

Not all the evidence points in the same direction. Some of it
suggests that the tenants are the Jewish leaders rather than the
people as a whole. According to 11:27, for example, Jesus is ad-
dressing the scribes and elders in this section of the Gospel, so one
might be inclined to identify the tenant farmers with them. This
identification is supported by the transition to 12:10, where the
violent tenants become the builders who reject the stone; 'builders',
however, is a common rabbinic image for *scribes*, who build Jerusalem or the Torah by applying God's original Sinaitic revelation
to contemporary problems (see e.g. *Midr. Cant.* 1.5).[9] Mark 12:12
might also be thought to link the tenants with the leaders rather
than with the people as a whole, since it contrasts the negative reaction of the leaders with the positive reaction of the crowd.

This identification is also supported by intertextual evidence
from Isaiah. A couple of chapters before the passage that underlies the Markan parable, the Lord enters into judgement with the
elders and rulers of the people for devouring the *vineyard* (Isa. 3:14).
There is therefore a scriptural linkage between the destruction
of the Isaianic vineyard and a judgement on the elders of Israel.[10]
There are some strong arguments, therefore, for identifying the
Markan tenants with the Jewish leaders (scribes and elders).

But there are also indicators that Mark understands the violent
tenant farmers more broadly. These indicators have to do with the
Markan context, the general attitude of the early church, and intertextual biblical considerations.

The strongest evidence for a broader interpretation of the tenants comes from the parable itself, seen in its probable historical
context. As we shall see in a moment, a strong case can be made
for the view that the occasion for the composition of Mark's
Gospel is the great Jewish revolt against the Romans in 66–74 CE,
and in a setting strongly stamped by the war it would be hard not
to see Mark 12:9 as a reference to the catastrophic end of the revolt, when not only the Jewish leadership but also the people as a
whole was decimated. Similarly, the transfer of the vineyard to
'others' corresponds to the predominantly Gentile church's consciousness of itself as the new Israel,[11] a consciousness which was
no doubt strengthened by the end of Jewish sovereignty in Eretz
Israel.[12]

If the 'others' to whom the vineyard is transferred, however, are the church of the Gentiles, then the tenants from whom it is transferred must be a similarly broad group: the Jewish people, not just its leaders. This broader interpretation of the tenants and the 'others' corresponds to the dominant attitude in early Christian sources; as Charles Carlston puts it, 'In general ... it is hardly the early Christian belief that the people had only to change their leaders to become once again God's people ...'[13] And this is certainly how Matthew takes Mark 12:9, as is shown by his famous addition to his Markan source: 'Therefore I tell you, the kingdom of God will be taken away from you and given to a nation (ἔθνει) producing the fruits of it' (Matt. 21:43).

Passages elsewhere in Mark's Gospel also support the broad interpretation of the tenants. In 15:11–15, for example, the crowd joins up with the Jewish leadership in condemning Jesus, thus implicitly shouldering part of the responsibility for his death, which is what the tenants accomplish in 12:8. While it is true, therefore, that 12:12 suggests a division between the leaders and the crowd in their reactions to Jesus, by the end of the Gospel this division seems to have disappeared.

Intertextual Old Testament considerations also point towards an identification of the tenants with the people rather than just with its leaders. Verses 2–5 of our parable, for example, seem to reflect the Old Testament theme of the rejection of the prophets, and almost all the New Testament passages that deal with this theme, as well as about half of the Old Testament passages, put the blame for this rejection on the people as a whole.[14] More importantly, in Isaiah 5, the passage which lies most directly in the background to Mark 12:1–9, the vineyard is not simply the leadership of Israel but 'the inhabitants of Jerusalem', 'the men of Judah' and 'the house of Israel' (Isa. 5:3, 7) – i.e. Israel as a whole. Both the general theme of prophetic rejection and the particular background in Isaiah 5, then, point towards the Markan tenants being the people as a whole.

Mark 12:9, then, should be understood as a reference to the destruction of Jewish sovereignty in Eretz Israel and the transfer of the salvation-historical prerogatives of Israel to the church. While the scribes and elders are certainly included in the group symbolized by the tenant farmers from whom the vineyard is removed, that group is probably broader than the leadership. Mark, rather, understands it to be the Jewish people as a whole, or at least that large majority of the people that has rejected the gospel message. That may not be a conclusion one feels comfortable reaching, but I am afraid it is the conclusion to which the exegetical evidence drives us.

MARK VERSUS ISAIAH

The peculiar harshness of the attitude expressed by the Parable of the Vineyard in its Markan form becomes clear when we observe that Mark 12:1–9 is not just a straightforward repetition of the vineyard song in Isaiah 5; rather, the Markan passage distorts the Old Testament narrative at the same time that it appropriates it. In Mark, differently from Isaiah, it is not the vineyard but the tenants who are devastated, the vineyard itself being transferred, apparently intact, to 'others'. This alteration of the Isaian source seems to be deliberately designed to make the vineyard image more congenial to the theme of transference of salvation-historical privilege and less supportive of the idea of Israel's permanent election.

The adaptation is necessary because in some ways the Isaian image works against the transference theme. For in Isaiah 5, as we have already noted, the people of Israel are specifically identified as the Lord's vineyard. This vineyard has been lovingly created by God and belongs to him; even if he lays it waste in his wounded anger at its sin, ultimately he will not forsake it, as the reuse of vineyard imagery in Isaiah 27:2–9 shows. Here, in what seems to be a deliberate allusion to, and eschatological reversal of, the earlier vineyard song,[15] Israel has again become a pleasant vineyard guarded by God, blossoming, putting forth shoots and filling the whole world with her fruit. The strength of God's commitment to his vineyard, which was implicit even in the pain he suffered on its behalf in the earlier chapter, has now, in chapter 27, won the day; even her disobedience cannot cause him to cast her off, because he has chosen her.

This interpretation of Isaiah 5 as implying the eternal election of Israel is supported by later Jewish exegesis of the passage. For example, in the Dead Sea Scrolls, 4Q500, which is based on Isaiah 5, links the Lord's vineyard with the fruitfulness of the Garden of Eden,[16] and the 'shoot of an eternal planting' in 1QH 8 is reminiscent both of the Garden of Eden story and of Isaiah 5:1–7, as well as of Isaiah 27:6.[17]

Rabbinic allusions to Isaiah 5:1–7, similarly, tend to emphasize the 'graceful' aspect of the passage and to omit or downplay the aspect of judgement.[18] Most interest is centred on Isaiah 5:1, where God is called Israel's beloved, and on Isaiah 5:7.[19] In treatments of the latter verse attention is overwhelmingly concentrated on the positive message of the first half ('for the vineyard of the LORD of hosts is the house of Israel, and the men of Judah are his pleasant planting'), to the exclusion of the critical message of the second half ('and he looked for justice, but behold, bloodshed; for righteousness, but behold, a cry!').[20] *Pesiq. Rab. Kah.* 16.9 is perhaps typical when it cites Isaiah 5:7a to show that Israel is God's vineyard, then turns the Isaian context on its head by portraying Israel not as responsible for its own destruction but as the innocent victim of enemies (= pagans), who vandalize the vineyard out of hatred for its owner (= God).[21] Salvation-historical continuity is strongly emphasized; for several ancient Jewish exegetes, the message of Isaiah's vineyard parable is God's eternal love for 'the seed of Abraham'.[22]

This Jewish tendency to accentuate the positive (i.e. pro-Israel) aspects of Isaiah's vineyard parable could not be more strikingly different from Mark's usage of the passage. The Markan parable, by altering the Isaian imagery, distances Israel from the intimate covenantal relationship with God that is presupposed by Isaiah 5 and emphasized in Jewish exegesis of that passage. Now Israel is not the vineyard itself but only *tenants* who work the vineyard (12:1).[23] Their continued tenancy in the vineyard is therefore not assured but contingent on their satisfactory completion of the job for which they have been hired, namely the delivery to the owner of the vineyard's produce at the proper time (12:2). Unlike the fulsome description of Isaiah 5:1–4, which lingers lovingly over the tender care of the vineyard owner (= God) for his vineyard (= Israel), the description in Mark 12:1–2 is clipped and business-like: a man plants a vineyard and digs a winepress, protects his investment with fortifications, rents the vineyard out to tenants, and later sends a servant to collect the crop. Since the whole relationship is based on mutual contractual obligation rather than on loving nurture, the tenants' treacherous violence dissolves the compact and leads to the removal of the vineyard from their control as well as to their justified execution. These punishments, too, are described laconically and almost impassively, as if they were merely the natural penalty for the tenants' treachery; the description forms a marked contrast to the pathos attributed to the divine vineyard owner in Isaiah 5:1–7.[24] In Mark, the vineyard owner's passion is confined to his son, whom he loves (Mark 12:5); for the tenant farmers he seems to feel nothing.

Thus, instead of the intimate and unbreakable personal relationship between God and Israel that is implied by the vineyard image of Isaiah 5 and 27, we see in the vineyard image of Mark 12:1–9 an impersonal contractual relationship that is readily dissolved when Israel defaults on her side of the bargain. A sharper challenge to the notion of God's eternal covenant with Israel could scarcely be imagined; the Isaian image has been strained to the point that it threatens to become a parody of itself. What accounts for this difference in theme and tone between Isaiah 5 and Mark 12?

In his study of Jewish responses to catastrophe throughout history, *Against the Apocalypse*, David Roskies speaks of 'the survivor's tactic of inverting Scripture ... as a means of keeping faith'. This inversion, which Roskies calls a 'sacred parody', is triggered by the desire of the sufferer 'to imitate the sacrilege, to disrupt the received order of the text in the same way as the enemy, acting at the behest of God, [has] disrupted the order of the world'.[25] I believe that these remarks illuminate the distortion of Isaiah 5 in Mark. Scripture has been twisted in a way that imitates the disruption of the world by a shattering historical event; indeed, the distortion almost demands the hypothesis of a catastrophe to explain its existence, as the sight of a twisted piece of metal might demand the hypothesis of an explosion or a high-speed collision.

THE GREAT REVOLT AND THE MARKAN COMMUNITY

The catastrophe in view in the present instance is the event that most profoundly disrupted the order of the world for both Jews and Christians in the first century – the Great Revolt against the Romans. I have argued elsewhere[26] that this revolt provides the historical occasion for the composition of Mark's Gospel. It was a shattering event for Mark and his fellow Jewish Christians, not so much because of the destruction of the Temple and the crushing of the revolt but because, prior to those events, Jewish Christians were caught in a profound conflict of loyalty between their Jewish background, on the one hand, and their belief in Jesus' messiahship and their membership in the Christian community, on the other.

Mark and other Jewish Christians in Jerusalem would not have been able to enter fully into the revolt for at least two reasons. First, the revolt seems to have been catalysed by messianic expectation, as Josephus explicitly says (*War* 6.313), and it is probable that two of the revolutionary leaders, Judas the Galilean and Simon bar Giora, claimed to be the Messiah and/or were so proclaimed by their followers.[27] Such claims, however, would have clashed with the Christian conviction that Jesus was the Messiah, and the resultant conflict is probably reflected in Mark 13:6, 22, where Christians are warned against being led astray by false prophets and false Messiahs who proclaim, 'I am he!'[28] Second, it is probable that the theology of a substantial part of the revolutionary movement was not only anti-Roman but also anti-Gentile;[29] therefore a movement like early Christianity, which by 70 CE was strongly characterized by openness to Gentiles, would have run foul of it.

For these reasons, Mark and other Jewish Christians probably opposed the revolutionary movement from its inception, and this conflict must have reached the boiling-point after the Zealots occupied the Temple in Jerusalem in the winter of 67–8 CE and inaugurated a reign of terror (Josephus, *War* 4.151ff.) – an event to which Mark explicitly alludes twice in his Gospel (11:17; 13:14). Decimated by arrests, trials before revolutionary tribunals and martyrdoms, the survivors of Jerusalem Christianity fled from the city before the Romans closed the vice, and joined up with a group of Gentile Christians, perhaps in Pella.[30]

Reflections of this recent traumatic history can be seen in a passage such as 13:9–13. Here 'prophecies' are put into Jesus' mouth that seem to reflect the revolutionary reign of terror in a quite graphic way: Christians will be betrayed by family members, handed over to sanhedrins, beaten in synagogues, brought before rulers for judicial enquiry, even put to death. The catalyst for these persecutions will be the Christian outreach to non-Jews: 'The good news must first be preached to all the Gentiles' (13:10, my translation). In response to such breaking of revolutionary ranks, the animosity towards the Christians will become so general that their existence in the world can be characterized as being 'hated

by all' for the sake of Jesus' name. The situation, indeed, will
grow so dark that the Christians will be on the verge of losing
hope, desperately needing the reassurance that 'he who endures to
the end will be saved'.

THE MARKAN SOCIAL SITUATION AND
THE TRANSFORMATION OF ISAIAH 5:1–7

It is not difficult to see how the traumatic experiences described
in Mark 13:9–13, which reflect the revolutionary situation, could
have forced a new reading of the Isaian vineyard parable. Betrayed to revolutionary authorities by family members fervent in
their support for the revolution, even facing death for their opposition, the Christians may have found it easy to believe that there
was something rotten in the state of Israel and that the nation and
the family structure that supported it had lost their primacy as de-
finers of identity and had been supplanted by a new family and a
new nation (cf. 3:31–5; 10:29–30). Their 'kinsmen according to the
flesh', therefore, could not be identical with the Lord's vineyard.
Beaten in synagogues, arrested and even executed for the 'crime'
of believing in Jesus, the Christians may have found it easy to believe that a just God would not pass lightly over such palpably unjust treatment, but would reverse the trial process and judge their
enemies without mercy.[31] This judgement on the tenants, who had
permanently excluded them from the vineyard of national life,
would be their own permanent exclusion from the vineyard.

This hypothesis is supported both by linkages between the two
passages and by internal evidence found in the parable itself. The
linkages between the two passages include the fact that both Mark
12:1–9 and 13:9–13 speak of the beating of the servants of God
(12:3, 5; 13:9), of hateful treatment being meted out to them (12:4;
13:13) and of persecution unto death (12:5, 7, 8; 13:12), and both
have in view the Christian mission to Gentiles (12:9; 13:10). The
internal evidence is the striking parallel between the events described in Mark 12:8 and those described in 12:9:

v. 8 tenants kill son   tenants cast son out of vineyard
v. 9 owner destroys tenants   owner gives vineyard to others

In each case, the first event is a killing and the second is a separation from the vineyard. The judgement on the tenants in v. 9,

therefore, is a *lex talionis* for their action in v. 8; just as they have destroyed, so will they be destroyed, and just as they have thrown out of the vineyard, so will they be dispossessed of it.

In the parable's allegory, of course, v. 8 refers most directly to the killing of Jesus, who is God's 'beloved son' (cf. 1:11; 9:7).[32] But in early Christian theology, including Markan theology, the death of Jesus is closely associated with the martyrdom of Christians, who are called to take up their cross, follow Jesus and find their life by losing it for his sake (cf. Mark 8:34–5). It is easy, therefore, to see in Mark 12:8 not only a reference to Jesus' death but also, secondarily, a reference to the experience of Christian disciples, including Mark and some of the members of his community, who for Jesus' sake (13:9) and on account of his name (13:13) have suffered exclusion from Israel and even, in some cases, death. Indeed, the violence and social ostracism experienced by the Markan Christian community in 13:9–13 could well be encapsulated in the pregnant imagery of 12:8: 'killed ... and cast out of the vineyard'. The Markan readers of 12:8, therefore, would undoubtedly hear in this verse an echo of their own experience.

The judgement on Israel described in 12:9, therefore, could be described as a reversal of the Markan community's own recent experience of being cast out of the vineyard. Interestingly, both 12:8b ('and cast him out of the vineyard') and the prophecy of the tenants' destruction and replacement in the vineyard in 12:9 are absent from the *Gospel of Thomas* logion 65, suggesting that Mark himself may be responsible for 12:8b, as we have previously argued that he is responsible for 12:9. Whether or not this redactional conclusion is accepted, the parallelism of the two verses is itself strong evidence that the Markan community's experience of violent ejection from the Jewish community, which is mirrored in 12:8, has triggered its theology of Jewish expulsion from the vineyard, which is expressed in 12:9.

'THIS IS THE HEIR'

Once we have learned to read the Markan parable against the background of Christian difficulties during the Jewish War, another verse in the parable comes alive in a new way. In Mark 12:7, the wicked tenants clearly recognize the identity of the heir, who is the vineyard owner's beloved son and obviously corresponds to

Jesus, the Son of God. Οὗτός ἐστιν ὁ κληρονόμος, they say: 'This
is the heir.' Thus, like the demons elsewhere in Mark (1:24, 34;
3:11; 5:7), they unwittingly confess Jesus' identity even as they
oppose him. The tenants' subsequent statement is even more significant: 'Let us kill him', they say, 'and then the inheritance (ἡ
κληρονομία) will be ours' (Mark 12:7). Thus their murder of the
owner's son is motivated by their desire to usurp the κληρονομία,
the inheritance, that rightfully belongs to the son.

    In the parable, this inheritance, for which the tenants are willing
to kill, corresponds to the vineyard, which we have seen to be a
symbol of Israel. But anyone who speaks to a biblically literate
audience about Israel as an inheritance immediately evokes a
series of biblical texts in which the land is spoken of as a possession that the people inherit from Abraham (e.g. Num. 26:52–
6). This biblical tradition looks back to Genesis 15:7, where God
promises Abraham that he will give him the land of Canaan to inherit (κληρονομῆσαι).[33] The other side of the κληρονομία in this
fountainhead passage is the promise of descendants (Gen. 15:4–
5).[34] Both these aspects of the Abrahamic inheritance, land and
descendants, seem to be in view in the Markan vineyard parable,
since the passage, as we have seen, refers both to the Jewish loss of
the land and to the loss of the right to be called the true Israel, the
seed of Abraham. This detection of an Abrahamic nuance in the
Markan vineyard parable is supported by the Jewish texts that
speak of Abraham in exegeting the vineyard parable of Isaiah 5
(see above, n. 22). Such an association is natural given that both
Isaiah 5 and Mark 12 begin with the planting of the vineyard, and
this image would spontaneously evoke Abraham because of his
position as the founding father of Israel and the agricultural nuance of the stereotyped phrase 'seed of Abraham'.

    Thus, although the terms κληρονόμος and κληρονομία in Mark
12:7 are a basic part of the story, they also seem to have a figurative sense,[35] a large part of which is drawn from their association
with Abraham.[36] If this is so, however, it is likely that these terms,
like the usages of κληρονόμος, κληρονομία and κληρονομεῖν in
association with the Abraham story in Galatians 3 and Romans
4,[37] reflect debates between Christians and Jews (or Christian
Jews) about the identity of the inheritor of the promise to Abraham.[38] For in both Galatians and Romans the use of κληρονομία
seems to be a reaction to Jewish or Jewish-Christian claims that

only those who have joined the community of Israel through circumcision are Abraham's true heirs.

The usage of κληρονομία language in Mark 12, similarly, could very well be polemical, especially since we have discerned so many other polemical elements in our passage. It may, in other words, be a response to Jewish charges that Christians have usurped an inheritance that does not rightfully belong to them. Christians claim to be children of Abraham when many of them are not, claim to be Israel when they have discarded the vital element of ethnic continuity, claim to be the people of God when they have ignored or rejected God's law, which has held the Jewish community together for centuries and for which that community has suffered and died. From the Jewish point of view, then, it is the Christians who have usurped the inheritance. Our parable turns this charge on its head by making the Jews into rootless tenants who have no legitimate claim to the vineyard, the usurpers of the inheritance that rightfully belongs to Christ and through him to the Christians – as the usurpers themselves acknowledge.

This usurpation, which ends in the murder of the 'son', is answered in the Markan parable by the coming of 'the lord of the vineyard' to destroy the tenants and give the vineyard to others.[39] This description of the owner's 'coming', which as we have seen probably refers to the Roman destruction of Jerusalem and liquidation of the revolt, uses standard holy-war imagery ('coming', destruction). Again, however, it may represent a deliberate reversal of the Jewish revolutionary understanding, for the revolutionaries expected God to 'come' to their aid, destroy the pagan armies that surrounded them, and restore to them the inheritance, the κληρονομία, which for them meant first and foremost the land itself. Such a Markan reversal of the revolutionaries' holy-war theology, by the way, would be similar to that of Josephus, who polemically asserts that God fought on the Roman side rather than on the Jewish one.[40]

HERMENEUTICAL CONCLUSION

The Markan Parable of the Vineyard, then, is a thoroughly polemical rereading of the Isaian vineyard song which inverts the standard Jewish understanding of the scriptural passage under the impact of a chaotic social situation. To repeat Roskies' terminol-

ogy, Mark's distortion of Isaian imagery here is probably a reaction to the way in which the enemy, acting ultimately at the behest
of God,[41] has disrupted the world and forced a new reading of the
scriptural story. The story becomes a parody, because history has
become a parody of itself, or of what it was supposed to be; for
instead of accepting its Messiah, Israel has rejected him, followed
other Messiahs who have led her down the road to revolution, and
persecuted the followers of the true Messiah. In light of this unexpected turn of events, Mark teaches his community to see the
horrific sufferings of the Jewish people in the Great Revolt as
God's just judgement upon them. In the process he transforms the
Isaian vineyard from a symbol of God's suffering love for Israel, of
his commitment to the seed of Abraham, into a symbol of Israel's
lost inheritance and forfeited relationship with God.

The reuse of Isaiah 5 in Mark 12, then, illustrates how highly
charged the inheritance dispute between Jews and Christians became in the first century. We all know how messy inheritance disputes can get; tolerance is not usually to be expected from those
caught up in them. Such a realization may help us to gain some
understanding of, and distance from, the fierce language of Mark
12:1–9.

The continuing problem for the church, however, is that this
inheritance dispute has become enshrined in its sacred Scriptures.[42] By giving Mark scriptural status, the church has canonized
a denial of the Jews' salvation-historical role that grows out of a
very particular historical situation. This situation no longer corresponds to our own, in which, for the past sixteen centuries or so, it
has not usually been the case that it is Jews who are persecuting
Christians but the other way round. Yet our Christian Scripture
still retains passages, such as the present one, which reflect this
archaic situation and transform Israel from the tenderly nurtured
vineyard of Isaiah into a gang of hired workers who are without
roots in the vineyard. And as we know from Christian history, it is
an uncomfortably small step from a theology of salvation-historical
disinheritance to a concrete policy of eviction, or from the latter
to genocide. Nor are Christians the only ones who have skidded
down this slippery slope; all three monotheistic religions number
among their adherents people who espouse similar theologies of
salvation-historical disinheritance, or of the denial of salvation-
historical inheritance. These theologies have a basically similar

structure and effect, whether the disinheritors are from the German Christian movement, Islamic Jihad, or Meir Kahane's Kach.

But, as Lenin once said, what is to be done? How shall we deal with this theology of disinheritance, which in all three religions has roots in the canon of Scripture? In the present instance, at least, one way forward is perhaps the way backwards – backwards from Mark to Isaiah, which after all is also part of our canon. It may be helpful for us to follow the roots of Mark's rented and forfeited vineyard backwards into Isaiah's tenderly nurtured vineyard that has sprung Eden-like from God's hand, and to which he remains committed in spite of all the wild growth that has sprung up there and that grieves his heart – as he also remains committed to us in spite of all the wildness and murder that have sprung up in ours.[43]

NOTES

1 RSV altered; unless otherwise noted, all biblical quotations are from RSV.
2 Cf. Marcus, *The Way of the Lord*, 112–14, in which four stages in the development of Mark 12:1–12 are reconstructed.
3 Crossan (*In Parables*, 86–96, 111) argues compellingly that the original parable was similar to the *Gospel of Thomas* 65 and therefore lacked the vineyard owner's revenge; the parable, rather, approved of the bold action of the tenants who, like the unjust steward in Luke 16:1–7, recognized the critical moment in which they stood and acted decisively.
4 See e.g. 7:24–30; 8:1–9; 11:17; 13:10; 14:9; 15:39. Of these, at least 11:17; 13:10; and 14:9 are probably redactional; see Marcus, 'The Jewish War and the Sitz in Leben of Mark', 448–9 and n. 56. On the identity of the 'others' in 12:9 as Gentiles, see below.
5 See Scott, *Hear Then the Parable*, 238–41.
6 In the original draft of this paper, I cited Klauck (*Allegorie und Allegorese in synoptischen Gleichnistexten*, 288) for another argument against the originality of 12:9: the way in which the parable ends with a rhetorical question by Jesus, which Jesus himself then answers. While in Israel for the conference at which an abbreviated form of this paper was delivered, however, I noticed that our excellent tour guide, Yiska Harani, often adopted precisely this method of rhetorical question and self-supplied answer ('So why did they build the buildings this way? They built them this way because ... '). Perhaps more pertinently, the method has precedent in the OT prophets; see e.g. Isa. 37:23; Jer. 8:12.

7 See Taylor (*The Gospel According to Saint Mark*, 473), who lists ἀμπελών, φυτεύω, περιτίθημι, φραγμός, ὀρύσσω, ὑπολήνιον (Isaiah προλήν-ιον), οἰκοδομέω and πύργος. Although the tower may be symbolic of the Temple (see Evans, 'On the Vineyard Parables of Isaiah 5 and Mark 12'), the hedge and the winepress are of no independent significance in the story (cf. Carlston, *The Parables of the Triple Tradition*, 77); they therefore may be included mainly to evoke Isa. 5.

8 Under the influence of Jülicher, NT scholars claimed in the past that parables make only a single point. More recent scholarship has rightly emphasized that NT parables, like their OT predecessors, often have allegorical features; see e.g. Brown, 'Parable and Allegory Reconsidered'.

9 For other examples, see Derrett, 'The Stone That the Builders Rejected'.

10 *Exodus Rabbah* 5:12 links the two Isaian passages, though in a way that exculpates the elders. The LXX rendering of Isa. 3:14, 'elders of the people' (οἱ πρεσβύτεροι τοῦ λαοῦ), is echoed in the Matthean parallel to Mark 11:27 (Matt. 21:23) as well as elsewhere in Matthew's Gospel. See also Jer. 12:10, where the shepherds of Israel, i.e. her leaders, devour the vineyard.

11 See e.g. Gal. 6:16, Justin, *Dialogue* 11.5.

12 Cf. Justin (*Dialogue* 52), who links the fulfilment of Gen. 49:10 LXX ('a ruler shall not depart from Judah, or a leader from his thighs, until that which is laid up in store for him shall come; and he shall be the desire of nations') with the end of Jewish sovereignty in Eretz Israel and the coming of Gentiles to faith in Jesus.

13 Carlston, *Parables*, 43, citing Bonnard.

14 The people are blamed in 1 Kings 19:10, 14; 2 Chron. 24:21; Neh. 9:26; Jer. 2:30; 11:21; 26:8–11; 1 Thess. 2:15; Matt. 5:12; Luke 6:23; Luke 13:33–4//Matt. 23:37; Acts 7:52. The leaders are blamed in 1 Kings 18:4, 13; 22:27; 2 Chron. 16:10; Jer. 20:2; 26:20–3; 37:15–16; 38:4–6; Matt. 23:31, 34//Luke 11:47–9.

15 Cf. Jensen and Irwin, 'Isaiah', 245.

16 Baumgarten, '4Q500 and the Ancient Conception of the Lord's Vineyard', 6.

17 Dupont-Sommer, *The Essene Writings from Qumran*, 229 n. 1.

18 Cf. Klauck (*Allegorie*, 300) for a general discussion of the rabbinic development of the biblical vineyard image: polemical features are reduced, while the aspect of election and promise is brought out more strongly.

19 This is clear from a glance at Hyman, *Torah Haketubah Vehamessurah*, 2.125.

20 Similarly, Philo (*On Dreams* 2.173) develops the positive aspect of Isa. 5:7 without mentioning the negative aspect (the passage is noted by Klauck, *Allegorie*, 299–300).

21 See also *Yalqut Shimoni* (חי"ב רמז תתרסו, citing the Midrash on Psalms), where God's grace to Israel, the Lord's vineyard, provokes the jealousy of pagans, who consequently persecute Israel.

22 See e.g. *Tg. Isa.* 5.1–2: 'The prophet said, I will sing now for Israel – which is like a vineyard, the seed of Abraham, my friend – my friend's song for his vineyard: My people, my beloved Israel ... I sanctified them and I glorified them and I established them as the plant of a choice vine ... ' (translation from Chilton, *The Isaiah Targum*). *Yalqut Shimoni* on Isa. 5:1 (חי"ב רמז תא), citing *Lamentations Rabbah*, interprets קרן בן-שמן (RSV 'very fertile hill'; lit. 'horn of a son of fatness') as קרנו של אברהם (= 'the horn of Abraham').

23 For an acknowledgement of this difference, see Carlston, *Parables*, 185.

24 On the pathos of God in the prophets, see Heschel, *The Prophets*, index under 'Pathos, divine'.

25 Roskies, *Against the Apocalypse*, 19–20.

26 Marcus, 'Jewish War'.

27 See Marcus, 'Jewish War', 458–9 for the evidence.

28 A similar conflict seems to have occurred in the second Jewish revolt against the Romans, when Jewish Christians were persecuted for refusing to acknowledge Bar Kochba's messianic status (see Justin, *1 Apology* 31.6 and cf. Hengel, *The Zealots*, 300–1).

29 See Marcus, 'Jewish War', 450–1 n. 47 for the evidence.

30 See again 13:14, and cf. Eusebius, *H. E.* 3.5.3; Epiphanius, *Panarion* 29.7.7–8; 30.2.7; *Weights and Measures* 15.

31 We might compare Acts 23:3, where Paul, after being struck for declaring his innocence, immediately prophesies divine retribution on his attacker: 'God will strike you, you whitewashed wall!'

32 This identification of the parable's beloved son with Jesus is probably the reason that both Matthew and Luke switch the Markan order and have the son thrown out of the vineyard, then killed (Matt. 21:39// Luke 20:15). This switch reflects their awareness that Jesus was executed outside the walls of Jerusalem (cf. Heb. 13:12 and Fitzmyer, *The Gospel According to Luke*, 2.1284–5).

33 Ἐγὼ ὁ Ѳεὸς ὁ ἐξαγαγών σε ἐκ χώρας Χαλδαίων ὥστε δοῦναι τὴν γῆν ταύτην κληρονομῆσαι.

34 Οὐ κληρονομήσει σε οὗτος, ἀλλ' ὃς ἐξελεύσεται ἐκ σοῦ, οὗτος κληρονομήσει σε ... On these two aspects of the κληρονομία in Gen. 15, see Friedrich, 'κληρονομέω'.

35 Cf. Friedrich, 'κληρονομέω'.

36 Perhaps not all, however; cf. Heb. 1:2, where Christ is called the heir of God, and Rom. 8:17, where Christians are called joint-heirs with Christ; neither passage seems to have Abrahamic resonances.

37 Gal. 3:18, 29; 4:1, 7, 30; Rom. 4:13–14; 8:17.

38 This question was of concern to first-century Jews even apart from debates with Christians; see the title of Philo's treatise, which takes its

point of departure from Gen. 15:2–18: *Who is the Heir?* (Τίς ὁ Τῶν Θειῶν Ἔστιν Κληρονομία).

39 Our parable, then, suggests both salvation-historical continuity and discontinuity: continuity, because the inheritance belongs to Christ, and by implication to the Christians (12:7; cf. Rom. 8:17); discontinuity, because the vineyard is given to people different from its original tenants (12:9).

40 See e.g. *War* 2.390; 5.412; 6.110; 7.319; I am grateful to my Glasgow colleague John Barclay for these references. If we believe in intertextual echoes and respect for context in NT quotation of the OT, Mark's quotation of Ps. 118:22–3 in the immediately following verses (Mark 12:10–11) may reflect the revolutionaries' use of that psalm in their holy-war theology, for earlier in the psalm there is a classic expression of the hope for divine victory against the heathen: 'All nations surrounded me; in the name of the Lord I cut them off' (Ps. 118:10–12). See Marcus, *Way*, 114–15.

41 This despite the naive narrative device in 12:6, where the vineyard owner seems to hope and expect that the tenants will respect his son. Elsewhere, especially in 4:10–12, Mark makes it clear that those who oppose Jesus and the Christians have been blinded by God.

42 For other reflections of this dispute, see Siker, *Disinheriting the Jews*.

43 Cf. the discussion of Rom. 9–11 in Hays, *Echoes of Scripture in the Letters of Paul*, 63–73. In this section of Romans, Paul employs prophetic texts (Jer. 18:3–6; Hos. 2:1, 25) which imply the divine restoration of sinful Israel. In Rom. 9 Paul deconstructs these oracles in a way that dismantles Israel's privilege and transfers it to the Gentiles (see vv. 21–6), but then in Rom. 11 he 'dialectically deconstructs the deconstructive reading' and returns to something like the original meaning of the OT texts when he concludes that 'all Israel shall be saved' (11:25–6).

My proposal for dealing with Mark 12:9 is something like this Pauline return to the original sense of the prophetic texts. On the other hand, I would not want to deny that there are times when the Spirit may call people to challenge in the strongest possible terms an assumption of salvation-historical privilege, especially when that assumption is used to justify the oppression of others. I think that if I lived in Israel today, I would be tempted to proclaim the bad news of disinheritance to those who justify violence against Arabs by citing the biblical conquest traditions, etc. But discerning the καιρός – as well as the τόπος – is everything (cf. Rom. 13:11).

BIBLIOGRAPHY

Baumgarten, J. M., '4Q500 and the Ancient Conception of the Lord's Vineyard', *JJS* 40 (1989), 1–6.

Brown, R. E., 'Parable and Allegory Reconsidered', in his *New Testament Essays*, New York, 1968; orig. 1962, 321–33.

Carlston, C. E., *The Parables of the Triple Tradition*, Philadelphia, 1975.

Chilton, B. D., *The Isaiah Targum: Introduction, Translation, Apparatus and Notes*, The Aramaic Bible, Wilmington, 1987.

Crossan, J. D., *In Parables: The Challenge of the Historical Jesus*, New York, 1973.

Derrett, J. D. M., 'The Stone that the Builders Rejected,' in *Studies in the New Testament*, Leiden, 1978, vol. II, 64–5.

Dupont-Sommer, A., *The Essene Writings from Qumran*, Gloucester, Mass., 1973; orig. 1961.

Evans, C. A., 'On the Vineyard Parables of Isaiah 5 and Mark 12', *BZ* 28 (1984), 82–6.

Fitzmyer, J. A., *The Gospel According to Luke*, 2 vols., AB 28 and 28A, New York, 1981–5.

Friedrich, J. H., 'κληρονομέω', in H. Balz and G. Schneider (eds.), *Exegetical Dictionary of the New Testament*, Grand Rapids, 1993, vol. II, 298–9.

Hays, R. B., *Echoes of Scripture in the Letters of Paul*, New Haven, 1989.

Hengel, M., *The Zealots: Investigations into the Jewish Freedom Movement in the Period from Herod I Until 70 A.D.*, Edinburgh, 1989; orig. 1961.

Heschel, A. J., *The Prophets*, New York, 1975; orig. 1962.

Hyman, A., *Torah Haketubah Vehamessurah*, Tel Aviv, 1979.

Jensen, J., and Irwin, W. H., 'Isaiah', in R. E. Brown, J. A. Fitzmyer and R. E. Murphy (eds.), *The New Jerome Biblical Commentary*, Englewood Cliffs, N. J., 1990, 229–48.

Klauck, H. J., *Allegorie und Allegorese in synoptischen Gleichnistexten*, NTAbh 13, Münster, 1978.

Marcus, J., 'The Jewish War and the Sitz im Leben of Mark', *JBL* 111 (1992), 441–62.

    The Way of the Lord: Christological Exegesis of the Old Testament in the Gospel of Mark, Louisville, 1992.

Roskies, D. R., *Against the Apocalypse: Responses to Catastrophe in Modern Jewish Culture*, Cambridge, Mass., and London, 1984.

Scott, B. B., *Hear Then the Parable: A Commentary on the Parables of Jesus*, Minneapolis, 1989.

Siker, J., *Disinheriting the Jews: Abraham in Early Christian Controversy*, Louisville, 1991.

Taylor, V., *The Gospel According to Saint Mark.*, 2nd edn, Grand Rapids, 1981; orig. 1950.

CHAPTER 13

Jews and Jewish Christians in the land of Israel at the time of the Bar Kochba war, with special reference to the Apocalypse of Peter

Richard Bauckham

Evidence for Jewish Christianity[1] in Palestine west of the Jordan during the second century is sparse.[2] One valuable piece of evidence is Justin Martyr's statement (*1 Apol.* 31.6) that 'in the Jewish war which happened just recently, Bar Kochba (βαρχωχέβας), the leader of the Jewish revolt, ordered that Christians alone should be led away to terrible punishments, unless they would deny Jesus the Messiah and blaspheme'. Although the context is, of course, polemical, it is unlikely that Justin should have cited this single instance of Jewish persecution of Christians unless he knew it to be true. He was writing no more than ten or twenty years after the events, and there are indications in his writings that he acquired information about the revolt from Jews who emigrated to Ephesus after the war (*Dial.* 1.3; 9.3). Moreover, his statement is substantially consistent with what we know of the revolt. We need not suppose that Bar Kochba's government executed Christians specifically because they were Christians. We need only suppose that, because Bar Kochba was widely regarded as the Messiah by his followers, it seemed to Christians that they could not support his revolt without denying the messiahship of Jesus. From the government's point of view they were executed for refusing to support the revolt; from their own point of view they were executed for refusing to deny Jesus as Messiah. The Bar Kochba letters show that severe measures were taken against Jews who refused to join the war.[3] Justin's assertion that Christians were singled out need not be taken literally, but it is credible that Christians constituted the one identifiable category of Jews who held aloof from the revolt and would not acknowledge the legitimacy of Bar Kochba's government. As such their numbers need not have been very large for them to have acquired the stigma of a group disloyal to the national religious cause.

As it happens, Justin's is the earliest reference to Shim'on bar

Kosiva by his messianic nickname Bar Kochba, alluding to the star of Numbers 24:17.[4] It must have been a standard usage, since Justin shows no knowledge of the meaning of the nickname and treats it simply as the Jewish leader's name. Since neither Jews nor Christians would have had any reason to originate this pun on Bar Kosiva's name after the failure of the revolt, its early currency is good evidence that he really was regarded by his followers during the revolt as the Messiah.[5] Since evidence for the extent of the revolt does not seem to suggest that it included Galilee,[6] Justin's remark probably also shows that there were Jewish Christians in Judaea at the time of the revolt, which is supported by the fact that there were Jewish-Christian bishops of Jerusalem down to the time of Bar Kochba.[7]

It seems a plausible hypothesis that the refusal of Jewish Christians to support the rebellion was a critical stage in their alienation from other Palestinian Jews. In my view, we can see this in much more detail than Justin's brief reference allows, because we have the good fortune to possess a work written by a Palestinian Jewish Christian during the Bar Kochba war: the *Apocalypse of Peter*.[8] I have argued for this place and date of origin of the *Apocalypse of Peter* in detail elsewhere.[9] In the present context I shall focus on explaining how the opening and closing sections of the work (chapters 1–2 and 15–17) fit this context during Bar Kochba's war against Rome and how they illuminate Jewish-Christian responses to that context.

Chapters 1–2[10] are the beginning of a discourse of Jesus to his disciples on the Mount of Olives after the resurrection, giving an apocalyptic revelation of the events of the end of history and the last judgement. The post-resurrection setting was a conventional one for writers who wished to develop the teaching of Jesus in the Gospels, relying on the notion that the risen Christ had explained to his disciples the full meaning of his teaching given during the ministry.[11] These two chapters draw on the Synoptic eschatological discourse in its Matthean form (Matt. 24), but they do so highly selectively. The author is interested only in certain very definite themes in Matthew 24, on which he expands by use of other traditional material relating to the same themes. He is not reproducing a standard apocalyptic scenario, but focusing on a few features of that scenario which he wishes to highlight and develop.

There are two main themes. The first is the need to distinguish the true Messiah from the false. Following Matthew 24, the talk is initially of false Messiahs in general, by whom the disciples are to be careful not to be deceived (1:5; 2:7),[12] but, departing from Matthew 24, the discourse then focuses on a single false Messiah (2:8–13), who is clearly the author's real concern. The need to distinguish this false Messiah from the true Messiah explains the emphasis in the elaborate description of the parousia (1:6–7), i.e. the eschatological coming of the true Messiah Jesus. Jesus' coming will be quite unmistakable: 'like a bolt of lightning flashes from east to west'.[13] In his parousia Jesus will shine in glory seven times brighter than the sun, and his cross will go before him, indicating unambiguously that the unmistakably true Messiah is Jesus who was crucified. Those who expect this parousia of Jesus the Messiah will not be taken in by the signs and wonders performed by the impostor (2:12). The way this theme is developed already suggests that the concern is not with a still future false Messiah, but with a contemporary figure whom the readers are in danger of crediting. Such a figure could only be either a Jewish messianic claimant or a Roman emperor, but the latter is unlikely since Christian apocalyptic texts which depict the emperors as eschatological Antichrist figures always make much of the imperial cult. Strikingly, the false Messiah of this text does not claim worship, but merely claims to be the Messiah. Moreover, the whole context is Jewish, as the references to 'the house of Israel' in 2:4, 7, 11 make clear. Those who are deceived by the false Messiah and those who reject him are Jews.

The second theme which dominates chapter 2 is martyrdom. The author finds this in Matthew 24 only by interpreting the parable of the fig tree (Matt. 24:32) in this sense: the fig tree is the house of Israel, and the sprouting of its twigs, which according to the parable heralds the end of the world, represents the many martyrs who will die at the hands of the false Messiah. This theme even more clearly enables us to see that the author situated himself and his readers at the time when the false Messiah had already appeared and had already put some Jewish Christians to death. Evidence elsewhere in the *Apocalypse of Peter* shows that persecution and martyrdom are a matter of vital current concern. Chapters 7–12 are a lengthy description of the various punishments which sinners will suffer in hell after the last judgement; the material is conventional, paralleled in other Jewish and Christian apocalypses.[14] Most of the categories of sinners can be paralleled in other descriptions of hell. But three categories which occur as a group in 9:1–4 are unique to the *Apocalypse of Peter* and reveal that aspect of future judgement which most concerned this writer: they are 'the persecutors and betrayers of my righteous ones' (those who put the martyrs to death), 'the blasphemers and betrayers of my righteousness' (those who apostatized in order to escape martyrdom; cf. Justin, *1 Apol.* 31.6: Christians who suffered under Bar Kochba were those who refused to 'blaspheme'), and 'those who put to death the martyrs with a lie' (those who informed on the martyrs). We shall later note a key reference to persecution also in 16:5.

The persecution of Christians by the false Messiah has begun, but is not yet over when the author writes. The reference to Enoch and Elijah, sent to expose the deception of the false Messiah (2:12), presumably refers to an event still in the future. So far some Jewish Christians who already reject the false Messiah have suffered. But the author expects many more Jews – those who are not yet believers in Jesus – to reject the false Messiah when Enoch and Elijah expose him. These will be the majority of the martyrs and they will be numbered with those Jewish Christians who have already died as martyrs (2:13). Thus the author, who still hopes for the widespread conversion of his people to faith in Jesus as Messiah, sees the crisis in which he lives as the immediate prelude to the fulfilment of this hope. It is important to notice that nothing at all is said as to the ultimate fate of the false Messiah himself. If he is Bar Kochba, as many scholars have agreed,[15] and the *Apocalypse of Peter* were written after his death and the failure of his revolt, then it is inconceivable that these should not have been mentioned as the clinching evidence of the falsity of his claims. Rather, the author must be writing at the time when Bar Kochba's military success against the Romans persuaded many Jews that he must be the Messiah[16] and some Jewish Christians were being carried away by this enthusiasm for an enterprise apparently blessed with divine aid. The author's concern is that his fellow Jews, Christian and non-Christian, should not be deceived, and he expects the time to be close when the claims of the true Messiah Jesus will be vindicated against those of the false Messiah Bar Kochba.

The revelation given by Jesus to the disciples on the Mount of Olives concludes with chapter 14, and in 15:1 the scene shifts. Jesus

and the disciples cross the Kidron valley to 'the holy mountain',
i.e. Mount Zion, the location of the Temple. In the following section the author again draws on material from Matthew's Gospel,
this time the transfiguration narrative, but again he makes his own
very distinctive use of this material. There is no transfiguration of
Jesus at all,[17] but other elements in the Matthean narrative become occasions for an apocalyptic revelation which again concerns the issue of the true Messiah, but also deals with two other
closely connected issues: the question of the true temple, and the
question of the true people of God who are destined to share with
the patriarchs in the eschatological promises to Israel.

This last question is the subject from 15:2 to 16:6. The disciples
see Moses and Elijah in their glorified state. The vision prompts
Peter to ask where Abraham, Isaac, Jacob and the other fathers of
Israel are, and Jesus in response grants him a vision of paradise.
The climax of this section of the revelation comes when Peter is
told (16:5) that this glorious destiny of the patriarchs is the destiny
that persecuted Christians are to share. We shall return shortly to
this theme of sharing in the eschatological destiny of Israel with
the patriarchs.

The narrative now turns to the theme of the true temple,[18]
though this may not be immediately obvious. The author borrows
from the Matthean transfiguration narrative Peter's suggestion
that he build three tents for Jesus, Moses and Elijah (16:7), but the
author then departs from his source. Peter's suggestion receives a
remarkably strong rebuke from Jesus – 'Satan wages war against
you and has veiled your understanding' (16:8) – along with a
promise of both a visionary revelation and an auditory revelation
– 'your eyes will be uncovered and your ears will be opened up'
(16:9). The vision is of the heavenly temple, the tent not made by
human hand, constructed by God for Jesus and his chosen ones
(16:9). (Jews used the Greek word σκηνή as equivalent to mishkān,
and so the meaning is not necessarily 'tent' so much as divine
dwelling-place, whether the tabernacle, the Temple, the future eschatological temple, to be built by God, or the heavenly temple,
built by God. Cf. Heb. 9:11, which contrasts the earthly tent, the
tabernacle, made with human hands, and the heavenly sanctuary,
'the greater and perfect tent, not made with hands, that is, not of
this creation'.) So Peter's error was to propose to build earthly
dwellings with his own hands, on Mount Zion, the site of the

Temple, instead of the heavenly temple, not made with hands, which God has already created for his Messiah and his people.

Following this revelation of the true temple, there is a revelation of the true Messiah (17:1), when the divine voice from heaven identifies Jesus as God's Messiah. Thus the theme of the true Messiah is resumed from chapters 1–2, but is now emphatically endorsed, at the climax of the whole book, by God's own declaration, while also being now closely linked with the theme of the true temple. By this double revelation – of the true temple and the true Messiah – the veil Satan had cast over Peter's mind is removed and he is shown the truth.

But why was Peter so severely rebuked, and why was his satanically inspired error corrected not simply by the vision of the heavenly temple, but also by the voice which identifies the true Messiah? The point must be that Peter's proposal to build three tents on Mount Zion associates him with the false Messiah. The whole passage makes excellent sense if the false Messiah was proposing to rebuild the Temple in Jerusalem. The author's distinction between the true and the false Messiahs is linked with a distinction between the kind of temple each promises his followers. The false Messiah offers a merely earthly temple, built with human hands on earth, while Jesus the true Messiah promises his people entry into the heavenly sanctuary provided by God. This polemic readily fits the context of the Bar Kochba war, the primary aim of which, as we know from the coins of the revolt, was not only to liberate Jerusalem but to rebuild the Temple and to restore the Temple worship.[19]

Thus we learn that Jewish Christians – or at least, those who agreed with our author – held aloof from Bar Kochba's movement, not only because they could not acknowledge him as Messiah, but also because they had no sympathy for his central aim of rebuilding the Temple. The *Apocalypse of Peter*'s answer to the question which also preoccupied non-Christian Jewish apocalyptists of the early second century – what, in the divine purpose, should replace the Temple destroyed in 70 CE? – was not, in essence, peculiarly Christian. The Greek/Slavonic *Apocalypse of Baruch* (*3 Baruch*), a Jewish apocalypse written sometime in the second century, also proposes that the earthly Temple is now replaced by the transcendent heavenly temple. But the *Apocalypse of Peter*'s insistence that only this transcendent temple can be asso-

ciated with Jesus as Messiah should probably be linked to Jesus'
prophecy of the destruction of the Temple, widely reported in
early Christian literature and certainly known to the author of the
Apocalypse of Peter at least from Matthew's Gospel. Jewish Christians who must certainly have seen the events of 70 CE as fulfilment of Jesus' prophecy had a motive not available to other Jews
for opposing any attempt to rebuild the Temple in Jerusalem. The
Temple destroyed by God was to be replaced not by human re-
construction, but only by the temple God himself has made. This
issue of the temple may well have motivated Jewish-Christian failure to support Bar Kochba's revolt just as much as the issue of his
messiahship.[20]

Finally,[21] I suggest that the first of the three themes which are
prominent in this closing section of the *Apocalypse of Peter* – the as-
surance that Christians will inherit the eschatological promises to
Israel along with the patriarchs – may have its background not
only in the Bar Kochba revolt, but also in the *birkat ha-minim* (the
benediction concerning the heretics or sectarians), which had been
in use in many synagogues for some time prior to the revolt. The
birkat ha-minim is a much debated subject.[22] I take the view that
the *birkat ha-minim,* while aimed generally at non-rabbinic versions
of Judaism, not exclusively at Christians, would have been perceived as targeting Jewish Christians in some places and excluding
them from the religious community of Israel. Two features of the
benediction are notable. First, it is aimed not only against *minim*
but also against 'the kingdom of arrogance',[23] that is, Rome. Most
likely it was conceived as a prayer for the judgement of all the
enemies of God's people, including both Jewish apostates and sectarians and also Gentile oppressors. This association of *minim* with
the Gentile oppressors would have gained greater force in the
context of the Bar Kochba revolt. Jewish Christians who failed to
support the revolt could be seen as renegades who were taking the
side of 'the kingdom of arrogance' against Israel.

Secondly, the *birkat ha-minim,* especially when seen in its context
in the whole *Amidah,* with its strong emphasis on an eschatology
of Jewish national restoration, is a prayer that the *minim* will perish along with the Gentile enemies of Israel and be excluded from
the people of God who will inherit the eschatological promises.
Appropriately, the Cairo Genizah text of the *birkat ha-minim*
quotes Psalm 69:28: 'Let them be blotted out of the book of life

and not be written with the righteous.' We cannot be sure whether this text of the benediction was in use in the early second century, but it is at least rather suggestive that the closing words of the *Apocalypse of Peter* read: 'We prayed, and went down from the mountain praising God who has written the names of the righteous in the book of life in heaven' (17:7). The fact that this is also an echo of Psalm 69:28[24] suggests that it is countering an assertion that the names of Jewish Christians have been erased from the book of life.

In conclusion, in the early second century Jewish Christians in the land of Israel will have suffered, though we do not know how consistently, a certain marginalization wherever the *birkat ha-minim* was employed in the rabbinic attempt to make the rabbinic form of Judaism normative. But even more decisive for the fate of Jewish Christianity west of the Jordan may have been the refusal of Jewish Christians to support Bar Kochba's revolt. A very wide spectrum of Palestinian Jews would have perceived this as a betrayal of the national religious cause, a betrayal by which Jewish Christians aligned themselves with the Roman oppressors. In the context of the extraordinarily severe measures taken by the Romans in Judaea after the war, surviving Jewish Christians would have been highly unpopular, as would Jewish Christians in Galilee, to which many Judaean Jews moved. This may even have been the end of distinctively Jewish Christianity west of the Jordan, though the nature of our evidence makes this no more than a plausible guess.

NOTES

1 I use the term 'Jewish Christianity' here merely to refer to communities of Christian Jews who maintained their Jewish identity.
2 But not quite as sparse as Taylor, *Christians and the Holy Places*, supposes.
3 Schürer, *The History of the Jewish People in the Age of Jesus Christ*, 546.
4 Cf. *y. Ta'an.* 4.8 (24a); *Lam. Rab.* 2.5. On the exegesis of Num. 24:17 attributed to R. Aqiva in these rabbinic texts, see Marks, *The Image of Bar Kokhba in Traditional Jewish Literature*, 14–20.
5 Rheinhartz, 'Rabbinic Perceptions of Simeon bar Kosiba', 176–7.
6 Schäfer, *Der Bar-Kokhba-Aufstand*, 102–34; Isaac and Oppenheimer, 'The Revolt of Bar Kokhba', 53–4.
7 See Bauckham, *Jude and the Relatives of Jesus in the Early Church*, 70–9, on the bishops list.

8 This work is not to be confused with the Coptic *Apocalypse of Peter* from Nag Hammadi (CG VII, 3), which is a Gnostic work. Our *Apocalypse of Peter* is known from some quotations in the Fathers, two small fragments of the Greek text, one substantial fragment of a secondary, redacted Greek form of the text (the Akhmim fragment), and the complete text in an Ethiopic version. For a survey of research up to 1982 and an exhaustive bibliography up to 1987, see Bauckham, 'The Apocalypse of Peter: An Account of Research'. Major recent studies of the work are Buchholz, *Your Eyes Will be Opened*, and Bauckham, '*The Apocalypse of Peter*: A Jewish Christian Apocalypse from the Time of Bar Kokhba'. Buchholz, *Your Eyes,* provides a critical edition of the Ethiopic text, based for the first time on both known manuscripts, along with two English translations (one literal, one free). The treatment of the *Apocalypse of Peter* in E. Hennecke, W. Schneemelcher and R. McL. Wilson, *New Testament Apocrypha* (revised edition; Cambridge and Louisville, 1992), vol. II 620–38, is very unsatisfactory: see my review in *JTS* 45 (1994), 270–8.

9 Bauckham, 'The Two Fig Tree Parables in the Apocalypse of Peter'; 'Jewish Christian Apocalypse', 24–43.

10 For the argument of the following discussion of chapters 1–2 in more detail, see Bauckham, 'Two Fig Tree Parables'; 'Jewish Christian Apocalypse', 24–39. On problems of text and translation in chapter 2, see Hills, 'Parables, Pretenders and Prophecies'.

11 Bauckham, 'Jewish Christian Apocalypse', 20–2.

12 Chapter and verse numbers are those of Buchholz, *Your Eyes* (who follows the standard division into chapters but adds division into verses).

13 Translations of the Ethiopic are from Buchholz, *Your Eyes.*

14 See Himmelfarb, *Tours of Hell*; Bauckham, 'Jewish Christian Apocalypse', 55–71; Bauckham, 'Early Jewish Visions of Hell'.

15 E.g. Buchholz, *Your Eyes*, 408–12; others listed in Bauckham, 'Account', 4733 n. 197; cf. 4738 n. 231.

16 Rheinhartz, 'Rabbinic Perceptions', argues that the claim that Bar Kochba was the Messiah was made during the war, as an explanation of his success, by some of his supporters, though not by all.

17 Bauckham, 'Account', 4735–6.

18 For the argument of the following two paragraphs in more detail, see Bauckham, 'Jewish Christian Apocalypse', 39–43.

19 Isaac and Oppenheimer, 'Revolt', 47–9; Mildenberg, *The Coinage of the Bar Kokhba Revolt*, 31–48.

20 Cf. Bauckham, 'The Parting of the Ways', 145–6.

21 For the argument of the following two paragraphs in more detail, see Bauckham, 'Jewish Christian Apocalypse', 86–97.

22 I am indebted especially to Schäfer, 'Die sogenannte Synod von Jabne'; Kimelman, '*Birkat Ha-Minim*'; Horbury, 'The Benediction of

the Minim'; Katz, 'Issues in the Separation of Judaism and Christianity'; Pritz, *Nazarene Jewish Christianity*, 102–7; Alexander, 'The Parting of the Ways'.

23 With this term for Rome, cf. 4 Ezra 11:43.

24 Cf. also Exod. 32:33; Dan. 12:1, but Ps. 69:28 is the only occurrence of the phrase 'the book of life' in the Hebrew Bible. The image was commonly used in early Jewish and Christian literature (cf. *Jub.* 30.22; *1 Enoch* 104.1; 108.3; *Jos. As.* 15.4; Luke 10:20; Phil. 4:3; Heb. 12:23; Rev. 3:5; 13:8; 17:8; 20:15; 21:27), but in stating that the names of *the righteous* are *written* in *the book of life*, Apoc. Pet. 17.7 is verbally closer to Ps. 69:28 than are any of these other texts.

BIBLIOGRAPHY

Alexander, P. S. '"The Parting of the Ways" from the Perspective of Rabbinic Judaism', in J. D. G. Dunn (ed.), *Jews and Christians: The Parting of the Ways A.D. 70 to 135* (WUNT 66; Tübingen, 1993), 1–25.

Bauckham, R., 'The Two Fig Tree Parables in the Apocalypse of Peter', *JBL* 104 (1985), 269–87.

'The Apocalypse of Peter: An Account of Research', in *ANRW*, part II, vol. 25/6, Berlin and New York, 1988, 4712–50.

Jude and the Relatives of Jesus in the Early Church, Edinburgh, 1990.

'Early Jewish Visions of Hell', *JTS* 41 (1990), 355–85.

'The Parting of the Ways', *ST* 47 (1993), 135–51.

'The *Apocalypse of Peter*: A Jewish Christian Apocalypse from the Time of Bar Kokhba', *Apocrypha* 5 (1994), 7–111.

Buchholz, D. D., *Your Eyes Will be Opened: A Study of the Greek (Ethiopic) Apocalypse of Peter*, SBLDS 97, Atlanta, Ga., 1988.

Hills, J. V., 'Parables, Pretenders and Prophecies: Translation and Interpretation in the *Apocalypse of Peter* 2', *RB* 98 (1991), 560–73.

Himmelfarb, M., *Tours of Hell: An Apocalyptic Form in Jewish and Christian Literature*, Philadelphia, 1983.

Horbury, W., 'The Benediction of the Minim and the Early Jewish–Christian Controversy', *JTS* 33 (1982), 19–61.

Isaac, B., and Oppenheimer, A., 'The Revolt of Bar Kokhba: Ideology and Modern Scholarship', *JJS* 36 (1985), 33–60.

Katz, S. T., 'Issues in the Separation of Judaism and Christianity after 70 CE: A Reconsideration', *JBL* 103 (1984), 43–76.

Kimelman, R., '*Birkat Ha-Minim* and the Lack of Evidence for an Anti-Christian Jewish Prayer in Late Antiquity', in E. P. Sanders, A. I. Baumgarten and A. Mendelson (eds.), *Jewish and Christian Self-Definition*, vol. II: *Aspects of Judaism in the Graeco-Roman Period*, London, 1981, 226–44.

Marks, R. G., *The Image of Bar Kokhba in Traditional Jewish Literature*, Pennsylvania, 1994.

Mildenberg, L., *The Coinage of the Bar Kokhba Revolt*, Aarau, Frankfurt am Main and Salzburg, 1984.

Pritz, R. A., *Nazarene Jewish Christianity*, SPB 37, Jerusalem and Leiden, 1988.

Rheinhartz, A., 'Rabbinic Perceptions of Simeon bar Kosiba', *JSJ* 20 (1989), 171–94.

Schäfer, P., 'Die sogenannte Synod von Jabne: Zur Trennung von Juden und Christen im ersten/zweiten Jh. n. Chr', *Judaica* 31 (1975), 54–64.

Der Bar-Kokhba-Aufstand, TSAJ 1, Tübingen, 1981.

Schürer, E. *The History of the Jewish People in the Age of Jesus Christ*, (175 BC–AD 135), revised and ed. G. Vermes and F. Millar, vol. 1, Edinburgh, 1973.

Taylor, J. E., *Christians and the Holy Places: The Myth of Jewish-Christian Origins*, Oxford, 1993.

CHAPTER 14

The Nazoreans: living at the boundary of Judaism and Christianity

Martinus C. de Boer

Patristic literature testifies to the existence of a number of Jewish-Christian groups (e.g., Ebionites, Elchasaites). In this essay, I want to pay some attention to one such group known from the ancient sources, the Nazoreans (Ναζωραῖοι), to see what light this group may shed on the formation of boundaries between Jews and Christians in the ancient world, from the first century onwards. The primary source for our knowledge of the Nazoreans is the Church Father Epiphanius (*Panarion* 29.7), though there are some others as well, particularly Jerome (*c*.342–420) whose life and career overlapped with that of Epiphanius (*c*.315–403) in the late fourth century CE.[1] Epiphanius and Jerome seem to have had independent access to sources or information about the Nazoreans, though, according to Klijn and Reinink, 'they had no first-hand knowledge of their beliefs.'[2]

I. THE NAZOREANS IN THE CHURCH FATHERS

In her recent survey of scholarship on Jewish Christianity, Joan E. Taylor writes that the Nazoreans are the only group, 'among all those described in patristic literature, which appears to have a good case for being an early Jewish Christian church'.[3] What the Church Fathers, primarily Epiphanius and Jerome, say about other supposed Jewish-Christian groups (especially Ebionites and Elchasaites) is *comparatively* much more confused and unreliable.[4] That the Nazoreans may be the only Jewish-Christian community, or church, about whom we have any reliable information, however, is not only a question of the sources (which are actually sparse and must be read with caution since they are second-hand and written by those who had little evident sympathy for Nazorean points of view), but also a matter of definition: what exactly *is* Jewish Christianity and why are the Nazoreans perhaps the best example of the phenomenon?[5]

For Taylor, Jewish Christians are *Christian Jews* and their converts (Gentile proselytes) who uphold Jewish praxis (sabbath observance along with other Jewish festivals, circumcision of sons, food laws).[6] In a recent article, S. C. Mimouni comes to a strikingly similar definition of Jewish Christianity.[7] For both Taylor and Mimouni, then, what distinguishes these Jewish Christians from other Christians are two things only: Jewish ethnicity and Jewish praxis, *not* their theology (especially christology) which may or may not conform with that of 'orthodox' or 'catholic' Christianity of the time.[8] Taylor insists, I think rightly, that the label 'Jewish Christian' should not be used to characterize either Christians of Jewish birth who had abandoned Jewish Mosaic praxis, as most such Christians probably had by the early second century, or the so-called 'Judaizers' mentioned by Ignatius and others, who were probably mostly Gentiles by the second century.[9]

Taylor's and Mimouni's definition of Jewish Christianity is consistent with what the ancient evidence discloses about the Nazoreans in particular. According to Epiphanius, the Nazoreans 'live according to the preaching of the Law as among the Jews: there is no fault to find with them [from the Jewish side] apart from the fact that they have come to believe in Christ' (*Pan.* 29.7.2).[10] Or again: 'Only in this respect do they differ from the Jews and the Christians: with the Jews they do not agree because of their belief in Christ, with the Christians because they are trained in the Law, in circumcision, the sabbath and other things' (*Pan.* 29.7.5 (K–R, 173)). Jerome puts it this way: 'the Nazoreans [Lat., *Nazaraei*] ... try to connect the observance of the Law with evangelical grace' (*In Hiez.* 16.16 (K–R, 223)). Or again: 'The Nazoreans (*Nazaraei*) ... accept Christ in such a way that they do not cease to observe the old Law' (*In Esaiam* 8.11 (K–R, 221)).[11]

With respect to their theology or christology, Epiphanius says he does not know whether the Nazoreans' understanding of Jesus was 'orthodox' or 'heretical': 'With regard to Christ I cannot say whether ... they believe that he is a mere man or whether, in agreement with the truth, they emphatically declare that he was born of the Holy Spirit from Mary' (*Pan.* 29.7.6 (K–R, 173)). According to Jerome, the Nazoreans (*Nazaraei*) evidently accepted the virgin birth, acknowledged Paul's preaching, and believed Jesus to be the Son of God (*Ep.* 112.13; *In Esaiam* 9.1–4; 11.1–3; 29.17–21; 31.6–9 (K–R, 201, 223)).[12]

The Nazoreans, then, seem to exemplify the proposal of Taylor and Mimouni that Jewish Christians are Christian *Jews* who observed Torah, whatever their precise beliefs about Jesus may or may not have been.[13] This common understanding lends some force to the suggestion of G. P. Luttikhuizen that it may be preferable to use the label 'early Christian *Judaism*' instead of the label 'Jewish *Christianity*' for the Nazoreans (and other similar groups).[14] Luttikhuizen observes that the term 'Jewish Christianity' has the disadvantage of implying that we are dealing with a heretical deviation from mainstream, 'Law-free' orthodox or catholic Christianity, as the Church Fathers believed. The term 'early Christian Judaism' would acknowledge the probability that the Nazoreans were regarded in the first instance as a heretical aberration not of Christianity but of Judaism, of Pharisaic or rabbinic Judaism. Jerome himself hints that such was the case in a letter to Augustine (404 CE), his earliest known mention of the Nazoreans: 'Until now a heresy is to be found in all parts of the East where Jews have their synagogues; it is called "of the Minaeans" [probably reflecting the Hebrew word for heretics, *minim*] and cursed by the Pharisees up to now. Usually they are called Nazoreans (*Nazaraei*)' (*Ep.* 112.13 (K–R, 201)).[15]

Luttikhuizen's point is thus well taken. But the matter is perhaps more complicated than that. There are three questions to be considered in coming to a right understanding of the Nazoreans:

1. How did they define or understand themselves?
2. How did their contemporaries, both Christian and Jewish, define and understand them?
3. How can we today best describe or define them?

There is no reason why the answers to these three questions should be the same.

For instance, Epiphanius observes that 'they called themselves Nazoreans' (*Pan.* 29.1.2 (K–R, 169)); they gave themselves this name because Jesus is called 'the Nazorean in the gospel' (*Pan.* 29.5.6, citing not a Gospel but Acts 2:22 (K–R, 169)), a name in turn derived, he says, from Nazareth (also *Pan.* 29.7.1 (K–R, 173)).

Most interestingly, Epiphanius reports that the Nazoreans 'did not keep the name Jews', on the one side, nor 'did they call themselves Christians', on the other (*Pan.* 29.7.1 (K–R, 173)).

Epiphanius here reports how the Nazoreans apparently understood themselves, and we have little reason to cast doubt on this report since it disagrees, at least in part, with what he himself thinks about them. From his point of view, 'they are rather Jews and nothing else' (*Pan.* 29.9.1 (K–R, 173)). They may have declined to call themselves 'Jews' and they may have claimed to be followers of Jesus by calling themselves Nazoreans, but 'actually they remained wholly Jewish and nothing else' (*Pan.* 29.7.1 (K–R, 173)). Jerome dismisses them with the pointed remark that 'since they want to be both Jews and Christians [by being Nazoreans], they are neither Jews nor Christians', from a viewpoint that evidently assumes that Judaism and Christianity are two different religions (*Ep.* 112.13 (K–R, 201)).

The rabbis in turn regarded the Nazoreans (*ha-Notzrim*) as *minim*, as heretics from rabbinic norms.[16] This is clear especially from the Palestinian recension of the *birkat ha-minim*, which reads in part: 'May the *Notzrim* and the *minim* perish in an instant.'[17] This version of the *birkat ha-minim* is consistent with Jerome's report, quoted earlier, that 'a heresy is to be found in all parts of the East where Jews have their synagogues; it is called "of the Minaeans" and cursed by the Pharisees up to now. Usually they are called Nazoreans' (*Ep.* 112.13). Epiphanius writes that the Nazoreans 'are very much hated by the Jews. For ... the people also stand up ... three times a day [which can only apply to the Prayer of Eighteen Benedictions], and they pronounce curses and maledictions over them [the Nazoreans] when they say their prayers in the synagogues. Three times a day they say, "May God curse the Nazoreans (Ναζωραῖοι)"' (*Pan.* 29.9.2 (K–R, 175)).

Of course, such ancient opinions need careful scrutiny and critical evaluation and ought not to determine how we today may most usefully describe or characterize the Nazoreans mentioned by the Church Fathers and the rabbis as a social and religious phenomenon of the ancient world (though such ancient opinions are hardly irrelevant to this matter either). The third question remains: are the Nazoreans best characterized by scholars today as Jewish Christians (Taylor and Mimouni) or as Christian Jews (Luttikhuizen)?

At this point, it may be instructive to mention the distinction between 'Jewish Christians' and 'Christian Jews' put forth by J. L. Martyn in his well-known attempt to sketch the history of Johannine Christianity. The Gospel of John mentions an expulsion from the synagogue of Jews confessing Jesus to be the Messiah (9:22; 12:42; 16:2). According to Martyn, the expulsion meant that a *group* of *Christian Jews* at home in the synagogue became a *community* of *Jewish Christians* separated, both socially and religiously, from the synagogue.[18] Thus, Johannine Christians were Christian *Jews*, a group within the synagogue before their expulsion, and Jewish *Christians*, a community distinguishable from the synagogue community, after that expulsion. The trauma of expulsion from the synagogue, in short, entailed a fundamental change of social circumstances and of religious identity, making the Gospel of John the literary legacy of a form of Jewish Christianity, the Johannine community, separated sociologically and alienated theologically from 'the parent synagogue'.[19]

This sociological and dynamic distinction between Jewish Christians and Christian Jews suggests that it is probably best (for us as historians today) to characterize the Nazoreans as *Jewish Christians*, however they may have understood themselves or been understood by their contemporaries. The Nazoreans about whom Epiphanius and Jerome write are, like the Johannine community reflected in the Fourth Gospel in Martyn's account, a community of Jewish Christians, sociologically separated from the synagogue community from which they came, not Christian Jews, a group still within the synagogue community.[20]

However, if the Nazoreans about whom Epiphanius and Jerome write were 'Jewish Christians', a community sociologically separated from the synagogue, is it possible that the Nazoreans were 'Christian Jews', a group within the synagogue, in an *earlier* period of their history (much like the Johannine Jewish-Christian community described by Martyn)? Acts 24:5 may provide an answer.

2. THE NAZOREANS IN THE NEW TESTAMENT

Acts 24:5 contains the only mention of Nazoreans in the New Testament. Of course, the term 'Nazorean' (Ναζωραῖος) is also applied to Jesus himself. He is called 'Jesus the Nazorean', Ἰησοῦς ὁ Ναζωραῖος (Matt. 2:23; 26:71; Luke 18:37; Acts 2:22; 3:6; 4:10;

6:14; 9:5?; 22:8; 26:9; John 18:5, 7; 19:19),[21] often translated simply as 'Jesus of Nazareth' (cf. Acts 10:38; John 1:45–6).

The prevailing view is that Acts was written towards the end of the first century (between 80 and 100 CE). There is thus early testimony for the existence of a group known as Nazoreans. Not much is said about these Nazoreans in Acts 24:5. What is said, however, seems important. The context is Paul's trial in Caesarea before Felix who was then the Roman governor of Judaea (c.58 CE). Tertullus, the prosecuting attorney for the Sanhedrin, accuses Paul of being 'a pestilent fellow, an agitator among all the Jews throughout the world, and a ringleader of the sect (αἵρεσις) of the Nazoreans (Ναζωραῖοι)'.

The Nazoreans are described as a αἵρεσις, here meaning 'sect' or 'party'.[22] Acts uses the same term to describe the Sadducees (5:17) and the Pharisees (15:5), as does Josephus, the Jewish historian writing at about the same time as the author of Acts (Ant. 13.171; 20.199; Vita 10; 12; 191). It is clear from Acts, as indeed from Josephus, that the term αἵρεσις refers to a group within Judaism. In 26:5, Paul describes Pharisaism as 'the strictest αἵρεσις of our religion [Judaism]', while in 28:22, Jewish leaders in Rome say to Paul that 'with regard to this αἵρεσις [i.e., Jews who embrace Jesus as the Messiah, Nazoreans] we know that everywhere it is spoken against'. Similarly, in response to Tertullus' charges, Paul says to Felix that 'according to the Way, which they [= the Jews, my accusers] call a αἵρεσις,[23] I worship the God of our ancestors' (24:14). Tertullus, the Jewish attorney (24:1), thus speaks of 'the αἵρεσις of the Nazoreans' (24:5). The Nazoreans of Acts 24:5 are not Christians in general, and certainly not Gentile Christians. The Nazoreans are a Jewish αἵρεσις centred in Jerusalem and Jewish Palestine prior to the revolt of 66–70.[24] They are thus properly speaking Christian Jews, a αἵρεσις, or party, of the 'common Judaism' of the time.[25]

Given Paul's own letters, it may seem curious that he is described as a 'ringleader' of these Nazoreans, but perhaps less so if one takes into account Acts' portrait of Paul as a pious, law-abiding Pharisaic Jew even after he becomes a Christian.[26] Paul begins his defence before Felix by reporting his desire to worship in Jerusalem (24:11) and he goes on to underscore his piety as a Jew (cf. 24:14–17; 25:8; 26:4–5). For the author of Acts, at any rate, Paul himself is a Nazorean, i.e., a Christian Jew from Palestine who observes

Torah,[27] whatever one may say of his Gentile converts out in the Diaspora (cf. 21:27–8). Luke's portrait of Paul shows that the *only* thing distinguishing Nazoreans from Pharisees in Acts is the belief that Jesus the Nazorean is the Messiah. Like the Pharisees, the Nazoreans are 'zealous for the Law' (21:20; cf. Phil. 3:5–6; Gal. 2:7–9, 11–12; 6:12–13). This picture of the Nazoreans in Acts seems to match the portrayal of the Nazoreans in Epiphanius and Jerome, as outlined previously.

Yet it is noteworthy that Paul here does not acknowledge the designation 'Nazorean' as a self-description. The name 'Nazoreans' has seemingly lost its importance for the author of Acts and his audience (which is not Jewish or Palestinian). The author of Acts seems to know about *pre-70* Nazoreans only. The reference to the Nazoreans is simply part of the tradition available to him.[28] Furthermore, the author of Acts appears to think that it is a name given to Christian Jews by other, non-Christian, Jews (cf. the discussion of 24:14; 28:22 above), undoubtedly to distinguish them from other Jewish 'sects' or 'groups' such as the Pharisees and Sadducees.

As we have seen, according to Epiphanius, the Nazoreans he knew about in the late fourth century gave themselves that name, evidently to distinguish themselves from (other) Christians as much as from (other) Jews (*Pan.* 29.7.1 (K–R, 173)). In his discussion of Acts 24:5, however, Epiphanius acknowledges the contrary in the earliest period of Nazorean history: 'When they heard the name Nazoreans *from others*, they did not reject it.' They did not reject it, 'because they saw what was meant by those who called them by this name, viz., that they called them by this name because of Christ, since our Lord himself was also called Jesus the Nazorean, as appears from the Gospels and the Acts of the Apostles' (*Pan.* 29.6.7 (K–R, 171)).[29] A name that was initially applied to these Christian Jews by others, by fellow Jews, became in time a self-designation as well.

Epiphanius himself strenuously attempts to undermine any historical connection between pre- and post-70 Nazoreans, because he regards those of his own time as heretical. He is obviously embarrassed that Paul, as he says, 'did not deny this name, although he was not a follower of their heresy (αἵρεσις), but he gladly accepted the name [!], which was inspired by the malice of his opponents because it had been borne by Christ'. Epiphanius claims

that all Christians were called Nazoreans in the early church. 'For
it is no wonder that the Apostle admitted he was a Nazorean
because everybody called Christians with that name at that time,
because of the city of Nazareth and because at that time there was
no other name in use' (*Pan.* 29.6.3 and 5 (K–R, 171)). This line of
argument is not entirely convincing in view of Acts 11:26 where it
is reported that 'it was in Antioch that the disciples were first
called "Christians"' (cf. 26:28; 1 Pet. 4:16; *Did.* 12.4; Ignatius). The
latter term presumably encompassed Gentile as well as Jewish believers in the Diaspora, who had a more relaxed attitude towards
the law as Christians. As 24:5 suggests, 'Nazoreans' was the name
by which (Palestinian, or at least Judaean) Christian Jews were
known.[30]

Epiphanius also claims that 'the heresy according to the Nazoreans' actually had 'its beginning' *after 70* (*Pan.* 29.7.8 (K–R, 173))
in the Transjordan (i.e., in Perea, an area extending south from
Pella along the east bank of the Jordan). Epiphanius' heresio-
logical agenda evidently here gets in the way of historical accu-
racy.[31] Epiphanius actually testifies, if indirectly, to the probability
that the Nazoreans of his own day are the direct descendants of
the Nazoreans of the apostolic period (30–70 CE). The historical
connection between the Nazoreans of Acts and the Nazoreans
of Epiphanius is evident from his discussion of the flight of the
Jerusalem church to Pella in the Transjordan during the Jewish
War (66–70 CE) when also discussing the Nazoreans (*Pan.* 29.7.8
(K–R, 173)).

Furthermore, both pre- and post-70 Nazoreans are located in
Palestine and know 'Hebrew', which probably means they knew
and spoke Aramaic (and/or Syriac) as well (cf. Acts 21:40; 22:2;
26:14; *Pan.* 29.7.4 7; 29.9.4 (K–R, 173, 175); Jerome, *De vir. ill.* III;
In Matt. 27.9–10; *In Esaiam* 11.1–3; *Adv. Pelag.* III.2 (K–R, 211, 217,
223, 227–9)).[32] Both are law-observant Christians (cf. Acts 21:20).
Both affirm the resurrection of the dead (Acts 2:24, 32; 3:15; 4:10;
Pan. 29.7.3 (K–R, 173)), God as the Creator (Acts 4:24; *Pan.* 29.7.3),
and Christ as the παῖς (child, son) of God (Acts 3:13, 26; 4:27, 30;
Pan. 29.7.3). The historical connections and similarities are evi-
dent, if troublesome to a heresiologist like Epiphanius.

But there is at least *one* notable difference between pre- and
post-70 Nazoreans: whereas the Nazoreans of the so-called apostolic age were Christian Jews, a sect or group within Judaism

(which was marked by 'sectarian' diversity in the first century), the Nazoreans of the late fourth century were Jewish Christians, a community socially and religiously distinguishable from rabbinic Judaism and isolated from it. To put it otherwise: the Nazoreans were Christian Jews, integrated into and at home in Jewish religious and institutional life, who *became* Jewish Christians, separated and alienated from Jewish religious and institutional life (at least as defined and determined by the rabbis).

3. THE NAZOREANS IN RABBINIC TRADITIONS

As noted above, rabbinic literature also knows of the existence of the Nazoreans (*ha-Notzrim*) and, aside from two possible and debatable allusions to them by Tertullian (*c*.200) and Eusebius (early fourth century), is the only real evidence we have for their existence between Acts 24:5 and the works of Epiphanius and Jerome.[33] Because of censorship, many of the original references to both Jesus the Nazorean and the Nazoreans have been lost or disguised.[34] But there yet remain a dozen passages (perhaps thirteen), in addition to the *birkat ha-minim*, in which *Yeshu ha-Notzri* (Jesus the Nazorean) or *ha-Notzrim* (the Nazoreans) are explicitly mentioned.[35] For reasons of space, we must confine ourselves to three of these. The first two both concern Sunday:[36]

On the eve of Sabbath they did not fast out of respect to the Sabbath; still less [did they fast] on the Sabbath itself. Why did they not fast on the day after Sabbath? R. Yohanan says, 'Because of the *Notzrim*'. (*Ta'anit* 27b)

For R. Tahlipha bar Abdimi said that Shemuel said 'The *Notzri* day, according to the words of R. Ishmael, is forbidden for ever.' (*Avodah Zarah* 6a)[37]

The first passage speaks in the *past* tense. R. Yohanan, a Palestinian rabbi from the third century, 'is answering a question of why something was done (or not done) while the Temple stood'.[38] The issue is fasting on the day before sabbath, on the sabbath day itself, and on the day after sabbath, Sunday. Here we are told that Jews did not fast on Sunday 'because of the *Notzrim*'. Pritz writes: 'If Friday and Saturday are avoided out of respect, consistency would dictate that avoidance of fasting on Sunday also indicated a respect for the day.'[39] Thus it would seem that Jews (of the pre-70

period) did not fast on Sunday out of respect for Nazorean sensibilities (a situation inconceivable in the third century CE). The
passage assumes, then, that the Nazoreans were once regarded as
Jews in good standing and that they participated in the Temple
cult, a picture consistent with what we find in Acts (e.g., 3:1). The
Nazoreans of which this passage speaks are the Nazoreans of Acts
24:5, that is to say, Christian Jews of the time when the Temple
still stood (pre-70 CE).

In the second passage, which occurs in a tractate devoted to
idolatry, a saying about the Nazorean observance of Sunday is
effectively attributed to three different authorities, living in different centuries. The earliest, R. Ishmael, was a contemporary of
Akiba in the early second century, though the actual form of
the saying (the specific reference to *Notzrim*) may originate with
Shemuel who lived in the early third century.[40] The context in
which the saying occurs shows that it forbids business dealings
with those who observe Sunday as a festival.[41] This exhibits an
attitude rather different from the attitude towards Nazoreans in the
first passage discussed. The *Notzrim* and their religious practices
are no longer to be respected. They are lumped together with
pagans and their idolatrous practices. The Nazoreans are no longer
Christian Jews; they are now Jewish Christians, a community distinct from the synagogue.

In another passage, *Avodah Zarah* 16b–17a, R. Eliezer, who lived
in the early second century, tells R. Akiba of once encountering 'a
man of the disciples of *Yeshu ha-Notzri*' on the high street of Sepphoris in Galilee. This disciple, whose name is Jacob of Cephar
Sechanja,[42] enters into a midrashic debate with R. Eliezer. From
the Torah, Jacob quotes a passage from Deuteronomy (23:18) and
then another passage from the prophet Micah (1:6), to which is
added an interpretative comment attributed to *Yeshu ha-Notzri* (in
effect a saying of Jesus, otherwise unattested). The interpretation
by Jesus pleases R. Eliezer, which puts him under suspicion of
minuth, of heresy, i.e., of having become a Nazorean.

This passage (of which an earlier version is found in *t. Hullin*
2.24) indicates that in the early second century rabbinic Jews and
Nazoreans lived in proximity to one another in Galilee and were
still conversing with one another. A rabbi could even allow himself to be pleased by a saying of Jesus, yet not without suspicion of
having become a *min*, a heretic. The Nazoreans are *minim* and are

to be avoided.[43] The Nazoreans in short are no longer simply Christian Jews but are, or are in the process of becoming, Jewish Christians.[44]

A similar testimony to the interaction between Nazoreans and rabbinic Jews in these times is attested by Jerome (*In Esaiam* 8.11– 15 (K–R, 221)), who reports the familiarity of the Nazoreans (*Nazaraei*) with the houses of Hillel and Shammai as well as other Jewish leaders from the first and second centuries.[45] Jerome here also discusses a Nazorean interpretation of Isaiah 8:14 (which speaks of two 'houses of Israel') the purpose of which is to condemn the two houses of Hillel and Shammai and their rabbinic successors. Jerome discusses other passages in Isaiah and his discussion preserves a portion of a Nazorean commentary on this prophet. Noteworthy about all these passages is the sharp polemic by these former synagogue Jews against Pharisaic, rabbinic Judaism and their rejection of its halakah.[46] As Pritz writes, 'the rejection was not solely from the Jewish side'. The Nazoreans 'refused to accept the authority established by the Pharisaic camp'.[47] Nevertheless, the Isaiah commentary preserves the hope on the part of the Nazoreans that rabbinic Jews would eventually come to see things their way (Jerome, *In Esaiam* 31.6–9 (K–R, 222–4)). Talmudic sources, according to Pritz, indicate that the Nazoreans 'may have conducted an active program of evangelism among Jews'.[48] As he notes in conclusion, 'The separation process was no sudden tear but a slow parting of company.'[49]

It would seem that the *birkat ha-minim* played some sort of role in this separation process, though much about this famous benediction is disputed (its original wording, the meaning and dating of the terms *minim* and *Notzrim*, its purpose and its actual function).[50] The benediction almost certainly antedates the late fourth century when Epiphanius and Jerome were writing. Rabbinic tradition itself traces the origins of the benediction to Jamnia and the late first century (*b. Ber.* 28b–29a [baraita]; *j. Ber.* 8a), though this tradition is scarcely decisive with respect to dating (there is no confirmation in the Mishnah).[51] Justin, however, in the middle of the second century, in his *Dialogue with Trypho, A Jew* (*c.*150–5), alludes to it numerous times (chs. 16, 93, 95, 96, 108, 123, 133; cf. 35, 47, 107, 137),[52] even if he does so in a confused way and without specifically mentioning 'Nazoreans'; he speaks instead of 'them that believe in Christ'.

Justin probably takes the benediction to refer to all Christians, not just Jewish Christians, and some scholars (notably W. Horbury, L. H. Schiffman and S. T. Katz) have taken Justin's statements to provide a clue to the intention and the scope of the benediction, at least in so far as it referred specifically to a curse upon *Notzrim*. That is, they take '*Notzrim*' to be Gentile or catholic Christians in the period after the Bar Kochba revolt.[53] Epiphanius, in this view, was mistaken in identifying the *Notzrim* of the benediction with Nazorean Jewish Christians. This conclusion appears to be supported by Jerome who in the four references to the benediction apart from *Ep.* 112.13 (previously quoted) seems to think that the benediction involved a curse on Christians in general.[54] R. Kimelman, on the other hand, thinks that it is Justin and Jerome who are mistaken.[55]

The term *Notzrim* probably did not have one and only one meaning or referent in its usage over the centuries, any more than the corresponding Greek and Latin terms did.[56] In post-talmudic times, when the Nazoreans/*Notzrim* seem to have disappeared from the social landscape, it probably did among Jews refer to Christians in general, as Horbury has shown.[57] Originally, however, it probably referred to Christian Jews, i.e., to Jews within the fellowship of the synagogue who believed Jesus the Nazorean, *Yeshu ha-Notzri*, to be the Messiah. That seems clear (if the previous argument is correct) from the references to the Nazoreans in Acts 24:5 and to the *Notzrim* in *Ta'anit* 27b. In the subsequent centuries it came to refer *also* and probably primarily to the Jewish Christians who had formed a separated community *outside* the institution of the synagogue, until by the time of Epiphanius and Jerome that was perhaps the sole meaning of the term (there being no more Christian Jewish groups within the synagogue). Thus I would agree with Kimelman that Nazorean Christians, and not Christians in general, were intended by the term *Notzrim* in the Twelfth Benediction, at least in the first four centuries.[58]

It is conceivable, however, that the *Notzrim* (Nazoreans) may have been regarded by the rabbis as *representatives* of a wider problem, i.e., the problem of Christianity as a growing phenomenon among the Gentiles in the Diaspora.[59] In that sense, I suppose, Justin or Jerome heard the reference to *Notzrim* 'correctly' as referring to themselves and other Christians.[60] From within their own standpoint, understandably, the curse uttered over the Nazoreans or *Notzrim*, to the extent they became aware of the existence of such a curse, would be tantamount to a curse over all Christians.[61] Nevertheless, it would be anachronistic to read the post-talmudic Jewish usage of the term into earlier occurrences, or to adopt without qualification what catholic Christian leaders such as Justin or Jerome (in some instances), who were not Jewish Christians, thought the primary reference of *Notzrim* to be. The *minim* of the benediction were clearly Jewish heretics from rabbinic norms; the same would appear to apply to the *Notzrim* mentioned in it (cf. Jerome, *Ep.* 112.13).

Not all extant versions of the benediction specifically mention *Notzrim*.[62] (The benediction was known as the *birkat ha-minim*, not as the *birkat ha-Notzrim*.) Paul Schäfer has argued that different versions mentioned different heretical groups by name depending upon the local situation. The *Notzrim* are mentioned only in the so-called Palestinian recension, a recension that probably predates Justin. Pritz emphasizes that 'any knowledge of the cursing of Christ or of Christians is only to be found among Christian writers who had spent time in the East' – Justin, Epiphanius, Jerome[63] – and justifiably concludes that the *Notzrim* were mentioned only in places where they presented a threat, i.e., in Palestine.[64] If so, the benediction as reformulated by the rabbis in Jamnia, a town in Palestine, may well have referred to *Notzrim* from the start.[65]

Furthermore, according to Alexander, the *Notzrim* presented a threat primarily to rabbinic authority and orthodoxy within the synagogue, though the synagogue was not a rabbinic institution and the rabbis did not have authority to impose their will upon synagogues, even in Palestine, before the third century.[66] However that may be, the evidence of Epiphanius and Jerome indicates that the process of parting company was indeed a long one. And this means that the term *Notzrim* shifted constantly between referring to Christian Jews still in the synagogue and Jewish Christians who had departed from it, living outside its institutional and communal life.

With this benediction, the rabbis effectively sought to exclude Nazoreans (and other *minim*) from participation in synagogue life, beginning with its worship life but extending *mutatis mutandis* to all other spheres of synagogue life.[67] Historically speaking, the benediction's effect at any rate was to make Nazorean Christian Jews who once felt at home in the synagogue into Nazorean Jewish

Christians separated from the synagogue and unwelcome there.[68]
From the evidence of Epiphanius and Jerome, it is clear that the
Nazoreans had become by the end of the fourth century a Jewish-
Christian community sociologically distinct from its Jewish parent.

4. CONCLUSION

In conclusion, then, we can perhaps say the following:

(1) Continuity between the Nazoreans discussed by Epiphanius
(and Jerome) and the Nazoreans of Acts, i.e., between the fourth
century and the first, is indicated by the *Notzrim* mentioned in rabbinic traditions.[69]

(2) The Nazoreans of Acts were Christian Jews, a messianic
group within the institutional and religious life of Judaism; the
Nazoreans of Epiphanius (and Jerome), however, were Jewish
Christians, a messianic community sociologically distinct and, in
some measure, theologically alienated from the synagogue.

(3) The Nazoreans first started to become a sociologically defin-
able, separated Jewish-Christian community in the early second
century, probably somewhat earlier, through the instrumentality
of the Benediction Against the Heretics, among other measures.
For this reason, the *Notzrim* of the rabbis were probably both
Christian Jews within the fellowship of the synagogue (especially
in the earlier references to them) and Jewish Christians outside
that fellowship (especially in the later references to them, up to the
fifth century).

(4) In contrast to rabbinic authorities, church leaders did not
really begin to polemicize against Jewish Christians until the end
of the second century, with the work of Irenaeus.[70] Indeed, the
Nazoreans are not mentioned (as a form of Jewish Christianity
and under that name) by any Church Father until Epiphanius. By
the time of Epiphanius, Christian leaders and authorities have
become as uncomfortable with the Nazoreans as the rabbinic authorities had been earlier. Christian leaders were uncomfortable
with the Nazoreans' adherence to Jewish practices, while Jewish
authorities were uncomfortable with their embrace of Jesus as the
Messiah. Both sides had come to regard the Nazoreans as heretics from their own norms. Historically considered, the Nazoreans
were neither, since their origin antedates the rise of both orthodox
Christianity and rabbinic Judaism.

Being religiously, socially, and even geographically isolated from the main currents of both Judaism and Christianity, the destiny of the Nazoreans was to disappear. Sharp boundaries are difficult enough; blurred boundaries are intolerable.[71]

NOTES

1 The pertinent material has been collected by Klijn and Reinink, *Patristic Evidence for Jewish-Christian Sects*. Pritz has written what is apparently the only monograph devoted to the Nazoreans, *Nazarene Jewish Christianity*. See Blanchetière, 'Le "Secte des Nazaréens" ou les débuts du Christianisme'. Epiphanius always uses the term Ναζωραῖοι (= Nazoreans), never the term Ναζαρηνοί (= Nazarenes), for the Jewish-Christian group under discussion. I have been able to find only a single instance of the latter in Greek texts (Eusebius, *onomasticon*). Jerome and other Latin writers use both *Nazaraei* (= Ναζωραῖοι) and *Nazareni* (= Ναζαρηνοί) frequently and these terms seem to be interchangeable. See further Klijn and Reinink, *Patristic Evidence*, 44 n. 2.

2 Klijn and Reinink, *Patristic Evidence*, 52. Pritz writes (*Nazarene Jewish Christianity*, 44): 'It is only in *Pan.* 29,7 that he [Epiphanius] has preserved for us the testimony of a knowledgeable source.' Jerome seems to have had access to a commentary on Isaiah by the Nazoreans. On the minimal value of other patristic information about the Nazoreans, see Klijn and Reinink, *Patristic Evidence*, 50–2, and Pritz, *Nazarene Jewish Christianity*, 71–82.

3 Taylor, 'The Phenomenon of Early Jewish-Christianity', 326; see also her book, *Christians and Holy Places*.

4 Taylor, 'Phenomenon', 322–5.

5 For surveys of attempts to define Jewish-Christianity, see Taylor, 'Phenomenon'; Kaestli, 'Où en est le débat sur le judéo-christianisme?'; Mimouni, 'Pour une définition nouvelle du judéo-christianisme ancien', 161–86.

6 Taylor, 'Phenomenon', 314, 320, 327. She insists on a hyphen (Jewish-Christianity) to indicate this understanding of the phenomenon. I regard the designation 'Judaeo-Christianity' as a synonym of 'Jewish Christianity' (with or without the hyphen).

7 Mimouni, 'Pour une définition nouvelle', 162, 184.

8 Taylor, 'Phenomenon', 317, 327. Taylor, Mimouni and Kaestli all severely criticize attempts to define Jewish Christianity on the basis of theological concepts or themes, an approach associated especially with Daniélou, *The Theology of Jewish Christianity*. Appealing to Daniélou, Dunn (*The Partings of the Ways*, 234) can then rightly insist that 'Christianity as a whole can in some measure be described as "Jewish Christianity"'. But Jewish Christianity as defined by Taylor and Mimouni is something more limited.

9 Taylor, 'Phenomenon', 320.

10 Klijn and Reinink, *Patristic Evidence* (henceforth K–R), 173.

11 See also the *anacephaliosis* (to Epiphanius) 2.9 (K–R, 161), written in the early fifth century (Pritz, *Nazarene Jewish Christianity*, 29), and Augustine, *De baptismo* VII.I.I (K–R, 237); *Contra Faustem* XIX.4 (K–R, 237), *De haer.* 9 (K–R, 239).

12 See further on the variety of beliefs about Jesus among Jewish Christians, Strecker, 'On the Problem of Jewish Christianity', 273–4; Blanchetière, 'Secte des Nazaréens', 72–8. Two distinct tendencies are discernible, one 'adoptionist', the other 'orthodox'. See already Justin, *Dial.* 46–7, discussed by Strecker, Blanchetière and Pritz, *Nazarene Jewish Christianity*, 19–21.

13 Kaestli's views are akin to those of Taylor and Mimouni, but he, following Strecker ('Jewish Christianity') and Lüdemann (*Opposition to Paul in Jewish Christianity*), thinks anti-Paulinism was a defining characteristic of Jewish-Christianity. But no anti-Pauline sentiments are preserved in any of the reports about the Nazoreans, and, if Jerome is to be believed (*In Esaiam* 9.1–4 (K–R, 223)), the Nazoreans actually approved of Paul's mission.

14 Luttikhuizen, 'Vroeg-christelijk Jodendom', 163.

15 Jerome thinks these Nazoreans are to be identified with the Ebionites. But the reference to 'Minaeans' (= *minim*) and to Pharisees indicates that they were, as Jerome correctly indicates, Nazoreans, i.e., *Notzrim*. Taylor, following Klijn and Reinink, points out that the Church Fathers tended to refer to anything Jewish Christian as Ebionite. See further below on the rabbinic evidence.

16 See Alexander ('The Parting of the Ways', 9) for the definition of *min* as a heretic from rabbinic norms.

17 I take *Notzrim* here to refer to Nazoreans, not to Gentile Christians, or Christians in general, as did some Church Fathers and some scholars do today. I address this matter further below.

18 Martyn, 'Glimpses into the History of the Johannine Community', 104; cf. *History and Theology in the Fourth Gospel*, 66.

19 I have sought to explore the possible points of contact between Johannine Christianity and the Nazoreans in 'L'Evangile de Jean et le Christianisme juif (nazoréen)', 179–202.

20 Their sociological separation is indicative of where the primary determinant of their identity lay, in their messianic faith rather than in their law-observance, at least as the latter was defined by the rabbis. However, it is important to observe that the Nazoreans as Jewish Christians were also sociologically separate from the Great Church.

21 Mark prefers the term Ναζαρῆνος (Nazarene) for Jesus (1:24; 10:47; 14:67; 16:6), which Luke uses twice (4:34; 24:19), though the manuscript evidence often attests both. The two terms are probably synonyms.

22 This term was also used to designate a philosophical 'school (of

thought)', e.g., the Stoics, and later came to mean 'heresy' (cf. 2 Pet. 2:1), being so used by Epiphanius in his account of the Nazoreans. I use the term 'sect' here as a synonym for 'party' (or 'group').

23 This use of the term on the part of Jews is still evident in Justin, *Dial.* 17, 108. See Stanton, *A Gospel for a New People*, 237, 244.

24 I read Acts 24:5 to say two distinguishable things about Paul: (1) that he is 'an agitator among all the Jews [not the Gentiles!] throughout the world' (cf. 21:21, where he is charged with teaching 'all the Jews living among the Gentiles' to forsake Moses, i.e., the law, a charge the author of Acts regards as false), and (2) that he is a 'ringleader' of the Nazoreans, i.e., of Christian Jews located in Jerusalem and Palestine.

25 Pritz, *Nazarene Jewish Christianity*, 15. On 'common Judaism', see Sanders, *Judaism*, 47.

26 Cf. de Boer, 'Images of Paul in the Post-Apostolic Period' (1980). It is interesting that according to Jerome, *in Esaiam* 9.1–4 (K–R, 223), Paul seems to have been regarded positively by the Nazoreans, unlike other Jewish Christians. See Pritz, *Nazarene Jewish Christianity*, 109.

27 Paul may have been a Jew born in the Diaspora (Tarsus), but he was, according to the author of Acts, brought up in Jerusalem and educated there, at the feet of Gamaliel no less (22:3).

28 The author of Acts also does not explicitly indicate whether Christian Jews were called Nazoreans among Diaspora Jews (though 28:22 could perhaps be taken this way). By the same token, 'Nazorean' as an appellative for Jesus himself is not all that prominent in the Gospels and Acts, except as part of the earliest tradition about him. In all other NT literature, this appellative is absent and he is known generally by the double name 'Jesus Christ'.

29 Cf. note 54 below for similar testimony from Tertullian, Eusebius, Jerome and the rabbis.

30 There seems to me no reason to limit the Nazoreans to the Jerusalem church led by James, as Pritz is inclined to do, under the influence of Epiphanius (*Pan* 29.7.8 (K–R, 173)). Cf. Gal. 1:22: 'the churches of Judaea'. Acts of course depicts a successful series of missions by Aramaic-speaking Christians (Nazoreans) beyond the boundaries of Jerusalem and Judaea (cf. Acts 9:1), as emphasized by Taylor, 'Phenomenon', 316.

31 See Luttikhuizen, 'Vroeg-christelijk Jodendom', 176.

32 See Taylor, 'Phenomenon', 326; Luttikhuizen, 'Vroeg-christelijk Jodendom', 176. In this essay, 'Palestine' encompasses the general area south and east of Syrian Antioch down to Jerusalem. See Epiphanius, *Pan.* 29.7.7 (K–R, 173).

33 Pritz, *Nazarene Jewish Christianity*, 107. Of course, rabbinic literature presents great difficulties with respect to dating and historical reliability. Nevertheless, much of it must at least be earlier than Epiphanius or Jerome and reflects events and controversies in the history of

rabbinic Judaism after 70 CE. Pritz surmises (p. 109) that the Nazoreans (or Nazarenes, as he calls them) were not mentioned in earlier heretical lists by Church Fathers because they were not deemed 'heretical enough or a threat to "orthodoxy"' until the fourth century: 'Church writers do not mention Nazarenes by name until such a time as the Church was free from persecution and began to refine its own narrowed orthodoxy.'

34 Names for Jesus in the Talmud include Jesus ben Pantiri (the spelling varies), Ben Stada and Balaam. Nazoreans are often called simply *minim* (see Herford, *Christianity in Talmud and Midrash*, 361–97), even if this term is also used to cover other Jews deemed heretical by the rabbis.

35 All these are from the Babylonian Talmud (Gemara): *Sanhedrin* 107b (twice), 103a, 43a (four times); *Soṭa* 47a; *Avodah Zarah* 6a, 16b–17a (twice); *Ta'anit* 27b. These passages (among others) are discussed by Herford, *Christianity in Talmud and Midrash*, 50f., 56f., 83, 97, 138f., 171f., and by Pritz, *Nazarene Jewish Christianity*, 95–102, who (like others) also includes *Gittin* 57a on the basis of an emendation suggested by Samuel Klein (Pritz, 107): *Notzrim*, for *Mitzraim* (Egypt). According to Pritz, *Notzrim* as such are explicitly mentioned only in *Avodah Zarah* 6a, *Ta'anit* 27b, and *Gittin* 57a.

36 The text is from Herford, *Christianity in Talmud and Midrash*, 171–2.

37 Herford, followed by Pritz, thinks the term *Notzrim* in these two passages probably refers to catholic Christians. See Herford, *Christianity in Talmud and Midrash*, 172; Pritz, *Nazarene Jewish Christianity*, 98–9. This is not so clear, however, as the following argument will indicate. See Kimelman, 'Birkat ha-Minim', 241–3. Pritz dates both traditions back to the third century, but I shall argue that the first at least reflects much earlier traditions.

38 Pritz, *Nazarene Jewish Christianity*, 99, who adds the dubious comment 'at a time effectively before the *nozrim* [sic] were any factor', a claim belied by Acts 24:5. Pritz then goes on to consider the possibility that Yohanan 'is speaking about *nozrim* in a Temple activity long after the Temple was destroyed', but concludes that there seems to be an anachronism here. Pritz is right of course in claiming that 'there is no evidence of a Sunday fast unless, doubtfully, it might be 1 Cor. 11:33–34' (98 n. 17). However that may be, there is evidence of fasting among Jewish believers in earliest Christianity in Palestine: Matt. 6:16–18; 17:21; Acts 13:3; 14:23; *Did.* 1.3; cf. Mark 2:20 par. (There is no evidence of fasting in Pauline churches.) For later evidence, see *Acts of Thomas* 29, *Didascalia Apostolorum* 21, *Apostolic Constitutions* 4.3.15; 5.3.20 (discussed by Kimelman, 'Birkat', 243–4, 402 n. 121).

39 Pritz, *Nazarene Jewish Christianity*, 98. Pritz does not adopt this view, however, for he immediately and confidently adds: 'But this cannot

be the sense intended by R. Yohanan. There would have been no respectful treatment of the holy day' of Christians, whether Nazorean or catholic. This assessment, which may be correct for the third-century situation, is probably anachronistic with respect to Nazoreans as a group still *within* (Palestinian) Judaism prior to the second century CE.

40 See Pritz, *Nazarene Jewish Christianity*, 98; Herford, *Christianity in Talmud and Midrash*, 172.

41 Herford, *Christianity in Talmud and Midrash*, 172.

42 This Jacob is probably neither James the brother of Jesus nor James the son of Zebedee. See Herford, *Christianity in Talmud and Midrash*, 106.

43 See Pritz, *Nazarene Jewish Christianity*, 102.

44 See further Pritz, *Nazarene Jewish Christianity*, 99–102; Herford, *Christianity in Talmud and Midrash*, 97–137.

45 Pritz surmises that this information (much of it confused) possibly 'came from a convert from rabbinic Judaism' (*Nazarene Jewish Christianity*, 62; see his discussion, pp. 58–62).

46 See Pritz, *Nazarene Jewish Christianity*, 57–70; Klijn and Reinink, *Patristic Evidence*, 220–5.

47 Pritz, *Nazarene Jewish Christianity*, 110. See also Alexander, 'Parting'.

48 Pritz, *Nazarene Jewish Christianity*, 110.

49 *Ibid.*, 102. So also Alexander, 'Parting', 3.

50 See the brief review of the debate by van der Horst, 'The Birkat ha-Minim in Recent Research'.

51 But cf. *t. Ber.* 3.25 (Herford, *Christianity in Talmud and Midrash*, 136).

52 See Alexander, 'Parting', 7; Horbury, 'The Benediction of the Minim', 19–23; Schiffman, *Who was a Jew?*, 51–61, esp. 57.

53 See Horbury, 'Benediction', 28, 51, 60–1; Schiffman, *Who was a Jew?*, 58, 60–1; Katz, 'Issues in the Separation of Judaism and Christianity', 71–2.

54 See *In Amos* 1.11–12 ('until today in their synagogues they blaspheme the Christian people under the name *Nazareni*'); *In Esaiam* 5.18–19 ('up to the present they persevere in blasphemy and three times a day in all the synagogues they anathematize the Christian name under the name of *Nazareni*'); 49.7 ('they curse him three times a day under the name of *Nazareni*'); 52.4–6 ('in your synagogues they utter curses against the Christians three times a day, as I have said, under the name of *Nazareni*, who night and day blaspheme the Saviour) (K–R, 218–28). This would appear to find support in two brief notices found in Tertullian and Eusebius. In *Adv. Marc.* IV.8 (K–R, 108–9), Tertullian writes that 'Christ had to be called *Nazaraeus* according to the prophecy of the Creator [cf. Matt. 2:23]. Therefore also by this very name the Jews call us *Nazareni*.' Similarly, Eusebius, *onomasticon* (K–R,

150–1): 'From this name [Nazareth] Christ was called Ναζωραῖος [cf. Matt. 2:23], and we who are now called Christians received in the past the name Ναζαρῆνοι.'

55 Kimelman, 'Birkat', 238. Cf. also van der Horst, 'Birkat', 111.

56 See Vizotsky, 'Prolegomenon to the Study of Jewish-Christianities in Rabbinic Literature', 64: 'technical terminology does not remain static in the literature. Thus a term may mean one thing in tannaitic times (c.70–200) and quite another in Amoraic literature (c.200–500). Or a term may mean one thing in Babylonia and another in Palestine.' He then lists seven examples to which these observations probably apply, the first two being *min* and *Notzri*. On the changing meaning of *minim*, see Kimelman, 'Birkat', 228–32. Kimelman thinks that the Hebrew *Notzrim* was originally *Natzrim* (240, 399 n. 91).

57 Horbury, 'Benediction', 28.

58 Alexander writes: 'Rabbinic policy towards Christianity was aimed specifically at the Jewish Christians' ('Parting', 3).

59 Graham N. Stanton writes in this volume (p. 272): 'Sociologists remind us that where groups are in conflict, the sharpness of the reaction to the "inner enemy" is in proportion to the sharpness of the conflict with outer enemies.' He appeals to the work of Coser, *The Functions of Social Conflict*. See also the recent use of this work in Sanders, *Schismatics, Sectarians, Dissidents, Deviants*, 125–9.

60 The same would apply to Tertullian and Eusebius (note 56 above).

61 See Krauss, 'The Jews in the Works of the Church Fathers', 132 (cited by Kimelman, 'Birkat', 237, 398 n. 71), and Thornton, 'Christian Understandings of the *Birkath ha-Minim*'. Thornton argues that Jerome accurately reflected the actual scope of the benediction in *Ep.* 112.13. In *1 Apol.* 31, Justin takes the persecution of Christians by Bar Kochba to be a persecution of Christians in general when it seems rather more probable that Bar Kochba persecuted Jewish Christians, or Christian Jews. Cf. van der Horst, 'Birkat', 111.

62 See Schäfer, 'Die sogenannte Synode von Jabne'; Schürer, *The History of the Jewish People in the Age of Jesus Christ*, 454–63.

63 Justin was born in Samaria, Epiphanius in Judaea. Although he does not mention Nazoreans or the *birkat ha-minim*, Origen could be added to this list since he also spent much time in Palestine in the first half of the third century and mentions the cursing and blaspheming of Christ by Jews; cf. *Hom.* 118 *in Ps. 37 (38)* (*PG* 12.1387) and *Homilies on Jeremiah* 10.8.2; 19.12.31, which are discussed by Kimelman ('Birkat', 236–7). Kimelman points out that the *Homilies on Jeremiah* 'were composed during the 240s after Origen had spent over a decade in Palestine'. The precise import of Origen's statements on this matter is unclear (but see note 68 below).

64 Pritz, *Nazarene Jewish Christianity*, 106.

65 That could be one way to explain why *Notzrim*, rather than *minim*, stands first in the benediction. See Krauss, 'The Jews', 131–4. Krauss posited *Notzrim* as original to the benediction even before the Cairo Genizah specimens of the *birkat ha-minim* were found (see Pritz, *Nazarene Jewish Christianity*, 104). Contrast Kimelman, 'Birkat', 226–44, esp. 233; Katz, 'Issues', 43–76, esp. 68, 74. It seems to me that one could argue that the benediction against the *Notzrim* (usable in Palestine) *became* the benediction against the Heretics (usable elsewhere). The alternative is to take the reference to the *minim* as an explanatory gloss on the reference to the *Notzrim* ('the *Notzrim*, i.e., the *minim*'), though that still does not explain why *Notzrim* are mentioned before *minim*. In any event, Kimelman (like others) still observes that 'the Palestinian prayer against the *minim* was aimed at Jewish sectarians among whom Jewish Christians figured prominently' (232). Schiffman (*Who was a Jew?*, 54) thinks the *minim* of the benediction were primarily Jewish Christians (or, better, Christian Jews). Thus, the question of when the term *Notzrim* was introduced into the benediction may not be that important, since they were included under the term *minim* (see Herford, *Christianity in Talmud and Midrash*; Alexander, 'Parting'). However, the point may be important in view of the claim of Katz ('Issues', 74, 76) that the benediction functioned as 'a filter and a self-imposed ban'. If a person did not consider himself a heretic, the benediction would not present a threat and he could continue participation in synagogue worship and life. For 'the malediction actually to function to separate heretics it would be necessary for the term to have a clear and delimited meaning that was "inescapable"'. A similar claim is made by Kimelman, 'Birkat', 227. This claim is without weight of course if *Notzrim* was original to the Jamnian benediction. But even if it was not, Alexander rightly points out ('Parting', 9) that 'The power of cursing was taken seriously in antiquity; no-one would lightly curse himself or his associates or put himself voluntarily in the way of a curse', especially if everyone understood with a nod and wink who the *minim* cursed by the benediction were. See *Tanhuma Vayyiqra* 3, quoted by Alexander (p. 9 n. 14), and note 67 below.

66 Alexander, 'Parting'.

67 Cf. *t. Hullin* 2.20–1, which reads in part: 'We do not sell to them, nor do we buy from them. We do not take from them, we do not give to them.' See Alexander, 'Parting', 15–17, for this and other similar texts testifying, he believes, to attempts to ostracize Jewish Christians in particular. See esp. *b. Avodah Zarah* 27b, which counsels: 'A man shall have no dealing with the Minim, nor be cured by them, even for the sake of an hour of life.' The passage then goes on to recount how 'Jacob the Min of Cephar Sechanja', the same one mentioned in *b. Avodah Zarah* 16b–17a, discussed above, came to cure the nephew of

Rabbi Ishmael, who had been bitten by a serpent. But Rabbi Ishmael would not allow it and the nephew died (Herford, *Christianity in Talmud and Midrash*, 105). See also Justin, *Dialogue*, 38, 112.

68 Cf. Alexander, 'Parting'; Schiffman, *Who was a Jew?*, 54, 60–1; Katz, 'Issues', 51. According to Justin (*Dial.* 108), the Jews cursed both Christians and Jesus himself (cf. Acts 26:11; 1 Cor. 12:3). He thus seems to have understood, as did Jerome (*In Esaiam* 49.7: 'they curse him [Jesus] three times a day under the name of *Nazareni*' (K–R, 224–5)), if only in a confused way, that in reciting the Twelfth Benediction Nazoreans would in effect be cursing not only themselves (as Nazoreans) but also the Nazorean (Jesus) in whom they believed. This they evidently could not do. Origen may also be mentioned here (see note 63 above), despite Kimelman's attempt to distance Origen from any knowledge of the *birkat ha-minim* or anything analogous ('Birkat', 236–7). For Kimelman it is decisive that 'Origen makes no mention of Christians being cursed nor of any connection to the prayers' even though he does report 'Jews blaspheming Jesus'. Schiffman, on the other hand, sees 'allusions' to the *birkat ha-minim* in Origen as well as in Justin (*Who was a Jew?*, 61).

69 And by Tertullian, *Adv. Marc.* IV.8 (K–R, 108–9), cited in note 54 above, who at least indicates that the term was being used by Jews *c.*200 CE. Other Church Fathers (e.g. Justin, Irenaeus) could provide further evidence of such continuity, even though they do not mention 'Nazoreans' by name. See the intriguing discussion by Blanchetière, 'Secte des Nazaréens'.

70 Cf. Klijn and Reinink, *Patristic Evidence.* By comparison, Justin is remarkably open-minded about them in *Dial.* 46–7, though he knows of other Christians who are less tolerant than he is. Furthermore, he has his own reservations about Jewish Christians who seek to encourage Gentile Christians to keep the law; see the essay by G. N. Stanton in this volume, ch. 15 below.

71 Cf. the social dynamics of boundary formation and maintenance in Sanders, *Schismatics*, 129–51, esp. 150.

BIBLIOGRAPHY

Alexander, Philip S., '"The Parting of the Ways" from the Perspective of Rabbinic Judaism", in J. D. G. Dunn (ed.), *Jews and Christians: The Parting of the Ways AD 70 to 135*, WUNT 66, Tübingen, 1993, 1–25.

Baarda, T., de Jonge, H. J., and Menken, M. J. J. (eds.), *Jodendom en Vroeg Christendom: Continuiteit en Discontinuiteit*, Kampen, 1991.

Blanchetière, F., 'Le "Secte des Nazaréens" ou les débuts du christianisme', in F. Blanchetière and M. Herr (eds.), *Aux origines juives du christianisme*, Paris, 1993, 65–91.

Coser, Lewis, *The Functions of Social Conflict*, London, 1956.

Daniélou, Jean, *The Theology of Jewish Christianity*, London, 1964 (French, 1958).

De Boer, M. C., 'Images of Paul in the Post-Apostolic Period', *CBQ* 42 (1980), 359–80.

'L'Evangile de Jean et le Christianisme juif (nazoréen)', in D. Marguerat (ed.), *Le déchirement. Juifs et chrétiens au premier siècle*, Geneva, 1996, 179–202.

Dunn, J. D. G., *The Partings of the Ways Between Christianity and Judaism and their Significance for the Character of Christianity*, London, 1991.

Herford, R. Travers, *Christianity in Talmud and Midrash*, London, 1903.

Horbury, W., 'The Benediction of the *Minim* and Early Jewish–Christian Controversy', *JTS* 33 (1982), 19–61.

Kaestli, Jean-Daniel, 'Où en est le débat sur le judéo-christianisme?', in D. Marguerat (ed.), *Le déchirement. Juifs et chrétiens au premier siècle*, Geneva, 1996, 243–72.

Katz, S. T., 'Issues in the Separation of Judaism and Christianity after 70 CE: A Reconsideration', *JBL* 103 (1984), 43–76.

Kimelman, R., 'Birkat ha-Minim and the Lack of Evidence for an Anti-Christian Jewish Prayer in Late Antiquity', in E. P. Sanders (ed.), *Jewish and Christian Self-Definition*, Philadelphia, 1981, vol. II, 226–44, 391–403.

Klijn, A. F. J., and Reinink, G. J., *Patristic Evidence for Jewish-Christian Sects*, NovTSup, 36, Leiden, 1973.

Krauss, S., 'The Jews in the Works of the Church Fathers', *JQR* o.s. 5 (1892–3), 122–57.

Lüdemann, G., *Opposition to Paul in Jewish Christianity*, Minneapolis, 1989.

Luttikhuizen, G. P., 'Vroeg-christelijk Jodendom', in T. Baarda, H. J. de Jonge and M. J. J. Menken (eds.), *Jodendom en Vroeg Christendom: Continuiteit en Discontinuiteit*, Kampen, 1991.

Marguerat, D. (ed.), *Le déchirement. Juifs et chrétiens au premier siècle*, Le Monde de la Bible 32, Geneva, 1996.

Martyn, J. Louis, 'Glimpses into the History of the Johannine Community', in *The Gospel of John in Christian History*, New York, 1978, 90–121. First published in M. de Jonge (ed.), *L'Evangile de Jean. Sources, rédaction, theologie*, BETL 14, Leuven, 1977.

History and Theology in the Fourth Gospel, Nashville, 1979 (1968).

Mimouni, S. C., 'Pour une définition nouvelle du Judéo-Christianisme ancien', *NTS* 38 (1992), 161–86.

Pritz, Ray A., *Nazarene Jewish Christianity*, Jerusalem and Leiden, 1988.

Sanders, E. P., *Judaism: Practice and Belief 63* BCE–66 CE, London and Philadelphia, 1992.

Sanders, Jack T., *Schismatics, Sectarians, Dissidents, Deviants: The First One Hundred Years of Jewish–Christian Relations*, London, 1993.

Schäfer, P., 'Die sogenannte Synode von Jabne', *Judaica* 31 (1975), 54–64.

Schiffman, Lawrence H., *Who was a Jew? Rabbinic and Halakhic Perspectives on the Jewish Christian Schism*, Hoboken, NJ, 1985.

Schürer, E., *The History of the Jewish People in the age of Jesus Christ (175 BC–AD 135)*, vol. II, rev. and ed. by G. Vermes, F. Millar and M. Goodman, Edinburgh, 1979.

Stanton, G., *A Gospel for a New People: Studies in Matthew*, Edinburgh, 1992.

Strecker, G., 'On the Problem of Jewish Christianity' (1971; German, 1964), in W. Bauer (ed.), *Orthodoxy and Heresy in Earliest Christianity*, Philadelphia, 1971 (German 1934, 1964²), 241–85 (app. 1).

Taylor, Joan E., 'The Phenomenon of Early Jewish-Christianity: Reality or Scholarly Invention?', *VC* 44 (1990), 313–34.

Christians and Holy Places. The Myth of Jewish-Christian Origins, Oxford, 1993.

Thornton, T. C. G., 'Christian Understandings of the *Birkath ha-Minim* in the Eastern Roman Empire', *JTS* 38 (1987), 419–31.

Van der Horst, P. W., 'The Birkat ha-Minim in Recent Research', in his *Hellenism–Judaism–Christianity. Essays on their Interaction.* Contributions to Biblical Exegesis & Theology 8, Kampen, 1994, 99–111. Also published in *Expository Times* 105 (1994), 363–8.

Vizotsky, Burton L., 'Prolegomenon to the Study of Jewish-Christianities in Rabbinic Literature', *AJS Review. Journal of the Association of Jewish Studies* 14 (1989), 47–70.

CHAPTER 15

Justin Martyr's Dialogue with Trypho: *group boundaries, 'proselytes' and 'God-fearers'*

Graham N. Stanton

Justin's *Dialogue* is the earliest surviving writing which sets out fully the issues which separated Christians and Jews. This fascinating *Dialogue* was written about 160 CE. It draws on earlier Christian exegetical traditions; in places it has very deep roots in Jewish–Christian polemic and apologetic.

Although Justin and Trypho argue vigorously, they do not resort to personal abuse or to name-calling. At the end of the *Dialogue*, they agree to disagree; after praying for one another they go their separate ways. Most later Christian anti-Jewish writings are less moderate in tone; unlike Trypho, the Jewish opponent(s) often cave in and accept the 'truth' of Christianity. However, if we have twentieth-century understandings of 'tolerance' in mind, it would not be appropriate to claim either Justin or Trypho as models of 'tolerance'. Both the Christian and his Jewish partner in dialogue not only set out their respective very different religious positions, they go further: they appeal vigorously to one another to change sides, with the clear implication that the other side is wrong-headed.

How plausible is Justin's claim that his *Dialogue* records an extended discussion he had with a learned Jew, Trypho, shortly after the second Jewish revolt? Opinions have differed widely. My own view is that the *Dialogue* is neither a verbatim account of a two-day debate which took place in Ephesus between a Christian and a Jew, nor a wholly artificial compilation of Christian polemical traditions which is unrelated to discussions between Christians and Jews in the middle decades of the second century. There are points at which Trypho is little more than a puppet: he is allowed to say only what Justin wants him to say. However, many of the arguments and responses of both Justin and Trypho are found in other writings from this period. In several key passages Trypho echoes widely held Jewish objections to Christian claims and sets out Jewish basic convictions or interpretations of Scripture which are well attested elsewhere.

In this chapter I shall discuss a set of passages which set out Justin's view of the boundaries marked out by both Judaism and Christianity, i.e. passages which are directly relevant to the theme of this volume. The *Dialogue* undoubtedly reflects one prominent Christian's perception of the Judaism and the Christianity of his own day. Within the space available it will not be possible to discuss the extent to which Justin's views correspond to historical reality. I shall have to content myself with the assertion that at least as far as the themes of this chapter are concerned, Justin rarely misleads us. As we shall see, the *Dialogue* contains important references both to 'God-fearers' and to 'proselytes' which have been overlooked in recent scholarly discussion of these topics.

If my reading of a set of key passages in the *Dialogue* is in certain respects fresh, then it is the result not of any new evidence which has come to hand, but rather of my use of two methods which have been used to good effect in recent studies of the Gospels. I shall draw on some of the insights of modern literary critics by emphasizing the relationship of Justin's characterization of Trypho's companions to his overall purposes.[1] I shall also appeal briefly to sociological insights, in particular to social conflict theory and to the varying levels of commitment often found in groups.

I. TRYPHO'S COMPANIONS

Several scholars have commented on Justin's characterization of Trypho the Jew. They have stressed that Trypho is a pleasant courteous Jew, and that, unlike many later Christian and Jewish disputants, Justin and Trypho respect one another. However, the role in the *Dialogue* of Trypho's *companions* has usually been quietly ignored, from Eusebius right up to the present.

In the very first extant sentence of the *Dialogue* Justin is met by an unidentified man who is accompanied by companions; the latter are referred to in the second sentence as the man's 'friends'.[2] The reader's curiosity is aroused immediately. Who is the person who engages Justin in conversation, and who are his companions? Before Trypho identifies himself and states that he is a circumcised

Jew who has recently fled from the Bar Kochba war, his 'followers and companions' inform Justin (and the reader of the *Dialogue*) that they are keen to hear 'some profitable discourse' from Justin. But we are *not* told anything about the background of Trypho's companions at this point. This silence turns out to be significant.

The extended discussions between Justin and Trypho take place on two days, on both of which Trypho (but not Justin) is accompanied by friends. Indeed, Justin notes that some additional companions turned up with Trypho on the second day.[3] Occasionally the companions intervene in the discussions to remind the reader of their presence. They never defend a point of view which differs from that of Trypho, but, as we shall see, they are distinguished from Trypho in important respects. In the very last chapter (142), Trypho is still accompanied by his companions as he and Justin go their separate ways after praying for one another.

Although the companions are firmly in Trypho's court, Justin takes pains to distinguish between their reaction to Justin's Christian claims and Trypho's own reaction. Trypho's companions are portrayed as being more cynical about Justin's Christian claims than Trypho himself: they are therefore even less likely to become Christians.

This distinction is set out clearly in the opening chapters, and maintained consistently thereafter. In the first seven chapters, which are a prologue to the *Dialogue* as a whole, Justin tells Trypho about his intellectual pilgrimage and his conversion to Christianity. In response Trypho smiles and replies courteously, but his companions 'laugh aloud' (8.3). In the next chapter the reader is told that they 'laughed aloud again and began to shout quite rudely' (9.2). Not surprisingly, Justin is offended and starts to break off the discussion. Trypho urges him to keep his promise and to continue. Justin agrees, with the proviso that the companions must behave themselves and listen quietly. At this point two of the companions disappear, 'with some jokes, and some jests at our zeal', Justin says ruefully. The remaining companions sit down quietly with Justin and Trypho, and after a brief conversation about the Bar Kochba war, they listen to the discussions between Justin and Trypho.

The hostility of Trypho's companions is not confined to the opening chapters. Towards the end of the second day of the discussions their rudeness is referred to again: 'some of those who had come on the second day' protested at one of Justin's claims, and 'cried out as though in a theatre' (122.4).

Justin has taken pains to portray Trypho's companions carefully. Hence they are not simply part of the stage scenery – merely a convention of the dialogue genre which goes back to Plato and Xenophon, a genre which reappeared in the second century CE. For example, in Plutarch's *Moralia* we have dinner-party conversations of a group of wise men. In the only extant work of Athenaeus, *The Learned Banquet*, which was written at the end of the second century, a Cynic philosopher is introduced as a foil to the twenty-three men at the banquet. But the dialogue tradition does not usually contain the sharp differentiation between two groups *on the same side* which is so striking in Justin's *Dialogue*.

Just like Justin himself, for the time being I shall leave my readers in suspense concerning the identity of Trypho's companions.

2. *DIALOGUE* 8 AND 9: GROUP BOUNDARIES

In terms of the literary structure of the *Dialogue*, these two chapters are programmatic. They mark the transition from the Prologue to the main body of the *Dialogue*. Their structural role is confirmed by the fact that only here (8.3), and at the beginning[4] and the end (141.5) of the whole *Dialogue* does Justin address Marcus Pompeius, the person to whom the *Dialogue* is dedicated. Most of the themes which will be discussed in the 133 chapters which follow are foreshadowed here.

Justin appeals to Trypho to become a Christian: 'If you seek salvation seriously and have trusted in God, it is open to you, once you know the Christ of God and have become an initiate,[5] to live happily.'

Trypho immediately makes a counter-appeal to Justin. 'When you have forsaken God (καταλιπόντι τὸν θεόν)[6] and placed your hope on a man, what kind of hope yet remains (περιλείπεται) for you?' Trypho acknowledges Justin as a friend and then urges him to be circumcised, then (as is commanded in the law) to keep the sabbath and the feasts and God's new moons, and, in short, to do all the things that are written in the law, and then perchance he will find mercy from God (8.4). Trypho then summarizes his own views concerning the Messiah, and alleges that Christians have shaped a kind of Messiah for themselves. A little later Trypho criticizes Christians for their failure to mark out a boundary between themselves and pagans (10.3).

The issues which separate Justin and Trypho are set out clearly: Justin appeals to Trypho 'to know the Christ of God'; Trypho urges Justin to 'do all the things that are written in the law'. Their agendas are very different. Both refer to a rather different 'rite of entry' into their respective communities, baptism and circumcision.

Both claim that the other person has been led astray by false teachers. Trypho claims that Justin has been led astray (ἐξαπα-τᾶθῆναι) by false speeches, and has followed men of no account.[7] Justin claims that Trypho has 'obeyed teachers who do not understand the Scriptures, and has prophesied falsely (ἀπομαντευόμε-νος), saying whatever comes into his mind' (9.1). Justin then insists that he wants to show Trypho that Christians have not been led astray (πεπλανήμεθα); the context suggests that false teachers are in mind. I have tried to show elsewhere that these charges and countercharges of 'false prophecy' and 'leading astray' have deep roots in early Christian–Jewish polemic and apologetic.[8]

For my present purposes, however, I want to focus on another striking feature of this passage. In these two programmatic chapters the 'group boundaries' and the 'rites of initiation' of the rival religious communities are set out. In both cases the social boundaries are tight, but that does not preclude openness to outsiders. This is confirmed by the parallel appeals to change sides, and by the references to false teachers. Justin and Trypho do not write one another off absolutely. Both single out false teachers as responsible for the false stance taken by the other.[9] Both hope that once the sway of the false teachers is shaken off, their rival will be able to change sides. In other words, from Justin's perspective, both synagogue and church hope that adherents of the rival community will be won over. In spite of tight social boundaries on both sides of the divide, movement is possible. As we shall see, the language of movement, 'going over', is found more explicitly in *Dialogue* 47.

3. *DIALOGUE* 23: 'GOD-FEARERS'

At the end of a series of scriptural citations in chapters 21 and 22, Justin brings his argument to a climax by challenging Trypho and his companions: 'If this is not so, tell me what you all think about the matters under discussion.' And when no one answers, Justin adds: 'Therefore to you, Trypho, *and to those who wish to become proselytes* (καὶ τοῖς βουλομένοις προσηλύτοις γενέσθαι) I proclaim the Divine message ...' (23.3).

This is the *first time* the reader is given any specific information about the companions: they 'want to become proselytes'. This phrase can be understood in three ways: the companions could be either Jews or Gentiles who want to become proselytes to Christianity; or they could be Gentiles who want to become proselytes to Judaism.

Perhaps our first inclination is to assume that Trypho's companions are fellow Jews who are seriously interested in becoming Christians. That might seem appropriate in view of Justin's opening appeal to Trypho which we have just noted. However, the sustained hostility and cynicism of the companions makes this unlikely. In addition, the immediate context rules out the possibility that the companions are Jews. This passage comes at the climax of an extended discussion about circumcision which follows the programmatic chapters 8 and 9. Two sentences after the reference to the companions who wish to become proselytes, Justin makes an impassioned plea to them: 'Stay as you have been born' (μείνατε ὡς γεγένησθε). And a familiar line of argument about Abraham's justification before circumcision then follows: the latter was just a sign. If Trypho's companions were Jews, there would not be any need to urge them to stay as they are and not to bother with circumcision. *So the companions must be Gentiles.*

Do they wish to become proselytes (i.e. convert fully) to Judaism, or to Christianity? The latter view has been influential, largely as a result of the most widely available English translation, by A. L. Williams (1930). Williams clarifies the ambiguous Greek by adding in brackets after 'proselytes' the phrase 'to the true faith'. In other words Williams thinks that Trypho's companions are keen to become 'proselytes' to Christianity.

Although this interpretation has been defended by Stylianopoulos, his arguments are unconvincing.[10] (i) Stylianopoulos places great emphasis on two passages in the *Dialogue* which refer to Christian proselytes. First, at 28.2, Justin states that there is only a short time left for 'proselytizing' to us (προσηλύσεως), i.e. for becoming Christians.[11] But this is a desperate plea in the form of a *threat* to Trypho and his companions; there is no suggestion that the companions are at all keen or likely to become Christians – on the contrary. Secondly, in the only passage in the *Dialogue* in which προσήλυτος refers to 'proselytes to Christianity' (122.5), Justin is referring to himself and to fellow Gentile Christians – certainly not to Trypho's companions. As far as I can discover, this is the first time in extant writings in which προσήλυτος is used to refer to converts to Christianity.[12] In this highly rhetorical passage Justin contrasts 'the old law and its proselytes' with 'Christ and his proselytes'. The reference to Christian proselytes is modelled on the well-established Jewish usage. With this single exception, in the *Dialogue* the noun 'proselyte' (ten out of eleven times) always means 'convert completely to Judaism by means of circumcision'.

(ii) Sylianopoulos claims that Justin does not distinguish between Trypho and his companions – and thus misses the point I have emphasized above. On his view the appeal, 'Stay as you have been born', is addressed to both Trypho and his *Jewish* companions. However, Stylianopoulos does not explain what this appeal would mean if addressed to Jews. The context is a discussion concerning circumcision. In that context why would Justin urge circumcised Jews (Trypho and his companions) to remain as they were born?

On my interpretation (which now has the weighty support of L. H. Feldman, even if only in one sentence),[13] Justin is keen to dissuade Trypho's companions from taking the final step of circumcision, for he knows (probably from experience) that it is even more difficult to convert to Christ those have become proselytes to Judaism than it is to convert Jews like Trypho. So he argues vigorously and at length that circumcision was not part of God's original purposes.

At the beginning of their lengthy discussion on this topic Justin lets Trypho have first say. Justin seems to be generous in allowing Trypho to deal the first card, but, as we shall see, Justin himself holds the trump card. Trypho's first card, (10.3) is the very first of the numerous explicit citations of Scripture in the *Dialogue*, Genesis 17:14: 'The person who has *not* been circumcised on the eighth day shall be cut off from God's people.' Trypho then claims that this command refers not only to born Israelites, but also *to foreigners* (including Justin himself) (ἀλλογενῶν), and to purchased slaves. In interpreting Genesis 17:14 to refer to three groups, Trypho goes further than the MT or the LXX which refer to only two groups: born Israelites and (foreign) purchased slaves.

But Justin ignores the point at this stage in the *Dialogue* and concentrates on his own arguments concerning circumcision. At the climax Justin attempts to trump Trypho's card concerning Genesis 17:14: he insists once again that circumcision was given as a sign, but not for righteousness. The sentences which follow are highly rhetorical:

Understand that the blood of that circumcision has been made useless, and we have believed the blood that brings salvation ... Jesus Christ circumcises all those who will ... Come with me, *all who fear God* (φοβούμε-νοι τὸν θεόν), who wish to see the good things of Jerusalem. Come, let us go in the light of the Lord, for he has set his people free, even the house of Jacob ... (24.3)

These words are addressed directly to Trypho and his companions. The plea, 'Come with me, *all who fear God*', is intriguing. These words *may* be addressed directly to the companions: they fear God, and wish to see the good things of Jerusalem – and Justin urges them to join his side. I think it is possible, but far from certain, that Trypho's companions are referred to here as 'those who fear God', a phrase found in several passages in Acts (10:2, 22, 35; 13:16, 26).

I am more confident that at *Dialogue* 10.4 the phrase 'those who fear God' refers to Gentiles sympathetic to Judaism.[14] In this passage Trypho complains that Christians who claim to know God, do not keep the commandments – yet even those who fear God do (οἱ φοβούμενοι τὸν θεόν). Perhaps Trypho even has in mind his own companions, as well as other Gentiles sympathetic to Judaism. It is important to note that in both 10.4 and 24.3 the phrase 'those who fear God' is a very general way of referring to those sympathetic to Judaism; it is not a technical term.[15]

Justin's identification of Trypho's companions as Gentiles closely attached to Judaism who wish to become proselytes is striking. The companions are 'God-fearers', even though Justin does not explicitly refer to them as such. In recent years (especially since the discovery of the Aphrodisias inscription) literature on 'God-fearers' has become a growth industry.[16] As far as I can see, none of the recent writers on this topic makes more than a passing reference to Justin. This is unfortunate. I am convinced that when Justin's evidence is set alongside the other varied and often baffling evidence, we are forced to conclude that Gentiles were attracted to Judaism for many reasons and that their relationship to Judaism took many forms. In short, we are not to think of 'God-fearers' as a technical term which refers to one distinct group whose status remained constant. I hope to show below that the same is true of 'proselytes'.

Before we leave chapter 23, we must ask why Justin has so much to say about circumcision in his opening exchanges with Trypho. First, he is responding to Jewish criticisms, well grounded in Scripture, of Christian claims. Secondly, he is deliberately ringing alarm bells for his Christian readers, some of whom were attracted to Judaism. Thirdly, and most important of all for my present purposes, he is appealing to Gentiles who have some form of attachment to Judaism not to become proselytes, for he knew that proselytes were even less likely than Jews such as Trypho to respond to Christian preaching.

4. *DIALOGUE* 47: TOLERANCE AND INTOLERANCE

Several observations made so far are confirmed in *Dialogue* 47. We have already seen that the programmatic chapters 8 and 9 imply that there is movement in both directions between Judaism and Christianity: this is what both Justin and Trypho assume in their opening appeals to one another. At 47.1 Justin reminds his readers of Trypho's initial appeal to him in 8.4 to become a proselyte.

In response to a question from Trypho, Justin concedes that Jews who have become Christians and still wish to keep the law fully are to be accepted as long as they do not persuade Gentiles (μὴ πείθοντες αὐτούς) to keep the law, and as long as they have full fellowship with Gentile Christians. Justin refers to this issue three times in this one fairly short but very important chapter.[17] The third reference is particularly important. Justin concedes, somewhat reluctantly, that perhaps Gentile Christians who have been persuaded by Jewish Christians to keep the law will be saved (σωθήσεσθαι ἴσως ὑπολαμβάνω). Justin notes that there are some Gentile Christians who are much less tolerant than he is: they will not converse or share table-fellowship with those who acknowledge Christ and keep the law.

Why is Justin himself so cautious about Jewish Christians, and why are some of his fellow Christians so intolerant? Justin gives one answer himself: Jewish Christians who insist on keeping the law arouse the suspicion of Gentile Christians because they may try to persuade Gentile Christians to keep the law, a position Justin will not tolerate (47.3).

But this answer is not entirely satisfactory. Why should Gentiles who 'believe on this Christ' not be encouraged by Jewish Christians to 'live in accordance with the law appointed by Moses'? Why is Justin, tolerant in many other respects, so intolerant at precisely this point? Perhaps some Jewish Christians are insisting that the law should be kept as a *sine qua non* as far as salvation is concerned. However, Justin does not say that this is their position. He implies that they are encouraging Gentiles to keep the law *alongside* their faith in Christ.

I suspect that there is a partly hidden agenda at this point. The clue to a probable explanation comes in 47.4: Justin notes that some Gentile Christians who have been persuaded to keep the law have moved over completely to the Jewish polity (μεταβάντες ἐπὶ τὴν ἔννομον πολιτείαν); they have denied that 'this is the Christ', and therefore cannot be saved. Justin suspects that some Jewish Christians who encourage Gentile Christians to keep the law may in fact be responsible for turning them into proselytes to Judaism. The continuing attraction of Judaism to Gentiles, whether Christian or not, suggests that this is a plausible explanation. So I suggest that Justin is extremely sensitive concerning the status of Jews who have become Christians because he fears that some of them will encourage Gentile Christians to keep the law – and that will prove to be the crucial step on the path towards a complete transfer to Judaism.

This explanation is strengthened by sociological considerations. Justin's *Dialogue* provides ample evidence that in his day Judaism and Christianity were such keen rivals that sporadic conflict was always likely. Sociologists remind us that where groups are in conflict, the sharpness of the reaction to the 'inner enemy' is in proportion to the sharpness of the conflict with the outer enemies. A group at odds with its arch-rival will react with even more hostility to a heretic than to an apostate, for a heretic still shares many of the goals of his former fellow members.[18] Hatred is directed, not in the first place against opponents of its own view of the world order, but against the dreaded 'internal enemy' who is competing for the same end.[19]

In these terms, Jewish Christians who seek to persuade Gentile Christians to keep the law are an 'inner enemy', 'heretics', whose influence is to be feared. Trypho (and other Jews who do not 'anathematize' Christians) are 'apostates' who can be portrayed comparatively sympathetically. Not surprisingly, in this chapter and elsewhere, Justin is very hostile towards the 'outer enemy', Jews who, he claims, have 'anathematized and still anathematize' (καταναναθεματίζοντας) in the synagogues those who believe in 'this Christ' (47.4).

5. *DIALOGUE* 122–3: 'PROSELYTES'

These two chapters contain a set of vigorous exchanges over the interpretation of Isaiah 49:6 and 42:6ff., passages which refer to Israel as a 'light for the Gentiles'. Justin says to Trypho (and his companions): 'You all indeed suppose that this [i.e. Isa. 49:6] was said of the stranger and the proselytes (τὸν γηόραν καὶ τοὺς προσηλύτους). But in reality these words were said of us who have been enlightened through Jesus …' (121.1). Justin continues, 'These things also [Isa 42:6ff.], Gentlemen, have been spoken with reference to the Christ, and concerning the Gentiles that have been enlightened. Or will you say again: with reference to the Law and the proselytes he says these things?' (122.3).

Then some of those who had come on the second day cried out as though in a theatre: 'What then? Does He [God] not say them with reference to the Law and those that have been enlightened by it? Now these are the proselytes' (122.4). In his reply Justin insists that Isaiah 42:6ff. does not refer to 'the old law and its proselytes, but Christ and His proselytes, us Gentiles, whom he enlightened …'

There are several points of particular interest in this passage. (i) When Justin denies that the two passages from Isaiah refer to proselytes to Judaism, Trypho's companions fly into a rage. Their reaction suggests that they set great store by these passages: they insist that they themselves, as would-be proselytes, are enlightened by the law. A number of passages in Jewish writings state that *the law* is the light of the world, especially for proselytes.[20] Trypho and his companions quote this well-established Jewish exegetical tradition and insist that it refers to them. Justin, however, takes it over and replaces the law with Christ. In short, Justin and Trypho are rivals, both seeking 'proselytes' among Gentiles; both claim that Scripture supports their appeal to Gentiles.

(ii) Justin claims that proselytes not only do not believe, but utter blasphemies against Christ's name doubly more than Trypho himself, and wish both to kill and to torment those who believe on him (122.2). No doubt the reference to the excessive enthusiasm of proselytes is rhetorical exaggeration. Justin immediately adds his own wry, but perceptive, comment: 'For they [proselytes] are eager to become like you [Trypho and his fellow Jews] in everything.' This suggests that proselytes are uneasy about their status and need to prove themselves, even though Justin alludes to the well-known rabbinic tradition that a circumcised proselyte 'is like one who is native born' (123.1; cf. *b. Yeb.* 47b and 62a). In his recent important article on proselytes, Shaye Cohen concludes that 'the proselyte probably has an ambiguous status in the Jewish community'.[21] Although Cohen does not refer to Justin, this passage in the *Dialogue* supports his conclusion.

(iii) Most important of all for my present purposes, in 122.1 (quoted above) 'the stranger' is at least partly distinct from 'the proselytes'. Here we have further evidence for two groups with different levels of attachment to Judaism.

6. CONCLUDING OBSERVATIONS

Justin's *Dialogue* indicates that in the middle of the second century both Judaism and Christianity were concerned to maintain tight boundaries. Trypho complains that Christians (unlike Jews) do not mark themselves off from pagans. He also mentions that some Jewish teachers forbid Jews to enter into conversation with Christians – lest they be persuaded by 'blasphemous' Christian claims (38.1; 112.4). Justin's references to alleged Jewish persecution of Christians also point to Jewish anxiety lest community boundaries be breached.

Justin is concerned to maintain tight boundaries on the Christian side. He will not tolerate Jewish Christians who are not in full fellowship with Gentile Christians. Justin is very sensitive about Jewish Christians who persuade Gentile Christians to keep the law: he suspects that under their influence some Gentile Christians may move over completely to the Jewish polity (47.3–4).

And yet in spite of the concerns of both 'synagogue' and 'church' to maintain tight boundaries, there is movement across both boundary lines. This has happened in the past, and there is an expectation that it will happen in the future. In short, there is keen 'on the ground' rivalry – and this is surely the mainspring of the intolerance expressed on both sides.

Justin's *Dialogue* suggests that there were different levels of attachment to both communities. On the Jewish side there were proselytes whose status was often ambiguous; would-be proselytes, such as Trypho's companions; other Gentile sympathizers or 'God-fearers'; some Jews who acknowledged Christ, but were not in full fellowship with Gentile Christians; and some Gentile Christians who had 'gone over' to Judaism. It is surely a mistake to think of two groups which can be clearly defined, 'proselytes' and 'God-fearers'.

On the Christian side there were two kinds of Jewish Christians, one acceptable to Justin, and one not; there were also Gentile Christians who seemed likely to go over to Judaism (47.1–4).

No doubt both sides hoped to consolidate the level of commitment of those on the 'fringes' of their communities. From a later period a tradition expresses what is likely to have been the case in Justin's 'school' as well as in synagogues: 'when the sage takes his seat to expound doctrine, many strangers become proselytes' (*Cant. Rab.* 1.15; cf. 1.3 and 4.2).

As we have seen, the *Dialogue* contains important neglected evidence for the existence in the middle of the second century of 'God-fearers', even though Justin does not use a specific term for Gentiles who already have some attachment to the synagogue.

Why did Justin write his *Dialogue*? I do not think that his *main* aim was to 'win over' Jews such as Trypho. If that had been his hope and expectation, he would not have allowed Trypho to go his own way. Justin must have recognized that some Gentiles (such as Trypho's companions) were so strongly attached to Judaism that their conversion was unlikely. Perhaps his primary appeal (via his Christian 'school') was to Gentiles who were broadly sympathetic to both Judaism and Christianity – Gentiles who did not appreciate the differences, Gentiles with a weak level of attachment either to Christianity or to Judaism.

NOTES

1 I also accept that in the study of Justin's *Dialogue*, ancient literary conventions need to be considered much more fully than they have been recently.

2 Most scholars accept that the expected opening dedication is missing and that it probably mentioned Ephesus as the location of the dialogue; see Eusebius, *H.E.* 94.18.6.

3 'One of those who had come *with them* on the second day, called Mnaseas, said: "We are glad that you undertake to repeat your words again for us"' (85.6). At 56.13, the fourth of those who had remained with Trypho contributes to the discussion.

4 Marcus Pompeius was probably addressed in the missing opening lines of the *Dialogue*.

5 τελείῳ γενομένῳ, a phrase not used elsewhere in the *Dialogue*. W. Bauer, W. F. Arndt and F. W. Gingrich, *A Greek Lexicon of the New Testament and other Early Christian Literature*, note (with references) that τέλειος is used as a technical term to refer to one initiated into the rites of the mystery religions. Here Justin is referring to Christian baptism. Cf. also 14.1–2.

6 Cf. 17.1 and 108.2. From Trypho's perspective the failure of Christians to keep the law confirms that they are 'godless'.

7 This is an allusion to Justin's account in the opening chapters of his encounter with a venerable old man through whom he is introduced to Christian claims.

8 See Stanton, *A Gospel for a New People*, 237–42, and 'Jesus of Nazareth'.

9 In a series of passages Justin tries to separate Trypho from Jewish teachers: 9.1; 36.2; 38.1–2; 43.5; 48.2; 62.2; 68.7; 71.1; 110.1; 112.4–5; 117.4; 120.5; 133.3; 134.1; 137.2; 140.2; 142.2.

10 Stylianopoulos, *Justin Martyr and the Mosaic Law*, 174–6.

11 The noun προσήλυσις is not found elsewhere in Justin.

12 προσήλυτος is in fact used only comparatively rarely to refer to Christian converts. The next example is in Clement of Alexandria. See G. W. H. Lampe, *A Patristic Greek Lexicon*, Oxford 1961–8.

13 Feldman, *Jew and Gentile in the Ancient World*, 402. After coming to the conclusion defended above I discovered that it was first proposed by Zahn (1886), whose view is accepted (without discussion) by Skarsaune, *The Proof from Prophecy*, 258.

14 So too Feldman, *Jew and Gentile*, 357.

15 The other examples of this phrase in the *Dialogue* (1.5; 98.5; 106.1, 2) are almost certainly not relevant.

16 For full recent discussions, see Feldman, *Jew and Gentile*, 342–83; Wander, *Trennungsprozesse zwischen Frühem Christentum und Judentum*, 173–91.

17 In his very detailed study, *Proof from Prophecy*, O. Skarsaune refers only once in passing to chapter 47!

18 Lewis Coser, *The Functions of Social Conflict*, London, 1956, 169 n. 4 and 70–1. See also H. Himmelweit, 'Deviant Behaviour', in J. Gould and W. L. Kolb (eds.), *A Dictionary of the Social Sciences*, New York, 1964, 196.

19 Coser, *Social Conflict*, 70. Coser refers to the work of Robert Michels in order to establish this point. Michels is primarily concerned with political rivalries, but his observation has wider relevance.
20 See Skarsaune, *Proof from Prophecy*, 353–4, who refers to passages in Philo; *Joseph and Asenath*; the *Testament of the Twelve Patriarchs*; rabbinic traditions; Rom. 2:17–20.
21 Cohen, 'Crossing the Boundary and Becoming a Jew', 29.

BIBLIOGRAPHY

Editions used

Otto, J. C. Th., *Corpus Apologetarum Christianorum Saeculi Secundi*, 1, Jena, 2nd edn 1847 (Greek text, with translation and notes in Latin).
Williams, A. Lukyn, *Justin Martyr, the Dialogue with Trypho*, London, 1930 (English translation, introduction and brief notes).

Secondary sources

Barnard, L. W., *Justin Martyr, His Life and Thought*, Cambridge, 1967.
Bauer, W., Arndt, W. F., and Gingrich, F. W. (eds.), *A Greek Lexicon of the New Testament and other Early Christian Literature*, 4th edn, Cambridge, 1952.
Chadwick, H., 'Justin Martyr's Defence of Christianity', *BJRL* 47 (1965), 275–97.
Cohen, Shaye, 'Crossing the Boundary and Becoming a Jew', *HTR* 82 (1989), 13–33.
Feldman, L. H., *Jew and Gentile in the Ancient World. Attitudes and Interactions from Alexander to Justinian*, Princeton, 1993.
Hulen, A. B., 'Dialogues with the Jews as Sources for the Early Jewish Argument against Christianity', *JBL* 51 (1932), 58–71.
Prigent, P., *Justin et l'Ancient Testament*, Paris, 1964.
Remus, Harold, 'Justin Martyr's Argument with Judaism', in S. G. Wilson (ed.), *Anti-Judaism in Early Christianity*, Waterloo, Ontario, *1986*, II, 59–80.
Shotwell, H. A., *The Biblical Exegesis of Justin Martyr*, London, 1965.
Skarsaune, O., *The Proof from Prophecy: A Study in Justin Martyr*, Leiden, 1987.
Stanton, G. N., 'Aspects of Early Christian–Jewish Polemic and Apologetic', *NTS* 31 (1985), 377–92; now reprinted in *A Gospel for a New People: Studies in Matthew*, Edinburgh, 1992.
'The Two Parousias of Christ: Justin Martyr and Matthew', in M. C. de Boer (ed.), *From Jesus to John: Essays on Jesus and New Testament Christology in Honour of Marinus de Jonge*, Sheffield, 1993, 183–95.
'Jesus of Nazareth: A Magician and a False Prophet who Deceived

God's People?', in J. B. Green and M. M. B. Turner (eds.), *Jesus of Nazareth: Lord and Christ*, Grand Rapids, 1994, 166–82.

Stylianopoulos, T., *Justin Martyr and the Mosaic Law*, Missoula, 1975.

Wander, B., *Trennungsprozesse zwischen Frühem Christentum und Judentum im 1. Jahrhundert n. Chr.*, Tübingen and Basel, 1994.

Wilson, S. G., *Related Strangers. Jews and Christians 70–170 CE*, Minneapolis, 1995.

CHAPTER 16

Accusations of Jewish persecution in early Christian sources, with particular reference to Justin Martyr and the Martyrdom of Polycarp

Judith M. Lieu

For in truth your hand was lifted high to do evil, for even when you had killed the Christ you did not repent, but you also hate and murder us...

(Justin Martyr, *Dialogue* 133.6)

The charge that the Jews actively sought the death of Christians lies at the heart of the oft-rehearsed scholarly debate over Jewish involvement in the persecution of Christians, a debate which need only be cursorily signalled here. Harnack's vivid account, summarized in his words 'as a rule [*sic*], whenever bloody persecutions are afoot in later days, the Jews are either in the background or in the foreground',[1] offers a useful starting-point. True, it is an account which easily can be shown to rely more on rhetoric than on wealth of evidence, which even when taken as historical record is remarkable for its paucity:[2] in fact, it was not historical evidence so much as Harnack's own understanding of Christianity's discovery of its true identity which shaped his narrative. Yet it is an account which has left a long legacy. W. H. C. Frend's rhetoric is equally well known: 'In the persecutions which were to wrack Asia in the reign of Marcus Aurelius the Jew was often in the background [note the echo of Harnack]. For nearly another century he [*sic*] continued to stir up trouble wherever he could.'[3] This is only a high point of a continuing theme in the early part of Frend's account, and has evoked an angry response from the critics, one which betrays that more than historical fidelity to the sources is at stake.[4]

The historical question cannot be ignored, and it is undoubtedly one that has been obscured by an inappropriate tendency to see Jewish – Christian interaction, even in the Diaspora, in isolation from the wider context of the Graeco-Roman city, despite the emphasis in recent study of Jewish communities on their social

integration within the city. However, a better starting-point might
be not 'Jewish persecution of Christians' but 'Christian accusations of Jewish persecution'. Most of our sources for the former,
'historical', question are those accusations, yet rarely, if ever, do
they come in 'historical' contexts. Hence the primary task must be
to analyse the literary and theological nature and function of such
accusations. Thus the initial question must be not about the Jews
– 'Did they persecute Christians?' – but about the Christians –
'Why did they perceive Jews as persecutors?' This may be part of
a much wider debate: the precise nature of the persecution of
Christians, its legal – or otherwise – base, and its extent before
250 CE are heavily contested.[5] However, what is beyond dispute is
that Christians perceived and presented themselves as persecuted.[6]
Again, it is important to ask why this was so and how this self-
presentation functioned.

In exploring this issue we shall leave aside the New Testament
material because of the ambiguity as to when and whether it is
appropriate there to speak of 'internal' or of 'external' action or
perception, a problem exemplified by Gallio's response to Jewish
complaints in Acts 18:12–17. Only from a later perspective could
such tensions be seen unequivocally as defining 'the synagogues of
the Jews [as] the fount-heads of persecution'.[7] We may also leave
aside the hostile role of the Jews in the later *Acts* of martyrdom of
the saints, a role which frequently led to generalizing statements
about Jewish responsibility by those who edited them: sixty years
ago James Parkes exposed the flimsy grounds on which such statements were made and demonstrated how few *early Acts* lay the
blame at the feet of the Jews, and that even in these few instances
the tendency is to the general rather than to the specific.[8] So too,
it is only accusations of persecution that are relevant, and not the
ubiquitous complaints of Jewish rejection of Christian preaching;
similarly, charges that the Jews spread their own 'slanders' concerning Jesus or his followers, some of which may be traced in the
sources, or the more questionable assertion that they were responsible for pagan slanders against Christians, are not enough to
establish *persecution*.[9]

THE PERSECUTION OF THE RIGHTEOUS

Despite Christian attempts to deny any parallel between their own
experience and that of the Jews, both the fact of persecution as a

response to their perceived exclusivity, and their interpretation of it through the martyrological tradition, can only be understood within a Jewish framework.[10] This is something that Christian authors – and we shall start with Justin Martyr – were able to affirm, but only when refracted through their own interpretative lens:

> For you murdered the righteous one and the prophets before him [cf. Isa. 57:1; Jas. 5:6]. And now you reject those who put their hope in him and in God, the almighty and creator of all, who sent him. (*Dial.* 16.4)

Here Justin stands within a tradition concerning the fate of the prophets that early Christianity inherited from Judaism, a tradition in which it is characteristic of a prophet to be rejected, persecuted and even murdered by his (*sic*) contemporaries. In its original context, this portrayal is an integral element within and inseparable from the broader tradition of the obstinacy of those to whom the prophet is sent, of the warnings and judgement given by God, and of the climactic appeal for repentance; in Christian hands it easily became a demonstration of Jewish inveterate rejection of God's message, a rejection which might even have reached the point of no return. Justin, of course, was not the first to use the theme: whether or not part of Jesus' own self-understanding, it is taken up by New Testament (cf. Luke 6:23; Matt. 23:29–31; Luke 11:49f.) and later writers.[11] In Justin, however, it offers a key to the understanding of Jewish rejection both of Jesus and of those who followed him, which is developed in a number of directions.

First, to extend the passage just quoted:

> Accordingly, these things have happened to you in fairness and justice, for you have murdered *the righteous one* and the prophets before him. And now you reject those who put their hope in him and in God, the almighty and creator of all, who sent him, and, as far as you can (ὅσον ἐφ' ὑμῖν), you insult, cursing in your synagogues those who believe in the Christ. For you do not have authority to act murderously against us, on account of those who now hold power, but as often as you were able, that you did. Wherefore God through Isaiah calls to you, 'Behold how *the righteous one* is destroyed ... [Isa. 57:1–4]' (*Dial.* 16.4)[12]

In the next chapter Justin goes on to accuse them not only of murdering 'the only blameless and righteous man', but that when 'you knew that he had risen from the dead ... you not only did not repent of the wicked deeds you had committed' – the prophetic theme is again unmistakable – but sent out messengers with charges against Christianity 'so that you might make not only yourselves guilty of injustice but also all other people' (17.1). This charge is further substantiated by Isaiah 52:5, 'Through you my name is blasphemed among the nations', by Isaiah 3:9–11, 'Let us bind the *righteous one* for he is distasteful to us', and by Isaiah 5:18–20.

Similarly, in *Dialogue* 93.4 the litany starts with '*your*' rejection of God, continues that '*you* proved to be always idolaters and murderers of the righteous [pl.]', and proceeds via '*your*' killing of Christ to '*your*' cursing of those who prove him to be the Christ and even '*your*' attempt to show him to be cursed.[13] The second person plural, 'you/your', does not only belong to the *Dialogue* form; it establishes a continuity of character and responsibility which has its roots and authority in the Scriptures and which reaches, without a break, to the present. In 136.3–137.4, Justin again starts from Isaiah 3:9–11, this time appealing to what he claims to be the LXX text, 'Let us *do away* with the righteous'; once more he traces a history of disobedience which continues through their rejection of Jesus to their infamous 'reviling of the son of God ... and despising of the King of Israel, as your rulers of the synagogue teach, after the prayer' (137.2).

In this material a number of themes are being developed, each of which could be traced further through other early Christian writings: first, the 'murder of the prophets' is extended to include both Jesus and his messengers, a process which encourages or colludes with the suppression of any role by the Roman authorities in the death of Jesus; secondly, a significant step in the argument is provided by the appeal to Isaiah 57:1, the murder of the *righteous one*, a text that Justin had already used as a proof-text in *Apology* 48.5, but which is now combined with Isaiah 3:9–11; thirdly, this tradition can be used either as a basis for an appeal to repent or, and more frequently, as an assertion that they rejected the opportunity to repent; and fourthly, Isaiah 52:5 is here used by Justin – as it is later by Tertullian (*Adv. Iud.* 13.26; *Adv. Marc.* III.23.3) – of Jewish defamation of Christians. Much later, Jerome still uses the same passage, but has to acknowledge that the words 'among the nations' are not part of the Hebrew text; therefore he refers the verse instead to Jewish cursing of Christians in the synagogue (*In Esaiam* 14.52.4), an issue with which it had been already rhetorically associated, but not as a proof-text!

That Justin was seriously convinced of Jewish hostility to Christians is not to be doubted; however, the *frequent repetition* of the theme owes as much to its function within one (or more than one) theological schema, as it does to its historical primacy.

FULFILMENT OF PROPHECY

If the charge of 'always' murdering the righteous belongs to direct polemic, the appeal to the fulfilment of prophecy had a wider potency, and its significance in Justin's *Apologies* shows how much was at stake. There he appeals again to Isaiah 5:20:

> For evidence that these slanders which are uttered against those who confess the Christ were foreknown and that those who slander him and say it is good to keep the old customs would be afflicted, hear what is succinctly said through Isaiah, 'Woe to those who call what is sweet bitter, and what is bitter sweet' [Isa. 5:20]. (*Apol.* 49.7)

Despite this assertion, Justin explicitly blames the Jews for persecution at only two points in the *Apology*, 31.6; 36.3. In both cases the contexts are important: in chapter 31 he is establishing the credibility of Christianity by an appeal to prophecy, and the credibility of that appeal by reference to the *Jewish* Scriptures which are authenticated by a double line of tradition. Here he recounts the story of their translation into Greek by the Egyptians, 'among whom the books have remained even to this day', and also claims their universal distribution among the Jews.[14] He pre-empts this from becoming a counter-argument in favour of the Jews by continuing, 'However, the Jews when they read do not understand what has been said, but consider us enemies and hostile, killing and punishing us, like you do, whenever they can, as you can be persuaded' (*Apol.* 31.5). To support this claim he asserts that Bar Kochba ordered that '*only* the Christians should be subjected to fearsome tortures if they did not deny that Jesus was the Messiah' (31.6). In Roman ears, when the war was still a living memory, the example would be a persuasive one; no one would be likely to voice the objection that Bar Kochba was acting within the bounds of permitted Jewish self-regulation. In fact, that *only* Christians suffered seems improbable, and it is noteworthy that Justin does not make the same claim in the *Dialogue* where it could have served him well.[15]

His second reference, this time only to Jewish hatred of Christians, again comes when Justin appeals to the proper understanding of prophecy which is inspired by the divine *logos* (36.1–3). Once again the Jews are explicitly those 'who possess the books of the prophets' but who fail to understand them; instead they respond with hatred to Christian demonstration that they crucified the one whose coming the prophets foretold.

Thus Jewish hostility serves an apologetic function in the appeal to fulfilment of prophecy, which qualifies the necessary recognition of their prior claim to the Scriptures. The competitive element which is implicit here is explicit in the *Dialogue*. As is well known, Justin finds in prophecy the promise of two parousias of Christ, the first in obscurity, the second in glory. In an exegesis of Micah 4:1–7 in these terms (*Dial.* 109–10) he interprets 'I shall make her that is driven out a remnant and her that is oppressed a strong nation' (v. 6) as a reference to the Christians, 'driven out even from the world as far as you and all other people can, not permitting any Christian to live' (110.5). Yet he acknowledges that the Jews, perhaps in the aftermath of the Bar Kochba revolt, interpret this passage of themselves, 'that this has happened to your people'. This he cannot allow: *they* suffer deservedly as all the Scriptures testify, *Christians* suffer in company with Christ and in fulfilment of Isaiah 57:1 ('See how the righteous one is destroyed'). Thus Jewish involvement in Christian suffering is an important element in delegitimating not only any Jewish appeal to scriptural fulfilment but also Jewish suffering itself.

SCRIPTURAL MODELS

The contribution of scriptural exegesis to charges of persecution could also take other forms. Irenaeus uses the well-known theme of brotherly rivalry, Esau representing the Jews, Jacob the Christians: 'Jacob took the blessings of Esau as the latter people has snatched the blessings of the former. For which cause his brother suffered the plots and persecutions of a brother, just as the Church suffers this self-same thing from the Jews' (Iren., *Adv. haer.* 4.21.3).[16] For Hippolytus the two elders who spied on Susannah represent 'the two peoples (δύο λαοί), one from the circumcision, the other from the nations', who still seek false witness against Christians in the hope of stirring up destructive persecution (*Ad Danielem* 1.13–15). The editors of the text in *Sources Chrétiennes* take this as evidence of contemporary Jewish involvement in persecution, citing Harnack in support,[17] but, as always with exegetically rooted assertions, it would be better to ask whether the exegeted text has been more creative than historical experience: modern experience of the use of the Bible easily demonstrates both that suitable texts can be found which mirror reality, but also that reality becomes shaped in its presentation and language by the text. Thus Hippolytus goes on to describe how the action of the elders is fulfilled when on a suitable day 'the two peoples' come into the house of God where all are praying and singing hymns, and drag them out, saying, 'worship the gods with us or we will testify against you', and, so saying, drag them for judgement and condemnation (1.20).[18]

UNIVERSAL WITNESS

The generalizing 'two peoples' and the improbability that Jews would use such terms – 'worship the gods with us' – introduce a further theme. A similar scenario appears in an apparently narrative context in the *Martyrdom of Polycarp*, often seen as guilty of an 'undisguised anti-semitism'.[19] In the initial account of the persecution which broke out at Smyrna no mention is made of the Jews; it is the crowd (τὸ πλῆθος) who are astounded by the bravery of the earlier martyrs and who cry 'Away with the godless (ἄθεοι); let Polycarp be sought!' (3.2), with no hint that Jewish voices were added to (never mind loudest in) that cry. It is only when the narrative focuses on Polycarp that they appear: when, after his arrest and refusal to renounce his Christian confession, the herald is sent into the stadium or amphitheatre to announce to those who had been waiting that 'Polycarp has confessed three times that he is a Christian',

the whole crowd of Gentiles and Jews (ἅπαν τὸ πλῆθος ἐθνῶν τε καὶ Ἰουδαίων) dwelling in Smyrna cried out in uncontrollable anger and with a great shout, 'This is the teacher of Asia [*or* of impiety],[20] the father of the Christians, the destroyer of our gods, the one who teaches many to neither sacrifice nor worship!' (12.2)

The description fills a number of literary functions as the drama of the moment betrays. These we cannot pursue except to note that it is irrelevant, albeit true, that the words are unlikely to have been found on Jewish lips – they would not have claimed the city gods as 'theirs' nor ventured to accuse someone else of avoiding their worship without running the risk of having the same charge turned against themselves. It is equally pointless to allocate the cries to the groups involved, so that the Jews contribute only the first two affirmations, or to debate the 'orthodoxy' of the Jews involved or the official nature of their involvement.[21] From the point of view of the narrative Polycarp's clear testimony must have a universal audience and he himself must stand alone against the gathered forces of the opposition.

This theme of the universality of the audience of the Christian witness – and a martyr is a witness – appears to be a traditional one. It is already there in the promise that the disciples will be 'scourged in their synagogues and led before rulers and kings ... as a witness to them and the gentiles' (Matt. 10:17–18 par.), a passage echoed in the legitimating avowal that none of the Montanists 'had been persecuted by the Jews or killed by the lawless' (Eusebius, *H.E.* 5.16.12).[22] In a more neutral context Acts uses similar language to *Mart. Poly.* when 'all those dwelling in Asia ... Jews and Greeks' came to hear Paul's preaching (19:10, 17; cf. 14:1, 5).[23] According to Hegesippus' account of his martyrdom, James, the brother of Jesus, was invited to persuade those who had come to Jerusalem for the Passover, namely 'all the tribes together with the Gentiles' (Eusebius, *H.E.* 2.23.11).[24] After his death and burial James is declared to be a true witness 'to both Jews and Greeks that Jesus is the Christ' (*H.E.* 2.23.18):[25] in James' case the focus of the testimony is christological, in *Mart. Poly.* it is Polycarp himself as teacher and as martyr. Although not a martyrdom, Peter is told in his eponymous *Acts* that he will have a 'trial of faith' with Simon Magus before 'many more of the Gentiles and Jews', although in the event those gathered in the forum are addressed only as 'men of Rome' (*Acts of Peter* 16; 30). The third-century *Martyrdom of Pionius*, which both contains much authentic tradition and is explicitly rooted in the theological and literary tradition of *Mart. Poly.*, marks a further development when it identifies the crowd witnessing Pionius' testimony as composed of 'Greeks and Jews and women' (*Mart. Pionius* 3.6). The theme becomes a truism and formulaic: Cyprian speaks about Christian patient hope of vindication in the midst of the changing tumults and persecutions of Jews, Gentiles or heretics (*De bono pat.* 21; cf. *Epist.* 59.2); Tertul-

lian declares 'we have as many enemies as there are outsiders ...
Jews from envy, soldiers from extortion, even our own servants
from their nature itself. Daily we are besieged ... ' (*Apol.* 7.3). Even
Tertullian's much-quoted description of the Jewish synagogues as
'fount-heads of persecution' is immediately followed by the 'peoples of the nations with that circus of theirs' (*Scorp.* 10.9).[26]

The cry of these 'peoples of the nations', 'How long the third
race (*usquequo genus tertium*)?', serves to underline that this picture
of universal opposition is only the obverse of the awareness by
Christians that they constitute a new people or even a third race
over against Greeks and Jews, an idea already hinted at in Hippolytus' 'two peoples'. The tendency for the Jews to merge into or
emerge out of an otherwise undifferentiated crowd of the lawless in
Mart. Poly. (13.1; 17.2–18.1) and elsewhere is a reflection of the way
this Christian self-identity oscillates between a model of the '*third
race*' and a dualist contrast between the righteous and the unrigh-
teous. Thus the charge of Jewish involvement in persecution is
deeply implicated in Christian apologetics of self-identity, and,
considering the dialectical relationship with Judaism within those
apologetics, claiming their antiquity and heritage while denying
their legitimacy, we may be surprised that it is not found more
frequently.

THE ACTIVITY OF THE DEVIL

The *Martyrdom of Polycarp* brings us to another ominous theme: the
ultimate source of all this opposition is not the proconsul nor the
mob nor even the Jews, although we shall return to them, but
the devil.[27] Already at the beginning of the account the colourful
variety of tortures endured by the earlier martyrs was recognized
as the devices of the devil trying by many means to subvert them
to denial (*Mart. Poly.* 2.4–3.1). At that point he appears merely as
'the devil',[28] but in the final scenes after Polycarp's death, and in
opposition to 'the greatness of Polycarp's martyrdom, his blameless
life and the crown of immortality he has now won', his true identity is manifested: as 'the jealous and envious and evil one, the one
who opposes the race of the righteous', he determines that the
Christians will be deprived at least of the 'poor body' of the martyr. To this end he incites Nicetas, the father of the police chief
Herod and, incidentally, brother of a certain Alce, to ask the

magistrate that the body not be handed over on request, as was usually possible, 'lest abandoning the crucified one, they begin to worship this man' (17.1–2).

At this point (17.2) 'the Jews' reappear, 'inciting and urging'.[29] Showing his hand ever more clearly, the author continues,

> they[30] also kept watch as we were about to take him from the fire, not realising that we shall never be able to desert the Christ, who, for the sake of the salvation of the whole world of the saved, suffered blameless for sinners, and so to worship some other one ... At this, the centurion, seeing the contentiousness of the Jews, placed him in public, as is their custom, and burnt him

– although he first would have had to reignite the fire which a little while ago had been quenched by Polycarp's blood! However, the Christians are not prevented from later gathering 'the precious bones' and putting them in an appropriate place (18.2).

Again, a number of concerns have shaped the text and probably contributed to its unevenness in its present form. We may only note and pass by the concern about the veneration of the martyr's remains in relation to the worship of Christ which seems to be reflecting an inner-Christian debate under the guise of objections made by Jews or pagans: it is after all improbable that either group would fear that, or be worried whether, Christians might desert Jesus in favour of Polycarp; projecting the problem onto the crowd would be a rhetorically effective way of dealing with it. We can also only note the role played by Nicetas who requests the magistrate that the body not be surrendered; we are reminded here for the second time (cf. 8.2) that he is the father of Herod, the police chief, a piece of information given not just for biographical interest but to recall for us the role played by Herod in the (Lukan) Passion narrative. Polycarp's martyrdom is explicitly 'according to the gospel' (1.1), and at a number of points echoes Jesus' own arrest, trial and death, in which of course the Jews inevitably featured. It is unlikely that the imitation theme has created the presence of the Jews entirely – if it had, more explicit verbal echoes could be expected – but that a 'Herod', even if not a Jew, should be closely related to the activity of the Jews should against this background cause no surprise.

For our purposes it is the way the role played by the Jews is presented which is most important. Here they are no longer one group within the crowd, as in the earlier references, but initiators of the attempt to thwart the influence of Polycarp, even after his death. Their activity is explicitly parallel to, or perhaps the earthly counterpart of, that of the 'evil one who opposes the race of the righteous'; just as he 'incited' (ὑπέβαλεν) Nicetas, so too they are all the while 'inciting' (ὑποβαλλόντων) these things.

Blaming persecution on the demons is not an exclusively 'anti-Jewish' theme. Indeed, like other themes we have traced, it may have Jewish roots: in the *Martyrdom of Isaiah* the prophet's suffering at the hands of Manasseh is attributed to the latter's 'ally' the devil (3.11f.; 5.1).[31] Where martyrdom, or even faithful perseverance, is seen as part of a conflict waged with the devil, it is natural to identify the agents of persecution as in some way doing the work of the devil.

But there are other sources too: in *Apology* 5 Justin argues that it was demons who engineered Socrates' death when he exposed by reason (*logos*) the deception by which the people had come to worship them as gods; the charge against him was atheism. Justin then blames the persecution of Christians on the same demons, for Christians too expose them in the name of the Logos incarnate, Jesus Christ.[32] The theme is repeated in *2 Apology* 8 where Justin adds Heraclitus and Musonius to the list of those who lived by reason and suffered the murderous hatred of the demons. He would probably have included also Abraham, Elijah and the Three Young Men of Daniel 3, whom he also lists as 'living by reason' and who were also martyrs or near martyrs (*Apol.* 5).[33] Demons are also responsible for apparent pagan anticipations or imitations of Christian concepts, for heresy and for disbelief; it is no surprise that they continue their opposition through inciting *pagans* to persecute Christians (57.1), while they had already engineered the death of Jesus 'at the hands of the foolish Jews' (63.10).

A different schema is followed in the *Dialogue*, where, as we have seen, the emphasis is much more on Jewish opposition. The contribution of demonic inspiration to persecution by pagan outsiders is less important (*Dial.* 18; 39), but at a highly significant point Justin speaks of Christian fidelity in the face of the 'punishments even to death which have been inflicted on us by demons and by the host of the devil, through the aid given to them by you' (131.2). This comes in the introduction to his long judgement-history, a sort of inverted salvation-history (131–3); it cannot be separated from Justin's assertion that the Jews ('*you*') repeatedly sacrificed their children to demons (133.1; cf. 19; 27; 117), a crime he aligns with the making of the golden calf, with the slaying of the prophets, and with their supposed 'mutilation' of the Greek translation of the Scriptures (73.6) – a suggestive juxtaposition of the themes that we have already discussed. In telling contrast, Gentile Christians are those who by their conversion have turned away from demons (30; 78). Thus, in the *Dialogue*, blaming the devil for persecution does nothing to alleviate the Jews of responsibility; instead it gives their opposition a more comprehensive character in both creating and defining Jewish identity.

There are, of course, some New Testament roots to this: there it is Judas who is suborned by Satan (Luke 22:3; John 13:2, 27), although John can speak of the Jews as stemming from their father the devil who was 'a murderer from the beginning' (8:44); particularly significant is the letter to the church at Smyrna in Revelation 2:8–11 which speaks of the slanders 'of those who call themselves Jews but are not, being rather the synagogue of Satan' (v. 9), and in the next verse warns of the suffering to come when the 'devil' (διάβολος, as in *Mart. Poly.* 3.1) will cast some of them into prison. In Justin these separate elements are being shaped into a more comprehensive, and so rhetorically more persuasive, whole.[34]

DEFINING BY OPPOSITION AND *IMITATIO CHRISTI*

Christians thus share in the experience of Christ, and this too may demand a role for the Jews, at least in Polycarp's martyrdom which is 'a testimony according to the gospel' by which he becomes a 'partaker of Christ' (*Mart. Poly.* 1.1; 6.2; cf. above, p. 288). Yet also on a broader base, persecution – and here Jewish persecution must play a special role – is but the necessary condition and foil for a Christian response which defines their new identity and values.[35] Already in Justin's *Apology*, Christian readiness to pray for their enemies is a matter of pride, and demonstrates their conversion from past ways, and indeed from enslavement to demons (*Apol.* 14). In the *Dialogue*, the charge of Jewish *cursing* of both Jesus and Christians, which is the regular preliminary to accusations of more active persecution (16.4; 95.4; 96.2; 133.6),[36] plays a prominent role in this. The issues raised by this charge are too complex to be treated here in detail, although again they would have to be looked at first not in relation to some supposed external reality,[37] but in relation to the rhetorical reasons why Justin not only claims that it happened but does so repeatedly (16.4; 93.4; 95.4; 96.2; 108.3; 133.2). Thus, for example, Justin's focus on cursing is not to be divorced from his exegesis of the Old Testament, including his long discussion of Deuteronomy 21:23 in *Dialogue* 89–96.[38] On the one hand, the scriptural 'cursed be everyone who hangs on a tree' anticipated how the Jews would treat both Christ and Christians, yet, on the other, it also sets into sharp relief the Christian response of steadfastness and forgiveness, as they meet cursing with prayer and forgiveness (96.1–3).

A final passage both draws this out and evokes a number of the themes we have considered. At the end of that reverse judgement-history in *Dialogue* 131–3 alluded to earlier, Justin reaches a climax following a quotation of Isaiah 3:9–15; 5:18–25:

> For in truth your hand was lifted high to do evil, for even when you had killed the Christ you did not then repent, but you also hate and murder us who believe through him in the God and Father of all, as often as you get the power, and unceasingly you curse both him himself and those of his, while all of us pray for you and for all people, even as we have been taught to do by our Christ and Lord, when he instructed us to pray for our enemies, and to love those who hate us and to bless those who curse [Luke 6.18]. (133.6)

In all these texts we have been listening to rhetoric, even in the deceptively narrative *Martyrdom of Polycarp*. Such rhetoric served to create a persuasive world or symbolic universe for insiders if not for outsiders; the role of the Jews in the persecution of Christians becomes part of that world, but a surprisingly less central part than might have been expected. It is one which must have been rooted in *perceived* experience, although what sort of experience these texts alone cannot tell us. We have seen how exegesis could be an interpretative response to experience, but might in turn create 'reality' for an immediate audience or for subsequent interpreters, thus shaping their 'experience'. This is a process which is an intrinsic part of early Christian – Jewish interaction, and demands of the modern interpreter a path between a simple historicism and a sceptical dismissal of theological fantasy.[39]

NOTES

1 A. Harnack, *The Expansion of Christianity in the First Three Centuries*, I, 64–7, quotation from p. 66.

2 See D. Hare, *The Theme of Jewish Persecution of Christians in the Gospel according to St Matthew*, 66–79.

3 W. H. C. Frend, *Martyrdom and Persecution in the Early Church*, 259.

4 See the review by F. Millar in *JRS* 56 (1966) 231–6; T. Barnes, 'Tertullian's "*Scorpiae*"', 132; and the spirited self-defence by Frend, 'A Note on Tertullian and the Jews'. A summary and assessment of this aspect of the debate is made by D. M. Scholer, 'Tertullian on Jewish Persecution of Christians'.

5 See the classic debate between de Ste Croix, 'Why were Early Christians Persecuted?', 'A Rejoinder', and Sherwin-White, 'An Amendment'.

6 See Perkins, 'The Apocryphal Acts of the Apostles and the Early Christian Martyrdom', 222.

7 Tertullian, *Scorp.* 10: this passage has inspired much of the debate referred to in n. 4, although the next words, 'among whom the apostles suffered beatings', does seem to restrict the reference to apostolic times.

8 J. Parkes, *The Conflict of the Church and the Synagogue*, 121–50.

9 On the former see already Justin, *Dial.* 17.1; 108.2; 117.3; Maier, *Jesus von Nazareth in der talmudischen Überlieferung*; for the latter, particularly that Christians participated in cannibalistic and sexual orgies, see Tertullian, *Ad. Nat.* 1.14; Origen, *C. Cels.* VI.14; A. Henrichs, 'Pagan Ritual and the Alleged Crimes of the Early Christians'.

10 See Frend, *Martyrdom and Persecution*, 31–78.

11 See O. Steck, *Israel und das gewaltsame Geschick der Propheten*; on the early Christian use of the tradition (99–109), Steck adds 1 Thess. 2:15; Jas. 5:10; *Barn.* 5.11; Ignatius, *Magn.* 8.2; *3 Cor.* 9f., and the passages from Justin to be discussed below.

12 For the recognition they do not have the power they would like, see 95.4.

13 In 96.2 'your cursing' is activated by the Gentiles in the killing of Christians; see below, pp. 290–1.

14 On Justin's contribution to the development of this legend see M. Müller, 'Graeca sive Hebraica Veritas?'.

15 Neither does he capitalize on these Christians' failure to support Bar Kochba's own messianic pretensions – as later scholars have done; see also R. Bauckham, in this volume.

16 In Jewish exegesis Jacob represents the Jewish people, Esau the Roman (and later Christian) Empire.

17 G. Bardy and M. Lefèvre (eds.), *Hippolyte, Commentaire sur Daniel*, 99.

18 The editors take the specific reference to 'acting against the decree of Caesar' as a reference to Sulpicius Severus' edict according to *Hist. Aug.* XVII against *Jewish* proselytizing and against Christianity (p. 111).

19 H. Musurillo, *The Acts of the Christian Martyrs*, xiv.

20 All the Greek manuscripts except M(oscow) read 'teacher of impiety'; 'of Asia' has the support of M, Eusebius and the Latin translation.
21 Musurillo, *Christian Martyrs*, 11, n. 16, attributes the accusations to different groups in the throng; Parkes, *Church and Synagogue*, 137, ascribes the action to Jewish 'lewd fellows of the baser sort' and denies its official character – however 'official' might be defined.
22 The passage continues that none had been scourged in the synagogues or stoned; an exegesis of Matt. 10:17 is more probable here than a reference to contemporary Jewish persecution.
23 Acts 19:10, 17 anticipate the apparently redundant 'dwelling in Smyrna' in *Mart. Poly.*
24 It is not clear whether 'gentiles' (ἔθνη) here are non-Jews or Jews from the Diaspora.
25 K. Beyschlag, 'Das Jakobsmartyrium und seine Verwandten in der frühchristlichen Literatur', argues for a common tradition underlying the martyrdom of James, that of Polycarp, and other Christian martyr traditions.
26 On this passage see n. 7 above.
27 This is a standard theme in martyr accounts, compare the Martyrs of Lyons in Eusebius, *H.E.* 5.1.16
28 And possibly as 'the tyrant' (ὁ τύραννος) which is read in 2.4 by the majority of Greek MSS (except M). Although often seen as secondary, it is not a common term in Christian martyrologies while it is used of the earthly opponent and persecutor in Jewish martyr stories (4 Macc. 9:1, 10 etc.), and so perhaps should be preserved.
29 In 13.1 they had appeared as contributing with customary enthusiasm to the gathering of wood for the fire. The exact connection at 17.2 is obscured by grammatical unevenness (smoothed out in Eusebius *H.E.* 4.15.41) although the general sense is clear. I subject all these passages to a detailed analysis in *Image and Reality*.
30 Still the Jews, although the motive which follows has just been attributed to Nicetas.
31 See T. Baumeister, *Die Anfänge der Theologie des Martyriums*, 288; 60.
32 See T. Baumeister, 'Das Martyrium in der Sicht Justins des Märtyrers', 633.
33 Ibid. On the importance of demons in Justin's scheme see E. Osborn, *Justin Martyr*, 55–65.
34 Baumeister, 'Das Martyrium', asks whether the motivating force was the tradition from which Justin spoke, the real experience of Jewish opposition, or even his hope that this might bring about repentance; he continues, 'He speaks from the position of the persecuted, not the powerful. It is tragic that the thought developed by him, later, when the former persecuted were in possession of state power, produced such devastating consequences' (638).
35 Perkins, 'Apocryphal Acts', 222.

294 JUDITH M. LIEU

36 122.2 associates proselytes blaspheming his name with their seeking to kill 'us'.
37 Most frequently in relation to the *birkat-ha-minim*, although most of Justin's references seem too general for this.
38 This is why, although Justin also speaks of Jews reviling, blaspheming and profaning, 'cursing' plays such a major role; see further J. Lieu, 'Reading in Canon and Community'.
39 See further Judith M. Lieu, *Image and Reality*.

BIBLIOGRAPHY

Bardy, G., and Lefèvre, M. (eds.) *Hippolyte, Commentaire sur Daniel*, SC 14, Paris, 1947.
Barnes, T., 'Tertullian's *"Scorpiae"*', *JTS* 20 (1969), 105–32.
Baumeister, T., *Die Anfänge der Theologie des Martyriums*, MBTh 45, Münster, 1980.
'Das Martyrium in der Sicht Justins des Märtyrers', in E. Livingstone (ed.), *Studia Patristica* XVII.2, Oxford, 1982, 631–42.
Beyschlag, K. 'Das Jakobsmartyrium und seine Verwandten in der frühchristlichen Literatur', *ZNW* 56 (1965), 149–78.
Finley, M. I. (ed.), *Studies in Ancient Society*, London and Boston, 1974.
Frend, W. H. C., *Martyrdom and Persecution in the Early Church*, Oxford, 1965.
'A Note on Tertullian and the Jews', in F. L. Cross (ed.) *Studia Patristica* X, TU 107, Berlin, 1970, 291–6.
Hare, D., *The Theme of Jewish Persecution of Christians in the Gospel according to St Matthew*, SNTSMS 6, Cambridge, 1967.
Harnack, A. von, *The Expansion of Christianity in the First Three Centuries*, E. tr. J. Moffatt, London, 1904.
Henrichs, A., 'Pagan Ritual and the Alleged Crimes of the Early Christians', in P. Granfield and J. Jungmann (eds.), *Kyriakon* (FS. J. Quasten), Münster, 1970, I, 18–35.
Lieu, Judith M., 'Reading in Canon and Community: Deut. 21.22–23, A Test Case for Dialogue', in M. D. Carroll, D. Clines and P. Davies (eds.), *The Bible in Human Society. Essays in Honour of John Rogerson*, JSOTSS 200, Sheffield, 1995, 317–34.
Image and Reality: The Jews in the World of the Christians in the Second Century, Edinburgh, 1996.
Maier, J., *Jesus von Nazareth in der talmudischen Überlieferung*, Darmstadt, 1978.
Müller, M., 'Graeca sive Hebraica Veritas? The Defense of the Septuagint in the Early Church', *SJOT* 1989/1 (1989), 103–24.
Musurillo, H., *The Acts of the Christian Martyrs*, Oxford, 1972.
Osborn, E., *Justin Martyr*, BhTh 47, Tübingen, 1973.
Parkes, J., *The Conflict of the Church and the Synagogue*, London, 1934.
Perkins, J., 'The Apocryphal Acts of the Apostles and the Early Christian Martyrdom', *Arethusa* 18 (1985), 211–30.

Ste Croix, G. M. de, 'Why were Early Christians Persecuted?', in M. I. Finley (ed.), *Studies in Ancient Society*, London and Boston, 1974, 210–49.

'Why were Early Christians Persecuted? A Rejoinder', in M. I. Finley (ed.), *Studies in Ancient Society*, London and Boston, 1974, 256–62.

Scholer, D. M., 'Tertullian on Jewish Persecution of Christians', in E. Livingstone (ed.), *Studia Patristica* xvii.2, Oxford, 1982, 821–8.

Sherwin-White, A. N., 'Why were Early Christians Persecuted? An Amendment', in M. I. Finley (ed.), *Studies in Ancient Society*, London and Boston, 1974, 250–5.

Steck, O., *Israel und das gewaltsame Geschick der Propheten. Untersuchungen zur Überlieferung des deuteronomischen Geschichtsbildes im Alten Testament, Spätjudentum und Urchristentum*, Neukirchen-Vluyn, 1967.

CHAPTER 17

Early Christians on synagogue prayer and imprecation

William Horbury

The synagogue was tolerated under Christian rule in antiquity and the Middle Ages, but much New Testament and patristic authority, including some texts reviewed below, would have weighed on the side of restriction. Early Christian comment on contemporary Jewish worship had intertwined roots in inner-Jewish controversy and in Greek and Roman anti-Jewish polemic.[1]

Yet such comment, despite its polemical character, included some genuine observation.[2] This aspect is illustrated here with two aims in view. First, evidence on Jewish worship in the ancient world is patchy, whether Jewish or non-Jewish. Christian texts are therefore potentially important to the historian of the ancient synagogue, as S. J. D. Cohen has emphasized.[3] Here some passages are reconsidered which may throw light on the rise of the synagogue and the development of Jewish prayer, including the question of anti-Christian imprecations in the synagogue. Secondly, the potentially misleading character of the image of Judaism in Christian polemic has long been noted.[4] Assessment of the Christian sources should also reckon, however, with the keen if hostile observation which they sometimes reflect.

In modern liturgical study, it has often been assumed that Christians knew a good deal about Jewish worship – enough to be deeply influenced by it in their own prayers, down to the relatively late date of the *Apostolic Constitutions*. A strong support for this view is the dismay expressed by a series of Church Fathers at synagogue attendance by Christians; the witnesses include Origen, Aphrahat, Chrysostom and Jerome. In the West, at the end of the second century, Callistus is said to have gone into a synagogue in Rome, creating disturbance and claiming to be a Christian; whatever the truth of this story, it shows what could be envisaged as plausible (Hippolytus, *Ref.* 9.7, 7–9). In third-century Smyrna, according to the *Acts of Pionius* (13.1), Jews invited Christians in a time of persecution 'into the synagogues', and those who accepted would give up their Christianity.[5]

Comparably, canons of the fourth century include prohibitions of sharing feasts with Jews (Elvira 50, Laodicea 37–8 (360; also forbids acceptance of gifts from Jews for Christian feasts), Apostolic Canon 69 (also forbids fasting with Jews)), with special reference to the Passover (Canon 1 of Antioch, 341) and to taking oil into the synagogue for a festival (Apostolic Canon 70), and prohibitions of entering a synagogue (Apostolic Canon 63) or having fields blessed by Jews (Elvira 49).[6] Moreover, after Constantine the Christians were only too well aware of synagogues and their prestige; zealous Christians constantly sought to annex or destroy them, and by the sixth century compulsory sermons for Jews had become normal, although the earliest known examples appear to have been preached in the open or in church, not in the synagogue.[7] Bishops occasionally moderated these actions, but often tolerated or encouraged them, as Ambrose did by his stance in the Callinicum affair. All this points to long-standing Christian acquaintance with synagogues and their rites, but the need for caution can be exemplified by J. van der Lof's conclusion that, perhaps contrary to expectation, the evidence for the cult of the Maccabees does not evince close links between Christians and local synagogues in the third and fourth centuries.[8]

The limited historical enquiry undertaken here can conveniently start from the conclusions of S. J. D. Cohen, as cited above. First, looking at archaeological and literary evidence as a whole, he notes that earlier Church Fathers rarely mention the synagogue or proseuche, and in his view it is rarely mentioned by pagan authors. On the other hand, he says, it gets fuller Christian discussion in the second part of the fourth century, notably from Chrysostom and Jerome; similarly, archaeological evidence for synagogues becomes more abundant from the late third century onwards. He infers from this convergence of archaeological and patristic evidence that synagogues did not in fact attain institutional prominence until this period, when there is also evidence for authority exercised in synagogues by the Jewish patriarch. Secondly, he says that patristic authors are important witnesses to the view that synagogues were regarded as temple-like holy places – a view found also, he notes, in Jewish inscriptions and rabbinic literature. Thirdly, he judges that Christian references to Jewish customs and rites are sparse, but notes that they include mention of the public reading of the law by Roman permission (Hippolytus, in connection with the story of Callistus), of the alleged theatricality of synagogue services, with particular reference to trumpet-blowing (Chrysostom), of an Antiochene synagogue built over the remains of the Maccabean martyrs (John Malalas), and of a Jewish ethnarch and Jewish patriarchs (Origen and Epiphanius); in all these points, he says, the Christian sources can be supported from other evidence.

I. THE RISE OF THE SYNAGOGUE

First, then, on the general question of the rise of the synagogue, it may be noted that Christian sources set a question mark against the relatively late dating for the emergence of the synagogue into institutional prominence which Cohen and others favour, in so far as they presuppose its familiarity at an earlier time in the homeland as well as the Diaspora. With regard to the Second Temple period, although there is much in favour of the view that synagogue buildings were known in Judaea as well as in the Diaspora by the time of Herod the Great,[9] the lack of pre-Roman archaeological and literary evidence leads some to judge that they would have been far less familiar in Herodian Judaea and Galilee than in the contemporary Western Diaspora, where inscriptions and literature amply attest the buildings of the proseuche;[10] at this period the name συναγωγή appears to be associated with the homeland rather than the Diaspora, but in any case it would have been understood there, on this view of the development of the synagogue, primarily as 'assembly' rather than 'house of assembly'.[11] It is true that in the Mishnah, reflecting conditions in Judaea and Galilee, the 'house of assembly' is taken for granted; thus Akiba is said to appeal in an argument to usage in bet ha-kᵉnesset (Ber. 7.3). A synagogue assembly could also occur, however, in the 'open place (rᵉhôb) of the town' (Meg. 3.1, if the open place is sold, a house of assembly must be bought with the price; cf. Ta'an. 2.1, where on fast-days the ark is carried to the open place); and the survival of this information in a work compiled seventy years after the Bar Kochba revolt would be consistent with the view that common earlier practice was to meet in the 'open place', not a synagogue building.[12]

Cohen's summary of the evidence designedly omits New Testament texts, but their contribution on this point is important, as they refer to Judaea and Galilee as well as the Diaspora, and antedate the Mishnah by a century or more. In Matthew, Luke-Acts and John the term συναγωγή, 'assembly' or 'house of assembly', appears without any special explanation; a synagogue has been 'built' in Capernaum according to Luke 7.5, and the term can most naturally be taken to refer to a building, not simply an assembly, in a number of other passages (for example, Mark 1:21, 29; 12:39, and parallels; Luke 4:16, 44; 13:10; Acts 13:14; 18:7). In Acts 6:9, on the other hand, 'the synagogue of the *libertini*' in Jerusalem is primarily an assembly or corporation formed by a particular group (compare the synagogues of the Augustesians and the Agrippesians in Rome), and including Cyrenians, Alexandrians and others;[13] yet in a rabbinic tradition, by contrast, it happens that a '*house* of assembly (*bet ha-k^enesset*) of the Alexandrians who were in Jerusalem' (*t. Meg.* 3.6, compare *y Meg.* 3.1, 73d) is mentioned, by the second-century teacher Judah b. Ilai, in a discussion of the uses to which a former synagogue can be put – a discussion presupposing that it was, and may still be, in some sense a holy place.[14] This rabbinic passage is a reminder that an attestation of συναγωγή in the sense of 'assembly' by no means rules out the possibility of a room or building for the assembly. Similarly, the synagogue environment can be implied where the word does not occur at all, as in Paul's reference to the ἀνάγνωσις of the Pentateuch at 2 Corinthians 3.14–15.[15] Finally, the organization of the assembly or corporation under ἀρχισυνάγωγοι is assumed as entirely familiar, once again with regard to the homeland as well as the Diaspora (Mark 5:22 and parallels; Luke 13:14; Acts 13:15; 18:8, 17).

The New Testament texts bear on the question of the rise of the synagogue in at least three ways. First, they combine with Justin Martyr, Tertullian and Hippolytus to suggest that synagogues, including synagogue buildings, were taken for granted by the time of Christian origins, in the homeland as well as the Diaspora, and continued to be prominent and familiar to Christians in the second century. Justin Martyr mentions synagogues as repositories of the biblical books (Justin, *Dial.* 72.3). Tertullian calls them *templa*

(*Iei.* 16.6, discussed below), as Tacitus did (*Hist.* 5.5); and they are implied, but not mentioned by name, when Tertullian says of the biblical readings of the Jews 'vulgo aditur sabbatis omnibus' (*Apol.* 18.8); he doubtless echoes Acts 15:21 on the sabbath reading from Moses (compare 2 Cor. 3:14–15, cited above), but the contemporary character of his observation emerges from his bitter allusion to Roman protection of the Jewish assemblies – 'a liberty paid for by tribute' (attested at about the same time in Hippolytus on the Roman synagogue visited by Callistus, as cited above).

Secondly, New Testament and early patristic passages cohere with and amplify Jewish and pagan evidence for the synagogue as an accepted institution about the time of Christian origins. Thus the New Testament assumption that synagogues were familiar in the Holy Land is fully consistent with Josephus on events at synagogue buildings at Dora in Phoenicia, on the coast between Caesarea and Mount Carmel, under Agrippa I, and at Caesarea and Tiberias in 66–7 (Josephus, *Ant.* 19.300–11; *War* 2.285–92; *Vita* 277–303). He uses συναγωγή for the first two, προσευχή for the third (which was a μέγιστον οἴκημα, *Vita* 277); in the Caesarean narrative he implies the holiness of the place (the Jews believed it to be defiled, he says, by the Greeks who sacrificed at the entrance), and he mentions the removal of 'the laws' by the Jews for safety (*War* 2.289, 291). This last point recalls Justin Martyr on the synagogue books. Perhaps not far away in time from Josephus' narrative are the founder's inscriptions from the synagogue of Theodotus in Jerusalem and the proseuche of Papous in Egypt.[16] Again, Acts mentions Diaspora synagogues in Syria, Cyprus, Asia Minor and Greece, but not in Italy. Its overlap with other sources is not complete. Thus Josephus mentions the Jews of Cyprus, but not their synagogues (*Ant.* 13.284–7). On the other hand, the Roman proseuchae are relatively well attested outside Acts. For the Augustan period, Philo on the proseuchae in Rome tolerated by Augustus (*Leg. ad Gaium* 156) is corroborated by Ovid, implying their existence without naming them (and indicating attendance by women) when he tells his pupil in the art of love:

> Nec te praetereat Veneri ploratus Adonis,
> cultaque Iudaeo septima sacra Syro.   (*A. A.* 1.76)[17]

No doubt, then, in Acts 28 it is assumed that the reader will know of the unmentioned Roman synagogues, and will note that Paul seems not to have received permission to speak in them. This phenomenon of coherence without full overlap with other sources, evident as regards both the homeland and the Diaspora, commends the New Testament material on the synagogue.

Thirdly, the New Testament writers might perhaps be expected to impose a Diaspora or gentilic viewpoint, but they employ the term συναγωγή which seems to be less characteristic of the Diaspora; it is used only once in Philo, and then of the Essenes in Palestine (*Quod omnis probus*, 81, again noting the synagogue as a sacred place).

The Christian sources, then, when set beside the epigraphic material and the Jewish and pagan literary evidence for the period up to about 200 CE, do much to turn the scale towards the position represented by Hengel, Levine and Sanders (n. 9, above). They suggest that the synagogue was established at home as well as abroad by the time of Christian origins. The familiarity of the synagogue building in the homeland is assumed in the New Testament and Josephus as well as the Mishnah, and its acceptance as an institution throughout the Jewish world is assumed in the New Testament, Justin Martyr, Tertullian and Hippolytus as well as Philo and Josephus. Yet the Christian texts give their own particular information, and do not simply echo the other sources.

2. THE SYNAGOGUE ARK

Now, secondly, the area which Cohen regards as more sparsely attested in the Church Fathers, that of rites and customs, can be considered with reference to prayer. It has appeared already that Christians sometimes entered synagogue assemblies, and that the general public could do so; 'vulgo aditur', says Tertullian, suggesting a continuation of the access by non-Jews attested earlier in Ovid and elsewhere. Christians by Tertullian's time were inclined to perceive the synagogue as a temple-like holy place, and its worship as continuous with the ancient sacrificial service described in the Pentateuch. Familiarity with the Old Testament would encourage such impressions, and they might be discounted were it not for their agreement with inner-Jewish views, as Cohen among others has noted; thus the holiness of the synagogue emerges from Philo, Josephus and the Mishnah, as cited above. The Christian impressions also remind one that, up to the third century, the synagogue was likely to be a much grander building than any used for Christian gatherings. This emerges from Josephus on Tiberias (cited above), with Philo's reference (*Leg. ad Gaium* 134) to 'the largest and most famous' of the Alexandrian proseuchae, and rabbinic tradition on the basilica-synagogue of Alexandria (*t. Sukk.* 4.6 and parallels).[18] The synagogue might be very large, and, at least at Alexandria, a basilica on the scale of the fourth-century basilican churches. (For Jewish use of this structural form compare Herod's great basilica, the 'Royal Porch', on the south side of the Temple site in Jerusalem.) Even a smaller synagogue such as has been discovered at Ostia could display considerable elegance. The appeal of a 'holy and beautiful house' will have been among the factors encouraging pagans to embrace Judaism without considering Christian claims, a practice deplored by Origen (*In Matt. ser.* 16).[19]

Within this sometimes impressive synagogue setting, a group of Christian references attest the public reading of the law (Acts, Tertullian and Hippolytus, as cited already), the keeping of the holy books in the synagogue (Justin, *Dial.* 72.3, cited above; Ps.-Justin, *Cohortatio* xiii), and in particular the ark of the law, which was central both in the biblical reading and the public prayers. In Palestine at this period, according to rabbinic texts, the ark was carried in and out of the hall in which the assembly gathered, not kept there permanently. The Mishnah prescribes that, on a fast-day, the ark should be carried into the 'open place of the town' for public prayers (*Ta'an.* 2.1). The prayer-leader in the Amidah (Eighteen Benedictions) was said to 'pass before the ark', to take up a position in front of it (*m. Ber.* 5.3–4, etc.).[20] Diaspora usage need not have been identical, but passages in Tertullian noted below are illuminated if similar customs can be presupposed.

A visual impression of the synagogue ark in late antiquity can be gathered from representations in stone-carving, mural painting, mosaic and gold-glass, from the homeland and the Diaspora. Temple imagery is used in them, and it is not clear whether the ark intended is the synagogue ark or that of Solomon's Temple.[21] The representations will in any case, however, bear on the appearance of the synagogue ark, which was popularly connected with the ark of the covenant, as noted below. E. L. Sukenik wrote:

It is a sort of double-doored chest with a gabled or rounded roof. Each of the door-wings was divided horizontally into a number of square or oblong panels. The door-posts were sometimes shaped like columns. The pediment was also ornamented, sometimes with a shell in the centre. A view of the interior of the ark is offered by the Jewish gilt glass vessels found in the catacombs of Rome. Here the ark is as a rule represented with open doors, showing the scrolls, each rolled about a rod ... lying in rows on shelves.[22]

With this in mind, it can be seen that Tertullian probably means the synagogue ark when he mentions that the book of Enoch is not admitted to 'the Jewish chest', *armarium iudaicum*, in which biblical books are kept (*Cult. fem.* 1.3).[23] This interpretation of the phrase is supported by Tertullian's references to two specific occasions on which the ark might have been seen by Christians. First, Tertullian was familiar with the sabbath biblical reading, as already noted. Secondly, he knew that on a Jewish fast[24] the Jews leave their 'templa', as he calls them, and pray in the open on the sea-shore, and he vividly describes, not without a note of satire, how they wait for the evening star to signal the end of the fast (*Iei.* 16.6); for the mockery implied in the thought that Jewish practice is governed by star-rise, compare the *Preaching of Peter* 2, on Jewish dependence on the observation of the new moon. Such 'sea-shore prayers' (*Nat.* 1.13, 4 'orationes littorales') were authentically Jewish, for (among other evidences) a decree quoted by Josephus calls it a Jewish custom to offer prayers by the sea (*Ant.* 14.258), and synagogue remains have been found by the shore in both Galilee and the Diaspora. Tertullian does not mention the ark when he describes the Jewish fast-day prayers, but perhaps it was brought out, in accord with the custom mentioned at about the same time in the Mishnah, and he had the chance of seeing it.

In the fourth century, Aphrahat and Chrysostom both take some trouble to belittle the synagogue ark. Aphrahat points out how Jeremiah prophesied that the ark of the covenant shall no more be remembered or made (*Hom.* 12, quoting Jer. 3:16);[25] contrast other writers who use this prophecy without making that particular point (Eusebius, Jerome, Theodoret). Chrysostom calls the ark no better than the little boxes you can get in the market (*Adv. Iud.* 6.7). Chrysostom is worried lest Christians, assured of the sanctity of the ark and its sacred books, regard it as making the synagogue holy, and he argues first against their logic (Did the ark when captured by the Philistines make the temple of Dagon holy?) and secondly against the sanctity of the contemporary ark itself (Where are the mercy-seat, the Urim, the tables of the covenant, the holy of holies, and all the other glories that went with the original ark in the first Temple?).

Chrysostom's two arguments show how the deep-rooted Christian respect for the sanctity of the Bible embraced the ark, and consequently the synagogue; but they also suggest that Christians and Jews thought about the synagogue ark on the same lines. For Jewish association of the synagogue ark with the ark brought up to Jerusalem by David, compare the 'song of the kine' (Babylonian Talmud, *Avodah Zarah* 24b; *Ber. R.* 54.4), perhaps linked with a synagogue ark procession,[26] and a carving from the frieze of the Capernaum synagogue which probably represents the ark being brought up on its new cart into Zion.[27] Chrysostom's word κιβω-τός appears in the late second century in an inscription of the Ostia synagogue recording how Mindius Faustus 'set up the ark for the holy law';[28] the emphasis here on the fundamental holiness of the law exactly corresponds to the belief which Chrysostom imputes to his own flock. The same emphasis occurs in the Mishnah, where a list in ascending order of esteem runs: open place, house of assembly, ark, scroll wrappings, holy books, a copy of the Torah (*Meg.* 3.1, cited above). Against this background it seems likely, as argued elsewhere, that the probably third-century reference to Israel's loss of the candlestick, the ark of the covenant, the priestly vessels and the trumpets, in the pseudo-Cyprianic *Adversus Iudaeos*, corresponds to frequently encountered Jewish symbols, and includes an attack on the synagogue ark.[29]

Patristic writings therefore show some familiarity with the ark, from which the biblical scrolls read in public were taken and before which, according to the Mishnah, the prayer-leader stood; this familiarity corresponds with the ancient biblical as well as contemporary liturgical associations of the ark, yet customs in which the ark was prominent themselves appear to have been known. Further, in the fourth century some Christians were inclined to the view that the ark was a focus of holiness, as the receptacle of the sacred books, and that its holiness was imparted to the synagogue as a whole, and this view corresponds to Jewish views attested earlier both in Galilee and in Italy (Mishnah, Megillah and the Ostia inscription, cited above). Christian polemic directed at the ark suggests a non-legal dimension of the Christian treatment of the

Jewish scriptures as an 'old' and superseded testament, found in St Paul (2 Cor. 3:14–15, cited above) and in the Epistle to the Hebrews (especially 8:6–13) and thenceforth; it was probably not simply the Scriptures that were in view, but the Scriptures surrounded by the numinous aura of the ark, the synagogue and the synagogue assembly. Some of the Christian anxiety to prove the abrogation of the law would then have been based not simply on the need to justify Christian practice over diet and worship, but also on the attraction of the awe-inspiring atmosphere of holiness connected with the ark and the synagogue.

3. PUBLIC PRAYER

What further light do Christian texts throw on Jewish prayer? From Jewish sources it seems likely that some prayer was conjoined with the public reading of the law, in both the homeland and the Diaspora, by the second century CE, although – as S. C. Reif emphasizes – this was certainly not the only setting for common prayer.[30] Notable evidence includes the benediction and Amen described before the reading of the law in Nehemiah 8:5–7, Agatharchides on prayer as the sabbath duty (cited above), Philo's use of the term *proseuche* for the place in which the law was read (*Leg. ad Gaium* 156) (compare the use of προσεύχεσθαι for common prayer away from the homeland in 1 Kings 8:44, 48, LXX), and Josephus' association of daily prayers with the septennial public reading of the law in his exposition of the commandments (*Ant.* 4.209–12); at the end of the second century the Mishnah, in a list of rites which need a quorum of ten, brings together – in a way which would be natural if they were already associated in practice – the Shema and the Amidah, the reading of the law and the prophets, and the priestly blessing (*Meg.* 4:1–5). The large number of texts of Jewish prayers and hymns from the late pre-Christian and early Christian period (for example, the Prayer of Manasses, the psalm of Tobit, the Song of the Three Children, the communal confession in the book of Baruch, the benedictions for every morning and evening of a month in 4Q503, and the responses and canticles intermingled with the psalms in 11QPs[a]) indicates the importance of prayer in Judaism at this time, even though the texts also suggest variety in the places and times of prayer. Comparably, M. P. Weitzman argues that the importance of the service of prayer in the Peshitta reflects its importance in Jewish life at the time of Christian origins, especially but not only in the Diaspora.[31] Even when full weight is given to reservations expressed by writers on prayer,[32] Josephus' evidence in particular, in the context of the earlier and later sources noted above, suggests public prayer in conjunction with the reading of the law in Judaea at the end of the Second Temple period.

Three early allusions to Jewish prayer by Christians may be considered against this background. First, in the *Didache* 'Pray not with the hypocrites' (8.2) follows on the warning 'Let not your fasts be with the hypocrites'; the writer knows that they fast on Mondays and Thursdays. (Compare the strong awareness of contemporary Jewish fasting practice evinced in the *Epistle of Barnabas*, chapter 3.[33]) Prayer is integral to fast-days, as already noted, and the transition to prayer is natural. Just as Wednesdays and Fridays are ordained as distinctively Christian fast-days, so, on prayer, the Lord's Prayer is given as the distinctively Christian form of prayer to use – perhaps by contrast with a Jewish form like one of the daily benedictions found in Qumran texts (4Q503), or with a compressed form of the Amidah – and the *Didache* directs the Lord's Prayer to be used thrice daily; compare the Mishnaic direction that the Amidah is to be prayed thrice daily by every Israelite (*Ber.* 3.3; 4.1). Here there is a sense that communal prayer is a characteristic aspect of Jewish common life, and that Christians must have something comparable but different. It has of course been independently surmised that the prayers in *Didache* 9–10 were originally Jewish, a conclusion which would well fit the situation suggested by chapter 3.[34] Irrespective of 9–10, however, it could be inferred from chapter 3 alone that common prayer was established and central in the Jewish life known to the writer, perhaps in the early second century.

Secondly, Justin Martyr objects to the Jewish view that Malachi 1:11, on the pure offering to be made in every place and among the Gentiles, referred to the prayers offered by Israelites in the dispersion (*Dial.* 117.2, 4); this application of the verse occurs in the Targum and the Midrash (*Num. Rab.* 13, on 7:12), but Justin's is the earliest datable attestation. This Jewish interpretation will have seemed weighty if its background included not only biblical passages on Diaspora prayer (such as 1 Kings 8:44, 48; Jer. 29:7, 12; and Baruch 3:6–7), but also the prayers currently offered in the proseuche. Such prayer is more definitely mentioned in a famous passage of Justin which also bears on imprecation. 'After the prayer' (μετὰ τὴν προσευχήν) the rulers of synagogue teach mockery of Christ – whether in a discourse or by means of a curse is unclear (*Dial.* 137.2). In Luke 13:14 an ἀρχισυνάγωγος disputes with Christ, but the gospel narrative differs too much from Justin's allegation to be the source of it. Justin's use of the article shows that 'the prayer' had an accepted place. The Greek might correspond to the determinate Hebrew *ha-t^ephillah*, used in the Mishnah (e.g. *Ber.* 4.1) to designate *the* prayer, the Amidah; given the Diaspora currency of texts exhibiting antecedents of the Amidah (Ecclus. 36:1–17; 2 Macc. 1:27–9), it is a reasonable conjecture that the topics of 'the prayer' as known to Justin would have resembled those which were prevalent in contemporary forms of the Amidah. At any rate Justin here provides, soon after 150, one of the earliest clear indications that prayer was regular in a synagogue assembly.

Lastly, Tertullian (*Orat.* 14) makes the striking claim that the Jews do not raise their hands to the Lord in prayer – indeed they dare not, lest some Isaiah should cry out that their hands are full of blood (Isa. 1:15). This claim is combined with an attack on Jewish purificatory washing, and it might perhaps be dismissed as an effort to justify the attached polemic, for the practice of lifting up the hands in prayer, often mentioned in the Hebrew Scriptures, was common to Jews and non-Jews in antiquity (compare the raised hands carved over the incised Jewish imprecation of Rheneia, CIJ 725). The raising of hands is mentioned in descriptions of Egyptian Jews at prayer (3 Macc. 5:25 (supplication); Philo, *Flacc.* 121 (thanksgiving)). Scripture also attests the *expansion* of the hands in prayer (Exod. 9:29, etc.). This gesture can of course merge into elevation (1 Kings 8:22). It is noteworthy, however, that in the later second century BCE the Judaean Jews are described by Agatharchides of Cnidus (quoted by Josephus, *Ap.* 2.209) as *expanding* their hands in prayer on the sabbath until the evening (ἐκτετακότες τὰς χεῖρας εὔχεσθαι μέχρι τῆς ἑσπέρας); and perhaps at about the same time or somewhat earlier 'I have spread out my hands' is the biblical expression echoed in the third of the apocryphal psalms preserved in Syriac (Ps. 155), verse 2 (Hebrew text in 11Q Ps^a, col. 24, line 3). Christians likewise lifted up hands in prayer (1 Tim. 2:8; *1 Clem.* 29.1), but they also associated the raising and expansion of their hands with the cross, implying the custom of spreading out rather than raising only (Tertullian, ibid.; *Odes. Sol.* 27; 43.1–2).[35]

Yet Tertullian's claim is perhaps too unexpected to be totally dismissed. Can it be accounted for by a trend among many Jews towards restricting such gestures? This would accord with the stress on decorum evinced both in Philo on the sabbath assembly and in the Mishnah on the Amidah (and reflected in the Pauline 'decently and in order' in 1 Cor. 14:40).[36] Tertullian himself does not want Christians to raise their hands too high (*Orat.* 17). There are hints of a comparable Jewish feeling. As already noted, the expansion rather than the raising of the hands is mentioned by Agatharchides and in an apocryphal psalm. In 3 Maccabees and Philo, as cited above, the raising of hands is mentioned not as normal prayer practice, but as a sign of exceptionally intense emotion; the same consideration perhaps applies to the Rheneia hands, represented over a call for divine vengeance. One of the biblical phrases for raising the hands, 'to lift up the palms (*kappayim*)' (Ps. 63:4, etc.), has in the Mishnah (e.g. *Ber.* 5.4) already become a technical term for giving the priestly blessing; the alternative phrase 'to lift up the hands (*yadayim*)' is linked in Scripture itself with priestly blessing (Lev. 9:22; Ecclus. 1:20), and in the LXX both phrases alike are rendered with χεῖρες, 'hands'. Development of the biblical phrase into a technical term suggests that by the second century in the circles concerned it was not favoured as a general description of prayer.

Some reluctance to take the raising of hands as a description of prayer is also suggested by interpretations of Scripture. Biblical references to the practice are sometimes but not always straightforwardly interpreted as such. In the Targum of Psalms only 141:2 survives as raising of hands in prayer; at 28.2 and 63.5 'lifting up' in the Hebrew significantly becomes 'spreading out' in the Targum, and 134.2 is referred to the priestly blessing. In the haggadah Psalm 63:4 is referred to the Amidah (Babylonian Talmud, *Ber.* 16b), but this is because the lifting up of the palms is taken as a reference to the priestly blessing at the close of the prayer. In Exodus, comparably, the *expansion* of Moses' hands is prayer (9:29 in Targums *Neofiti*, *Pseudo-Jonathan* and *Onqelos*, and Midrash *Exod. Rab.* 12.7); but there is variation over the great Jewish and Christian pattern of prayer, the *raising* of his hands with the help of Aaron and Hur (17:11–12).[37] In the *Fragment Targum* and *Targum*

Neofiti the hands are specifically said to be raised in prayer, in both verses. In *Targum Pseudo-Jonathan* the hands are raised in prayer in verse 11, but they are *expanded* in prayer in verse 12. Finally, in *Targum Onqelos* the raising of the hands in verse 11 is mentioned but not specified as prayer, and in 12 the hands are said to be expanded in prayer. It was by no more than a very slight addition to existing interpretation that Christians found in this passage prayer with raised and expanded hands, in the form of the cross (so, among others, *Barn.* 12.2; Justin, *Dial.* 90.4–5; Tertullian, *Adv. Marc.* III.18, 6). The caution evinced in the Jewish renderings is all the more striking because the narrative itself suggests that the hands cannot have been raised high.

From Jewish interpretation here and elsewhere, therefore, one can infer some feeling against taking the raising of the hands as a standard prayer posture, and a preference for spreading out the hands without raising them high. Such feeling, no doubt historically continuous with the sense of decorum evinced by Philo, was perhaps enhanced among Jews in Tertullian's environment by reaction against the Christianization of lifting up the hands; but Tertullian's own restrictions on raising the hands suggest a care for decorum which is not unlikely also to have been present among Jews. If this conjecture is on the right lines, Tertullian's startling claim that Jews do not raise their hands in prayer will attest a preference among Jews in Carthage for spreading out the hands rather than raising them, comparable with rabbinic stress on reverent prayer, and rooted in pre-rabbinic practice.

4. IMPRECATION

These are three early instances of a more widely attested Christian acquaintance with Jewish prayer custom. Against this background the much-discussed patristic passages on Jewish imprecations against Christ and the Christians seem likely to offer some reflection of practice, despite their polemical character. This view is supported by the fact that they find correspondence in other sources. Thus in Justin Martyr the cursing of *Christ* probably reflects a purgation formula used by Jews and Romans (compare Acts 26:11; 1 Cor. 12:3; also Pliny, *Ep.* 10:96, 5–6, on *Christo maledicere* as one of the tests of those denounced as Christians). Justin once puts this curse on Christ 'after the prayer', as noted above, and in

this respect his report can be compared with much later midrashic
evidence for a curse on *Christians* uttered after the Amidah.[38]

The cursing of Christians mentioned by Justin himself, however,
seems likely to correspond to a form of the curse on apostates
included in the Amidah, specially mentioning *minim*, 'heretics' –
whence the Twelfth Benediction of the Amidah became known as
birkat ha-minim. In contemporary Judaea and Galilee it seems that
a benediction 'of the *minim*' could be used in the Amidah either on
its own or in combination with another benediction, 'of the separatists' or 'of the wicked'; extant texts of the Twelfth Benediction
show the results of such a combination.[39] The general context was
a prayer for national redemption and judgement. Association of
Justin's curse on Christians with the Amidah, in its fluid second-
century shape as reflected in his milieu, is encouraged by the later
reports of Jerome noted below, where the Amidah is almost certainly the Jewish prayer in view.

Nevertheless, Justin is widely considered to have mistaken the
scope of the benediction 'of the *minim*'. He assumes that the curse
applied to all Christians, but many judge that, in so far as it
touched the Christian church, it would have applied to Jewish
members only.[40] This judgement seems, however, not to reckon
fully with the position of the church at this period as a minority
closely linked with the non-Christian Jewish majority (compare
Tertullian, *Apol.* 21.1, quoted in n. 5, above). The single Christian
body of Jews and Gentiles, within which Gentiles claimed to have
been made one with Jews (Eph. 2:11–3:11), was widely regarded by
outsiders as an aberrant form of the majority Jewish community,
which also had a substantial number of Gentile adherents. So the
Christians as a body were considered by Jews and pagans a αἵρεσις (Acts 24:5; Justin, *Dial.* 108) or faction (Celsus in Origen, *Contra Celsum* 3.1, 5; 8.14) of the Jewish community. A Jewish attitude
of special hostility directed towards *minim* is suggested also by
Trypho's bitter disapproval of Gentile conversion to Christianity
and of Gentile Christians, as represented in Justin's *Dialogue*; it
would have been better for the Gentile Justin to have continued as
a pagan, when he might have had some hope, than to be deceived
by Christian error, and it would have been better if Trypho himself had obeyed the ordinance of the Jewish teachers, who forbid
discussion with Christians (*Dial.* 8; 38). The *Dialogue* in these passages recalls the Tosefta, on *minim* as people who are worse than

idolaters, and should be steadfastly shunned (*Shabb.* 13.5; *Hullin* 2.20–4, where anecdotes of Christians are told to support the ban on converse with *minim*).[41]

The allegations of thrice-daily maledictions in Epiphanius and Jerome (who are perhaps indebted here to Apollinaris of Laodicaea) are likely to reflect the *birkat ha-minim* when repeated thrice daily as the Twelfth Benediction of the Amidah. In Jerome these allegations are part of his unceasing all-round polemic against opponents of his ecclesiastical position. Yet, as Samuel Krauss showed, Jerome had some familiarity with Jewish prayer.[42] T. C. G. Thornton has argued, nevertheless, that the allegations were invented, because the imperial authorities would have forbidden any such public prayer.[43] Yet the authorities were not always anxious to act against the Jewish communities, as the initial imperial resistance to Ambrose's pressure in the Callinicum incident shows. It has long been thought likely, however, that imperial action on the Eighteen Benedictions was indeed eventually taken in the sixth or early seventh century, perhaps in connection with Justinian's *Novella* of 553 on Jewish public reading of the Scriptures. Pirqoi ben Baboi (eighth century) reports a tradition that the 'evil kingdom' prohibited the *Shema* and the *Tefillah* in the land of Israel before the Arab conquest. This will refer to a Byzantine measure, banning both these prayers as anti-Christian,[44] in an extension of the prohibition of objectionable Jewish interpretation in the *Novella*.[45]

The Christian notices of synagogue prayer illustrated above have something to offer, it has been suggested, not only on topics in Jewish – Christian relations, such as the cursing of Christians, but also on the rise of the synagogue, the significance of the ark and the development of Jewish public prayer. Christian texts are important among the early attestations of synagogues, they cohere with archaeological and other indications of the impressive architecture of synagogues, and they show the prevalence of common prayer at an earlier date than most Jewish sources permit. They can also give glimpses of the style of prayer; Tertullian's notices suggest an esteem for decorum and *gravitas* recalling Philo and the Mishnah. Moreover, it is of significance for the study of the western Diaspora if such Christian reports can be illuminated by rabbinic and targumic texts, as was attempted above. Links of some strength between the west and the homeland can then be presupposed. Lastly, the fact that Christian texts can offer material for

consideration in the study of Jewish prayer suggests that, although
Christians saw the synagogue through Old and New Testament
spectacles, their eyes were not wholly blinded to their contemporary Jewish neighbours.

NOTES

1 For the latter see especially Juster, *Les juifs dans l'empire romain*, 1, 45,
  n. 1.
2 This point is brought out by Lieu, 'History and Theology in Christian
  Views of Judaism', 85–7.
3 Cohen, 'Pagan and Christian Evidence on the Ancient Synagogue',
  159–60.
4 See for example Harnack, *Die Altercatio Simonis et Theophili*, 57, 64–5
  (allowing that some Christian texts reflect real contact with Jews, 73–
  4, 78. n. 59); Tränkle, *Tertulliani Adversus Iudaeos*, lxx–lxxi, n. 6; Lieu,
  'History'; Taylor, *Anti-Judaism and Early Christian Identity*.
5 According to Goodman, *Mission and Conversion*, 118–19, they could only
  have become godfearers, not proselytes, since Roman legislation for-
  bade the circumcision of Gentiles; but this inference is doubtful, for
  Jews were forbidden to circumcise those 'non eiusdem religionis' (by
  Antoninus Pius, according to Modestinus, quoted in *Digest* 48.8, 11),
  but Christians might well be considered as aberrant Jews, sharing the
  Jewish *religio*. So Tertullian acknowledges that they might seem to
  shelter 'sub umbraculo insignissimae religionis, certe licitae' – Judaism (*Apol.* 21.1). Goodman's stimulating argument against identification of Jewish enthusiasm for proselytizing before the third century CE seems to me in general to underrate the closeness of
  Christians to Jews, and the implications of earlier evidence for Jewish
  welcome to proselytes, for example in Philo and the Thirteenth Benediction of the Amidah.
6 Parkes, *The Conflict of the Church and the Synagogue*, 381–2.
7 Blumenkranz, *Juifs et chrétiens dans le monde occidental*, 93–4.
8 Van der Lof, 'Les liens des chrétiens avec les synagogues locales'.
9 See Hengel, 'Proseuche und Synagoge'; Levine, 'The Second Temple
  Synagogue'; Sanders, *Jewish Law from Jesus to the Mishnah*, 77–9;
  Judaism, 198–202.
10 For similar views see Meyers and Strange, *Archaeology, the Rabbis and
  Early Christianity*, 140–1; Kee, 'The Transformation of the Synagogue
  after 70 CE', exhaustively criticized by Sanders, *Jewish Law*, 341–3, nn.
  28–9 (with special reference to archaeology, Philo and Josephus) and
  by Oster, 'Supposed Anachronism in Luke–Acts' Use of συναγωγή'
  (questioning Kee's assessment of Luke–Acts); also Kee, 'The Changing Meaning of Synagogue' (inter alia, setting the Theodotus inscrip-

tion found on Mount Ophel in the fourth century or later, as opposed to the usual dating before 66 CE; the later date raises many difficulties, as noted by Sanders, *Jewish Law*, 341, n. 28).

11 So Reif, *Judaism and Hebrew Prayer*, 73–5, with nn. 42–3 (literature); on nomenclature see especially Hengel, 'Proseuche', and the summary of names by Levine, 'The Second Temple Synagogue', 13–14.

12 Compare the αἰθρίοι προσευχαί said by Apion to have been built by Moses (Apion, quoted by Josephus, *Ap.* 2.10); did some old proseuchae in Egypt approximate to the 'open place' by providing a courtyard used for assembly?

13 On the interpretation of the Greek see Barrett, *Acts*, I, 323–4.

14 The Mishnah in this context quotes Lev. 26:31, 'And I will bring their sanctuaries into desolation', to show that the holiness of the synagogues abides even when they are forsaken (*Meg.* 3.3).

15 This view is further encouraged if Paul's stress on the veil alludes to scroll wrappings (*m. Meg.* 3.1) or reflects some early form of the practice of shielding the ark with a veil (attested from the third century CE, see Z. Safrai, 'Dukhan, Aron and Teva', 72, 74, and n. 29), as is urged by Knox, *St Paul and the Church of the Gentiles*, 131 (noting the symbolism of the temple veil in Philo); but the hint at synagogue practice depends on the mention of reading (Acts 13:15; 15:21; Philo, *Hyp.* 7.12–13) rather than the question of the veil.

16 On Theodotus see Sanders, *Jewish Law*, 341, n. 28, cited above; on Papous, Noy, 'A Jewish Place of Prayer in Roman Egypt'.

17 A. S. Hollis (ed.), *Ovid, Ars Amatoria, Book I*, Oxford, 1977, notes that although an occasion rather than a place is mentioned, synagogues are envisaged.

18 Smallwood, *Philonis Alexandrini Legatio ad Gaium*, 222–3, discusses rabbinic passages together with Philo.

19 Goodman, *Mission*, 137–8, rightly notes that motives other than proselytization will have influenced the construction of great synagogues, but the attractive power of such buildings is unlikely to have gone unnoticed by those responsible for them.

20 On usages concerning the ark in the rabbinic period see Elbogen, *Jewish Liturgy*, 359–63 (including later developments); Safrai, 'Dukhan', 71–7 (with special reference to archaeology).

21 The former view is represented by Sukenik, *Ancient Synagogues in Palestine and Greece*, 52–3, and Dothan, *Hammath Tiberias*, 32–7, with plate 27 (mosaic panel of ark); the latter by Dequeker, 'L'iconographie de l'arche de la Torah'. The doors incised on ossuaries cannot be interpreted with confidence as representing the ark (Figueras, *Decorated Jewish Ossuaries*, 57–8).

22 Sukenik, *Synagogues*, 53.

23 This interpretation is given without argument by Beckwith, *The Old Testament Canon of the New Testament Church*, 391. On rolls of Enoch in

Tertullian's time see Hengel, with Deines, 'Die Septuaginta als "christliche Schriftensammlung"', 216–18.

24 Perhaps the Day of Atonement (so Aziza, *Tertullien et le judaïsme*, 29–30), but not necessarily so, since days of fasting were common in Jewish practice at this period, as noted in connection with the *Didache*, below.

25 This passage is judged by Safrai, 'Dukhan', 76, to attest a single synagogue ark-chest, and not the use of the ark together with a central chest or platform which is found in Geonic Babylonia.

26 The text is interpreted by Krauss, *Synagogale Altertümer*, 369–71.

27 Sukenik, *Synagogues*, 17–18, note, was against this interpretation, but it is accepted by Dothan, *Tiberias*, 36, with comparison of a Dura Europos representation.

28 Noy, *Jewish Inscriptions of Western Europe*, 1, no. 13 and plate vi.

29 Horbury, 'The Purpose of Pseudo-Cyprian', 310–11.

30 Reif, *Hebrew Prayer*, 83.

31 Weitzman, 'From Judaism to Christianity'.

32 Sanders, *Judaism*, 202–8, accepts that there will have been prayer in Judaean synagogues before the destruction of the Temple, but stresses that it was more probably individual than unified. Salzmann, *Lehren und Ermahnen*, 451–2, judges that prayer will have been regular in the Diaspora before 70, but leaves open the question whether in Jerusalem and its neighbourhood there was synagogue prayer while the Temple stood. Nitzan, *Qumran Prayer and Religious Poetry*, 14, 40–5, allows slight beginnings only of fixed common prayer before the destruction of the Temple.

33 Horbury, 'Jewish–Christian Relations in Barnabas and Justin Martyr', 323–6; on the importance of this point in assessment of the Epistle, Carleton Paget, *The Epistle of Barnabas*, 109–10.

34 Sandelin, *Wisdom as Nourisher*, 186–228 (literature), reconstructs Hebrew forms of the prayers, holding that they were essentially Jewish thanksgivings used at common meals; they would have been used in Hebrew in Palestine, and in Greek among Egyptian Jews, whence they would have passed to Christians.

35 On Christian practice see von Severus, 'Gebet 1', cols. 1231–2.

36 Philo, *Somn.* 2.127, *Hyp.* 7.12–13; in rabbinic opinion the prayer-leader in the Amidah is to display gravity (*m. Ber.* 5.1) and a disciplined stance (feet straight, like those of the living creatures in Ezek. 1:7: Babylonian Talmud, *Ber.* 10b).

37 In the *Mekhilta* and in *Targum Pseudo-Jonathan* it is taken to be fast-day prayer 'until the going down of the sun' (verse 12) (compare Tertullian on prayer until star-rise), and a pattern for the officiating of three prayer-leaders on fast-days; Philo (*Mos.* 1.216) similarly views it as supplication, adding that Moses purified himself beforehand (compare Tertullian's attack on Jewish washing before prayer).

38 For fuller discussion see Horbury, 'The Benediction of the *Minim*', 54–8, and 'Barnabas', 342–3.
39 Elbogen and Heinemann, *Liturgy*, 33–5, with n. 22; Horbury, 'Benediction', 36–9, 46–7.
40 So Van der Horst, *Hellenism–Judaism–Christianity*, 111 (literature); for the considerations in the text below see Horbury, 'Benediction', 28, 50–1, 58–9.
41 Goodman, *Mission*, 142, suggests that the measure of acceptance of paganism in *Dial.* 8 dilutes Trypho's counsel that Justin should be circumcised; but Trypho is represented as thinking that *even* a pagan is better than a Christian, not as doubting that Justin ought to accept Judaism.
42 Krauss, 'The Jews in the Works of the Church Fathers', 233–4.
43 Thornton, 'Christian Understanding of the *Birkath Ha-Minim*'.
44 The prominence of the Shema (Deut. 6:4) in medieval anti-Christian polemic is noted by Lasker, *Jewish Philosophical Polemics*, 189, n. 19; comparably, in a Byzantine Christian work, the fifth- or sixth-century Greek Dialogue of Timothy and Aquila, Deut. 6:4 is the first text quoted against Christian beliefs by the Jewish spokesman (F. C. Conybeare (ed.), *The Dialogues of Athanasius and Zacchaeus, and of Timothy and Aquila*, Oxford, 1898, 65).
45 Horbury, 'Benediction', 29 (on Pirqoi ben Baboi in the series of references to the Benediction of the *Minim*); Mann, 'Changes in the Divine Service of the Synagogue', 252–4, 277–8, ascribes the measure to Heraclius; Veltri, 'Novelle', 129 (literature), ascribes it to Justinian, whom he regards as seeking the conversion of the Jews.

BIBLIOGRAPHY

Aziza, C., *Tertullien et le judaïsme*, Nice, 1977.
Barrett, C. K., *A Critical and Exegetical Commentary on the Acts of the Apostles*, I, Edinburgh, 1994.
Beckwith, R. T., *The Old Testament Canon of the New Testament Church*, London, 1985.
Blumenkranz, B., *Juifs et chrétiens dans le monde occidental*, Paris, 1960.
Carleton Paget, J. N. B., *The Epistle of Barnabas: Outlook and Background*, Tübingen, 1994.
Cohen, S. J. D., 'Pagan and Christian Evidence on the Ancient Synagogue', in L. I. Levine (ed.), *The Synagogue in Late Antiquity*, Philadelphia, 1987, 159–81.
Dequeker, L., 'L'iconographie de l'arche de la Torah dans les catacombes juives de Rome', *Augustinianum* 28 (1988), 437–60.
Dothan, M., *Hammath Tiberias*, Jerusalem, 1983.
Elbogen, I., *Der jüdische Gottesdienst in seiner geschichtlichen Entwicklung* (1913), Hebrew translation edited and supplemented by J. Heinemann and

others (1972), E. tr. from Hebrew and German by R. P. Scheindlin, *Jewish Liturgy: A Comprehensive History*, Philadelphia, New York and Jerusalem, 1993.

Figueras, P., *Decorated Jewish Ossuaries*, Leiden, 1983.

Goodman, M., *Mission and Conversion: Proselytizing in the Religious History of the Roman Empire*, Oxford, 1994.

Harnack, A., *Die Altercatio Simonis et Theophili, nebst Untersuchungen über die antijüdische Polemik in der alten Kirche*, TU i 3, Leipzig, 1883, 1–136.

Hengel, M., 'Proseuche und Synagoge', in G. Jeremias, H.-W. Kuhn and H. Stegemann (eds.), *Tradition und Glaube ... Festgabe für K. G. Kuhn zum 65. Geburtstag*, Göttingen, 1971, 157–83.

with R. Deines, 'Die Septuaginta als "christliche Schriftensammlung", ihre Vorgeschichte und das Problem ihres Kanons', in M. Hengel and A. M. Schwemer (eds.), *Die Septuaginta zwischen Judentum und Christentum*, Tübingen, 1994, 182–284.

Horbury, W., 'The Benediction of the *Minim* and Jewish–Christian Controversy', *JTS* N.S. 3 (1982), 19–61.

'The Purpose of Pseudo-Cyprian, *Adversus Iudaeos*', in E. A. Livingstone (ed.), *Studia Patristica* xviii, 3, Kalamazoo and Leuven, 1989, 291–317.

'Jewish–Christian Relations in Barnabas and Justin Martyr', in J. D. G. Dunn (ed.), *Jews and Christians: The Parting of the Ways A.D. 70 to 135*, Tübingen, 1992, 315–45.

Juster, J., *Les juifs dans l'empire romain*, 2 vols., Paris, 1914.

Kee, H. C., 'The Transformation of the Synagogue after 70 CE: Its Import for Early Christianity', *NTS* 36 (1990), 1–24.

'The Changing Meaning of Synagogue: A Response to Richard Oster', *NTS* 40 (1994), 281–3.

Knox, W. L., *St Paul and the Church of the Gentiles*, Cambridge, 1939.

Krauss, S., 'The Jews in the Works of the Church Fathers', iii, *JQR* 6 (1894), 225–6.

Synagogale Altertümer, Berlin and Vienna, 1922.

Lasker, D. J., *Jewish Philosophical Polemics Against Christianity in the Middle Ages*, New York, 1977.

Levine, L. I., 'The Second Temple Synagogue: The Formative Years', in L. I. Levine (ed.), *The Synagogue in Late Antiquity*, Philadelphia, 1987, 7–31.

Lieu, J., 'History and Theology in Christian Views of Judaism', in J. Lieu, J. North and T. Rajak (eds.), *The Jews among Pagans and Christians in the Roman Empire*, London and New York, 1992, 79–96.

Lof, J. van der, 'Les liens des chrétiens avec les synagogues locales du temps de saint Cyprien et saint Augustin', *NAK* N.S. 56 (1975–6), 385–95.

Mann, J., 'Changes in the Divine Service of the Synagogue due to Religious Persecution', *HUCA* 4 (1927), 241–310.

Meyers, E. M., and Strange, J. F., *Archaeology, the Rabbis and Early Christianity*, London, 1981.

Nitzan, B., *Qumran Prayer and Religious Poetry*, E. tr. by J. Chipman, Leiden, New York and Cologne, 1994.

Noy, David, 'A Jewish Place of Prayer in Roman Egypt', *JTS* N.S. 43 (1992), 118–22

Jewish Inscriptions of Western Europe, I, Cambridge, 1993.

Oster, R. E., 'Supposed Anachronism in Luke–Acts' Use of συναγωγή: A Rejoinder to H. C. Kee', *NTS* 39 (1993), 178–208.

Parkes, James, *The Conflict of the Church and the Synagogue*, London, 1934.

Reif, S. C., *Judaism and Hebrew Prayer*, Cambridge, 1993.

Safrai, Z., 'Dukhan, Aron and Teva: How was the Ancient Synagogue Furnished?', in R. Hachlili (ed.), *Ancient Synagogues in Israel, Third–Seventh Century C.E.*, BAR International Series 499, Oxford, 1989, 69–84.

Salzmann, J. C., *Lehren und Ermahnen: Zur Geschichte des christlichen Wortgottesdienstes in den ersten drei Jahrhunderten*, Tübingen, 1994.

Sandelin, K.-G., *Wisdom as Nourisher*, Åbo, 1986.

Sanders, E. P., *Jewish Law from Jesus to the Mishnah*, London and Philadelphia, 1990.

Judaism: Practice and Belief, 63 BCE-66 CE, London and Philadelphia, 1992.

Severus, E. von, 'Gebet 1', RAC VIII (1972), cols. 1134–256.

Smallwood, E. M., *Philonis Alexandrini Legatio ad Gaium*, Leiden, 1961.

Sukenik, E. L., *Ancient Synagogues in Palestine and Greece*, London, 1934.

Taylor, Miriam, *Anti-Judaism and Early Christian Identity*, Leiden, 1995.

Thornton, T. C. G., 'Christian Understanding of the *Birkath Ha-Minim* in the Eastern Roman Empire', *JTS* N.S. 38 (1987), 419–31.

Tränkle, H., *Q. S. F. Tertulliani Adversus Iudaeos*, Wiesbaden, 1964.

Van der Horst, P. W., *Hellenism–Judaism–Christianity*, Kampen, 1994.

Veltri, G., 'Die Novelle 146 περὶ 'Εβραίων', in M. Hengel and A. M. Schwemer (eds.), *Die Septuaginta zwischen Judentum und Christentum*, Tübingen, 1994, 116–30.

Weitzman, M. P., 'From Judaism to Christianity: The Syriac Version of the Hebrew Bible', in J. Lieu, J. North and T. Rajak (eds.), *The Jews among Pagans and Christians in the Roman Empire*, London and New York, 147–73.

CHAPTER 18

Messianism, Torah and early Christian tradition

Andrew Chester

I. INTRODUCTION

Christianity, in origin, is a Jewish messianic movement.[1] Hence, clearly, Jewish messianic expectations and movements provide one particular context within which the early Christian movement is to be understood.[2] One issue of potential significance for early Christianity as a messianic movement is that of concern with and traditions about law (or Torah), and related issues.

This may not seem a very promising theme to take, both because it has already been investigated by a number of scholars (especially W. D. Davies and Díez Macho)[3] and also because the results of their studies have been mostly meagre and unconvincing. But this is at least partly, I would want to argue, because their approach has been both too limited and also in many ways the wrong way round. That is, they have only looked at the issue of the 'messianic Torah', and not more extensively at the wider issues involved, and they have also tried to accumulate all the possible Jewish evidence, including rabbinic material, in order to demonstrate the existence of a Jewish doctrine of a 'messianic Torah' as the background for the use and developments of this theme in the New Testament in the first century CE. In fact, in his original essay, Davies is suitably modest about the results of his work, and admits that the evidence is sparse and scanty, even though he still wants to hold on to it to produce some form of this 'doctrine' of a messianic Torah.[4] He does indeed perform a reasonably valuable service in taking up the texts already discussed by earlier writers and showing the severe limitations of the conclusions that can be drawn from them. But in the later version of his work, under the influence of Díez Macho (and now arguing much the same case as the latter), he holds that the Jewish evidence as a whole, and the rabbinic in particular, points to the expectation of the abrogation of the Mosaic Torah and the bringing in of the messianic Torah in the messianic or final age.[5] This argument, however, is fatally flawed. There are two main problems: first, that there is little or nothing in the whole of rabbinic literature about abolishing Torah or introducing a new Torah in the messianic age; and secondly, that even if there were, it would not in itself provide background or proof for claims that this is what we find in the case of Jesus or the New Testament more generally.

This does not, however, mean that Jewish, including rabbinic, sources have no significance for the issues involved here, and I shall return to them briefly at the end of the chapter. At this point I want only to note a few scriptural passages (several of them discussed by Davies) that are of potential importance for this theme. First, Isaiah 2:2–4 (and the parallel in Micah 4:1–4): the setting is the 'latter days'; the vision, especially of 2:4, is close to that of Isaiah 11, which is taken up in later Jewish (and Christian) tradition as pointing to the idyllic messianic age. The focus is on Jerusalem and the Temple, to which the Gentiles come; and it is out of Zion (or Jerusalem) that the law (or word of the Lord) goes. It is not certain, in the original context, what sense 'Torah' would have, but it is obviously easy to see how the idea of Torah being given to the Gentiles in the final age could develop from this. There are further sections in Isaiah that are potentially important, especially 42:1–4: the Servant has the spirit put on him, and will bring forth justice to the nations (v. 1), 'the coastlands wait for his law' (v. 4, cf. also v. 6). The context is not specifically eschatological, though it could obviously be interpreted thus. So also 49:1–6; 51:4–5 (v. 4: 'a law will go forth from me'), which might be understood as implicitly eschatological; 55:3, and 56:1–8 (cf 2:2–4; the reference now is specifically to the covenant, but is not eschatological).

The most famous passage is Jeremiah 31:31–4. Again, it is not clear precisely what 'Torah' would mean in its context here; nor is it said that it is a new law, in contrast to the old. The main point is that it will be internalized, and perfectly obeyed, in the context of the (new) covenant God will make. But it obviously offers considerable scope for developed understanding and interpretation concerning the covenant, law and final (or, in certain contexts, messianic) age.

There are also passages in Ezekiel (not considered in Davies 1952/64) that may be important: 36:22–32 (especially vv. 27 and 29: a vision of the keeping of the law in the age of the restoration to the land) and 37:24–8 (which speaks of an 'everlasting covenant' and 'covenant of peace', and of keeping the law).

All this does not amount to much, as far as the theme of Torah in the final (or, potentially, messianic) age is concerned, although Isaiah 2 (and Micah 4) and Jeremiah 31 especially are potentially of great significance and easily able to be drawn on as resources concerning the future hope and vision of the final age. There is, however, a wider theme evident here which is worth drawing attention to; that is, the emphasis, negatively, on the failure of Israel to obey God and keep the law, and the promise that in the 'end' God will make this obedience possible (as for example by his gift of the spirit).[6] This is clear in Jeremiah 31, where the contrast is drawn between, on the one hand, the covenant they have broken (31:32) and, on the other, the new covenant, and the law and knowledge of God they will then have within them, along with God's forgiveness of their sin. The same basic theme, the contrast between sin and keeping the law or covenant, is found in Isaiah 55:3–8; 56:1–8; 65 (the new heaven and the new earth, where the vision of the final age and transformation is set in contrast to the failure to obey God). It is also a theme that is evident in Ezekiel (especially 20; also 16; 23; 36) and the eighth-century prophets (Amos 4; Hos. 4; Isa. 1). The same basic theme is found much more widely, in the Pentateuch (especially Lev. 26; Deut. 29–30), Psalms (e.g. 78; 105; 106; 143) and 1 and 2 Chronicles, as well as in later Jewish writings: the Qumran texts (1QH 1; 11; 17; 18; 1QS 4; 11; CD 3; at least in terms of the 'precepts' of God), and *1 Enoch* (1–10), *Jubilees* (1.22–5), *Psalms of Solomon* 17, *Testament of Moses*, 4 Ezra 8, and *Testament of the Twelve Patriarchs* (*T. Lev.* 14–18; *T. Dan.* 5) and the main traditions of the Pentateuchal Targums for Deuteronomy 29–30; Leviticus 26.

The significance of this theme will become clear shortly. For the present, however, it needs to be noted that no 'doctrine' of a new Torah in the messianic or final age can be demonstrated from Jewish Scripture or from subsequent Jewish tradition. It is in most respects a false construct. There is not a great deal, for example, either in Scripture or in the rabbinic writings, about the messianic age more generally. Quite plausibly, there would be an assumption that when this new age actually arrived, it would be made clear (by God or the Messiah), or would at any rate become clear, what should happen, and specifically whether the Torah was still fully in force and whether any particular conditions obtained.

From this basis, I shall first examine early Christian texts and developments, before considering what issues they would raise within a Jewish context, and whether and to what extent they would appear disjunctive.

2. MATTHEW, JAMES AND THE *DIDACHE*

This first group of texts belongs mainly within, rather than in outright opposition to, Judaism or Jewish tradition.

2.1 Matthew

The main relevant section is 5:17–48, and especially 5:17–20. It is emphasized here that Jesus does not abrogate or set aside the law (v. 17), but reaffirms and intensifies it (v. 19). The law is made an integral and essential part of the messianic (final) age (or the kingdom). There is no possibility of it being set aside until the final fulfilment, beyond the messianic age or kingdom (5:18). Until then, the fulfilment, the (perfect or full) practice, teaching and continuation of Torah, in its detailed precepts, is insisted on. What is demanded is thus made potentially much more rigorous. The apparent contradiction of this by the continuation in 5:21–48 is only apparent; the so-called 'antitheses' are not for the most part antitheses as such at all.[7] Again, they primarily represent an intensification of the law, a heightened demand. They do not set the Mosaic Torah aside, but insist on attending to the spirit as well as the letter of the law, drawing out the deeper implications of Torah. Hence what is envisaged is not a new law, or a different law, but more of the same law, although it would certainly be possible to understand this section in Matthew as implicitly developing the theme of the 'law on the heart' from Jeremiah 31.31–4, since the understanding of the law is now set at the level of intention as well as action. Thus 5:17–48 does not undermine but reinforces Torah in the final (or messianic) age, and the section culminates, quite consistently, in the demand for *perfection* (5:48).

This is very closely related to the demand for *righteousness* in

5:20, a further key theme in Matthew,[8] bound up with Torah (and covenant), and a further part of the insistence on the need for the observance and practice of Torah. That is, it needs to be seen to be done, to be shown in action, and not merely affirmed verbally. This fits with the strong emphasis on righteousness in 5–7 as a whole. It is introduced as an important focus of the Beatitudes (5:6, 10). This theme (integral to the covenant and Torah) is made into a central aspect of the community's self-identity, and its urgent, intensified existence in the final age. Specifically, it is made a category (and perhaps a condition) for belonging to the kingdom of God (or messianic kingdom). And the kingdom is in a real sense the main point of reference for the whole of the Beatitudes, with the reference to it at the beginning and end (5:3, 10; excluding 5:11). So also at 6:33, the urgent demand for intense living and quasi-perfection makes attaining the kingdom and righteousness virtually synonymous.

All this does certainly set an 'impossible' ideal or demand, as is immediately obvious from the reference to 'perfection' (5:48; cf. 19:21). But it belongs to the intense, urgent demands of the onset of the final or messianic age (or kingdom),[9] and it is also tied very closely to specific action, conduct and response (as at 19:21, and very obviously the whole of 5–7). Hence the themes of the messianic kingdom, Torah, righteousness and perfection are integrally caught up with each other, and help us understand the self-definition of the Matthean community. These themes are further illuminated, and thrown into relief, by 11:25–30 (especially the 'easy yoke' of vv. 29–30: the demands of the messianic kingdom and Torah are made possible for those who properly belong in the community; and the specific nature of this community is further implicitly defined by 18:1–35 and 25:31–46, amongst other passages).

2.2 James

In 2:8 James speaks of fulfilling the νόμος βασιλικός; this is usually rendered the 'royal law', but it is much more plausibly to be understood as 'the law concerning the king, or kingdom'.[10] If, then, we have here what is effectively a reference to the law of the (messianic) kingdom, it is notable that this law is specified as love of neighbour. This is concrete, specific and practical in its emphasis, in keeping with James more generally; it is also a specific precept of Torah. The Torah, or messianic law, is not limited to this one precept (perhaps in contrast to Paul in Rom. 13:10), but it is nevertheless significant that James makes *this* particular precept central and determinative for the Torah of the messianic age or kingdom (or the prospect of this, at least).

It is consistent with this that 2:5 speaks of the messianic kingdom belonging to the poor. This would naturally imply the materially poor,[11] and the rest of the letter confirms that this is what is intended. Thus it further defines the true nature of the community (over against its present state). The writer thus calls the community to an ideal, in relation to the Torah and kingdom, but this demand is also portrayed as a practical and urgent necessity.

It is also striking that James has a very high and positive understanding of the law.[12] Thus 1:25 speaks of the 'perfect law' and 'law of freedom', which must be observed; and 2:12 the 'law of freedom' by which they are to be judged. This whole section, 2:8–13, in fact starts with the reference to the law of the kingdom, and then makes clear that the law in full remains in force, before coming to the theme of judgement by the law of freedom. It is usually assumed that James in 2:9–11 means that it is only the moral, not the cultic, law that continues in force, but the distinction between moral and cultic is itself dubious as far as Torah is concerned,[13] and James provides no clear evidence for limiting the scope of the law here. In any case, what we have here is a powerful statement of the law's continuing validity and effect. Thus in 2:8–13 as a whole, there is strong eschatological emphasis in connection with the Torah. That is, fulfilling the law of the kingdom shows, implicitly, the right to belong in the messianic kingdom, while failure to fulfil it brings eschatological judgement on the offender. The idea here, then, is clearly of an eschatological Torah, or Torah of the messianic age or kingdom that has eschatological effect. It is not clear how much, if at all, this Torah differs from the Mosaic Torah presently in force. James 4:11–12 is the antithesis of 2:8: to act negatively, as judge, against one's fellow is to usurp God's role as judge, and the divine judgement enshrined and set out in the Torah. It thus involves setting oneself up over against the law, and again implicitly bringing divine judgement back upon oneself.

There are brief hints in James of a demand for perfection, especially at 1:4, where the call to attain a 'perfect' state is set in the urgent situation of final testing. Implicitly, attaining perfection

will allow those addressed to withstand the imminent eschatological threat. At any rate, 2:10, in relation to the law, makes very
high demands (keeping the whole law; cf. Matt. 5:17–20!), and the
emphasis on doing and action in 1:22–5, in the context of the
'perfect law', and on action in 2:8–13, ties in closely with the main
emphasis on works in 2:14–26. This theme belongs integrally to
the understanding of the fulfilment of the Torah (2:8–13), and the
covenant and righteousness (and justification; 2:14–26, esp. vv. 21–
6). The theme of the covenant and, especially, righteousness is
implicitly sharpened considerably by the eschatological emphasis
on judgement,[14] which provides the cutting edge of the election
and covenant in the final age.

Thus there is constant emphasis in James on the way of life that
is necessary as the basis for and vindication of the claims that are
made. Implicitly, these concern the Messiah and messianic age,
and it is the perspective of final judgement, kingdom and messianic Torah that underlies the continual demand for action and
conduct that is appropriate to this.

2.3 Didache

The strong eschatological emphasis of the *Didache* is evident especially in 9–10, 16, with its main concerns of kingdom, parousia
and indeed church.[15] It has much in common throughout with the
tradition of Matthew and James, especially (amongst others). Thus
16.1–2 emphasizes the need to be fully ready, or 'perfect' (τέλειος)
at the end, or else their faith will have been in vain.[16] This same
demand for perfection is also found at 1.4 (part of a secondary development of the tradition), in conjunction with the command to
turn the other cheek. Much of the body of the work fills out how
the demand for perfection of 16.1–2 (and 1.4) is to be met.

This is clearly so in the sustained collection of teaching in the
'Two Ways' section of 1–6. Much of it is stereotyped, traditional
Jewish wisdom[17] (as is James), setting out detailed standards for
conduct for the community addressed. Thus 4.13 gives the impression of a 'new law' for the kingdom or church. That impression is
confirmed by the conclusion to the Way of Death (6.1–2): '... if
you are able to bear the Lord's yoke in its entirety, you will be
perfect; but if you are not able, do what you can'. The precise

sense of 'the Lord's yoke' is disputed; it has been taken to refer to
Matthew 11:29–30, or to a stringent, ascetic prohibition of marriage. But the most plausible alternatives are either that it denotes
the Mosaic or Jewish law (cultic as well as ethical), thus making
very extensive demands (especially on any Gentile or proselyte
members of the community), or else that it should be understood
as 'the yoke of Christ', not as in Matthew 11:29–30 but with reference to the specific teaching, or (effectively) 'new law' of Christ,
set out at the start of the Two Ways section of the *Didache*, with
teaching from the Sermon on the Mount, in particular.[18] In this
case, the clause qualifying the reference to perfection may be a
recognition of the 'impossibility' of the Sermon on the Mount (or
the 'law', as Jesus, according to Matthew, represents it), and thus
a deliberate mitigation of the demands made in Matthew. There
may in fact be more overlap between these two alternatives than
might at first appear, especially if the 'yoke of Christ' were understood to refer to more than the very start of the Way of Life, since
much of the material used here is (as in Matthew and James)
drawn from Jewish Scripture.

At any rate, 'perfection' is here linked directly to teaching and
law (whether specifically the 'law of Christ' or not). And again (as
in Matthew and James), however much the understanding of 'perfection' is qualified or mitigated in 6.2, a place in the final kingdom is dependent on the fulfilment of specific law and teaching,
and (according to 16.2) being 'perfect' at the end. What is demanded, then, is the specific observance of specific demands, and
precise kinds of action (as especially for the poor and needy); it
may also involve observance of cultic as well as ethical aspects of
the law. The demands made on this 'community of the final age'
are, then, clear enough in general at least.

Hence it is apparent that Matthew, James and the *Didache* are
all, to a greater or lesser extent, still set within Judaism, however
much they are in tension with it or its leaders (as obviously Matthew and probably the *Didache*, for example with its reference to
the hypocrites, in relation to fasting, in 8.1–2; the tension is much
less evident in James). They are all clearly eschatologically orientated, directed, that is, towards the fulfilment of the messianic or
final age. There is strong emphasis in all three on (the continuing
validity of) Torah. This is in detailed form, not just in general.

The specific injunctions are prescriptive, and present what amounts to an intensified demand for perfection. All this strongly suggests that all three writings, to a greater or lesser extent, feel the need to vindicate and validate their distinctive claims, and their existence as a 'separate' community, above all by their action, or their whole way of life.

3. HEBREWS AND *BARNABAS*

It is next worth considering briefly the issues raised by a much more disjunctive (although not homogeneous) tradition, that represented by Hebrews and *Barnabas*.

3.1 Hebrews

The radical rejection in Hebrews of the cult and temple goes beyond most of the rest of the New Testament. The law is not the main theme as such, but obviously the radical rejection of cult and priesthood means that a large part of Torah is rejected as ineffective and outmoded (so, specifically, 7:18–19; 10:1–8); the law achieves nothing and is a mere shadow. Yet at the same time there is a positive interpretation of the covenant tradition. It is of course a new covenant, brought in by Jesus (8:6–13), but it is specifically based on the prophecy of Jeremiah 31 (8:8–12; 10:16–17). It is also represented specifically as a fulfilment or continuation of the Mosaic covenant: the 'blood of the covenant' (9:20 and other passages) represents the new covenant brought in by Jesus' death. Hence it is a covenant that is radically and disjunctively new, but one which is also deliberately linked to Jeremiah 31 and Exodus 24 (the sealing or making of the covenant).

Hence what we have here is a phenomenon we also encounter in Justin (as will be seen: section 6.1 below), and more generally in much of early Christian tradition. What is radically rejected at one level, and judged negatively, is appropriated at another, and used, positively and typologically, to define the distinctive nature of the new community. It thus specifically establishes a boundary or barrier between the new community and (the rest of) Judaism, but it does so by usurping concepts or 'territory' that still overlap or are held in common. Hence Hebrews, by its radical rejection of cult, temple and covenant, removes itself from the Judaism in which it originates; yet at the same time (in contrast to Justin and other later developments) it remains in critical tension with it.

In portraying the 'new covenant', Hebrews does not specifically take up the theme of the 'law written on the heart'. But (and here of course it has strong affinities with Matthew, James and the *Didache*) it sets strong and dramatic emphasis on conduct, and makes heightened and intensified demands. These are related above all to the final judgement and threat of rejection: salvation is not certain, and there is need for 'works' and a fully consistent way of life. So the remarkable vision of 12:18–24, concerned with the fulfilment of hope and the denouement of the eschatological age, has integral reference to the covenant and is hedged on both sides by strong references to conduct (as throughout: e.g. 3:7–4:13; 5:11–6:12). Hebrews represents an urgent final demand and warning to those it addresses; and the radical nature of its rejection and the barrier it thus creates may be correspondingly and deliberately exaggerated.

3.2 Barnabas

Barnabas is theologically crude, compared to Hebrews, and its attitude to and attack on Judaism is correspondingly crass and crude. It has close links with the tradition of Hebrews, although it is much more negative and hostile in its rejection of Judaism. Thus in 7–8, it claims that the Jews were wrong to understand sacrifice literally; its true meaning is the prefigurement of Christ's death. So also 16 (cf. 6.15) spiritualizes the temple, so the true temple is made to mean what the Christians have in themselves. *Barnabas* 16.5 specifically disallows claims about the temple, city and land, and thus comes sharply into conflict with Jewish eschatological hopes for the (messianic) kingdom.

Consistent with this treatment of Jewish tradition is what is perhaps the most striking feature of the whole work, in 4, and 13–14: that is, there is not a new covenant, brought in by Jesus (in contrast to Hebrews), but only one, single covenant. That is, the Christians do not have a new covenant or better promise, but simply the same covenant that is set out in Scripture. It was rejected by the Jews and now it properly belongs to the Christians. This argument is as disjunctive as it is bizarre but one correlative of this position is that *Barnabas* accepts (Jewish!) Scripture as the word of God, and fully valid; specifically, Scripture, when it is properly understood by means of *Barnabas'* allegorical method, shows that all that *Barnabas* claims is true.

It is in the light of this that we can perhaps make sense of the enigmatic 2.6: 'These things [sacrifices] he has superseded; it was intended that the new law of our Lord Jesus Christ should dispense with yoke and compulsion, and that its oblation should not be a man-made one.' It is certainly possible that the 'new law of our Lord Jesus Christ' denotes Jesus' own teaching (as, for example, in the Sermon on the Mount), or the summary of this as the 'law of love'. But, if so, this is not made clear, and it is plausible that *Barnabas* intends it to mean scriptural (Mosaic) law, properly (that is, allegorically) interpreted, so that it is not tied to the practice of Judaism that Christ has shown to be false.[19]

If so, there may be some links with *Didache* 6.1–2, although *Barnabas* is much more negative and disjunctive in his development of this tradition. The whole work is hostile to Judaism, and reflects embittered relations. It appropriates the Jewish heritage entirely, without trace, and erects an absolute barrier. What should be still held in common is completely denied to the Jews. Yet, as with other writings caught in conflict with (some of) Judaism, it has inevitably to operate with Jewish categories; hence, amongst other things, the double-edged nature of its understanding of Jewish Scripture (and law), in making it find its fulfilment in the Christian community. It is not clear that *Barnabas* is working with a concept of a messianic kingdom (or specific new age), but it is obviously acquainted with this tradition in some form. Thus, for example, *Barnabas* uses the language of the kingdom at 7.11, citing a saying of Jesus. And although it certainly does not emphasize the theme of a '(new) law for the messianic age', 2.6 remains striking. Again, although detailed 'law' is not a central emphasis of the work, prescriptive, moral instruction is clearly important, although not original, as with the 'Two Ways' teaching taken over from the *Didache*. Thus *Barnabas* does not simply jettison the law; just as he accepts Scripture as valid, so also he strikingly says that Moses 'legislated splendidly' (10.11). It is as part of his reinterpretation and appropriation of Torah that *Barnabas* produces specific ethical prescriptions for the Christian community (for example, 2.6–10; 3.6; 9.4ff.; 10.1ff.). He also, at 9.4ff., provides a positive interpretation of the covenant in connection with the law.[20]

4. JUSTIN AND IRENAEUS

4.1 Justin

Justin is clearly familiar with traditions of Matthew.[21] He is probably acquainted with Paul also, though notoriously he makes no reference to his writings; most plausibly this is because he needs to argue directly from Scripture itself.[22] Not surprisingly, the *Dialogue* provides the most interesting evidence. Thus it is striking that Jesus is portrayed as a 'new lawgiver' (14.3; cf. 12.2). Even more striking is the fact that in the same context Justin actually says that Jesus *is* the new law and new covenant[23] (11.2; 11.4).

Confusingly, then, at least as it appears, Christ both *brings* the new law and also *is* the new law and covenant in himself. Justin intends this, as these passages make clear, at least partly in the sense that he represents the fulfilment and true end of Torah, and has now taken its place. Thus Jeremiah 31:31ff. is specifically seen as fulfilled in Christ (*Dial.* 11), as are important passages from Isaiah concerning Torah (potentially set in the messianic age), for example 51:4–5; 55:3–5 (*Dial.* 11, 12).

So also Isaiah 2:2–4 (or, specifically, the parallel in Mic. 4:1–4) is seen as being fulfilled in Christ: *Dialogue* 109 cites the whole of Micah 4:1–7, and 110 interprets it as referring to Jesus and the proclamation about Jesus (cf. *1 Apol.* 39; 45.5). The law here, then, is understood as Jesus' message of repentance, or the apostolic proclamation of Jesus. In *Dialogue* 122 Justin interprets Isaiah 42:6–7; 49:8 to show Jesus as taking the place of Torah.

However, it is not simply that the true law is now fulfilled in Christ. It is also the case, as for example *Dialogue* 11, 110 and *1 Apol.* 39 make clear, that Christ as the true law causes people to turn from evil and idolatry, and instead worship God and practise piety (εὐσέβεια). Thus Justin clearly means that Christ as the new law fulfils the ethical requirement of the law, while the cultic or ceremonial aspects of the law are not fulfilled but superseded. They were only ever temporary and limited in nature (*Dial.* 18–30).

These laws were only given to Israel because of their hardness of heart, when they lapsed into idolatry in the incident of the Golden Calf.

Justin takes this theme of the limited, temporary and negative purpose of the ceremonial aspects of the law further in *Dialogue* 23.3, arguing that because circumcision was not necessary before Abraham, or sabbath before Moses, so they are not needed now. So, more generally, he interprets Jewish practice (sacrifice, sabbath, circumcision) as no longer valid as such, but as having its true meaning and fulfilment in the practice of the Christian community: baptism, eucharist and their whole way of life.

This is a strikingly disjunctive theme. Hence it is worth taking seriously Skarsaune's thesis:[24] the point of Justin's argument is essentially polemical. Gentiles can be seen as fully valid members of the Christian community, and (fellow) Jews are called, in the aftermath of the Bar Kochba revolt, to come over to the Christian community. That is, they are called to accept the true Messiah, the real fulfilment of Torah, and the real promise of the kingdom and land; this will include specifically the return to Jerusalem, since after 135 only Gentiles, not Jews, can enter it. This is, then, potentially a sharp and contentious argument, setting the Christian community in place of the Jewish, and claiming the Jewish heritage for itself.

There are potentially interesting links with Justin in the tantalizingly brief fragments of the *Kerygma Petrou*. As this is reported by Clement of Alexandria, Jesus is here called 'Law and Logos', which Clement sees as directly related to Isaiah 2:2–4, while it also applies Jeremiah 31:31–4 to the Christian community. It is also striking that Hermas in *Sim.* 8.3 identifies the divine law as 'God's son, preached to the ends of the earth', which may again apply Isaiah 2:2–4 to Christ, while the *Didascalia* specifically speaks of Christ giving the law.[25]

4.2 Irenaeus

Irenaeus' main treatment of the law comes in *Adv. Haer.* 4.[26] He is familiar with Justin's work, and shares several of the same themes. Thus he argues (4.15) that the Mosaic law and special commands were only given to the Jews because of their hardness of heart and the idolatry of the Golden Calf. In 4.16 he argues that circumcision and sabbath were given simply as signs, specifically, that is, of the covenant and kingdom: in themselves they cannot save and have no use. So also, he argues, the Patriarchs did not have the Mosaic law, circumcision or sabbath. Instead, they had the meaning of the Decalogue written on their hearts, and hence had no need of a written form.

The main purpose of Irenaeus' work is to combat Marcion and the Gnostics. Hence he is concerned with the status of Scripture, the understanding of the God of the 'Old Testament', and the nature of the Christian dispensation. For this reason, he constantly argues that Christ has come to fulfil and extend the law and covenant (4.2; 4.4; 4.13). It is also the same God who speaks through Moses and Jesus (thus 4.2, and especially 4.2.3: 'the writings of Moses are the words of Christ'). Similarly, Irenaeus also portrays the law as having a positive purpose. Thus in 4.2.7 he argues that the law actually exhorts the Jews to believe in Jesus as the Son of God.

Nevertheless, even here the understanding of the law can easily be seen as ambivalent or negative. Thus whereas in 4.12 he speaks of Christ as the end of the law in the sense of him being the final cause of it, and of the Decalogue as still in force, in 4.2 he portrays Christ as bringing an end to the law, when the new covenant is revealed, while in 4.9 he speaks of Christ as delivering a law and giving precepts. Here (cf. 4.2.7) the contrast is drawn between the two covenants: the old, concerned with the giving of the law that took place formerly, and the new, where Christ points out the way of life required by the gospel, which is seen as the fulfilment of Jeremiah 31:31–4. It is clearly consistent with this emphasis when he says: 'Greater, therefore, is the legislation that has been given for liberty than that for bondage.'

Hence, in the end, the positive understanding of the law is very limited, and Irenaeus gives an essentially negative verdict and polemical treatment. Distinctive Jewish law and tradition are denigrated. The true will of God is now to be found in the new covenant and law given by Christ. The Decalogue remains in force, but Jewish law otherwise is essentially superseded. From now on, the focus is on the distinctive themes of the Christian community. Jesus' new law or teaching has the specific way of life and ethical demands for the community contained within it. Clearly Irenaeus is caught in a tension. On the one hand, he needs to hold on to the

Jewish Scriptures as an integral part of the Christian dispensation, but on the other hand he wants as much as possible to leave aside Mosaic law, and shift the focus to Christ and his teaching. Thus he opens up what has become a perennial problem for the Christian church.

5. JEWISH TEXTS

5.1 Rabbinic evidence

Despite claims that have been made, there is no evidence in rabbinic sources for the cessation or abrogation of Torah in the final or messianic age. There is a little more as far as modification of Torah is concerned: *Way. R.* 13.3 and, especially, *Midr. Teh.* 146.4 open up the possibility of a change of specific laws, for the end-time (and they specifically use the phrase, תּוֹרָה חֲדָשָׁה/חִדֵּגֹשׁ תּוֹרָה, however that is to be understood). Both are late texts, however, and the evidence here is extremely limited within the context of rabbinic literature as a whole.[27]

5.2 Qumran texts

5.2.1 1QS/CD

At least parts of these (as indeed other) Qumran texts can be understood as introducing an intensification of Torah, setting new demands and conditions for the final age.[28] The overall perspective for 1QS, as for the Qumran community more generally, is thoroughly eschatological and messianic (e.g. 1QS 4 end: 9.). In this context, 1QS 5.8–10; cf. 5.20–2; 1.11–18 requires those who join to observe not only every detail of the Mosaic Torah, but also the distinctive interpretation of this within the community. This interpretation is detailed, intense and rigorous; it applies to the whole of the everyday life of the individual and the community, and has obvious ethical implications.

5.2.2 11QT

The Temple Scroll is in many ways the most fascinating of the Qumran texts, whether or not it was originally composed at Qumran. One remarkable, perhaps unique, feature is that the scroll throughout has God speaking in the first person, setting out laws and requirements which go well beyond what is contained in the Mosaic Torah. Thus it is presented as an even more direct divine revelation than the Torah that Exodus, and the Pentateuch more generally, present God as giving to Moses at Sinai, and contains more detailed and rigorous demands. Hence it has been argued by Wacholder and others, against Yadin,[29] that it should be designated the Torah Scroll rather than the Temple Scroll, since it represents a deliberate attempt to create a new, and radically different, Mosaic Torah. Certainly it is striking that it presents such radical innovations, differing so markedly from the Pentateuch as we know it and presented as the direct words of God. All this is orientated towards the future; in its Qumran context, at least, this future is specifically the final age, and the scroll effectively offers Israel a final chance.

5.3 Messianic movements and revolts

The evidence here, even for the major revolts of 66–73, 115–17 and 132–5 CE, is unfortunately very sparse. Potentially there is a great deal for 66–73, but our main source of information, Josephus, is a hostile witness. He portrays the revolutionaries as committing ἀνομία, that is, hostility to Torah and desecration of the Temple. This might be plausible for isolated incidents, but otherwise the reverse is almost certainly the case. That is, most probably the revolutionaries practised zeal for Torah (including the Temple), and effected an intensification of the demands of Torah for the final age. Thus, for example, there are indications that they rejected all images, including those on coins, enforced rigorous laws concerning intercourse with non-Jews, and demanded the circumcision (forced if necessary) of pagans.[30] The evidence for the other two revolts is extraordinarily scant by comparison, and as far as 115–17 is concerned nothing can be gathered about attitudes to Torah on the part of the messianic leader of the revolt or his followers. For 132–5, however, although the evidence is very limited, the documents as far as they go indicate that the messianic leader, Bar Kochba, and the other leaders of the revolt demanded strict and intensified observance of Torah, for example with tithing and the prohibition of travel on the sabbath.[31]

5.4 Jubilees

The *Book of Jubilees* is difficult to interpret in a number of respects, although its close relation with some of the Qumran literature has helped illuminate some of its obscurities. It uses Genesis 1–Exodus 12 as its basis, expanding and commenting on the biblical narrative. Throughout it stresses the importance of Torah, both in general and also especially in developed halakhic requirements developed from specific biblical laws. Jubilees also contains a number of developed eschatological sections.[32] One of the most striking passages in the work, where both these features are prominent, is 23.16–32. It is a strongly eschatological section, probably set against the immediate context of the threat to Torah and Temple posed by Antiochus Epiphanes and the Jewish supporters of the Seleucids in 169 and following. There is first a portrayal of the 'evil generation' (16–21), who have forsaken the covenant, followed by final divine judgement and retribution (22–5). This in turn gives way to a completely contrasting and positive picture of repentance, with a return to the law and commandments, and a perfect, paradisal new age of peace and divine blessing. There is no messianic figure here or elsewhere in *Jubilees*, and the judgement and restoration are carried out by God himself, but the striking point is that observance of Torah is set as the precondition and characteristic of belonging in the new age that God brings about. This theme is consistent with the rest of the work, but the way in which *Jubilees* describes the evil generation and final judgement and deliverance pushes this new age sharply into focus and almost makes it a present reality.

5.5 Prayer texts

There are some indications in various prayer forms and traditions that Torah has an integral and important part in the final or messianic age.[33] Thus, for example, in the *Birkat ha-Mazon* the second petition thanks God for, amongst other things, the land, covenant and Torah, and this is immediately followed in the third by a call to God to 'restore the kingdom of the house of David to its place in our days, and speedily build Jerusalem'. Again, at the end of the *Uba' le-siyyon* (recited after the reading from Torah) observance of Torah is seen as resulting in blessing in the days of the Messiah.

So also, the prayer following the Amidah stresses both the final deliverance (of the messianic age) and study of Torah, and both are related to a return to the original state where they worship God freely and observe Torah.

Overall, then, the evidence within this period for Jewish conceptions of Torah in the messianic or final age is quite limited and disparate; for rabbinic literature especially, there is very little indeed. Nevertheless, there are clear indications from different strands of Judaism that where the final or messianic age looms large, Torah is often seen as important; in some cases indeed, particularly at the level of claims to messiahship and of popular messianic movements, Torah is understood not only to continue in effect, but to be intensified as well.

6. CONCLUSION

It is evident that for the early Christian movement, which begins as a Jewish messianic movement, the question of Torah looms large. This is so at least as far as several main strands of the movement are concerned, but just as these early developments within the Christian movement are by no means homogeneous, so also there are very obvious differences in the attitudes to Torah.

6.1 Intensification of Torah

One option which is taken up is that of making Torah continue in force and intensifying its demands; this is what we find above all in Matthew, but it is a position which is probably reflected by James and perhaps the *Didache* as well. This attitude is closely related to the eschatological and messianic emphasis of the early Christian movement (or at least these strands of it), where the demand for heightened obedience to Torah, even approximating to perfection in regard to it, can be understood in the context of the brief, foreshortened time of the messianic age, together with the need to demonstrate the true messianic character of the early Christian movement, and the validity of its claims, *vis-à-vis* the Judaism to which it either still belongs or else is still closely related. It is also possible to see this perspective as important for understanding Paul.[34] The continuity and intensification of Torah in relation to the final or messianic age is a theme that is evident in various strands of Judaism and Jewish tradition, as for example in some of the Qumran texts, in evidence available for the Bar Kochba revolt (and, probably, other messianic movements as well), in *Jubilees* and in part of the Targumic tradition.

6.2 Fulfilment of Torah

A second position for which we find evidence within various parts of the early Christian tradition is that Torah finds its true fulfilment in Christ, or even that Torah is actually to be identified with Christ. The 'fulfilment' theme represents one main line of interpretation for Paul, and Christ is specifically identified with the law in subsequent Christian sources, at least partly dependent on Paul. This is most strikingly so in Justin, but is a tradition also found in Hermas and the *Kerygma Petrou*. The fulfilment theme more generally is also evident in Justin, and in Irenaeus as well. The identification of Torah with Wisdom, and hence of Torah taking on the very developed theological understanding that Wisdom had acquired by this stage, is found within Jewish sources from much earlier.

6.3 New Torah

A third distinctive position, or emphasis, is that Christ brings a new law. This has been a main way of interpreting Matthew, despite the apparent disclaimer of 5:17–20. It is found quite specifically and unambiguously in Justin, as also in Irenaeus and the later *Didascalia*. Obviously, in one main sense at least, it can be seen as a variation of the 'fulfilment' position; that is, Christ represents continuity with and fulfilment of Torah, since it is he who brings the true, perfect and final Torah. On this basis it would also be possible to understand distinctive aspects of the Johannine letters, the Fourth Gospel and indeed Paul. Obviously there is nothing in Jewish tradition that corresponds directly to this. Perhaps the closest analogy is 11QT, if it should properly be understood to represent an attempt to create a new, and radically different, Torah. There are also the brief hints within rabbinic tradition of modifications or changes to Torah being envisaged for the messianic age; but it needs to be said that these do not provide evidence for a completely new or radically different Torah.

6.4 Rejection of Torah

Fourthly, and most disjunctively, some strands of the early Christian movement represent a deliberate rejection, or at least superseding, of Torah altogether. This position is represented in its starkest and most uncompromising form by *Barnabas*; it is also to a large extent what is represented by Hebrews, although the attack here is primarily focused on the Temple and sacrificial cult. It is this radically disjunctive attitude that Paul has often also been understood as advocating. The ambiguity of Paul's position is to an extent what we also find reflected in Justin and Irenaeus. Thus on the one hand they portray, as we have seen, continuity and fulfilment, but the theme of fulfilment does itself, especially as it points to the new law that Christ brings in, in many ways lead to a negative emphasis. In both, the cultic aspect of the law at least is superseded, and Irenaeus in particular is negative and polemical about Jewish law more generally. There is, as far as I can see, no evidence within Jewish sources of the cessation or abrogation of Torah within the final or messianic age, despite claims that have been made especially as far as rabbinic literature is concerned. It has to be admitted that the evidence from Jewish sources as a whole for the status of Torah in the final age is very limited, but it appears plausible that the negative, disjunctive attitude in some early Christian writings does itself reflect the way that parts of that movement are beginning to break away from Judaism or have already done so.

These four positions are not all mutually exclusive, of course, and there is indeed considerable overlap between them (so, for example, Justin represents three of the categories), although obviously the negative thrust of the fourth is incompatible with at least the positive aspects of the first three. It is important in any case to note that these various positions and attitudes are not thought out in the abstract, but integrally bound up with the life and practice of the particular community. It is also the case, as we have noted, that the early Christian movement begins as a messianic movement within Judaism, and for much of the evidence that we have been considering here continues to be part of Judaism. Hence it is not surprising that apart from the overlap within the early Christian movement on these various positions, there is also considerable common ground with Judaism.

This common ground with Judaism, however, also very easily constitutes the problem. That is, the various strands of the early Christian movement have to take up the question of Torah, in one way or another, and find that, in doing so, they have raised large issues that they cannot readily resolve. This easily causes and reinforces tensions and divisions between Christianity and Judaism (at least as they come to be known: denoting them thus in some cases is probably anachronistic); the boundaries between the two, however, are often blurred. In a large part of the early Christian movement there is a clear struggle to understand how much of Torah still applies and in what way, and comparable questions clearly arise within Judaism, especially where messianic or eschatological hopes loom large. The issue of Torah (or the law) also has a wide range of reference in early Christianity, as of course it does in Judaism. Hence for the early Christian movement it involves not only christological and ethical categories, but those that we denote as ecclesiological and soteriological as well. A crucial question here, then, as for early Christianity and Judaism more widely, is whether the understanding of these various aspects is inclusive (that is, the Jewish categories of Torah and covenant are extended, to include potentially everyone, though for the early Christian movement they are obviously set in terms of Christ) or exclusive (that is, only faith in Christ can save, and only a completely new covenant and Torah can be of effect). As we have seen, there is no one single answer in the early Christian writings. Torah serves both to unite and to divide Judaism and Christianity in the first two centuries, and that is the legacy that has been bequeathed to contemporary discussion of these issues.

NOTES

1 It is not possible to discuss here arguments for the diminished importance, or limited definition, of the concept of 'messiah' in Second Temple Judaism, as e.g. in Neusner, Green and Frerichs 1987, e.g. ix–xiv, 1–13, but also in other essays in the book; Charlesworth 1987; 1992, 3–36. See further Chester 1991b, 17–19.
2 For discussion of various important themes in Jewish and Christian messianism, such as temple, land, kingdom, new heaven and new earth, cf. Wilcken 1986; Horbury 1988; Chester 1991a; 1992.
3 Davies 1952; 1964, 109–90, 446–50; Díez Macho 1953, 1954. Cf. also e.g. Schoeps 1961, 172; see further Bammel 1964, 120–3, for dis-

cussion of earlier treatments of the issue and reference to relevant works, especially concerning Paul's understanding of the law.

4 Davies 1952, 85–94.

5 Davies 1964, 446–7, and compare 1964, 187–90 with 1952, 90–4. Cf. also Díez Macho 1953, 1954.

6 See further Thielman 1989, 28–46.

7 For full discussion and bibliography, see Davies and Allison 1988, 504–71; certainly the last four 'antitheses' (5:31–48) can be seen as opposing what Scripture says, but they are best understood as making further, not contradictory, demands.

8 See Przybylski 1980 for further discussion; he rightly argues that righteousness is a theme that Matthew is forced to take up in context of the struggle with the Jewish community and leadership, and the demand for perfection here should be understood as part of the need for justification of the distinctive claims of the Matthean community.

9 See especially Davies 1964, 90–108, 187–90, 447 (although, as I have indicated, Davies' argument needs to be treated with caution); Davies and Allison 1988, 481–502.

10 Cf. Chester and Martin 1994, 19, and the further works referred to there.

11 Cf. Maynard-Reid 1987; Martin 1988; Chester and Martin 1994, 19, 32–4.

12 Cf. Chester and Martin 1994, 36–8.

13 Cf. e.g. Sanders 1992, 194–5.

14 Cf. Chester and Martin 1994, 16–28, and further works referred to there.

15 Cf. Clerici 1966, 61–4; O'Hagan 1966, 18–22; Wengst 1984; Niederwimmer 1989; Chester 1992, 278–92.

16 Cf. Wengst 1984, 59–61; Chester 1992, 284–7.

17 The most illuminating discussion of Jewish as well as early Christian traditions of the Two Ways is that of Brock 1990, who also provides reference to further literature.

18 Cf. Wengst 1984, 95–6; Niederwimmer 1989, 153–6.

19 Cf. e.g. Wengst 1984, 135–6. Carleton Paget 1994, 105–6, plausibly argues that the original tradition that *Barnabas* takes over may well have meant that a completely new law was brought in by Christ, but *Barnabas* reinterprets this tradition to make it conform to his view that there was only ever one law.

20 Cf. the excellent discussion, with further bibliography, in Carleton Paget 1994, 51–70, 101–24, 143–54.

21 For detailed treatment of this, see Massaux 1993, 11–44, 49–86.

22 So Lindemann 1979, 353–67, who gives a careful treatment of the issue, with full bibliographical references; cf. also Massaux 1993, 96–101, although even he doubts whether Justin uses Paul's writings directly.

23 Cf. Daniélou 1964, 164–5; Hengel 1992, 44.

24 Skarsaune 1987, esp. 326–74.

25 Cf. Daniélou 1964, 164; Hengel 1992, 44.
26 Cf. in general Lawson 1948, 232–40; Osborn 1973, 156–61.
27 The texts are set out and discussed by Davies 1952, 50–90; 1964, 156–90; cf. Díez Macho 1953, 1954, but, as I have indicated above, despite the careful reservations expressed by Davies, these works still need to be treated with caution.
28 For discussion in general, see Vermes 1977, 87–109.
29 Wacholder 1983, 1–32; Yadin 1977.
30 Cf. Hengel 1989, 183–228.
31 Cf. Schürer 1973, 544, with further works referred to there.
32 Cf. in general Nickelsburg 1981, 73–80. Davenport 1971 argues for a less developed understanding of the final age in *Jubilees*.
33 Cf. further Heinemann 1977, 256–69.
34 I have had to omit sections on Paul and on the Johannine literature (as also further sections on Jewish sources) from the original version of this essay, on grounds of length.

BIBLIOGRAPHY

Bammel, E., 1964, 'Νόμος Χριστοῦ', in F. L. Cross (ed.), *Studia Evangelica* vol. III, TU 88, Berlin, 120–8.
Brock, S., 1990, 'The Two Ways and the Palestinian Targum', in P. R. Davies and R. T. White (eds.), *A Tribute to Geza Vermes*, JSOTSS 100, Sheffield, 139–52.
Carleton Paget, J., 1994, *The Epistle of Barnabas*, Tübingen.
Charlesworth, J. H. (ed.) 1992, *The Messiah*, Philadelphia.
Chester, A., 1991a, 'The Sibyl and the Temple', in W. Horbury (ed.), *Templum Amicitiae*, JSNTSS 48, Sheffield, 37–69.
1991b, 'Jewish Messianic Expectations and Mediatorial Figures and Pauline Christology', in M. Hengel and U. Heckel (eds.), *Paulus und das antike Judentum*, Tübingen, 17–89.
1992, 'The Parting of the Ways: Eschatology and Messianic Hope', in J. D. G. Dunn (ed.), *Jews and Christians*, WUNT 66, Tübingen, 239–313.
Chester, A., and Martin, R. P., 1994, *The Theology of the Letters of James, Peter and Jude*, Cambridge.
Clerici, L., 1966, *Einsammlung der Zerstreuten. Liturgiegeschichtliche Untersuchung zur Vor- und Nachgeschichte der Fürbitte für die Kirche in Didache 9,4 und 10,5*, Münster.
Daniélou, J., 1964, *The Theology of Jewish Christianity*, E. tr. London.
Davenport, G. L., 1971, *The Eschatology of the Book of Jubilees*, SPB 20, Leiden.
Davies, W. D., 1952, *Torah in the Messianic Age and/or the Age to Come*, Philadelphia.
1964, *The Setting of the Sermon on the Mount*, Cambridge.

Davies, W. D., and Allison, D. C., 1988, *A Critical and Exegetical Commentary on the Gospel according to Saint Matthew*, vol. 1, Edinburgh.

Díez Macho, A., 1953, 1954, 'Cesara la Tora en la Edad Mesiánica?', *Estúdios Biblicos* 12 (1953), 115–18; 13 (1954), 5–51.

Heinemann, J., 1977, *Prayer in the Talmud. Forms and Patterns*, SJ IX, Berlin and New York.

Hengel, M., 1992, 'Die Septuaginta als von den Christen beanspruchte Schriftensammlung bei Justin und den Vätern vor Origenes', in J. D. G. Dunn (ed.), *Jews and Christians*, WUNT 66, Tübingen, 39–84.

Horbury, W., 1988, 'Messianism among Jews and Christians in the Second Century', *Augustinianum* 28:71–88.

Lawson, J., 1948, *The Biblical Theology of Saint Irenaeus*, London.

Lindemann, A., 1979, *Paulus im ältesten Christentum*, BhTh 58, Tübingen.

Martin, R. P., 1988, *James*, Waco.

Massaux, E., 1993, *The Influence of the Gospel of Saint Matthew on Christian Literature before Saint Irenaeus: Book 3: The Apologists and the Didache*, E. tr. Macon.

Maynard-Reid, P. U., 1987, *Poverty and Wealth in James*, Maryknoll.

Neusner, J., Green, W. S. and Frerichs, E. S., 1987, *Judaisms and their Messiahs at the Turn of the Christian Era*, Cambridge.

Nickelsburg, G. W. E., 1981, *Jewish Literature between the Bible and the Mishnah*, London.

Niederwimmer, K., 1989, *Didache*, KAV 1, Göttingen.

O'Hagan, A. P., 1966, *Material Re-Creation in the Apostolic Fathers*, TU 100, Berlin.

Osborn, E. F., 1973, *Justin Martyr*, BhTh 47, Tübingen.

Przybylski, B., 1980, *Righteousness in Matthew and his World of Thought*, SNTSMS 41, Cambridge.

Sanders, E. P., 1992, *Judaism: Practice and Belief 63 BCE–66 CE*, London and Philadelphia.

Schoeps, H. J., 1961, *Paul*, E. tr. London.

Schürer, E., 1973, *The History of the Jewish People in the Age of Jesus Christ (175 BC–AD 135)*, new English edn rev. and ed. G. Vermes, F. Vermes, F. Millar, M. Black and M. Goodman, vol. 1, Edinburgh.

Skarsaune, O., 1987, *The Proof from Prophecy*, NovTSup 56, Leiden.

Thielman, F., 1989, *From Plight to Solution*, NovTSup, Leiden.

Vermes, G., 1977, *The Dead Sea Scrolls. Qumran in Perspective*, London.

Wacholder, B. Z., 1983, *The Dawn of Qumran*, Cincinnati.

Wengst, K., 1984, *Didache (Apostellehre), Barnabasbrief, Zweiter Klemensbrief, Schrift an Diognet*, Darmstadt.

Wilcken, R. L., 1986, 'Early Christian Chiliasm, Jewish Messianism, and the Idea of the Holy Land', *HTR* 79:98–107.

Yadin, Y., 1977, *The Temple Scroll*, 3 vols., Jerusalem.

CHAPTER 19

Jewish and Christian public ethics in the early Roman Empire

Markus Bockmuehl

Among the issues defining the limits of corporate tolerance in Christianity and Judaism are matters of morality and lifestyle. In this context it can be quite revealing to examine the distinctive characteristics of how Jews and Christians explained and justified that morality in public discourse. By 'public' discourse I mean that which is carried on in terms that would be relevant to outsiders, within the early imperial environment of pluralistic paganism. Such public dialogue may be real or only notional, just as apologetics may be internal as well as external dialogue; indeed the difference between internal and external need not always be clear.[1] Ethics for present purposes is 'public' regardless of whether its communication to outsiders is intended to be persuasive, reassuring, or straightforwardly explanatory.

Before going on to look at some of the substantive questions on this subject, it is worth considering briefly the social *Sitz im Leben* of such public discourse. It must be admitted from the outset that for both Judaism and Christianity, deliberate thought about public ethics probably always remained a fringe activity on the part of a social and intellectual elite. What is more, Jewish life and practice at least in the larger centres like Palestine, Alexandria or Antioch was a sufficiently established reality on the ground to make popular preoccupation with this subject the exception rather than the rule.

However, it would be erroneous to conclude that the subject of public moral discourse is therefore only of marginal interest for the study of early Jewish and Christian attitudes to tolerance. There are in fact a number of points worth raising in reply. First, smaller Diaspora communities throughout the Empire would almost constantly have had to face the problem of justifying the Jewish way of life in terms intelligible to a hostile or indifferent

342

majority. The same consideration must have been true in *all* cases for the fledgling Gentile Christian churches.

But even for the larger communities it is clearly the case that apologetic efforts were periodically needed: 3 Maccabees and Philo's mission to Gaius demonstrate this for Alexandria, as Josephus arguably does for Rome (and perhaps for Jerusalem). Periodic imperial chicaneries in the province of Judaea and elsewhere would make the satisfactory public justification of Jewish customs and practices a matter of concern not just for an elite but for entire communities. A variety of other indicators show that apologetic concerns, including those relating to morality, were at times not just of academic interest but a matter of life and death and the very essence of Jewishness: additional examples of this can be found to range all the way from the book of Daniel (3:1ff.) and the Maccabean revolt (1 Macc. 1:45–8) to the Bar Kochba war and beyond. The widespread interest in such matters can further be seen in the didactic stereotype of rabbis in dialogue or dispute with Gentiles;[2] and the need for it appears in the echoes, in Juvenal and other writers,[3] of widespread popular bigotry against Jews. Finally, funerary inscriptions can provide another useful gauge of the public self-portrayal at least of the middle and upper classes; and here it is significant to note the many cases of eulogies in self-consciously popular Gentile terms of praise.[4]

Many of these arguments about the Jewish need for public ethics apply *a fortiori* to Christianity, which at no time in the first three centuries of our era enjoyed the civil and religious rights pertaining to an ancestral *religio licita*. The public face of Christian morality was a constant concern, as the pages of the New Testament, along with subsequent public opprobrium and persecution, make very clear.

THE PROBLEM OF HALAKAH IN JEWISH AND CHRISTIAN ETHICS

Before going on to comment specifically on public ethics, it is necessary to offer one or two more *general* comparative observations on the nature of Jewish and early Christian morality.

1. Ancient *Jewish* ethics in the broadest sense cannot properly be understood without reference to the concept of halakah. True, there are significant Graeco-Roman philosophical influences on the

form and presentation especially of Diaspora ethical texts. Jewish
Hellenistic virtue and vice lists do owe a great deal to Stoicism
and to the shape of popular Graeco-Roman philosophy.[5] But that
influence does not explain the *selection criteria* for how much pagan
morality is included and what is left out. At the end of the day
mainstream authors are rarely if ever prepared to step outside
recognized principles of binding halakah, whether these are based
on the written Torah or tradition or both. That much, I suspect, is
by and large uncontroversial.

2. On the *Christian* side, however, we run into difficulty as soon
as we attempt to say anything comparative. The basic rationale of
Christian ethics is generally assumed to be both straightforward
and yet manifestly distinctive. In particular, the New Testament
authors share a highly theological approach to ethics and often
explicitly ground their appeals on christology, pneumatology and
eschatology. Their view of Jewish law as a source of moral authority comes across as highly ambivalent: despite a certain undeniable
overlap in substance, explicit appeals to Jewish law are extremely
rare in these writers. What is more, both St Paul and the Jesus of
the Gospels frequently appear to criticize aspects either of the
Torah itself or of Torah observance.

Most commonly, therefore, textbooks of ethics assume a straightforward shift from Torah to Christ, from halakah to haggadah,
and so on.[6] Even if many writers would allow varying degrees of
influence of the Torah even on Paul's ethical teaching, it is in any
case very widely assumed that the Torah *qua law* no longer has any
normative place in the canonical writings of the New Testament.
(Matthew and James are sometimes allowed as partial exceptions.)

Nevertheless, the substantive peculiarity of the New Testament
approach to law and morality must still somehow be accounted
for. The single most important reason for this, I would submit, is
neither christology nor pneumatology nor eschatology, whether of
the realized or the millenarian kind. These matters by themselves
might perhaps *contribute* to a distinctive or sectarian outlook; and it
is of course true that the teaching and example of Christ sometimes serve as a significant ethical motif.[7] But they do not *ipso facto*
explain the New Testament's remarkable neglect or indeed outright antipathy towards what both Paul and 4QMMT appear to
call the 'works of the law':[8] circumcision, *kashrut, Toharot* and sac-

rificial regulations. Jewish Christianity presumably had all or much of the eschatology and messianology, but without being obstreperous about the things that make Jews Jewish. Much the same could be said for the authors of several of the Dead Sea Scrolls.

Similarly, no one nowadays would dispute the influence of *Hellenistic* patterns of moral instruction on the formulation of early Christian ethics. However, just as the use made of such material by Jewish authors is not indiscriminate but ultimately governed by halakhic criteria, so also it will not do to ignore the fundamental rationale behind its appearance in Christian ethical texts. The apostle Paul and others are in fact highly selective and specific in their adoption of Hellenistic moral principles, as e.g. John Barclay has shown for Galatians.[9] True, the *teaching and example* of Jesus do seem to contribute significantly to those Christian selection criteria. However, christology, pneumatology and eschatology supply at best the frame of reference and have relatively little direct bearing on the matter. Paul's Corinthian and Galatian correspondence offers eloquent testimony to the fact that the instruction to 'walk in the Spirit' by itself could mean rather different things to different people.

If, therefore, christology fails to account sufficiently for the substance and character of New Testament ethics, another explanation must be sought. It occurs to me that the most plausible alternative consists in the *Gentile audience* that is envisioned in most or all of the New Testament writings. In a recent study on the Noachide commandments[10] I attempted to argue that the New Testament authors make very substantial use of the traditional *halakah for Gentiles*, which can be traced from the Pentateuchal laws for resident aliens all the way to the rabbinic *Sheba* mitzvot benê Noah.* Ever since the Levitical Holiness Code and the prophets, these views had concentrated on the prohibitions of idolatry, sexual immorality and blood offences.

A study of the specific role of halakah in New Testament ethics must here be left for another occasion. For now, these short comments may suffice to alert us to the legitimacy and likely usefulness of a *comparative halakhic approach* to Jewish and early Christian ethics.

With this in mind, the next two sections of this chapter briefly address the substance of Jewish and Christian public ethics.

JEWISH PUBLIC ETHICS

I should like here for the sake of convenience to divide the material into (i) sources clearly intended for an internal Jewish audience and (ii) sources intended for an external or quasi-external audience.

(1) Internal discourse

We have no time to discuss all the relevant texts, but among the sources to be considered must be those which generally address what might be called Jewish international law. I mean of course the halakah for Gentiles, i.e. texts which in effect relate to the Noachide Commandments. In addition to the relevant biblical texts and the standard rabbinic passages on the *Sheba^c Mitzvot*,[11] an important early text is *Jubilees* 7.20ff., where the Noachide doctrine is explicitly referred to. This passage is particularly significant as it shows that Gentile morality was an important issue even in narrowly sectarian circles.

Moving on a little to somewhat more 'extrovert' literature, the most important sources include the *Letter of Aristeas*, Wisdom 14:12–31, the *Sibylline Oracles* 3–5, and Pseudo-Phocylides.[12] Scholars are now generally convinced that despite their adoption of secular Graeco-Roman literary *forms*, these documents are written by Jews and for Jews. At the same time, each one gives the appearance of being concerned with a minimum morality which, although addressed in the first instance to Jews, commends itself in principle even to Gentiles. Most (although not all) of the principles in question concern themselves with matters that fall broadly within the categories expected in a Noachide context: idolatry, sexual ethics, violence, property and blood offences.[13]

Two other examples of 'internal' ethics for Gentiles may be mentioned in passing. The first issue relates to the larger topic of *'abodah zarah*, i.e. pagan idolatry (lit. 'foreign worship'). Scholars have devoted considerable effort to the ancient debates about purchasing olive oil and other materials from potentially idolatrous Gentiles.[14] Does one assume with R. Eliezer ben Hyrcanus that the unspecified moral intention of Gentiles is always idolatrous, or not?[15] Opinions differed, but the issue clearly illustrates interest in how one should expect Gentiles to behave.

The second example is the issue of Gentile sabbath observance. This concerns halakhic questions about Gentiles ploughing fields in *Eretz Israel* on a sabbath, and could be said to comprise many of the classic controversies and traditions which eventually led to the doctrine of the 'Shabbes Goy': the Gentile may rightly do work for himself on the sabbath which is forbidden to the Jew – even if the Jew thereby benefits.[16]

A special subset of inner-Jewish concern about Gentile ethics is formed by those texts which speak to an internal audience about injustices and atrocities committed by pagan enemies or overlords. This is of course a commonplace concern whose antecedents are well attested in Scripture (Amos 1–2 etc.). The moral tenor of these is not prescriptive so much as plaintive: even Gentiles are subject to certain universal norms of justice and should have known better. Examples from the Second Temple and Tannaitic periods include 1–3 Maccabees, the campaigns of Holofernes in Judith, *Psalms of Solomon*, *2 Baruch* and several other apocalypses. Rabbinic passages about the bloodiness of the Bar Kochba revolt imply a similar perspective. The same is true of legends of martyrdom from Shadrach, Meshach and Abednego via the Maccabean revolt to Rabbi Akiba. It would also be worth exploring the attitudes towards the governmental policies of imperial Rome implied in the legends about R. Shim'on ben Yochai and rabbinic visitors to Rome.

(2) 'Public' Discourse

In addition to the frequently halakhic discussion intended for an internal audience, however, there is also the apologetic approach directed towards an *external* or quasi-external audience. In these contexts public ethics are propounded in terms intelligible to outsiders and intended either to persuade outsiders or to encourage insiders about the moral excellence or indeed superiority of the Jewish way of life.

The obvious examples of this perspective include a good deal of ethical material in Philo and Josephus; perhaps it is worth especially singling out Philo's *Legatio ad Gaium* and the *Hypothetica*; in Josephus the most obvious section is perhaps the summary of the law in *Contra Apionem* 2.190ff. Despite their stylized character, they reflect an engagement with genuine public challenges, including on the subject of Jewish morality. It is interesting to note the practical

Sitz im Leben of embassies to Roman authorities on behalf of endangered Jewish communities. Such appeals to the government stress the role of Jews as followers of an ancient and venerable religion, and as exemplary citizens whose way of life is outstanding and praiseworthy even by Roman standards. (This line of argument almost suggests a kind of Kantian approach to public ethics: 'we Jews live the kind of life which deserves universal respect, and which is beneficial for humanity as a whole'.)

Rabbinic literature offers mainly an internal perspective on public ethics, which has rather more to say about Jewish dealings with Gentiles than about how Gentile society ought to behave. Nevertheless, we do get the occasional glimpse of an 'internal moral apologetic'. A reflection of public dialogue about morality may well be found in some of the popular tales of encounter between famous rabbis and their Gentile interlocutors. Borrowing a phrase from *Mishnah Abot*, one might call these the '*el Epikuros*' stories. Perhaps the most famous example is Hillel's encounter with the (non-converting) Gentile who wants to learn the Torah while standing on one leg. Hillel replies by commending the Golden Rule[17] – once again a reply which, one suspects, would have pleased Immanuel Kant.

CHARACTERISTICS OF THE CHRISTIAN APPROACH

A treatment of early Christian public ethics is also subject to the distinction between internal and external discourse about the subject. On the one hand most of New Testament ethics is 'extrovert', in that it addresses Gentiles to whom the Torah does not apply in its entirety. Terms of reference are frequently taken from the familiar Jewish halakah for Gentiles.

On the other hand, from the perspective of the authors and their communities, they themselves are the new 'insiders' of the chosen people constituted by God's purposes in Jesus Christ; they are in turn very well aware of community boundaries and of the difference between themselves and the outside world, designated variously as 'Gentiles', 'the world', 'those outside', 'unbelievers' etc. (sometimes even 'the Jews'). Christians *were* once 'pagans' (1 Cor. 12:2) and 'aliens' (Eph. 2:19), but are so no longer, having converted from the service of idols to the living God (1 Thess. 1:9) and thus become part of the chosen people. New Testament moral instruction, therefore, is formulated as ethics *for insiders*, and it spells out ethical principles characteristic of self-conscious insiders. In that sense, therefore, New Testament ethics shows signs of being both 'public' or universal and yet internal.

The difference between Christian ethics and a universal morality explicable to outsiders is not always clear. In general, the substance of Christian public ethics does follow the Jewish pattern of ethics for Gentiles. The difference is that now there is a distinction not between Torah for insiders and *mitzvot benê Noah* for outsiders, but between the largely Jewish moral assessment of outsiders (Rom. 1:18–32; 13:1–7; 1 Thess. 1:9f.; Eph. 4:17ff. etc.) and an internal reformulation of the halakah for Gentiles in light of the person and work of Christ (NB Rom. 12–15) and of his parousia (1 Cor. 7; 1 Thess. 4).

As a result, therefore, Christian *public* ethics properly speaking is remarkably similar to Jewish public ethics. This is true especially for its negative or critical function: the very Jewishness of early Christianity's criteria of sin and evil has often been pointed out.[18] The wickedness of pagans and yet the usefulness of the restraining secular orders of Caesar, *polis* and *oikos* are all reiterated in traditional Jewish terms. Positively, we find in numerous New Testament authors[19] the familiar desire to present the Christian way of life publicly as blameless, concerned for the welfare of others, and morally superior to paganism. The difference here is that even in their public demeanour, Christians are also motivated by the teaching and example of Christ. It is worth noting that while New Testament vice lists are almost entirely conventional (Jewish Hellenistic and/or Stoic), there is a good deal of conceptual and theological innovation in the lists of *virtues*.

The same pattern continues in the second century with the writings of the Apologists. Aristides, Justin Martyr, Origen and others portray Christianity as actively sponsoring the welfare of all humanity and thereby of the Empire. Opponents accused Christianity of undermining the Empire by their supposed atheism, secret immorality and failure to render public service. In reply to this, the Christian writers followed the cue of the Lucan and Pauline corpus of the New Testament in arguing the public respectability of Christianity, indeed its benefit to society as a whole.

Most famously, perhaps, the *Epistle to Diognetus* affirms about Christians:

Every foreign country is their fatherland, and every fatherland is a foreign country. They marry as all do; they beget children, but they do not destroy their offspring. They have a common table but not a common bed. They are in the flesh, but do not live after the flesh ... They love all people, and are persecuted by all ... They are poor and make many rich ... They are abused and give blessing ... To put it shortly: what the soul is in the body, that the Christians are in the world ... Christians are in the world, but are not of the world ... Christians are confined in the world as in a prison, and yet they are the preservers of the world. (5–6)[20]

The impressiveness, if not the persuasive force, of such arguments of public ethics can be documented by occasional pagan acknowledgements, on the part of Pliny the Younger, Galen and others.[21]

One other issue of interest to the present symposium is worth highlighting before we conclude. The lines of distinction between insiders and outsiders are somewhat blurred on the subject of whether *Jews* are insiders or outsiders. This problem arises in Matthew and Paul and becomes painfully obvious in the Johannine corpus. Acts 21 specifically identifies the cause of opposition to Paul as significantly related to his attitude towards the *halakah*: he is accused of teaching Diaspora Jews to forsake Moses (ἀποστασίαν διδάσκεις ἀπὸ Μωϋσέως), circumcision and 'the customs' (μὴδε τοῖς ἔθεσιν περιπατεῖν). But even beyond this, we know that tensions between Palestinian Jewish Christians and Jews sometimes centred on halakhic disputes. Thus, in the year 62 CE, James the Just was executed by stoning on a Sadducean initiative as a transgressor of the law.[22] The Talmud further records an intriguing discussion at Sepphoris, between Eliezer ben Hyrcanus and Jacob of Sikhnin, concerning Jesus' supposed halakah on the tithe of prostitutes.[23]

More specifically, the Gospel of Matthew morally indicts an outside majority of Jewish Pharisees on numerous occasions for hypocrisy and failing to practise what they preach. Jews appear as persecutors in the Gospels and in Paul; in the second century there are several Christian sources complaining against the injustice of Jewish persecution of Christians in the Bar Kochba revolt (Justin Martyr, Jerome, Eusebius;[24] cf. *Apocalypse of Peter*[25]). The injustice of enemies was a theme of public morality for both Jews and

Jewish Christians, and it was met with denunciation and sometimes martyrdom. But while martyrdom for Jews was evidence of the general wickedness of pagans, Christian martyrdom could be due either to pagan or to Jewish injustice and impenitence.

Similarities of substance between the Jewish and Christian approaches abound, and time does not allow us to rehearse them here. Suffice it to say that there is very significant agreement between Jewish and Christian public ethics on the practical substance of a halakah for non-converting Gentiles; one might add that Jewish halakah for Gentiles also provides much of the chicken stock for the broth of internal Christian ethics. Even in the second century, some Christians explicitly acknowledged that their understanding of natural law was shared with Judaism.[26] I shall here concentrate on summing up the *distinctive* emphases in public ethics.

Specifically Christian contributions to public moral discourse were perhaps not many. But they include a greater apologetic emphasis on the exemplary lifestyle of Christianity, with a comparatively greater emphasis on Christian concern for the social welfare of outsiders. This was perhaps partly through pragmatic necessity and partly by explicit appeal to the person of Jesus.

Christians at least in the first two centuries also took a strong public stance in favour of pacifism, non-retaliation and refusal of military service, sometimes at considerable cost to themselves. Intolerance of public norms led to denunciation and often martyrdom. Christian resistance in the early centuries was consistently non-violent. Martyrdom was viewed not nationally, on behalf of the Jewish people, but as occurring for and through Christ. It is here that the teaching and example of Jesus had a powerful impact on Christian public ethics.

Perhaps the greatest social difference lies in the fact that despite periodic pogroms and endemic anti-Semitism, Judaism's presence on the Graeco-Roman scene was that of an established ethnic group with civic rights and privileges. Christianity, by contrast, was a newcomer on the scene and had no obvious claims to being *religio licita*. This necessitated a significant difference in the apologetic approach to matters of morality. As we find in sources as early as the second century BCE, Jewish apologists could afford to stress the ancient and venerable origin of their religion, its exalted ethical standards and achievements predating and excelling Homer and the great philosophers.

Many of the Church Fathers were fully aware of the force of this argument from antiquity. They, too, therefore, attempted to mount such a case based on their claim to be the true heirs of the Old Testament not just theologically but in terms of moral probity as well. For Christians, this argument served the threefold apologetic purpose of reassuring insiders, silencing pagan detractors and, more problematically, establishing the legitimacy of Christianity *vis-à-vis* Judaism.[27] From the perspective of Christian–Jewish ethical polemics, a particularly interesting reflection of the debate about Old Testament law may be present in the *baraita* about the removal of the Decalogue from the daily liturgy. This was said to be due to *minim* who claimed that only the Ten Commandments were spoken to Moses at Sinai.[28]

At the same time, however, early Christianity was a clearly recent and non-ethnic voluntary association, which therefore could not naturally mount a claim to the venerable antiquity of its moral teaching. Instead, while still paradoxically claiming to be the true heirs to the Old Testament, Christians also began to bank on the idea of progress and innovation. The Apologists stressed that they were the new chosen people from all nations, the 'third race' whose moral probity and unselfish love surpassed that of both Jew and Gentile.[29] This argument, which has its roots in the New Testament itself and its first clear occurrence in the *Kerygma Petrou*,[30] could be said to underlie much of the public self-definition of early Christianity, in terms not only of theology but also of moral argument. In this mode of discourse, the distinctiveness of Christian morality is publicly linked with the novelty of the gospel. This means that while the Apologists do commend Christianity's inherent attractiveness and persuasiveness,[31] the implied moral boundaries continue all the while to be determined by the Christian revelation. Whereas Paul can appeal to public convention in ethical instructions to his churches, Clement of Alexandria, in formulating an apologetic *vis-à-vis* paganism, explicitly pits the revealed truth of the gospel against the prevailing customs.[32]

At the end of the day, this same tacit priority of revelation over conventional reason in fact defines the limits of moral tolerance for both Jews and Christians. It finds its most graphic illustration in the acts of the martyrs: the same categorical resistance to the lie of idolatry is embodied, *mutatis mutandis*, in Akiba's dying confession of אחד ('one': Deut. 6:4) and in the words: *Christianus sum.*

NOTES

1 It is an intriguing but undeniable phenomenon that a good deal of Christian evangelism at the same time serves an apologetic purpose for believers; conversely, apologetics can also be evangelistic in effect.

2 Note the frequent colloquies between Rabbi and 'Antoninus' (Caracalla?): on this see Samuel Krauss, *Antoninus und Rabbi*, Frankfurt, 1910; Günter Stemberger, 'Die Beurteilung Roms in der rabbinischen Literatur', *ANRW* 2.19.2, Berlin and New York, 1979, 367–75. Similarly, one finds numerous encounters between rabbis and Roman matrons or pagan enquirers, e.g. in the tractate *Avodah Zarah* in both the Mishnah and the Talmud (see below).

3 Juvenal, *Satires* 14.96ff.; Tacitus, *Histories* 5.1–13; *Annals* 15.44.

4 Cf. William Horbury, 'Jewish Inscriptions and Jewish Literature in Egypt, with Special Reference to Ecclesiasticus', in J. W. van Henten and P. W. van der Horst (eds.), *Studies in Early Jewish Epigraphy*, Leiden, 1994, 9–43.

5 See, e.g., recently L. H. Feldman, *Jew and Gentile in the Ancient World. Attitudes and Interactions from Alexander to Justinian*, Princeton, 1993, 201–31, on Jewish use of the cardinal virtues.

6 See, e.g., Philipp Vielhauer, 'Paulus und das Alte Testament', in *Oikodome: Aufsätze zum Neuen Testament*, ed. G. Klein, vol. 2, Munich, 1979, 220; James A. Sanders, 'Torah and Christ', *Interpretation* 29 (1975), 373–4; W. D. Davies, *Paul and Rabbinic Judaism*, 3rd edn, Philadelphia, 1980, 147–76 and *passim*.

7 Messianism itself can arguably function as a catalyst in the development of a sectarian outlook. See the contribution by Albert Baumgarten in this volume.

8 See Gal. 2:15; 3:2, 5, 10, 12; 4QMMT C 29.

9 John Barclay, *Obeying The Truth: A Study of Paul's Ethics in Galatians*, SNTW, Edinburgh, 1988, esp. 170–7. On the need for selection see also Hans Dieter Betz, 'Das Problem der Grundlagen der paulinischen Ethik', *ZThK* 85 (1988), 200f.

10 Markus Bockmuehl, 'The Noachide Commandments and New Testament Ethics', *RB* 102 (1995), 72–101.

11 *T. Avod. Zar.* 8.4; other Tannaitic texts include *b. Sanh.* 56a bottom [Baraita]; Mekhilta *Bahodesh, Yitro* 5 (R. Simeon b. Eleazar; ed. Horovitz/Rabin, p. 221); *Sifre Deut.* 343 (Deut. 33:2; ed. Finkelstein, p. 396) cf. further *b. Avod. Zar.* 2b bottom; *Gen. R.* 34.8, etc.

12 Cf. e.g. *Sib. Or.* 3.36–45, 185–91, 235–45, 373–80, 593–6, 732–40, 758 ('the Immortal in the starry heaven will put in effect a common law

for people throughout the whole earth'), 762–6; 4.30–4; 5.165–74, 386–93, 430f. See also 12.110–12; and *Letter of Aristeas* 131–6, 168f., 171 and *passim*.

13 Some might wish to include in this category Jewish testamentary literature, especially the *Testaments of the Twelve Patriarchs*. However, despite their identifiable Hellenistic moral tone these documents do not in fact concern themselves in any sense with Gentiles, who indeed are almost always dismissed as morally irrelevant. E.g. *T. Dan* 5.5, 8; *T. Naph.* 4.1; but see *T. Sim.* 7.2, a Christian interpolation. The ethics in the *Testaments* may well be a kind of Jewish or Jewish-Christian edification for proselytes.

14 See e.g. E. P. Sanders, *Jewish Law from Jesus to the Mishnah*, London, 1990, 272–83; Peter J. Tomson, *Paul and the Jewish Law: Halakha in the Letters of the Apostle to the Gentiles*, CRINT 3:1, Assen and Maastricht; Minneapolis, 1990, 168–76.

15 *M. Hul.* 2.7. Compare the opinion in the Dead Sea *War Scroll* that clean animals may not be sold to Gentiles lest they sacrifice them to idols (CD 12.8).

16 Cf. in this regard Jacob Katz, *The Shabbes Goy: A Study in Halakhic Flexibility*, Philadelphia and New York, 1989.

We must leave aside here the disputed issue of the halakah strictly concerned with Jewish behaviour towards Gentiles, e.g. respecting business dealings and the charging of usury etc. Like the testamentary literature, this material is not strictly concerned with *Gentile* behaviour.

17 *A.R.N.* B 29 (ed. Schechter, pp. 61–2); *b. Šabb.* 31a. See also Rabban Gamliel and Proclus in *m. Avod. Zar.* 3.4.

18 See most recently Wayne A. Meeks, *The Origins of Christian Morality: The First Two Centuries*, New Haven and London, 1993, 122ff.

19 E.g. Matthew (5:16; 23:1ff.), Luke–Acts (Luke 19:8; Acts 2:44–7), Paul (1 Thess. 4:11f.; Rom. 13; Phil. 2:15f.); 1 Tim. 2:1–2; 3:7; Tit. 2:10; 3:2; 1 Pet. 2:13.

20 Cf. Origen *C. Cels.* 8.73–5; Robert L. Wilken, *The Christians as the Romans Saw Them*, New Haven, 1984, 118f., 124f.

21 E.g. Pliny, *Epistles* 10.96; Galen in Eusebius, *H.E.* 5.28.15

22 See Josephus, *Antiquities* 20.200.

23 See *t. Hul.* 2.24; *Qoh. R.* 1.1.8; *b. Avod. Zar.* 16b–17a.

24 Note on this subject William Horbury, 'The Benediction of the *Minim* and Early Jewish–Christian Controversy', *JTS* 33 (1982), 19–61; and his contribution to the present volume.

25 Note recently Julian V. Hills, 'Parables, Pretenders, and Prophecies: Translation and Interpretation in the *Apocalypse of Peter* 2', *RB* 98 (1991), 560–73; and see the contribution of Richard J. Bauckham to the present volume.

26 Irenaeus states unambiguously, 'Naturalia omnia praecepta communia sunt nobis et illis' (*Haer.* 4.13.4). For Tertullian, the Torah and the

Prophets merely reformed the *lex naturalis*, which was already given to Adam (*Adv. Iud.* 2).

27 See Marcel Simon, *Verus Israel: A Study of the Relations between Christians and Jews in the Roman Empire (135–425)*, trans. H. McKeating, The Littman Library, Oxford, 1986, 146–55 and *passim*; also Manlio Simonetti, *Biblical Interpretation in the Early Church: An Historical Introduction to Patristic Exegesis*, trans. J. A. Hughes, eds. A. Bergquist and M. Bockmuehl, Edinburgh, 1994, *passim*; and Peter Pilhofer, *Presbyteron kreitton: Der Altersbeweis der jüdischen und christlichen Apologeten und seine Vorgeschichte*, Tübingen, 1990.

28 See Ephraim E. Urbach, 'The Decalogue in Jewish Worship', in Ben-Zion Segal and Gershon Levi (eds.), *The Ten Commandments in History and Tradition*, Jerusalem, 1990, 166–81. Urbach wrongly rejects the link with early Christian claims: Geza Vermes points out the similarity of the argument of Stephen in Acts 7:53 (cf. Acts 7:38; Gal. 3:19) with that of the *Minim* ('The Decalogue and the Minim', in *Post-Biblical Jewish Studies*, SJLA 8, Leiden, 1975, 177). Furthermore, as early as *Barnabas* 4.7–8; Justin, *Dial.* 19–20; *Ps.-Clem. Rec.* 35–6 one finds the argument that the laws given after the Golden Calf incident (and hence after the Decalogue) serve only the inferior purpose of preventing idolatry.

29 On the Christian idea of innovation and progress in general see now Wolfram Kinzig, *Novitas Christiana: Die Idee des Fortschritts in der Alten Kirche bis Eusebius*, Forschungen zur Kirchen- und Dogmengeschichte 58, Göttingen, 1994.

30 Fragment quoted in Clement of Alexandria, *Stromateis* 6.5. See E. Hennecke, *New Testament Apocrypha*, ed. W. Schneemelcher, E.tr. ed. R. McL. Wilson, vol. II, London and Philadelphia, 1965, 100.

31 See e.g. the *Letter to Diognetus*, cited above; and cf. Aristides, *Apology* 15–16; Justin, *I Apol.* 16, 65; *Dial.* 110; Tertullian, *Apol.* 39.1–6.

32 See his *Protrepticus*. I am indebted for this observation to my colleague Dr James Carleton Paget.

Postscript: the future of intolerance

Guy G. Stroumsa

The chapters in this volume approach from various angles the different but related problems of identity and its boundaries, sectarianism, persecution, coexistence and *Kulturkampf* among Jews and Christians, in the Hellenistic world and under the early Empire. This was a world of competing and conflicting identities. Ethnic and religious groups, living in many ways according to similar life patterns, were at the same time involved in deep, even radical, arguments with one another (and among themselves) about religious truth and error, and about the components of their own identity versus outsiders of all sorts.

These chapters do not offer an overarching thesis or grand theory on religious tolerance and intolerance in ancient monotheistic religions. Since Edward Gibbon – perhaps even since Julian the Apostate – it has often been claimed that religious intolerance lies in the very nature of monotheism: to one single God corresponds one single truth, while all other views of the divinity reflect intellectual and moral error, and end in idolatry. The simplistic character of such a position has often been submitted to sharp criticism: polytheistic religions, too, could show clear signs of intolerance, while in many ways Christian and Jewish patterns of thought and behaviour reflected a tolerant attitude *vis-à-vis* outsiders. The purpose of this book is neither to refute nor to substantiate what can be called the neo-pagan conception of an inherent monotheistic intolerance.

What the essays collected here attempt to do, on the other hand, is to call attention to the various ways in which some crucial problems of religious identity and behaviour with which we are confronted at the end of the second millennium find their roots in the formative period of Judaism and Christianity. Indeed, if intolerance seems to us such an important concept when dealing with

356

religious phenomena, it is also because we are today witnesses to a fast and threatening growth in intolerance and violence both within and across religious boundaries.

To be sure, intolerance is not religious in nature: one can speak, for instance, of ethnic, political or sexual intolerance. Moreover, there is no reason to see religious intolerance as limited to monotheistic religions; contemporary violence on the part of Hindus or Buddhists in various Asian countries is a sad but eloquent commentary on this fact. But the kind of religious intolerance enhanced in monotheistic religions is certainly different from other forms of intolerance. It is my belief that the better we understand the mechanics of the growth of religious intolerance in the ancient world, the more we can hope to grasp, and hence fight, contemporary forms of religious intolerance.

Naturally, these essays represent case-studies, not theories or 'models'. Hence, attention should be called here to the caution with which terms like 'tolerance' and 'intolerance' should be used. 'Tolerance' seems to have been used first in John Locke's *De tolerantia*, published in 1689. One must be careful, therefore, in applying such terms to the study of ancient religion: tolerance was not a virtue in the ancient world.

Beyond the polemics between debunkers of and apologists for monotheism, however, the fact remains that the creation and development of new forms of religious identity among Jews and Christians in the Roman world brought to the fore attitudes towards 'the other' previously unknown. The reasons for this fact are complex, but stem partly from the new definition of identity in religious, rather than cultural, terms. It has often been noticed that the fourth century represents the major watershed. Tolerance and intolerance are not asked in the same terms after the Constantinian revolution. More precisely, one can observe, throughout the first Christian centuries and late antiquity, an increase in phenomena which can be diversely described as religious intolerance and violence. Christianity as a religious system of thought and doctrine is certainly not solely responsible for this sad development. Yet, the fact remains that religious intolerance would become part and parcel of medieval society, in the West as well as in Byzantium. In a sense, therefore, this volume seeks to uncover some deep roots of medieval religious intolerance.

A better term than 'intolerance' for describing various religious

phenomena in late antiquity would perhaps be 'exclusion'. The
definition and protection of religious boundaries had been a constant obsession of Jews since the days of Ezra and Nehemiah.
However, while Jews had found concrete ways of underlining
these boundaries through religious practice and law, early Christian intellectuals, who had rejected, precisely, Jewish religious
practice, were thrown into endless religious discussions in order to
define their new community and doctrine, still *religio illicita* in the
Empire. These discussions dealt with different although related
issues, confronting the pagans as idolaters and the Jews as blind to
the true meaning of their own Scriptures, while other Christians
were seen as clinging to wrong or even perverse interpretations of
the faith. Like the 'pagans', and later the Jews, these heretics were
perceived as being under the sway of Satan, who was in secret
implanting those strange opinions within them. Precisely because
there was so little in terms of religious law which could function as
a social definer for Christians, theological discussions received in
patristic literature a significance far greater than the one they ever
possessed among the Rabbis.

Idolaters, philosophers, heretics, Jews: of all the competitors of
nascent Christianity, only the Jews survived. By the late fourth or
early fifth century, the pagan danger appeared, if not to have
quite vanished, at least as being much weakened. Heretics of all
kinds had become outlaws, as shown by Book XVI of the *Theodosian
Codex*. In the late fourth century, the Jews were still often perceived
as a threat, as revealed in John Chrysostom's eight Homilies *kata
tôn Ioudaiôn*, i.e., 'against the Judaizers' (rather than 'against the
Jews'). In late antiquity, one witnesses the passage from early
Christian anti-Judaism to attitudes of hatred, sometimes combined
with a racial component, which one cannot avoid calling anti-
Semitism. One of the reasons for such a demonization of the
Jews, unknown in the early centuries, seems to be connected to
the disappearance, for all practical purposes, of the pagan threat:
the Jews inherited, as it were, some of the qualities previously
attributed to the believers in false gods, i.e., demons. But it should
be pointed out that, with some exceptions, the Jews remained
tolerated, being in their fall, throughout the Middle Ages, in the
West as in the East, a living proof of Christian truth. Actually,
one can even say that in the medieval world the Jews were the *only*
tolerated non-orthodox community.

One should not, however, imagine the late antique world as a place of constantly growing religious intolerance. Inability or unwillingness to accommodate the other, too, had its limits, and people belonging to different communities prayed, if not to the same God, at least for the same things: to escape the scourges of illness, drought, draft and tax. Hence a certain amount of what may be called *koinos bios*, which kept intolerance itself within limits. In daily life, after all, people did not only, or usually, function according to the sometimes radical demands of their theologies. Among neighbours, a *lingua franca* in most walks of life is an imperious necessity. The whole period came to its conclusion, as it were, with the rise of Islam. As is well known, a modicum of tolerance to other religious communities, provided they possess holy Scriptures (*ahl al-kitāb*), is extended by medieval Islamic law and practice, in fact as in theory, to Jews, Christians and Zoroastrians.

In seeking to understand the roots and the mechanism of religious intolerance among Jews and Christians, one should take some of the differences between Judaism and Christianity into account. The exclusivism fostered in ancient Judaism, rather than being a direct consequence of monotheism, appears to have been connected to the idea of a 'holy community' separated from the rest of humankind by its perception of itself and the behaviour of its members. In a sense, one may speak here of a sectarian attitude, which was brought to a paroxysm in various Jewish sects, such as the Qumran covenanters, during the second commonwealth. As we now recognize, the latter were quite intolerant and even hateful in their perception of outsiders.

Despite clear links with Qumran and various parallels between the two phenomena, nascent Christianity was built upon vastly different assumptions. Christianity can be called a 'secondary' religion, i.e., one born out of another religion, and in contrast and opposition to it. In particular, Christianity rejected from the start, and in radical fashion at that, Jewish ethnicity and the Law. Mainstream Christianity, hence, believed it had suppressed religious exclusivism. The religious structures of Christianity were different from those of Judaism; for the clearly defined collective boundaries was substituted the ambiguity of a dogma intended for all, but which excluded many. In this context, we should remember that there were different kinds of religious exclusion in the ancient world. Although Hellenistic and Roman societies did not share with Jews and Christians the claim for the uniqueness of religious truth, they had other ways of limiting religious freedom, even showing, from time to time, intolerance for religious outsiders appearing to threaten social coherence.

From the second to the late fourth century of the Common Era, however, religious freedom certainly appears to have shrunk in the Empire. One cannot avoid connecting this fact to the rise and victory of Christianity, originally a *religio illicita*, which earned the status of tolerated religion, at last vanquishing traditional religions. Until the third century, Christian intellectuals had developed cogent and impressive arguments in support of religious toleration. In the fourth century, it was the turn of Hellenic and Roman intellectuals to argue in such a fashion: a clear sign that they were now on the defensive. The Christians, on their side, feeling or knowing that time was on their side in the grand battle for hearts and power, soon forgot their earlier arguments.

Among the causes which explain how the religion of love eventually came to propound intolerant attitudes towards outsiders, one should mention, close to the top of the list, what can be called the 'internalization' of religion during the first Christian centuries. It is often assumed that an 'internalized' or 'spiritualized' religion is less prone to develop intolerant trends than an earlier, more 'exteriorized', religion. Such a conception, itself a hidden heir of early Christian anti-Jewish theology, is patently false. Suffice it here to remember that Augustine, the great discoverer of the inner man, is also one of the very first proponents of ecclesiastical collusion with 'the secular hand' in order to break dissent by force. Upon investigation, the two trends in his thought do not appear to be quite disconnected from one another.

Discourse is one thing, behaviour is another. The historian of religion should certainly take great care when moving from one to the other. But he or she should also remember that the world of theological ideas is not quite distinct from the world of day-to-day life and action. It certainly influences it as much as it is shaped by it. And radical religious ideas which might have seemed innocuous in the context in which they were first propounded can grow dangerous in a later situation, when they become the new allies of political power. The heritage of ancient Judaism and of early Christianity is also the inheritance of their potentially disruptive or threatening power.

BIBLIOGRAPHY

Beatrice, P. F. (ed.), *L'intolleranza cristiana nei confronti dei pagani* (= *Cristianesimo nella storia* 11 [1990]).

Brown, P., *Authority and the Sacred*, Cambridge, 1995, ch. 2: 'The Limits of Intolerance', 29–54.

Stroumsa, G. G., 'Interiorization and Intolerance in Early Christianity', in J. Assmann (ed.), *Die Efrindung des inneren Menschen*, Gütersloh, 1993, 168–82.

'Early Christianity as Radical Religion: Context and Implications', *IOS* 14 (1994), 173–93.

'From Anti-Judaism to Antisemitism in Early Christianity?', in O. Limor and G. G. Stroumsa (eds.), *Contra Iudaeos: Ancient and Medieval Polemics Between Jews and Christians*, Tübingen, 1996, 1–26.

General bibliography

Barclay, J. M. G., *Jews in the Mediterranean Diaspora from Alexander to Trajan (323 BCE–117 CE)*, Edinburgh, 1996.

Bauer, W., *Orthodoxy and Heresy in Earliest Christianity*, E.tr. Philadelphia, 1971.

Bickerman, E., *The God of the Maccabees. Studies in the Meaning and Origin of the Maccabean Revolt*, Leiden, 1979.

Cohen, S. J. D., 'Crossing the Boundary and Becoming a Jew', *HTR* 82 (1989), 13–33

Collins, J. J., *Between Athens and Jerusalem: Jewish Identity in the Hellenistic Diaspora*, New York, 1983.

Davies, W. D. and Finkelstein, L. (eds.), *The Cambridge History of Judaism. Vol. II: The Hellenistic Age*, Cambridge, 1989.

Droge, A. J., and Tabor, J. D., *A Noble Death: Suicide and Martyrdom among Christians and Jews in Antiquity*, San Francisco, 1992.

Dunn, J. D. G., *The Partings of the Ways Between Christianity and Judaism and their Significance for the Character of Christianity*, London, 1991.

Dunn, J. D. G. (ed.)., *Jews and Christians: The Parting of the Ways AD 70 to 135*, WUNT 66, Tübingen, 1992.

Evans, C. A., and Hagner, D. A. (eds.), *Anti-Semitism and Early Christianity: Issues of Polemic and Faith*, Minneapolis, 1993.

Feldman, L. H., *Jew and Gentile in the Ancient World. Attitudes and Interactions from Alexander to Justinian*, Princeton, 1993.

Feldmeier, R., and Heckel, U. (eds.), *Die Heiden, Juden, Christen und das Problem des Fremden*, WUNT 70, Tübingen, 1994.

Forkman, G., *The Limits of the Religious Community*, Lund, 1972.

Frend, W. H. C., *Martyrdom and Persecution in the Early Church*, Oxford, 1965.

Gager, J., *Kingdom and Community: The Social History of Early Christianity*, Englewood Cliffs, 1975.

Glover, T. R., *The Conflict of Religions in the Roman Empire*, London, 1909 and multiple later editions.

Goodman, M., *Mission and Conversion: Proselytizing in the Religious History of the Roman Empire*, Oxford, 1994.

Hengel, M., *The Zealots. Investigations into the Jewish Freedom Movement in the Period from Herod I until 70 AD*, E.tr. by David Smith of *Die Zeloten*, 2nd edn 1976, Edinburgh, 1989.

Hengel, M. (in collaboration with R. Deines), *The Pre-Christian Paul*, E.tr. by J. Bowden of *Der vorchristliche Paulus*, London and Philadelphia, 1991.

Horbury, W., 'Extirpation and Excommunication', *VT* 35 (1985), 13–38.

Johnson, L. T., 'The New Testament's Anti-Jewish Slander and the Conventions of Ancient Polemic', *JBL* 108 (1989), 419–41.

Klijn, A. F. J., and Reinink, G. J., *Patristic Evidence for Jewish-Christian Sects*, NovTSup 36, Leiden, 1973.

Lieu, Judith, *Image and Reality. Christian Perspectives on Jews and Judaism in the Second Century*, Edinburgh, 1996.

Lieu, J., North, J., and Rajak, T. (eds.), *The Jews among Pagans and Christians in the Roman Empire*, London and New York, 1992.

MacMullen, R., *Christianizing the Roman Empire, AD 100–400*, New Haven and London, 1984.

Marguerat, D. (ed.), *La grande déchirure. Chrétiens et juifs au premier siècle*, Geneva, 1995.

Mendus, S. (ed.), *Justifying Toleration. Conceptual and Historical Perspectives*, Cambridge, 1988.

Toleration and the Limits of Liberalism, London, 1989.

Neusner, J., and Frerichs, E. S. (eds.), *'To See Ourselves as Others See us': Christians, Jews, 'Others' in Late Antiquity*, Chico, CA, 1985.

Neusner, J. et al. (eds.), *The Social World of Formative Christianity and Judaism. Essays in Tribute to Howard Clark Kee*, Philadelphia, 1988.

Neusner, J., Green, W. S., and Frerichs, E. S., *Judaisms and their Messiahs at the Turn of the Christian Era*, Cambridge, 1987.

Parkes, J., *The Conflict of the Church and the Synagogue*, London, 1934.

Saldarini, A. J., *Pharisees, Scribes and Sadducees in Palestinian Society: A Sociological Approach*, Edinburgh, 1988.

Sanders, E. P. *Paul and Palestinian Judaism. A Comparison of Patterns of Religion*, London and Philadelphia, 1977.

Judaism: Practice and Belief 63 BCE–66 CE, London and Philadelphia, 1992.

Sanders, E. P., Baumgarten, A. I., and Mendelson, A. (eds.), *Jewish and Christian Self-Definition*, vol. II, London, 1981.

Sanders, J. T., *Schismatics, Sectarians, Dissidents, Deviants: The First One Hundred Years of Jewish–Christian Relations*, London, 1993.

Schürer, E., *The History of the Jewish People in the Age of Jesus Christ (175 BC–AD 135)*, new English edn rev. and ed. G. Vermes, F. Millar, M. Black and M. Goodman; 3 vols.; Edinburgh, 1973–87.

Schwartz, D. R., *Agrippa I*, Tübingen, 1990.

Studies in the Jewish Background of Christianity, Tübingen, 1992.

Segal, A. F., *Paul the Convert. The Apostolate and Apostasy of Saul the Pharisee*, New Haven, 1990.

Siker, J., *Disinheriting the Jews: Abraham in Early Christian Controversy*, Louisville, 1991.

Smallwood, E. M., *The Jews under Roman Rule. From Pompey to Diocletian*, 2nd edn, Leiden, 1981.

Sordi, M., *The Christians and the Roman Empire*, London, 1988.

Stanton, G. N., *A Gospel for a New People: Studies in Matthew*, Edinburgh, 1992.

Stone, M. E. (ed.), *Jewish Writings of the Second Temple Period*, Assen and Philadelphia, 1984.

Taylor, Miriam, *The Jews in the Writings of the Early Church Fathers*, Leiden, 1995.

Tcherikover, V., *Hellenistic Civilization and the Jews*, New York, 1985.

Van der Horst, P. W., *Hellenism–Judaism–Christianity. Essays on their Interaction*, Contributions to Biblical Exegesis and Theology 8, Kampen, 1994.

Vermes, G., *The Dead Sea Scrolls. Qumran in Perspective*, Cleveland, 1978.

Wander, Bernd, *Trennungsprozesse zwischen frühem Christentum und Judentum im 1. Jahrhundert n. Chr.*, Tübingen and Basel, 1994.

Wilson, S. G. (ed.), *Anti-Judaism in Early Christianity*, II, Waterloo, Ontario, 1986.

Wilson, S. G., *Related Strangers. Jews and Christians 70–170 CE*, Minneapolis, 1995.

Index

Index